Kitabu:
The Drum Still Cries

Earl L. Reifel

WestBow
PRESS
A DIVISION OF THOMAS NELSON

WestBow Press books may be ordered through booksellers or by contacting:

WestBow Press
A Division of Thomas Nelson
1663 Liberty Drive
Bloomington, IN 47403
www.westbowpress.com
1-(866) 928-1240

ISBN: 978-1-4497-3392-6 (sc)
ISBN: 978-1-4497-3391-9 (e)

Library of Congress Control Number: 2011962023

Printed in the United States of America

WestBow Press rev. date: 07/24/2012

Dedication

This book is lovingly and respectfully dedicated to my missionary heroes,
Rev. & Mrs. Arthur and Gladys Reifel

A man of integrity and vision, my father leaves to me:
The challenge I see in his heart of compassion for the lost,
The simplicity of his faith which he lived out every day,
And the privilege of being raised in the presence of a man of prayer.

The two words that I feel describe my mother best are wisdom and stability. I learned early that my mother possessed a brilliant mind, but it was not until I was a little older that I realized that God had given her a spiritual gift of teaching. She was able to take His Word and make it come alive to hundreds of Nigerian men and women who, over the past half-century, have passed it on to others in village churches throughout northern Nigeria. Her life demonstrates the faithfulness of our God as an unshakable foundation.

My thanks to both of you for being everything God wanted you to be, and for living it every day. You have given your children an incredible heritage. Thank you for you being you!!!

Contents

Part 3: Church Planting

Part 4: Evacuated

Part 4: Current Affairs

Introduction

In an attempt to span the generations of Kurankos that have lived in north eastern Sierra Leone, West Africa, I have created an imaginary figure in the tradition of the Kuranko oral historians. The Storyteller, named Finaba, is an unseen observer who tells the story of the ministry and the missionary. Because he is imaginary, he is not limited by time, and although imaginary, the story he tells is very real.

The names of nationals and the towns they live in have been changed to protect their identity. The country of Sierra Leone is very real, and so are the Kuranko people.

For the history of the people prior to our arrival in the Kamaron area in 1975, I have relied on conversations with the "old timers" and several oral historians. I have not been able to substantiate some of the information in documented form in any of the libraries through which I have searched. Yet, I have no reason to doubt the accuracy of their accounts. An example of this is the ancient iron smelting furnaces that stand today as solitary monuments of a forgotten past, hidden deep in the African bush. The art of smelting their own iron was forgotten several generations ago when Europeans began to bring in iron products. Yet the traditions and proverbs of that era still thread their way through Kuranko thinking. Although the art is no longer practiced, the physical remains of the smelting pots provide tangible evidence that confirms the traditions, proverbs, and wisdom of the ancients. Who am I to deny or question the lessons learned and passed on that emerged from the grueling task of transforming stones into iron? It is not mine to challenge the status of the blacksmith or to question his privileges which were established out of necessity in a bygone era but are still accepted today.

Some of the things outsiders do not understand are issues that everyone within the culture simply takes for granted. Off the beaten track, one has to learn to ask the right questions to get answers that reveal the truth, or the real meaning behind a thought or practice. The reason for this is simply because everyone within the culture assumes that you know the reason or the meaning, just as they do. Creating an imaginary "Storyteller" named Finaba enables me to observe the missionary from the outside, and makes it possible for me to portray, in a small way, the struggle of one missionary to learn to ask the right questions to discover the heartbeat of the people to whom God called him to minister.

The story told here deals with the development of the church among the Kuranko people in northeastern Sierra Leone between the years 1975 and 2010. During the years I ministered in Sierra Leone, there were two "church districts" among the Kuranko people. Due to the natural barrier of the rugged mountain terrain between them, the districts did not work closely together. The central area for the northern churches was a city which was home to people from almost all the tribes in the north, so although there were many Kuranko people living there it was not really a "Kuranko District" for the Church. When one considers the entire "Kuranko Nation" which would include all the Kuranko people in Sierra Leone and Guinea, the "Church District" which is the setting for this ministry is fairly close to the geographical center of this unreached people group. (The term "unreached," which appears here and elsewhere in this story, refers to a people group where less than five percent has heard the Gospel of Christ.) In this regard, the development of the church in this area is vitally important to reaching the people as a whole. (When a church was established under Kuranko leadership it was considered "initially reached".)

Originally the Kuranko people held to an animistic belief system. In this traditional African religion they believed that the world was held in balance by the "good spirits" opposed to the "evil spirits". However, since the "good spirits" would not harm them they developed a system of sacrifice in an endeavor to appease the "evil spirits" which would harm them. They held to the belief that all the spirits could, and did indeed, inhabit inanimate objects, and blessing or curses could be accrued through connecting with the spirits. They also held to a system of ancestral worship which carries with it all kinds of implications of demonization. Islam invaded this animistic world and the people found that they could combine the teaching of the Quran with their tribal belief system and as a result they developed a belief system of Folk Islam which allows both the traditional belief system as well as the teaching of Islam. In order to plant a Church among a people with such a world view one had to respond to the core beliefs of their world view as it has been taught to them by both Imans, Muslim teachers, as well as their traditional religious leaders. If we cannot present Biblical answers to the issues of life on the "heart level" we will end up with a Church that may be " a mile wide, but only skin deep". This is the story of a Church that stands on God's Word and answers the questions of the Kuranko heart.

Some might say that the story has been colored by my perspective. I guess every story has its color. The person seeing or experiencing it will pass it on as he, or she, sees it or remembers it. The "color" may vary depending on the person's background, perspective, or attitude, but the story can still be true.

There will always be those who look at a glass of water and say, "It is half empty," while others will look at it rejoicing and say, "The glass is still half full." Both are right!

There will be those, like me, who do not swim well, who will stand on the bank of the Atlantic and be intimidated by the roar of the water, the thunder of the waves, and the power of the ocean. Beside me are two young men, my sons, donned in snorkel or scuba diving gear, who will see the same scene as a challenge whose depths cradle adventure and beauty that one can never see from the sandy banks of the beach. All three of us are right, but our perspectives are so very, very different!

I believe that wherever God calls you to serve, He will offer to you the gift of a perspective that will enable you to enjoy the place, and the people, where He asks you to minister. It is from that perspective, or if you choose, "this coloring," that this true story is told. My goal is not to tell an entertaining story, although I trust that you will pick up that I had a great time serving where God called me to minister. My primary purpose is to give God the glory for what He has done, and to challenge you to become a part of the unfinished task of reaching our world with the Gospel of Jesus Christ. More specifically, I would like to challenge you to become a part of the Team to reach the rest of the Kuranko Nation for Jesus.

Acknowledgements

Above all I want to thank the Lord for the tremendous opportunity He has given me by allowing me to serve among the Kuranko people. May He receive all the praise, honor and glory for what has been, and for what will be accomplished. May the sharing of this story bring glory to His name for He alone is worthy of praise.

Secondly, I wish to express my deep appreciation to those who have encouraged me to record my journey on paper, chief among them were my parents and my children. I also want to thank those who took time to read and critique the rough draft so that it would be presentable in book form. My parents, (Art and Gladys Reifel), my sisters & their husbands, (Eva Mae Reifel & Colin and Connie, & Keith Gary), my daughter (Faith M. Hill), and several friends (Beverly Brogden and Wendy Clingan) gave valuable insight and encouragement to this project. My editor (Paul Woods) added sound advice and put a rough manuscript into a readable form. Thank you!

On the mission field I found those who encouraged and supported my ministry and often served as a sounding board for my ideas and endeavored to help me establish a truly effective ministry in a difficult area. Bill Harrigan and Jake Schierling have both gone home to glory. Stan and Valli Yoder are now ministering in the USA, and my brother and his wife (Elmer and Joann) who later joined the missionary staff in Sierra Leone ministered among the Kuranko on "the other side of the mountain." Thank you for your continued prayer support and encouragement that has meant more to me than I can express.

You will notice when walking with me that there were also those on the field whose most valuable gift to me was criticism. Although it was sometimes painful for me to listen to and to deal with, I do want to thank those individuals who offered this gift that challenged me to constantly evaluate my ministry and to find more effective ways to communicate the Gospel, so that I might disciple others in evangelism, discipleship and church planting. In doing so, they stimulated me to search the Scriptures, to study the lives of others that the world of missions recognizes as successful missionaries, and to read continually to keep myself on the cutting edge of missions. Thus they motivated me to evaluate my methods of ministry and stimulated me to remain in the center of God's will. I express my appreciation to them for helping me stay on the right track.

I thank my daughter, Faith, for her valuable insights: my son-in-law, Roy for his expertise on the computer; my sons for their support and encouragement in this project; and my new bride, Clare for the encouragement and help in bringing this project to completion.

I also express a special note of thanks to my publishers at West Bow Press who brought all the pieces together and turned it into a finished product.

Part 1: Dembeli and the Kuranko

Chapter 1: The Scattering of the Fire

Dusty brown feet hurried over the dry Judean hillside. As Amos scurried along the path, he wondered which of the messages he had delivered to his people had angered the king. Years before, God had spoken to Amos and told him that Jehovah would not do anything without first revealing His plan to the prophets. The first message God had given Amos didn't seem to disturb the status quo of his own community. But when God began to speak through him to the nation of Israel, it stirred things up.

As he hurried along, Amos was thinking about how God had commanded him to remind the people how Jehovah had tried to communicate with them: by withholding rain, sending hunger and plagues, and by challenging His people through the voice of the prophets to "Seek God and live." But the people were confident that—as God's chosen ones—whatever they did would be blessed by God. They proclaimed Jehovah's presence and power even as they ignored His statutes.

Almighty God had declared that He expected His people to "seek good and not evil, that they might live. Then God Almighty would be with them just as they claimed He was…" (Amos 5:14). Amos realized that in this message he had delivered, God was telling His people that no matter what claims they made about His presence being with them, if they lacked obedience in their hearts then Jehovah would not be there. Amos also wondered if the injustices he had cried out against were now the reason he was being summoned by the high priest. He had made a passionate plea for justice, but it had fallen on deaf ears.

God's response to the nation had come in the form of a vision, and Amos found himself pleading with Jehovah to be merciful to His people. As Amos stood in the breech between the Creator and the created, he was being unjustly accused of starting a conspiracy against the king of his nation. Amos was not afraid, but he wanted to avoid a confrontation with the religious leaders. Still, he knew in his heart that the God he served had called him and that it was the Creator who had given him the messages he had declared to his people. Now, standing before the priest at Bethel, Amos could hardly believe his ears. The thundering voice of the religious leader of his nation was telling him to "Get out… Go back to the land of Judah. Earn your bread there and do your prophesying there. Don't prophesy at Bethel anymore, because this is the king's sanctuary and the temple of the kingdom" (Amos 7:12-13).

In the stillness of his soul, Amos heard the now familiar voice of his Creator and declared to the nation his innocence and his obedience. "I was neither a prophet nor a prophet's son, but I was a shepherd and I also took care of sycamore-fig trees. But the Lord took me from tending the flock and said to me, 'Go, prophesy to my people Israel. Now then hear the word of the Lord'" (Amos 7:15-16). Amos' heart broke as God showed him the dark days that were ahead for the nation of Israel. He wept as he became the mouthpiece of the Lord declaring "The days are coming when I will send a famine through the land—not a famine for food or a thirst for water, but a famine of hearing the words of the Lord."

Generations later, in a land far, far away, another pair of dusty feet scurried down a rocky trail in response to the summons of a king. Finaba heard the echo of the king's drum as it reverberated through the hills with the familiar cadence that summoned all the men of the village to the compound of their king, known to his people as the "Paramount Chief." For generations Finaba's people had been called to important meetings by the sound of the huge drum. It had been hand-carved out of a log so large that it required a complete cowhide to cover it. As the deep, throbbing beat echoed and re-echoed through the valleys of his homeland Finaba mused that it was no wonder his people heard the drumbeat from miles away. But today the urgency in the rhythm set his young mind wondering why all the men of the village were being called to a meeting when the food supply was short and every able-bodied person was out gathering fruit, roots, herbs, and other edibles from the jungle that provided the sustenance for his people.

Upon arriving in the village, Finaba quickly found an obscure place a safe distance from the ring of men who sat nearest the chief, but close enough to hear every word. Somehow he sensed that today's discussions would change his life forever. In the past his position was out on the fringes of the crowd for he had been unimportant as a child. Now that he had gone through the initiation rites and had passed into manhood, he was entitled to move closer to the center of the circle where the men sat. The older women could no longer tell him to move back out of the way. Even so, he was pushing the boundaries by finding a place so close to the ring of elders now gathered around the great chief. Scanning the crowd, he noticed that the hunters had returned. Suddenly a tingle of excitement swept through his body as he realized that for the first time he might be allowed to take part in a major hunt led by the legendary Mende Fa Bore. His new status as a young man permitted him to enjoy such privileges.

The drumbeat stopped as one of the town criers strode to the center of the clearing surrounded by mud huts, the verandas of which were now crowded with people. As the musicians beat out the rhythm of praise on their homemade instruments, the crier sang the praises of their chief and Finaba's heart swelled with pride as the crier recalled the history and lineage of their great Paramount Chief. He knew that as a future Storyteller of the Kuranko people, he would one day learn all their history so he could pass it on through oral tradition to others. He dreamed of the day he would have the honored position of relating publicly the great names and events of the past, soon becoming lost in his own private world—musing about the great dynasty his people had established in Central Africa almost three hundred years before. It had been kept intact all those years, and only now were his people beginning to feel the threat of a foreign invasion.

Suddenly Finaba was jolted back to reality as the Paramount Chief rose to speak. Another crier strode onto the scene and began to loudly confirm the words of the chief through an abbreviated echo. More than the volume and quality of the speaker's voice, the very message the chief was conveying was what shook Finaba's being. Mende Fa Bore, the legendary hunter of his people, had disappeared.

Finaba's mind reeled at the thought that such a great hunter could possibly be gone. For all his young life he had known with pride that the master of all hunters lived among his people. Without the luxury of high-powered rifles, the fearless Mende Fa Bore had killed more animals than any other hunter. Even the elephant, leopard, and cape buffalo had fallen prey to his incredible skill. Finaba knew beyond any doubt that he had heard the stories of conquest from the greatest of all hunters, and now his mind failed to grasp the unthinkable: Mende Fa Bore was actually gone.

A search party of all able-bodied men set out to scour the hills for the missing hunter. Finaba joined in the endeavor, but as days became weeks, and weeks moved on through the months of the dry season, the legendary hunter was not found. By this time, Finaba was one of the few who still held onto hope that the hunter might someday come home, though admittedly he searched with a heavy heart. His people still foraged in the jungle for fruits, nuts, berries and herbs, but the abundant supply of meat that Mende Fa Bore had helped to supply was missing.

Finaba's mother and sisters would beat the leaves of a dry-season plant into a powder and join the other women as they scattered the concoction on the rivers and waited for stunned fish to float to the surface. With much laughter and more than the usual amount of gossip, the women followed in the wake of the poison, scooping up the paralyzed fish with nets woven from raffia. As the fish were caught in the nets, the women would take them out and put them in gourds attached to ropes hung over their shoulders. In spite of the fish, without the usual supply of meat, Finaba knew the hard times of hunger for the first time.

Dry season gave way to the refreshing showers of the rainy season. As the thirsty ground soaked up the water, plants that seemed dead spread their roots a little deeper to soak up the life-giving moisture. Edible leaves became abundant, and fruit, almost forgotten in the intense dry season heat, began to re-appear. The search for Mende Fa Bore was now a thing of the past. One by one the men of the tribe had reluctantly begun to accept that he was gone, and the hope of ever seeing him again was set aside. After all, the African bush had swallowed up many unfortunate hunters in the past. No one would ever know if it had been the charge of an enraged elephant, the nasty fangs of a wounded leopard, a seemingly slow-moving crocodile, or the meanest of all animals in the bush—the cape buffalo—that had claimed the life of their hero. Even in the re-telling of the legends that recounted the phenomenal exploits of Mende Fa Bore, men had to acknowledge in their hearts that Nature never forgives carelessness or forgetfulness, and maybe, just maybe, Mende Fa Bore—even in his greatness—had grown overconfident and misjudged his prey. The simple fact remained: he was gone.

—

One still, tropical evening was shattered when a drum began to beat. All other concerns were set aside as a spirit of expectation rippled through the town. The rhythm was picked up quickly by other drums, and like an electrical current sweeping through a city, the atmosphere was charged with excitement. Drums beat, youth danced, women sang as hands clapped, and Finaba strutted through the village on a beautiful night lit by a full moon. He enjoyed the festive atmosphere and the attention of certain young ladies who huddled together awaiting their turn to dance "the dance of the bird" and receive the applause of the crowd. They were also anxious to pick up the gifts that would be thrown to them as tokens of admiration for their skill as dancers, or for the view of their supple bodies, which were displayed to the maximum as the girls stomped their feet and shook to the rhythm of the drums. Finaba enjoyed the dancing every bit as much as they did on these full-moon nights when only the youngest, the weak, or the very old slept near the fires in their huts.

That night Finaba suddenly noticed that there were no elders at the festivities. Puzzled, he searched for his father and other family members, finally spotting an uncle in the shadow of the mango tree talking in hushed tones to the blacksmith. Unnoticed by the crowd, both men quietly left the gathering of people and strolled toward the chief's compound. Finaba followed, careful to remain unseen.

The throbbing of the drums and the stomping of dancing feet contrasted with the sharp sounds of clapping hands and squeals of delight coming from children, but it all faded into the background as Finaba stole quietly through the trees to the chief's hut. The other men there were waiting for the last of the elders to take his rightful place among the chief's advisors. Time meant nothing—Finaba knew that the meeting would not start until all the important men were on hand. For a while he tried to remain hidden, crouched in the shadows near the doorway, but he soon realized that he had nothing to worry about. The importance of the chief's summons to the elders demanded their full attention, and even if he had been noticed, his presence would not have been acknowledged. He watched as the chief quietly reached into the folds of his gown, withdrew a handful of cola nuts, and passed them around to the men.

Finaba listened attentively as the chief recalled the blessings of bygone days when food was plentiful and the hunters, under the leadership of Mende Fa Bore, had provided an abundant supply of meat. In those days, peace had reigned throughout the kingdom. But then the chief's face

7

grew long as he reminded them of the skirmishes on the border of the kingdom, the absence of meat, and how hard it was for families to find enough food. He shared honestly that even with all four of his wives out foraging for food, he had had difficulty providing for all the needs of his extended family and dignitaries from visiting clans. He concluded that the country was no longer able to support the growing population, for their wives had been fertile and the devils of disease had not attacked because they had been appeased through animal sacrifices and proper respect paid to ancestors.

To solve the problem, the chief challenged the head of each clan to take his family and spread out—to claim more territory and enlarge the kingdom so that they could once again experience the blessing of abundance and safety from foreign invasions. Pulling some coals from the fire, he first offered them to the elder on his right. Finaba watched, entranced, as the elder held out a piece of bamboo to accept the coals. The chief reminded them that they had to keep the coals alive and that the hand full of colas he was giving them represented the life-blood of their people. They had to keep a fire going to warm their huts, cook their food, and burn off the bush each year so they could forage farther and find a place to plant their meager gardens. Finaba's heart swelled with pride as he watched his own father solemnly hold out a large piece of bark and accept his portion of coals from the Paramount Chief on behalf of his clan. He watched and listened in breathless expectation as each elder solemnly accepted a share of coals from their chief. He knew that when they reached their destination his father would light a new fire and then share the coals with the head of each family in the clan. As long as he lived Finaba would never forget that night, for he had witnessed the challenge of the chief and had seen the scattering of the fire.

Finaba had never heard of the purifying fire of the Holy Spirit that cleanses from sin and sanctifies our hearts so we can stand before God. He had never heard of the Apostle Paul writing to young Timothy and saying "the gift of God is in your life like a handful of coals. Fan it. Blow on it. So that it will burst into flames and the light and warmth of it will draw other men to your Savior" (2 Timothy 1:6). Finaba knew nothing about the spiritual light, or Jesus, who is the Light of the World. He only knew that his people had to keep the fire going if they were to live, so he vowed that he would protect it at all costs. He also vowed to do everything within his power to fulfill the commission of the Paramount Chief to claim a new territory for his people.

Chapter 2: A Refuge from Danger

The chill of the morning air had forced even the hardiest of the dancers to find solace in the warmth of a communal fire which was fed with sticks children had brought back to the village as they returned from their foraging. But there was a sense of anticipation in the air, for the word had already circulated that the Paramount Chief had summoned the head of each clan to his hut for a meeting. The people were abuzz with speculation about what the meeting's topic might be, and Finaba chuckled to himself because he knew something his friends did not know. Finaba knew that it would not be long before everybody in the village would know what the meeting was about, because among his people secrets were only figments of one's imagination. Even the smallest child would soon hear what had been announced. Finaba did not have to wait long before his younger brother called him to the hut, and preparations for the journey began.

With his people, Finaba pushed south and west into the land known to us today as the countries of Guinea and Sierra Leone. They discovered that all their needs could be met in the foothills of the Konko Mountains, where the abundant forests, rivers, and swamps provided a more than adequate food supply for the animals of the forest and for their clan as well. They discovered the beauty of the rolling hills and explored the rugged mountain terrain. They drank from cool mountain streams in shady forests and fished the depths of uncharted rivers. They claimed an area so large it took a man five days to walk across it. It was a land where the hills were rich with "iron stones" from which tools could be made by melting them down and shaping the iron that flowed from them. It was a land where game was abundant and the forest so thick that a man could walk all day and never be struck by the direct light of the hot tropical sun. Like the rest of his clan, Finaba rejoiced in their new home.

They rejoiced until they began to hear rumors of some of the youth who had disappeared, apparently swallowed up by the land that had seemed so kind in meeting all their needs. Finaba had been taught from his earliest days that the world was held in balance by good spirits and by evil spirits. He was not overly concerned about the good spirits because he had learned that they would not harm anyone, but now he began to wonder what kind of sacrifice the elders would have to make to appease the evil spirits so no more youth would disappear. These evil spirits held his people in bondage of fear, for if they were not appeased, unspeakable evil would come upon the people to bring them into submission.

Finaba was still pondering these strange events when a summons came from the Paramount Chief to the heads of all the clans. Sensing that history was in the making, but motivated more by his curiosity, Finaba asked his father if he could accompany the elders on the journey back to the town of the Great Chief. Pride swelled in his heart, and maybe a little bit in his head, when he was reminded that he would one day be an oral historian for his people and that he would have the awesome responsibility of passing on to the next generation the story of his forefathers. His place in the clan now dictated that he attend all the important meetings, even if he was only an observer. Finaba sensed that his role as a historian was important. He no longer regretted that he had not been permitted to become an apprentice to the blacksmith to learn the secrets of melting the "iron stones" and the skills needed to shape the tools that served his people so well. As a child, he'd wished he had been born into a clan of blacksmiths so he could learn what he admired as a more honorable trade. Now he felt that he had an honorable calling.

As the elders prepared for the journey, Finaba realized that his place was now being acknowledged as honorable, for he could now begin to walk among his people with a status accorded to few. He purposed in his heart that he would be the best historian he could possibly be among a people who knew nothing of reading, writing, or filing of records. His people knew only the oldest and best means of communication known to man, the fine art of storytelling. And that was what Finaba's mind was being trained and disciplined to do.

A solemn group met three days later near the Paramount Chief's hut. The Chief listened carefully to reports from all over the chiefdom. He sensed the deep frustration of his people over the loss of so many youth. People argued about which of the spirits should be appeased to end the devastation that was creeping among his people. Finaba noticed that the chief would periodically slip out for a short time and then quietly return to enter into the discussions as if he had never been gone. After two days of discussion the chief displayed a look of confidence on his face. He called for the attention of his people and declared that a consensus had emerged. He pointed out that the people in the north felt that the disappearances were due to foreign invasions and skirmishes. The people on the southern edge of the newly formed kingdom were discovering that other tribes were also endeavoring to enlarge their territorial boundaries and were willing to fight for the same area now claimed by the Kuranko people. He concluded that the disappearances were caused by an even greater danger: the slavers who were coming into the area and taking youth away, never to return them to their homeland again. The chief felt that safety for his people was not a matter of appeasing the evil spirits, but of finding a way to defend themselves against invasion and the terrible aggression of slavery. He challenged the elders to consider how they could protect their people from foreign invasion.

Discussion continued long into the night, and Finaba took full advantage of the moonlight as he meandered from one group of elders to another to catch the essence of their discussions. He was appalled by stories of slavers that had come into a neighboring area and taken many of the young people. Fear gripped his heart as he heard how the slavers had laid a large chain on the ground in the middle of the village. Then they had taken a small chain and put it around the neck of each young man or woman, and padlocked the small chain into the big chain. One by one, young slaves were chained together by the neck only one step ahead of the slave behind them. Finaba asked what the slaver had done when he reached the end of the big chain. The elder explained that the slaver had simply padlocked another big chain to that one and had gone on chaining the youth by their necks. When all the youth of the village were chained, the slaver ordered the slaves to begin walking, and he herded them out of the village in total defeat.

Adding to his shock, Finaba discovered that the slaver purchased slaves from a neighboring Paramount Chief who had captured some young men during a tribal skirmish and sold them into slavery. The rumor was circulating that the slaves were being sold to men who carried them away in big boats—so far away that they could never come home again. Finaba's heart ached as he pictured the young people chained together, being marched for weeks to the coast where they would be sold to passing slavers who came on ships ready to carry their human cargo to the ends of the earth.

When asked why the slavers used such a method, the elder pointed out how the slaves still had their hands and feet free but could not escape because they were chained together so closely. Another elder spoke of when the Great Creator made the world and gave the angels a bag of rocks to scatter over all the earth. The angels began distributing the rocks all over the world, but the bag broke suddenly when they were flying over Sierra Leone. That's how they explained the rocks in the forest, rocks in the swamps, rocks on the plains, rocks on the hills and rocks everywhere. There did not seem to be a straight path anywhere, so the slavers had to find a way of getting their captives to the "big river" by a flexible means that would allow them to march along the bush paths, through the forests and swamps, and around the stones for almost three hundred miles to the coast.

Finaba had heard of the river that was so wide it did not have a bank on the other side, and was large enough that huge ships could float on it. Those ships carried hundreds of slaves to the end of the earth and left them somewhere so they could never come home again. Finaba was not sure about ships, and he certainly did not want to believe that a river could be that wide, but then Finaba had never stood on the shores of the Atlantic or seen the floating fortress that carried the human cargo to another world. He heard of a cottonwood tree where the slaves—his people—were taken and sold like goats in a market, and he wondered what kind of plan the great Paramount Chief could devise to protect his people against such powerful evil.

The sleepless night of fear and unease ended with the dawn of the new day, but the freshness of the morning did not lighten the ache in Finaba's heart as he and his father approached the meeting hut near the chief's compound. Apparently, like Finaba, the chief had wandered from one small group to another the evening before, or more likely, the groups had wandered over to the chief's compound and shared their fears and insights with him. In the morning meeting a variety of plans were suggested. After lengthly discussion a consensus began to emerge.

Finally the great chief called for the attention of all his people. He pointed out that caves had been discovered throughout the foothills of the mountains. He suggested that food be stashed in certain caves and that young men be posted as sentries where they could see long distances in every direction to warn the people when slavers were coming. When the warning was given, every man, woman, and child should immediately leave whatever they were doing, head for the cave closest to their area, and stay there until the slavers had passed. All of the clans quickly accepted the plan, and after a feast the elders began their journey back to their homes and families.

Several of Finaba's closest friends were designated as the sentries who kept constant watch for approaching slavers, but he never really thought that they would have to give the warning that would send his family into the cave. He thought that would only happen to the clans living farther south. One evening as Finaba and his friends sat around the fire, someone shared how he had met a sentry from the neighboring clan who told him that in the tribe south of them some people had been captured. Several escaped and ran away with the slavers hot on their trail. The young men found their way to the southern edge of the foothills and through the pass marked by huge pinnacles of granite. At that point the slavers turned back, knowing that the young man and his escaping companions could lose themselves in the hills and forest and never be seen again.

Finaba wondered how a person, if captured, might find his way to freedom. The scout advised that if he was ever captured and were able to escape, he should head for the foothills of the mountains and hike through "The Gates of Jubilee," those pinnacles of rock on the southern edge of the mountain range. Finaba also wondered about the hardships the escapees must have experienced, and how they had to learn another language to get along with the people from that neighboring tribe. He felt secure because he still figured the slavers would never make it this far from the big river.

A few days later, however, that security quickly vanished when the signal from his own clan's sentries echoed faintly in the distance. Finaba paused in his work to listen, thinking that all the stories had begun to work on his imagination and that he was just hearing things. But then the call came again and his heart skipped a beat. Suddenly, in his mind he pictured again the concern he'd seen on the face of the Paramount Chief as he talked to the elders and explained his plan for the safety of his people. Finaba remembered how the chief had felt it would be safer to hide in their own beloved hills than to fight the slavers who came with weapons far more advanced than the hunters had. Those weapons could speak harsh words to a resistant slave and leave that slave wounded, bleeding, or dead on the forest floor. So it was with a sense of fear that Finaba gathered his few simple farming tools and hurried off toward the hidden cave.

Scurrying past the sentries, Finaba did not even bother to wave as he had so often done in the past. As he rounded the corner and stepped into the mouth of the cave, his heart overflowed with relief when he saw every member of his family gathered there. In fact, most of the clan was there—but he feared that those missing were even now en route to the river so big that it did not have a bank on the other side.

The smell of smoke drew his attention to a few coals his uncle was trying to persuade to become a fire. Finaba watched as a tendril of smoke curled toward the rocky ceiling, and it slowly dawned on him that his whole clan was once again reduced to dependence on a handful of coals, remnants from the "scattering of the fire". The importance of those coals was not lost on him, for he knew better than most that his people had to keep that fire going. He knew that when the danger was past, his father— as the elder of the clan—would call the heads of the families and from that very fire would give a few coals to each so that when they returned home they could start their own fires.

The warning to be silent came as a whisper, and even the smallest of the children settled into an almost holy hush. They could hear the slavers in the distance, and the sound was drawing nearer. Finaba realized that it was probably fear that kept even the rowdiest children quiet. The slavers marched right up over the mountain and on to the next valley, never realizing that in the ground beneath them were the very people they had come to capture. It seemed an eternity before the all-clear signal came from the sentries. Like the others, Finaba treated his lungs to a breath of fresh mountain air and wondered how he had remembered to breathe during those hours when his people were in the gravest danger.

Then, just as Finaba had expected, his father called the heads of the families and solemnly gave a few coals to each. Looking around the cave, Finaba became genuinely grateful to the Paramount Chief for suggesting this successful plan of protection. The cave was a safe retreat where they could go and remain unharmed. It was the refuge they needed where danger could not reach them.

Finaba had never heard about a place called "heaven," and he knew nothing about an eternal refuge where he would be free from sickness, pain, sorrow, and death. He had never heard of Jesus telling His followers not to be afraid because He was going to heaven to prepare a mansion for each of them where He would give them eternal refuge (John 14:1-6). He had never heard of the new heaven that the Apostle John saw, where there would be no tears, crying, pain, or death (Rev. 21:1-4). Finaba only knew that he needed a place of physical refuge to shield him from the dangers around him. He did not know what would happen to him in the hereafter, but he did know that he needed—and had found—a refuge for the here and now.

Chapter 3: The Supreme Sacrifice

It is hard to say how long Finaba's people lived in the foothills of the mountains or how many generations passed into eternity without knowing about the Supreme Sacrifice that would end all their sacrificing. Generation after generation after generation marched their way through the hills, never having heard that Jesus had paid the price for sin and that they could be free from the bondage of their ancestral worship, consisting of fear, of sin, of death and of hell.

Finaba saw the generations of his people pass over the mountain and into eternity. He also continued to hear stories of young men and women who disappeared, never to be seen again. The reality of the possibility of being captured and taken to the coast as a slave cast a constant dark shadow over the lives of his people.

The story of a young man from a neighboring tribe stands out in Finaba's memory. This young man was journeying closer to the coast on a business venture. Finaba suspected that he was going after a wife, for what other business would be important enough to cause a man to travel that far. On his return trip the young man saw a slave chain coming and quickly hid in the bush so that he would not be noticed. As he hid in the bushes, he saw his older brother walk by with his head padlocked by a small chain into the big one. Anger gave the young man courage and he rushed to the slaver and demanded the life of his older brother.

Finaba mused that it must have been a bitter argument that followed as the young man declared that his older brother was born free in their hometown and that they would never be slaves to any man. The slaver, of course, mocked the idea and pointed out that the young man's brother was obviously somebody's slave. Finaba imagined the terrible argument that must have taken place as the young man endeavored to get his brother freed. At some point the slaver angrily held out his hand for money and told the young man that the older brother was his, and the young man would have to pay the price of freedom for the older brother to walk free again. Realizing that his anger was doing no good, the young man knelt in the dirt and begged for the life of his older brother. He was curtly dismissed by the slaver who said that he had no time for such "nonsense."

Darkness had fallen, and darker still were the feelings of the young man as he hurried home to tell his father what he had experienced. In the morning when he found his father and told him the news, his father hurried to the chief and asked him for help. The dull beat of the drum echoed through the hills, and soon all the men of the village had gathered at the summons of their chief. When told about the captive brother, people began to contribute what little they had so the young man could purchase him back from the slaver. Time dragged for the young man until he was assured that the chief had gathered enough and he was able to start his journey to the coast to purchase his brother's freedom.

Fortunately, the young man reached the coast before the slave traders, one of whom may have been John Newton, arrived for the auction held under the famous cottonwood tree on the Freetown Peninsula. John Newton is familiar to us because he was a slaver whose ships carried many from Africa to Europe and the Americas. His headquarters were on the Banana Islands just a few miles off the coast of Freetown, Sierra Leone, so he had easy access to the West African slave markets. A tropical disease laid him low and almost claimed his life, but in sickness he himself became a slave to others. While a slave, he was introduced to the person of Jesus Christ and saw his need for a Savior. His life was radically changed, and he later wrote the song, "Amazing Grace," his story and testimony.

Finaba pictured in his mind what the young man must have found when he reached the coast. Each slaver had a series of huts, where he would chain his "wares" until the slaving ships arrived. Many of the slaves, like the older brother, had been captured by the slavers. Others had been purchased from Paramount Chiefs who had taken them captive in battle against a neighboring tribe as they endeavored to enlarge their boundaries. All of these slaves were housed in the most miserable conditions imaginable, and Finaba's mind staggered at the unbelievable atrocities he had heard about. Finaba's people saw deeper than the mere physical pain of slavery, for it was reported that during the slave auctions one could see the demons and devils as they danced above the slaves in the branches of the great cottonwood tree which provided the shade for the illicit activity. Today that cottonwood tree still stands in the middle of Freetown, Sierra Leone's capital city. It is more then a reminder of the past. It is a monument to freedom, and a declaration of an independent people who can face the future with the confidence that they too can overcome.

Fortunately, the young man found his brother still alive in one of the huts owned by the swaggering slaver. It made him angry all over again. The ensuing discussion was likely not the most peaceful one carried on that day. The young man finally paid the required price for his brother. The slaver pulled out a string of keys, walked over to the older brother, and opened the padlock securing the chain around the older brother's neck. The chain fell off and the older brother threw his hands in the air shouting, "You pulled my head! You pulled my head! You pulled my head! I am free!"

Years later, this story became the basis for the contextualization of a Biblical principle. In the neighboring area, while translating the Scriptures into the language that belonged to the same linguistic group as the Kurnako, one of the early missionaries was looking for a word for "redeemed." The villagers could not think of a word like that in their language, even after the missionary explained the concept of redemption. As they continued to work their way through the translation of the New Testament, the missionary would occasionally bring up the issue again only to be told that they did not have that word. One day Finanba was visiting friends in the area and he decided to stop and when he heard that God's Word was being taught he decided to go and see what God had to say. He joined the group seated with the missionary and the subject of redemption came up again. The young men chuckled at the missionary's persistence in trying to find a word in their language that means "redeemed." But they settled back to listen to the story of redemption again, and wondered why it was so important to the white man that he have a word for "redeemed." As the missionary finished, Finaba spoke of the young man who had paid the price to free his older brother. Looking at the group of young men, Finaba, the Storyteller, concluded that the missionary was trying to say that we are bound by the chains of animism, ancestral worship, fear, sin, death, and hell. He explained that if we believe that Jesus died for us and that He is our Supreme Sacrifice, He will pull our heads from those chains of bondage and we will be forever free. The missionary's heart rejoiced as he heard the Storyteller conclude that the word for "redeemed" is "to have your head pulled." Now he could explain in terms they could understand the concept of redemption and salvation.

Time meant nothing to Finaba or his people as they marched on towards eternity. They knew nothing about the wars waged overseas, or about the Emancipation Proclamation declared by England in 1780 that set slaves free. They hadn't heard about American President Abraham Lincoln's declaration of Emancipation eighty years later on September 22, 1862. Finaba did hear the story of strange people who were dropped off at the coast. He heard about the thunder of the cannons. He heard about the strange languages those people spoke. But it was much later that he discovered they were freed slaves and that across the big river their king had emptied some of the jails and deported criminals and prostitutes along with many freed slaves, sending them to form a colony on the coast of Africa. He heard that when the king captured a ship bearing a cargo of slaves, his men would turn the ship around and release the cargo on the African coast. (The colony on the peninsula became known as "Freetown," for it was there that the captives knew again the joy of freedom.)

Finaba had no way of knowing that people from tribes he had never heard of were now living in his part of the world. He did know that they had to be able to communicate, and that over the years the neat-sounding words from each of the languages found their way into the vocabulary of the people on the peninsula. Using English as a base, and absorbing words from many other languages from all over West Africa, a unique and beautiful language was born which later became known as Krio.

In time, Finaba heard of the arrival of the white man. He knew that of the first nine who arrived in Sierra Leone, six died in a matter of weeks. In the first twenty five years of their ministry in Sierra Leone, the Church Missionary Society lost one hundred nine missionaries. The Christian and Missionary Alliance faced a similar situation. After twenty five years of ministry, thirty missionaries lay buried in African soil, with only forty two baptized believers as trophies of their labors (*Merging Streams*, by Eileen Lageer, Bethel Publishing Company, Elkhart Indiana 1978: pages 223 -224). Finaba knew that the diseases that claimed the lives of so many of his people were even harder on the white man. He heard that his part of the world soon came to be known as "The White Man's Grave Yard" as those diseases took a devastating toll on the early missionaries.

Soon Finaba heard that white men were coming into his area. Following the rivers, those early missionaries pushed into the interior with a persistence that caused Finaba no small amount of wonder. He knew that before long they would be coming through the foothills of the mountains, and he also knew the fear that gripped his people. All they had seen and known at the hands of the white man was dealt to them by the slavers and was not remembered with fondness. Even though many of the slavers in the interior were black, Finaba knew that his people saw the white man as the motivating force behind the disappearance of so many of their youth.

Courage and determination were the front-runners for the missionaries as they battled incredible odds en route to the interior. Finaba marveled that they would persist, for their graves often marked the trail for those who came behind. More graves of missionaries spotted the landscape than live missionaries, and Finaba wondered what could be so important in the interior of his country that men and women would lay down their lives to attain it. He learned years later that at that time many missionaries going out from America would pack their belongings in caskets to come to Africa because they realized that their chance of returning home in one was almost a certainty.

Finaba marveled at the commitment, and sometimes after a white man was laid to rest along the bank of the river and the rest of his people returned to their work, he would sit for a long time by the side of the grave and ponder the story that was in the making. He wished that he could have talked to the white man whose body lay beneath the sod so that he could ask, and perhaps be helped to understand, what had motivated them to come to such a harsh land. Finaba knew that the site of each grave would soon be forgotten and the white man's name possibly never remembered. He wondered about each man's family, his people, and why he had really come. He pondered even more as he considered what cause these white men considered worth dying for.

Soon the missionaries reached the end of the rivers, but they still pressed on. They marched overland, headed for the middle of what was known to them as "The Dark Continent." It was considered "dark" because the white man knew so little about it; "dark" because of the fear, superstition, and bondage that Satan had used to enslave the people for so long; "dark" because its people had never heard of the Fire (Light) of the Gospel, or of an eternal refuge called "heaven;" "dark" because their hearts and minds, had been blinded by the master of darkness, the devil himself; and "dark" because its people had marched, generation after generation after generation through the foothills of the mountains into an eternity for which they were not prepared.

The old familiar warning signal shocked Finaba back into reality. In former days that signal had sent his people scurrying into the caves in the hills. It had brought fear and dread to even the stoutest heart. Finaba knew that those days were supposed to have passed long ago, so he jumped up and hurried to discover what had caused such concern. Women and children quickly hid, but a few of the braver men advanced to see what the disturbance was about. There, coming into the southern edge of his village, was the first white man Finaba had ever seen. The stranger had blue eyes, and Finaba found himself wondering if the stranger could see out of eyes the color of the sky. How strange it was to see a man walking who had hair on his arms and head the color of the elephant grass at the beginning of dry season. In his amazement, Finaba chuckled when he thought that if the white man was friendly, even his own sons would soon want to feel the strange "feathers" that grew out of his arms and on his head.

The missionary settled in and began to learn the language. He sounded so nasal and ever so funny as he twisted his tongue around the simplest Kuranko words. What was even more amazing was that he wrote the sound on a paper and would later be able to repeat words back to the people. Soon his wife joined him and they were given a place to stay on a small hill at the edge of the town. Finaba heard that another missionary couple had arrived among the Kuranko people on the southern side of the Konko Mountains. He heard that they were planning to build a house and stay for a long time so that they could provide a resting spot for other missionaries who were coming overland. The mountains provided a natural barrier, and the rivers far inland were too small to be traveled by boat, so the missionaries' method of transportation into Central Africa would have to be on foot. The town chosen by the missionaries was a very logical transition point.

Finaba, like so many of the other elders in the tribe, was amazed at the stories the missionary told about a Man named Jesus, about His miracles, and about His teaching. They marveled at how quickly he learned to talk like they did, but how some of his customs and actions continued to remain so different. Then one day, death struck the home of the missionary like it had so many other homes in the little town of Samba. On the top of the hill among the rocks, a little white baby boy was laid to rest.

Finaba sensed that the missionaries had heavy hearts, but they pressed on in their efforts to learn his people's language and to enlarge the little books they were translating. However, the lingering diseases seemed to hinder their work, and Finaba was not surprised when after three years they told the gathered village elders that they had to return to their homeland for a period of time. It was obvious to the people that their missionaries had grown to love them and that they were leaving with heavy hearts, but only the Storyteller would live long enough to know that the young couple was never able to return and that many years would pass before another missionary would take up the ministry of love that they had left unfinished.

Years faded into history, and soon, only two tangible evidences of the missionary's presence in the village remained: a little grave among the rocks on the top of the hills and a small box of books that the missionary had given to little boy just before leaving Samba. Finaba knew that the little boy was the only one who had committed his heart and life to the God of the Book, who had become his Supreme Sacrifice and "pulled his head" from the bondage that ensnared the rest of his people. The Storyteller knew that was why the missionary had given the little boy the box of books. He knew that the boy harbored in his heart the hope that someday another missionary would come who would teach him to read so he could understand more about the incredible God who became man and died in his place. Finaba watched as the years went by and the little boy became a man, married, and had his own family, still treasuring that box of books. The young man still hoped God would send another missionary to open for him the Word of God written in the little books hidden safely away in the box he protected so carefully.

A generation passed, and then another. The little boy, now known as Samba Kei, had watched his children grow and he now had grandchildren. But no one had ever come back to teach him to read. Finally, as the oldest man in the village, he heard that missionaries had returned. But by then he was blind, and knew he would never be able to see the little scribbles on the yellowed pages in the box of books he had guarded so faithfully over the years.

Finaba knew that for one of his people the promises of the Book had been fulfilled. This old man had had his "head pulled" for he knew he had been redeemed. His heart had been set aflame by the Fire of the Holy Spirit. His feet had found the path that lead to an eternal refuge. The spiritual famine that had held his people in bondage for generations was over. A seed had been planted. A soul had been reborn. The harvest had begun! How long, Finaba wondered, before the rest of his people would hear.

Was this the beginning of the spiritual harvest foretold by the prophet Amos so long ago when he declared, "The days are coming, declares the Lord, when the reaper will be overtaken by the plowman, and the planter by the one treading grapes"? (Amos 9:13)

Chapter 4: Not Forgotten

Eighty years before the Emancipation Proclamation in America, the British Empire declared slavery illegal, and her navy began to do everything possible to stop the trafficking of human merchandise. The settlement formed by those freed slaves became known as Freetown and is today the capital city of Sierra Leone. Out of the rubble of slavery, a new nation emerged, forming its own customs and culture, becoming a unique and beautiful people. Just before the turn of the twentieth century, the Spirit of God moved in among those descendants of the slaves, and an incredible revival spread across the peninsula. Thousands, were brought into the kingdom of God. Bodies of believers joined together and stately churches were erected which stand today as a reminder of that Divine moment when the Spirit of God walked the coast of West Africa and started a revival fire stirring in the hearts of His people.

For many years Finaba knew nothing of the moving of the Spirit of God among the Krio people on the coast. When he finally did hear about it, he wondered why they did not press into the interior with the message of salvation. Although Finaba did not have any way of keeping track of the dates he did know how many generations passed since that revival which, in the white mans time, took place in the early 1900's. Maybe it was because they didn't know how many of his people were tucked away in the foothills of the mountains or hidden in the forests that bordered the rocky savanna land. Maybe rumors of tribal wars created fear in the hearts of the young Church on the coast so they never ventured beyond the confines of the peninsula. Whatever the reason, the awakening did not spread to the Kuranko people in the interior. However, the doors were now open for the arrival of more missionaries.

Due to hardship and disease, the life expectancy of a missionary in those early years was about ten months. It is estimated that for each missionary who laid down his or her life, less than one baptized convert remained (*Letters from the White Man's Grave : Pioneering on the Medical Missionary Frontier*, by Dr. Hugh L. Maclure, CREDO Publishing Corporation, White Rock, British Columbia, 1994, page 19). The causality rate was incredibly high, but the commitment so great that missionaries continued to come. They traveled the rivers and then pushed overland in their endeavor to reach beyond the mountains to carry the glorious message of salvation. Graves of the forerunners of today's missionaries still lie in the shade of the palm trees as silent monuments to hearts whose commitment was so great that they paid the ultimate sacrifice to declare the message of freedom to a people who, for generations, the devil had claimed as his own—hearts filled with a love for their Lord and the people of Africa.

During this time, sickness moved into one little corner of the Kuranko kingdom and claimed the lives of many of the residents of a little town called Heredugu tucked away on the edge of the foothills of the Konko Mountains. As animists they lived in fear, and in bondage, to the evil spirits and continually tried to appease them through ritual and sacrifice. But this time when sickness came, the people of Heredugu feared that the evil spirits were deeply offended and that they needed to move their town. As a result they fled from their homes and rebuilt new homes across the little river on a hill closer to the Ruwa River. Fortunately the disease left them and they settled in to life in their new location and continued to grow. They concluded that the change had appeased the spirits.

Finaba, the Storyteller, now centuries old, began to sense that times were beginning to change for his people forever. He watched with a little apprehension as he saw a missionary family move into Heredugu from the other side of the mountain, where the forest Kuranko lived. He was amazed at how quickly Jake and Ruth Schierling made the minor dialect changes in the language needed to effectively communicate the Gospel. And communicate they did! Finaba noticed that they did more than just talk, for they had a genuine interest in his people, their customs and their culture. The people respectfully called them "Pa" and "Ya" Schierling while the missionaries continued to refer to them as Jake and Ruth. Finaba laughed as Jake spent hours learning to play an indigenous game of math with the elders of the village who soon discovered that they could no longer defeat the white man at their own game. They held no animosity in their hearts for a man who so obviously cared for them.

Along with the rest of his people, Finaba was fascinated by the arrival of the jeep that the Schierlings brought along the winding road, if indeed one could call it a road. It was early 1951, and roads had not yet penetrated into the interior. The route the jeep traveled was actually not much more than a widened footpath through the bush that Jake had extended to reach their town. The Storyteller marveled at the loads the 4-wheeled monster could carry, and the speed at which it could travel through an area that for generations had known only the soft padding of bare or sandaled feet of travelers whose voices were raised in laughter, argument, or song, as they trudged the weary miles through the hills. The coming of the jeep brought other changes, for it was the forerunner of market vehicles that would bring produce, medicine, and cloth, and shortened the road to other towns and tribes. However, the vehicles also required that bridges be built, revealing another skill of the missionary as Jake began to supervise the construction of several major bridges in the area. Eventually the whole of the upper Kuranko territory would be accessible to the newfound means of transportation that could bring in goods for the weekly markets.

From generations of experience with people, Finaba sensed that the physical changes taking place as a result of the arrival of the missionaries was not nearly as great as the change that was beginning to take place because of the message that the missionaries brought. It was a message of love and of freedom, of Creator God who left all of heaven's glory to become a man so that he could be the Supreme Sacrifice for sin and pull their heads from the fear, superstition, and bondage of animism, ancestral worship, Islam, sin, death and hell. It was a message of deliverance, and as Finaba and his people listened to the Word of God being translated into their own language, they began to sense the stirring of the Spirit that generations earlier had moved along the coast and transformed the lives of the Krio people so long ago.

One by one, Kuranko people began to make a commitment to Christ as they heard the message of salvation. The Schierling's love for the culture and the people was evidenced, but their tremendous drive and commitment to Christ also came through loud and clear as they took the handful of believers and taught them the truths of God's Word. Soon God gave Jake and Ruth a vision for a Bible school, and a small classroom building was constructed under the shade of the trees on the mission compound. Along with the truths of Scripture, carpentry and more effective agriculture methods were taught. During those years of ministry (1951-1959), God used the Schierlings as instruments to plant His Church among the "upper" Kuranko people. A small church was established in the town of Heredugu. Finaba, saw the joys and the sorrow, the victories and the defeats, the changes and the conflicts of those early years of ministry among his people, but what he could not know until years later was that during those years the foundation was laid for a strong indigenous Church among his people.

Scriptures were translated, literacy classes were taught, seekers came—not alone—but with friends, and the Church began to grow. Years later, when the author moved into the area, he discovered evidence of the small beginning of a "people movement" among the Heredugu people at that time, but for some reason it never came into full blossom. When the Schierlings left there was one church in the area. The Schierlings had a vision of training national leadership, but when they went on furlough and were unable to return the small Bible school they had started in Heredugu became a memory.

Following the departure of the Schierlings for furlough, other missionaries came into the area for brief periods of ministry. None were able to stay for an extended period of time to do evangelism and church planting, or to build on the foundation that the Schierlings had laid. After a few years, a shortage of staff made it impossible for the Mission to station anyone in Heredugu, and for many years it stood vacant. Finaba saw the departure of the Schierlings, and he knew that the reason they did not return was because of the tremendous vision they carried in their hearts for a Bible school to train national leadership among his people. Years later when a Bible school was established in a city more centrally located to the overall work of the Mission, the Schierlings came back and lent their skills in the language, construction, translation, teaching, and organization to the development of that institution which has since trained most of the pastors now ministering among the Kuranko and Yalunka people groups. Their vision for the unreached people in the upper Kuranko area never dimmed, and they continued to make trips to Heredugu to encourage the Church and let them know that they still had a heart for the area. They assured the people that they were praying and that they would do everything they could to recruit others to take their place as area missionaries while they continued to train pastors at the Bible School who would help to reach the entire tribe.

Finaba sat musing under the shade of a mango tree, wondering if this time the rumors would be true that a young missionary couple was coming to take up residence in Heredugu. Could it be that once again he would hear the sounds of children's laughter echoing through the old mission house across the creek from town? Would the people really have one who would share their burdens, understand their tears, enjoy their laughter, and point them to an eternal refuge? Since the Schierlings left almost a generation ago, he had listened to the church pray that God would send an area missionary to take up the load of church planting among his people. But no one had come, and many had gone on into eternity without ever hearing the message that Finaba knew would change the hearts and lives of his people. Now "Pa" Jake Schierling was visiting the town again, and in the morning service he had announced that he needed help to fix up the road a little bit so that the new young couple could come and share Christmas with the Heredugu people.

Several days passed, and Finaba, along with the others, was finally convinced that a new family would soon be visiting. Pa Schierling, with the help of some of the Christians, had cleaned up the old mission house, repaired some needed furnishings, and fixed up the road. Then Pa Schierling took his truck and headed out to the big river where a bridge had washed out during the rainy season so that he could help the young missionaries ford the river. It was not long before Finaba could hear the sound of two vehicles coming, and he knew that God in His faithfulness had not forgotten the upper Kuranko people.

What a Christmas that was as Jake and Ruth Schierling introduced the Earl Reifel family to the Kuranko people (1975). Jake took them around town to meet the chief and the elders, the grannies and the big men. They were bombarded with qustions from curious children who had never seen white children before, let alone a white baby. It was the Christmas season, but for many, curiosity more than celebration was the reason they found their way to the missionary's home on the edge of town. Friendly chatter and laughter filled the air as they watched the new arrivals, especially the children.

Finaba chuckled quietly as he watched the preparations for the Christmas dinner. There was no turkey or ham, so Jake, his son Keith, and Earl went into the bush to invite a ham to come to dinner. Unfortunately word had gone through the animal kingdom that the new missionaries were hungry and so all the hams scurried off through the bush, taking a rain check on the invitation to dinner. However, one unfortunate python remained behind to welcome the visitors into his swamp. A well-placed invitation soon found him being carried back to the mission, and now Finaba had to laugh as he recalled the struggle those men had skinning that nine foot snake to prepare it for the coming banquet. Keith felt it would not be enough for the anticipated feast, so he took a motorcycle and headed out to the river in hopes of returning with some fish.

Having been to school, the fish had heard all about the Christmas feast and had moved on, leaving behind a crocodile that was gullible enough to be persuaded by a local fisherman to join the festivities. Keith returned home, proudly bearing the choicest section of the tail, his contribution to the upcoming event. Having been a missionary's kid in Nigeria, Earl did not have a problem with the preparations for the feast, but his wife was a little unsure of the gourmet cooking she saw underway. A curious bush fowl (quail) checked out the situation, and persuaded by Earl's invitation, decided to stay for dinner. Finaba suspected that the new missionary wife never closed her eyes as the prayer was being offered. Actually he suspected that her prayer was a little different than the others—a prayer that God would prevent that bird from leaving that platter because she perceived it to be the only edible potion of meat at the table. God heard her prayer. It stayed. She feasted.

The new couple, however, was not stationed in Heredugu until the book part of their language study was completed six months later and Earl had preached his first sermon in Kuranko, albeit a very brief one. During that time they lived in Kurela and studied the language under the tutelage of Jake and Ruth Schierling. In June, 1976, the Annual Field Council of missionaries stationed the Reifels at Heredugu, and they were free to begin moving to their new location to take up the ministry the Lord had called them to.

In the midst of the July rains, Earl began to transport their belongings to their new residence in Heredugu. The trip, although only one hundred miles, took a full day's drive in the truck. Finaba had helped some other men repair the bridge spanning the Soko river four miles out of town so that the truck could cross. Load after load of provisions came up from Kurela so the Reifels could begin to set up housekeeping. Earl made many trips without the family, transporting furnishings and supplies so that his family would have what they needed when they moved up to their new home with their three pre-school children. Finally Earl started out with the last truck load of supplies he would need to take before the rest of the family would be able to move in. He left Kurela on a beautiful tropical day, but about two hours out of Heredugu, a big beautiful tropical storm moved in.

A great tropical storm had driven the people of Heredugu onto their verandas and they were able to enjoy the hours of relaxed conversation in weather that prevented the continuation of their farm work. Suddenly they saw a bedraggled figure coming across the log bridge just out of town. Children skipped along in laughter to greet their new missionary friend who was coming into town with an obvious load over his shoulder. Could it really be that he had made the journey from Kurela in the storm? In response to their questions, Earl declared that he had indeed made the journey because it was not raining in Kurela when he left, but that the Soko river, four miles out of town was too flooded to get the truck through the river and across the bridge. He asked for volunteers to go back to the river with him and carry in a few of the bigger, more necessary loads. Finaba laughed as he examined the load tied across the missionary's shoulders. On his front there were six chickens with their legs tied together dangling from a rope running over his shoulder. Out of curiosity, Finaba walked around to the back of the missionary to see what could possibly be on the other end of the rope. Would you believe six more chickens were hanging there, just as soaked as the six in front! In his heart Finaba rejoiced at this evidence that the young missionary intended to stay awhile. Why else would he want to start a flock of chickens? Why else would he be willing to walk that four miles each direction from the bridge in the rain? Yes, it was beginning to look like they really were going to have an area missionary again.

Having completed the language lessons available in books, Earl settled in to learning how to communicate with his many newfound friends. He soon discovered that the children were an excellent source of information; first, because they are so friendly, and second because they are totally uninhibited. They would escort Earl to their farms chattering all along the way, often without realizing that their white friend did not have the slightest idea what the conversation was about. Often when he did talk he would make the funniest errors, which Finaba knew would be shared that evening as the children sat around the fire warming themselves. Earl would laugh right along with the people, and then ask how to say the word, or phrase, correctly so that he could be understood more clearly the next time. It seemed a slow process, but out under the mango trees, along the paths to the farms, and playing soccer with the children and youth, the language began to come together for Earl.

As Earl began to adjust to the people and the culture, so the people began to adjust to him and his strange ways too. Some of the people in town felt they had a new source of income and that they could go out to the mission house and borrow from an "unlimited supply." They discovered that Earl had a different idea. On the edge of the mission property was a forest where the young men had gone through their initiation rites for generations. The elders of the town felt that location should be moved, so another area of forest was chosen. One of the elders quickly seized the opportunity and asked permission to farm the little swamp where the forest was. Having been granted permission, he cut down the trees and planted rice.

By the time the Reifels arrived, the rice had been harvested and the grass had grown up over the logs from the trees that had been cut down. Earl asked some of the elders to help him, and took the four-wheel drive truck and some chains down to the edge of the swamp. The bewildered elders watched as Earl walked with them through the grass to the logs. At each log he would stop and ask them how much they would charge him to split that particular log into firewood. Then he would fasten a chain around it and drag it to higher ground. Soon he had four piles of logs. Finaba was puzzled by the activity of the young missionary until a couple of days later when a man came out to ask Earl for a loan. Earl talked to him as they walked toward the edge of the swamp, and then stooping at the first pile of logs he said, "You say you need $50. Well, you could split ten logs from that pile, or five from that pile, then I would pay you the $50 you need, and we would still be friends."

After several such visitors had checked out the new "loan officer," the ones in need found that they really could earn what they needed. Those who just wanted a handout disappeared, and Earl soon discovered that he had a very willing and able crew of workers. Some of the men saw him as the "banker" and they would split logs and take only half the money, leaving the rest in the "bank" until they had a desperate need, or until tax time came around. Some years the "bank" held the taxes for as many as thirty men. When the tax collector came they would come to the "bank", withdraw their hard-earned cash, and joyfully go back to town and pay their taxes.

The men in town soon realized that they needed to make other adjustments to the new missionary. Some had seen other missionaries take a can of insect spray and spray the chicken coop so that fleas would not be a problem. Earl opened the box of brand new spray cans only to discover

31

that the little spray nozzles were defective and would not work. However, he was not about to throw the cans away since he would have to travel all the way to the coast to get new ones. Finaba was amazed to see him set the can in the middle of the chicken coop, back up about twenty five yards, and then shoot it with a rifle. In one great poof the whole chicken coop was de-bugged. That method proved so effective that from then on he even used the good cans in the same manner.

When the Reifel kids were a little older, a problem arose with cockroaches in the latrine, which was a small mud-block building about forty yards behind the house. Toby and Andy tried to light a fire in the latrine to burn out the roaches, but they had trouble so they called their dad to help them. Together they poured gasoline into the latrine, which was sixteen feet deep. Then they lit a fuse and stood back. When the gasoline caught fire, there was a tremendous explosion. The latrine roof lifted slightly off the mud walls as flames shot out from underneath it. Bits and pieces of roaches were scattered all over. But when the smoke settled and the laughter subsided, there was only one response: "Do it again Dad! Do it again!" Of course they did it again—just to make sure that the entire cockroach population had been expelled.

The nationals were not the only ones making adjustments to a different way of doing things. The missionaries had to learn too. Sometimes there's not a clearly defined right way and wrong way of doing things. Sometimes it's just different. Earl recalled how in his youth growing up with missionary parents in Nigeria he had discovered this truth when he was talking to a nomadic cow herder. They were standing near some cows, and Earl asked his friend if it was time to milk the cows. The man told Earl that only women know how to milk cows.

Having helped on a dairy farm while on furlough in Michigan, Earl responded that he knew how to milk a cow. After a brief discussion, the Fulani cow herder led him over to one of the cows and invited Earl to go ahead and milk her. Earl no sooner touched the cow than she hauled off and kicked him soundly, proving the man's point and causing Earl to declare, "You are right. Only women know how to milk cows."

Often differences were a matter of perspective. Earl discovered this when the kerosene fridge quit working and he defrosted the freezer before relighting the fire. Finaba often heard Earl marvel at how a little fire in the bottom of a kerosene fridge could cause things above it to cool and the items in the freezer compartment at the top of the fridge to freeze. When he broke a large chunk of ice loose Earl took it outside. Several men were sitting on the veranda, so he asked Bande to help him. When Bande readily agreed, Earl handed the chunk of ice to Bande and asked him to hold it for a little bit. Never having seen ice before and not knowing what to expect, Bande reached out his hands and accepted his new role. It didn't take long before Bande experienced a sensation he had never felt before. He had no way to express it other than to exclaim, "It's hot! It's hot! It's hot!" Earl watched as the chunk of ice was passed from one man to the next so that they could experience what Bande was trying to tell them. Earl's children could not understand how the ice could be considered hot, and so Earl had to explain to them that their friends had no frame of reference in which to put the coldness of the ice, and as a result their perspective was totally different than those who have experienced cold as we know it in America.

Faith, Toby and Andy, also learned something about perspective when one of the men needed a job to earn extra money. Earl asked him to dig out an anthill in the front yard. All went well until the man came across the huge Queen Ant and brought it to the kids to show them. They were amazed because they had never seen such a gigantic ant. The man had the ant on a little dish, and he put it down and invited them to eat it with him. He suggested that before they eat they should thank God for the food. Although they said they were not interested in the meal, Faith, Toby and Andy did pray for the man's "lunch" and then, with Earl, watched him eat it. Although he smacked his lips and declared that it was delicious, the kids continued to pray for him and his tummy for the next three days until they were sure that he was not going to get sick.

The Kuranko children in town also learned to make some adjustments. They saw the truck moving through the one and only "street" in the middle of town as a challenge, and they would run and jump on. Earl would stop and reprimand them and tell them how dangerous it was to try and jump onto a moving vehicle, especially since some of them would try to climb on the tire to help them get over the back of the truck into the bed. Of course they could not relate to the danger since they did not have a context in which to put a fast-moving vehicle that could seriously hurt them if they fell under it. So Earl went to the town elders and the chief, and asked them to talk to·their children so they would not get hurt trying to jump on the moving vehicle. The men understood how dangerous it was, and told Earl simply to stop the truck, catch the children and beat them so that they would not do such a thing again. Earl said he would not spank their kids so the chief told him to bring the children to him and he would take care of it.

One evening as Earl headed out of town, a little boy used the back bumper as a stepping stone into the back of the truck and managed to hitch a ride. Earl saw him jump on, but did not want him to escape, so he kept going until he got to the chief's house. When he stopped, the chief came over and took the little fellow out of the back of the truck, and Earl continued on his journey.

Several hours later, a storm was moving in over the hills as Earl returned home. As he drove into town, he saw about a dozen little boys sitting on the veranda of the house across the road from the chief's house. He stopped to see what the problem was, and found the little boy who had jumped into the back of the truck was fastened in the stocks. The chief said he would not be released until he had paid a fine of about half a day's wages for a working man. All the little boys friends were sitting with him on the veranda because when they tried to pool all their pennies they still came up short. It was a pretty forlorn little group waiting for the storm to hit. Earl quickly paid the fine and the little guy was released. But word finally spread through town that the moving truck was "off limits," and one had to wait until it stopped and then get permission for a ride before jumping on.

Unfortunately it was not just the little boys who had the problem. Some time later, Earl was working with the Paramount Chief on building a bridge when several men jumped in the back of the truck while it was going by. One of the workers who was traveling with Earl told them that the chief had laid down the law that nobody was to climb in the truck, but that all the men were to go to their work site on foot since there were too many men for the vehicle. The worker who was riding in the back of the truck to care for the tools told the men what the chief would do if he found them in the back of the truck. They said they were not worried because Earl was going to the work site. When they found out that Earl had to go see the chief first, one of the men decided he would rather leave and walk back than have the chief find him in the back of the truck. Not having any concept of a fast-moving vehicle he stood up and simply stepped out of the truck. A Team member shouted for Earl to stop, and they found the poor man sprawled out in the middle of the road. Fortunately it was a new road that had recently been dug up with picks and shovels, so the man had a fairly decent landing in the soft dirt and was unhurt. But he was a whole lot wiser for his experience.

Finaba watched as Earl observed and learned. He would often ask why the Kuranko did something a certain way, or why they believed what they did. Then he would remind them that he wanted to watch until he discovered the real reason they were doing what they were doing because their core values and belief system would eventually be revealed. He knew that they were watching him just as closely to see why he did what he did and what he was really like.

Chapter 5: How Many Generations?

As Earl began to adapt to the Kuranko people and their culture, he began to analyze it. He soon came to the conclusion that there are three categories of cultural elements that one has to carefully consider. The first and most obvious category consists of the neutral issues like the food they eat, the homes they live in, the way they farm, and the basic items of everyday living that vary around the world due to climate, geography, and weather.

The second category involves the positive ingredients that make up a culture. The longer he lived among the Kuranko people, the more positive things Earl discovered in their culture. The first and most obvious to him was their tremendous hospitality. He marveled at how they could have so little—by American standards—yet share so much. A stranger passing through the town was always guaranteed a few free meals and a place to stay, no matter how difficult the times were or how poor the harvest had been. They shared what they had. Another positive aspect of the culture that quickly became obvious was the tremendous respect they show for the elderly. They see their elders as a source of knowledge and experience —almost as a fountain of wisdom — and honor them for that. Earl concluded that in a land where life expectancy is one of the lowest in the world, the aged do deserve a special place in the culture.

The third category is made up of the negative issues in the culture. Earl learned to define these as those aspects of the culture that run cross-grain to the Scriptures. Outsiders often have trouble identifying these because they tend to process everything through their own cultural grid and measure issues in light of what they have been taught or have experienced. Earl realized that he had to be extremely cautious about labeling something in his host culture as negative. He had to understand this negative aspect before he could plant an indigenous church, because if he could not properly identify the negative he would tangle with the wrong issues. The result would likely be a Church that looked very much like the sending Church back home, but one that would not be fully accepted in the host culture. He decided that the best way to analyze the culture was to observe and ask questions. He learned that one has to ask the right questions to get real answers. To do this, Earl needed to adapt to his host culture in an appropriate manner.

One of the negative issues he had to deal with was the fatalistic attitude that what happened simply happened, and there was nothing anyone could do about it. The declaration would then be that "God willed it." Finaba knew that in many cases this was true, but he sensed the total frustration that Earl felt when the wife of one of his friends refused to let her baby be treated with modern medicine. When the baby died, the woman simply said that what happened had happened, and that it was up to God. Earl's frustration was multiplied because his friend, the womans husband, had taken the baby to the clinic, where medicine was being given and the baby was recovering before the mother took the baby and walked seventeen miles home, leaving the medicine behind. Earl tried to ask the right questions and listen keenly to gain a better understanding of the situation. As the years passed he continued to encounter a fatalistic attitude in so many people in so many areas of their lives. In an effort to identify with his friends as closely as he could, he set out to learn how they thought and how they felt.

Earl knew that traditionally the missionaries were called by their American surname with a prefix of "Pa" (Mr.) added for the men, and "Ya" (Mrs.) for the women. He suspected however, that the Kurankos had their own names for the missionaries in their own language, and sometimes he would ask them what those names were. He figured that missionaries had come to be known by some characteristic, habit, or feature after the people had watched them closely for some time. Once the trust was strong enough, Earl figured that they would tell him some of those names. He soon discovered that as the trust relationship grew, they would actually do imitations of the missionaries. He figured they really trusted him when, although a little embarrassed to admit it at first, they imitated him. His laughter encouraged them, and later he was often privileged to see himself through their eyes as they did imitations of him along with the other missionaries.

One Sunday morning, the pastor decided it was time to let Earl know what they called him in Kuranko, and from then on he became known to most of the people in the area as "Dembeli." They would often ask what clan he was from, and Dembeli would laughingly respond with the Kuranko rendition of his American surname. But as time passed and relationships grew, Dembeli discovered that some of the people really wanted to be able to place him in one of their clans. An older man and Dembeli had formed a bond that many soon came to recognize as very special as the two of them discipled younger Christians together. Some time later an elder from a nearby town asked Dembeli what clan he was from. The Holy Spirit prompted Dembeli to respond by referring to his close friend as his older brother. He then asked the elder what reason there would be for him have a different clan name than that of his older brother. Dembeli's response brought surprising peace and acceptance. After that, people would occasionally call him by his clan name, and Dembeli discovered a new meaning to the bond that we have as brothers in Christ.

Shortly after arriving in the area, Dembeli was walking through a town and noticed a very elderly woman lying on the veranda of her hut so that the hot tropical sun would not be so punishing. Finaba watched in silence as Dembeli meandered over to the hut and greeted the lady with all the respect due her age and position. Once the greetings were completed, Finaba roared with laughter as Dembeli endeavored to share with the lady his faith in Christ. He got words mixed up and said the wrong thing, and it was really hard to understand his Kuranko. If the Storyteller could have stepped into real life, he could have told the lady what the young missionary was really trying to say. Realizing that he was not communicating, Dembeli asked the lady if she would allow him to pray with her. He prayed, and then headed home. It seemed to Finaba that with each step Dembeli took for the five miles home, he prayed one prayer over and over and over again. The young missionary was crying out to God with all his heart, "Lord, help me learn enough Kuranko to share the love of Jesus with these people." The God of all grace answered that prayer!

The elderly lady on the veranda was the first person Dembeli had tried to share his faith with one on one in Kuranko, and he felt the weight of failure. Interestingly enough, almost nineteen years later Dembeli was walking through another town and saw an elderly lady on her veranda. It brought back so many memories! Finaba watched to see if he would go and greet this granny as he had the other one so many years before. He did, but this time she responded, for she could understand. Finaba listened intently now with no need to interrupt as the wonderful story of the Gospel unfolded for the lady's listening ears. When Dembeli asked her if she understood, the lady responded that she had heard, but that she was not ready to make a commitment. Dembeli prayed with her, and then reminded her that any time she wanted to accept Jesus as her Savior and Lord that she could send word to him and he would come, or she could stop out at the house, and he would be more than happy to pray with her.

A few days later Finaba observed the granny picking her way ever so slowly along the path to the mission house. He sat in awed silence as he watched a scene unfold that confirmed in his mind that this was the real reason why the now not-so-young missionary had come to Finaba's people so long ago. After the preliminary greetings, Dembeli sat down beside the elderly lady on some boards that were stacked on the veranda. Pastor Dauda was nearby, and Dembeli called him to join them in the shade. Then with all respect Dembeli turned to the granny and asked her how he could help her that day. She stated her purpose so simply and yet so beautifully when she responded, "I am ready to walk with Jesus. I have come to have you pray with me." Finaba could almost see the little wheels of memory turning in Dembeli's mind, and was not surprised when he asked the lady to repeat why she had come. Then to make sure she understood what she was asking, Dembeli once again explained the plan of salvation. Three heads bowed in prayer as an old granny became a newborn child in the family of God. Shouts of joy and praise echoed through the halls of glory, and later Finaba witnessed the tears of joy and praise as Dembeli knelt in the silence of his own home and remembered the first elderly granny of so long ago. He thanked God that his prayer had been answered, and that the last person he would talk to about Jesus before leaving the country because of the war was another old granny who had just been born from above.

Finaba learned to enjoy following Dembeli around because he said and did some of the funniest things. Meeting a hunter, he asked if the hunt had been a good one. "No," replied the hunter, "I did not even see anything." Finaba thought Dembeli did well when he expressed sympathy to the hunter for his troubles, but when the hunter asked Dembeli if his hunt the day before had been successful, Finaba rolled with laughter at Dembeli's response. He said that the day before he had "shot three small smells. Thanks be to God." This rather confused the hunter, who asked him to repeat his statement—which Dembeli did. Then the confused hunter asked him what the "small smells" looked like. Finaba could have died laughing as the white man described an animal with long ears. "Oh," said the hunter, "you mean you shot an elephant." But the missionary shook his head and tried again to describe the "smells" he had shot.

The hunter tried again, and asked if he meant that he had shot a duiker (a small antelope). Once again Dembeli shook his head. Again Finaba roared as Dembeli tried to describe the "smells" that had found their way into his cooking pot. Finally, the hunter asked what the white man had done with the three smells he had shot. Dembeli assured the hunter that he had put them into his hunting bag and taken them home. By this time the hunter must have decided to just go along with the "smells" story and asked what had been done with them when he got them home. Dembeli proceeded with all diligence to convince the hunter that those three small smells had been cooked and that they made a delicious soup which he had eaten over rice earlier that day. Finaba would have loved to have stepped in and given the right word, but it seemed more fun to just let the hunter share the story until someone came from Heredugu a few days later and let him know that the "smells" with the big ears were really rabbits.

This encounter reminded Finaba of a recent journey he had taken with the Dembeli to Kurela, where he went twice a month to pick up the mail and to get fuel for the truck and kerosene for the fridge. It had really been a rather prosperous trip, for a variety of monkeys along the way had been rather forcefully persuaded by Dembeli's shotgun to join him on his excursion. One particular red monkey was too close when the Dembeli's gun spoke harsh words and the monkey had to listen to all of them. As a result, he looked like a sieve with "stuff" leaking out all over. The six hours the monkey spent bouncing along in the truck did not improve his looks by any stretch of the imagination.

By the time Dembeli reached Kurela that evening, the poor little monkey was a gory mess with blood and other "stuff" stuck to his fur, or leaking out of the holes in his anatomy. Within a few minutes of their arrival at the Bible school compound in Kurela, Dembeli was greeted by some good friends. Having persuaded several other monkeys to journey with him, he felt it would be appropriate to give one to a friend who had just come in off the farm. The students had not yet cooked the evening meal, and Dembeli knew that the meat would be greatly appreciated. Finaba watched as Dembeli took the yucky monkey out of the truck, and with all good intentions of friendliness, handed it to his friend meaning to say, "My friend, this is yours." Instead, with a big smile wrapped around his head and a warm note of friendship in his voice, Dembeli handed the monkey to his friend with the words, "My friend, this is you."

Dembeli made other major language goofs, too numerous to mention. Finaba especially enjoyed the day that Dembeli was alone on his motorcycle when he found a man lying in the road. The man was so drunk he had passed out on the way to his farm. Dembeli decided that the man really needed help, so he turned around and went back to the town nearest where he had found the man. However, Dembeli had not learned the word for "drunk" yet, and so he told the chief and several elders that were gathered there that a man was "sick" and lying in the road, and that he needed help. They quickly rounded up some young men and sent them out to bring the "sick" man home.

For the next several weeks each time Dembeli showed up in town, one or more of the young men would come staggering to meet him declaring loudly, "Oh I'm sick. I'm sick. I'm so sick." Nobody ever needed to tell the rest of the story, because like so many other stories among the Kuranko people, the punch line says it all.

Dembeli did learn through his language errors to be careful of what he said. One day as he was walking into town with his friend named Bande, they met Dembeli's sons playing with some of their little Kuranko friends. Dembeli was surprised to see Bande step off into the bush and come out with a switch. Some Kuranko boys from town were talking and Dembeli's sons were repeating the words they were saying. When the boys from town looked up and saw Bande with his switch, they took off running. They were not quite fast enough to get away from the switch or the tongue lashing, but whatever they were saying was not to be repeated because Bande would not even tell Dembeli the meaning of the words that his sons had just learned. When they got home, Toby and Andy explained that they had not learned the words yet so they could not repeat them correctly, but they were very willing to take them out their vocabulary. After that, Dembeli taught his kids never to repeat just any word, but to know what the new word meant before using it!

Dembeli continued to learn the language and customs of the people. The Storyteller noticed that the walks through the villages and the trips along the roads left Dembeli's heart heavy. He looked at the maps often and talked to the elders as best as he could, but could not discover how long the Kuranko people had been in the area. Then one day he was out alone when he started up a rocky hill. The path, like all the main paths through the bush to the villages, was easy to follow, for it had been worn into the hard gravel soil by many travelers. Dembeli seldom walked anywhere by himself, but on this particular day he was alone. He noticed that nearer to the top of the small mountain he was climbing that there was no path—only rock—and wondered how he would find his way. Finaba had watched him on many occasions and knew he would not turn back until he had reached the top of the hill. It seemed to the Storyteller that Dembeli simply had to see what was on the other side of the mountain and that to turn back before reaching the top would somehow offend his sense of accomplishing what he had set out to do. But this was different, for the dirt gave way to rock and the rock covered a large portion of the top of the hill. Yet Dembeli did not turn back.

At the edge of the rock he stopped, and the Storyteller watched as Dembeli gazed in amazement at the path that had been worn across solid rock by the generations of bare and sandaled feet that had walked that way before him. How many generations? How many bare feet? How long does it take to wear a path smooth across solid rock? Suddenly the thought struck Dembeli that all those generations of people, generation after generation after generation, had marched through the foothills of the mountains and had never known that they could have their heads pulled, that they could have within them the fire of the Holy Spirit and know that their feet were treading a path that led to the eternal refuge. All this is possible because God became man, lived among us, died as the Supreme Sacrifice for our sins, and rose again so that we can know we will spend eternity with Him. But how can they know if they have never heard? Finaba watched as Dembeli's heart broke and God gave him a new love for the Kuranko people as he asked his Lord, "How can one missionary reach such a big area with so many people for the Gospel?"

The Storyteller watched to see what response Dembeli would have to the realization that for generations the devil had considered the area his territory. He listened as Dembeli questioned the Paramount Chiefs and learned how many people and villages were actually in the area. Later he learned some new things when he found maps and census reports. Had he been asked, Finaba could have shared the facts that the area Dembeli was asking about was almost two thousand square miles, had over two hundred towns in it - - fewer than a quarter of which were accessible by motorized vehicle. An estimated 50,000 people lived in the area. He could have told Dembeli that he was living among a people group who were unreached by the Gospel.

Chapter 6: Gospel Teams

Finaba could not see what was happening in Dembeli's heart until one day Dembeli went to meet with Pastor Pita, the only pastor in the upper Kuranko area. He asked Pastor Pita a lot of questions. The facts he had been gathering were confirmed. One, there were no other missions, missionaries, or churches working in the whole of the up-country Kuranko area. Two, the closest missionaries, also with the same mission as Dembeli, were approximately a four to six hour drive away, depending on the season of the year. They were working among the Yalunka people. Three, no efforts of evangelism or church planting were being carried on in the area. Four, the area was basically unreached with the Gospel although there was one church, one pastor, and approximately thirty five or forty believers. God had richly blessed the earlier ministry of Jake and Ruth Schierling, and that one Church which He had planted through their ministry was a solid base of Bible-believing Christians. These were the facts.

In the middle of that vast area, along with the one church and one pastor, was now one church planter named Dembeli. Finaba sensed the excitement that Dembeli expressed as he shared with Pastor Pita God's response when he had asked God how he could reach that area with the Gospel. The Lord had told Dembeli that He would give him a "Gospel Team" he could work with, who would in turn reach their own people. Considering the Scriptures, Dembeli shared his belief that God gives all the gifts necessary to the Church for the building up of the body of Christ. He shared with Pastor Pita that if they really believed that, they would have to expect that God would give the gifts of evangelism, discipleship, and church planting to various individuals in the Heredugu Church so that

43

they could reach their people with the Gospel. Dembeli asked Pastor Pita to join him in prayer that God would do just that. Pastor Pita expressed his support and encouragement, and asked the young missionary to present his idea to the Church. The two friends prayed together, seeking God's will.

The following days were days of anticipation. Dembeli presented the concept of a Gospel Team to the Church and asked that the believers trust the Lord to give to the Body of Christ the gifts necessary to begin to reach the area with the Gospel. As Dembeli considered the monumental task ahead, he purposed in his heart to not ask for volunteers or to call on those he felt would do a great job. Pastor Pita agreed to this, and the Church began to pray with them. They never once approached the Church by saying, "Saturday morning we are going out on an evangelism trip to such and such a town and we would like some of you to go along. Meet here at the church at such and such a time." They never went to the Church and said, "You, you, and you have the gift of evangelism. Thursday evening let's go visit such and such a town and share the Gospel with them." The Storyteller wondered how they would ever get people on a Gospel Team if they did not advertise a little more aggressively.

But then it happened! On the same day at different times, two men came separately to Dembeli and asked if they could join him for a trip to Folote to share the Gospel. Dembeli set up a time for that evening to meet up with the men to walk to Folote together. Having watched the young missionary for the past few months, the Storyteller sensed his excitement as he anticipated the walk that evening. Then Dembeli noticed that a big, beautiful tropical storm was rolling in over the foothills of the mountains. Finaba watched as Dembeli went to the office and knelt in prayer, asking the Lord to hold off the storm long enough for them to get to Folote and back. For weeks he had been praying about the Gospel Team. Then the Church had joined him in prayer. Now there was a meager beginning, and he really expected the Lord to hold the storm off for a few hours until they could venture out and begin the fulfillment of a dream. Dembeli continued his work around the mission compound through the afternoon, but the Storyteller noticed that every once in a while he would turn and look at the bank of dark thunder clouds that was approaching on an ever increasing wind. He noticed that Dembeli would pause and pray again, asking the Lord to hold off the storm.

When evening rolled around, Dembeli prepared to go. On the way through town, he was joined by Dauda and Pa Suluku. They chattered joyfully as they walked though the hills. They waded through a little stream that was a mere trickle coming down out of the nearby hills. Dembeli did not even get the tops of his tennis shoes wet in the shallow water. They hardly slowed down in their anticipation of this first trip as a Gospel Team.

Arriving in town, the Team greeted the town chief and some of the elders who were seated on the veranda of his grass-thatched house. The chief and elders welcomed them and assured them that it would be fine if their words were shared with all the people who were willing to come and listen. The town crier was dispatched to announce to the people that there would be a general meeting at the chief's house and that all were invited. No sooner had the service started than it began to rain. Not just rain, but RAIN RAIN! Fortunately, one of the men from the town, an officer in the Sierra Leone army, was building a large pan-roofed house with a parlor big enough to hold a large crowd of people so the meeting was quickly transferred into that partially completed structure. For the next couple of hours the newly formed Gospel Team had a captive audience. It was a great time of sharing the Gospel Story. The Storyteller chuckled for he knew that nobody wanted to venture out into the downpour.

When the rain let up, the crowd began to disperse. The chief asked the Gospel Team if they wanted to stay a little longer until the rain had completely stopped, but they decided to head for home. They only had about three and a half miles to walk, and it was getting later than they had planned. As they started out of town they discovered that the tropical downpour had beaten down the elephant grass to such an extent that portions of the path were hidden from view. Clouds obscured the moon, so it was totally dark, except for the ring of light thrown out by the flickering flame of a kerosene storm lantern, which was faithfully trying to shine through rain-splattered glass. Spirits were high, and the three men pushed the grass aside and kept pressing for home. The elephant grass at that time of the year was already twelve to fifteen feet tall, and it was no easy task to find the footpath in some places.

When they reached the stream that had been only inches deep a few hours earlier, the Team discovered that the run-off water from the hills had swollen it to a river. The Storyteller almost laughed aloud at the expression on Dembeli's face as Dauda, who was leading, began to forge though the swollen current. Soon it was up to his chest, and Finaba wondered what Dembeli would do since he could not swim. Wading faster than any fish could swim, Dembeli pressed on through the current to the opposite bank of the river.

Have you ever had a good grumble session at God? At that point Dembeli began to express to God his disappointment that the Lord had not held off the storm. He pointed out to God that the storm was so bad it even hid the path from them so they had to struggle to get home. He observed that God changed that nice little stream into a raging torrent. Then they reached the bridge outside of Heredugu.

Just outside of their home town a peaceful little stream meandered its way through the bottleneck between two swamps as it headed downhill to the Ruwa River. In that bottleneck, a log bridge had been built. Only a few weeks earlier, Dembeli had helped men from the town drag in some large logs that served in the place of girders for the bridge. After being anchored on both sides of the river with large rocks, the huge logs were then covered with smaller logs that were then covered with elephant grass and dirt to form a bridge for the truck to come and go in and out of town. The storm had filled the swamp and the raging torrent had charged through the bottleneck tearing most of the smaller logs off the bridge and carrying them down to the river, leaving in their place a tangled mess of swamp grass, yuck, and an almost invisible bridge.

In the flickering circle of the kerosene lamp he was holding, Dauda began to feel under the water with his toes. In doing so he found one of the large logs that had been buried there, and he carefully picked his way through the wreckage of the bridge. Balancing on a log that he could not see because it was knee-deep under the raging torrent of the muddy swamp water that was now charging through the bottleneck, he crossed to the other side. Turning, he helped the others across, and then together the three men slogged through the mud the rest of the way into town.

Leaving the other two members of the newly formed Gospel Team in town, Dembeli headed on through town to his home on the mission. He went out to the office, knelt down by the desk, and expressed his feelings to the Lord about a storm that should have been held off. Finaba listened with a smile as the young missionary told the Lord how that what He had done was really not the way to do evangelism. He expressed his feeling of disappointment that the Lord had not held off the storm in answer to his prayers. He asked the Lord how he was supposed to do evangelism when God would not cooperate. He pointed out that the storm God had sent had knocked down the elephant grass and hidden the path. That God had turned a beautiful little stream into a rushing torrent that flooded a swamp, took away the bridge, and cut off the road. And what about the promised Gospel Team? Did the Lord know what those guys would say the next time Dembeli asked them to go out? Dembeli told the Lord he could already hear their answer. "Go out on evangelism with you? Why? That is bad stuff! You remember what the Lord did to us the last time we went out on evangelism? He hid the path, flooded the valley, took away the bridge, and we got our bodies soggy to the bone. No way, Man! We cannot go out with you again!" The Storyteller's smile almost turned to laughter as the young missionary advised the Lord on how to do evangelism!

The Lord waited until Dembeli was all done, and then He spoke. Finaba sensed that the Lord was answering Dembeli, but it wasn't until later that he found out what the Lord had said. In the stillness of the young missionary's heart the Lord asked, "Dembeli, whose people is this? Whose Church is this? Whose Gospel Team is this?" By then He had Dembeli's full attention and He could continue. "Dembeli," God said, "This is My People! This is My Church! This is My Gospel Team! All I want you to do is to disciple them!" The Storyteller could tell from the look of peace on Dembeli's face that the organization of the whole outfit had finally become clear.

Once the organization was in place, the Lord sent along more men to become part of the Gospel Team. Dembeli went back to the Lord and asked how he was expected to disciple them when six out of the eight that the Lord had sent to him could not read and write. After all, how do you disciple people who cannot read or write their own names, let alone read God's Word? But then again, with over two hundred towns in the area and only six schools, it was easy to understand why over 90% of the people in the area were illiterate. Then God planted the idea in Dembeli's mind of using pictures to train the Gospel Team and to help the men in their storytelling presentation of the Gospel.

Chapter 7: Kuranko Disciples

Dembeli had already learned that the Kuranko people are masters of communication. Most of them are adept at telling stories to entertain each other. This art had been honed through centuries of use in a culture where most people do not have access to modern technology. Dembeli realized that this art was the same as Jesus used to communicate deep Kingdom truths to disciple His followers so long ago. So Dembeli began to seek the basics of discipleship and try to understand how he could pass on the Lord's teachings in the simple and yet most powerful and effective means of communication known to man—storytelling. He knew that he needed the men who told the stories to stand on a firm foundation and that meant that they needed to learn a solid basis of Biblical truth before they told the stories.

Realizing that there are three basic elements to discipleship that transcend any culture, Dembeli began to implement them in a very simple form. The first principle that is so foundational is, "Saturate your soul with the Word of God." Finaba chuckled when he wondered how the new missionary would do this among his people who had never learned to read or write. Yet Dembeli had discovered early that the Kuranko people have oral traditions that have been passed down from generation to generation through countless tellings. Today the history of the Kuranko has remained intact in spite of the lack of books recording the message. The question was how to implement this principle of discipleship.

Dembeli began to meet with the team to teach them the Scriptures. The Gospel Team soon realized that they would have to commit God's Word to memory and that they needed to spend time in prayer together.

Each morning at sunrise, before the people went to their farms, one of the Team members rang the church bell and the believers gathered for morning prayers. The church bell was the rim of a seven-ton truck tire suspended by wire from the branch of a nearby tree. When struck with a broken leaf spring from a truck it gave forth a wonderful resonating gong that could be heard throughout the whole town. The brief meeting each morning was divided between Scripture memory and prayer.

In time, Dembeli was able to solicit the help of other missionaries in his endeavor to implement a Scripture memory program with illiterate people. The idea was that a picture would represent a Bible verse, and when the believers were taught the verse, the picture would trigger their memory. Faith has artistic talents that Dembeli can only dream of, and so she helped her dad by drawing pictures which could be used in a picture / verse association program. One of the missionaries stationed down-country later enlarged the idea and designed a Scripture memory program using this visual method. Before long, the prayer meeting leader could hold up a picture of a path and the people would quote, "I am the way the truth and the life. No one comes to the Father except through me" (John 14:6). A picture of a palm tree, a smiling face, a sad face, a bag of money, or a hoe all jogged their memory as the pictures became reminders of important portions of God's Word.

The early-morning prayer meeting caught on, and soon elders from the church joined the Gospel Team for those special times in God's Word each morning. The New Testament, translated by Hazel Shoup and a language assistant, had just recently been published, but the Old Testament being translated by Ruth Schierling, was not yet completed. Dembeli and the believers rejoiced in the portions of Scripture they had in Kuranko and concentrated their teaching on what they could read in their own language. Following the brief prayer meeting the believers would join their families and head out to their farms tucked away in the nearby hills. Many years later, in the summer of 2005, the revised translation of the whole Bible was completed by the translation team.

Finaba watched as the Gospel Team began to meet in a consistent discipleship program, in addition to the morning prayer-meeting which included the Scripture memory time. It began with Bible stories and the simple truths of God's Word, but discipleship soon took on more meaning as the men began to go out several nights a week to neighboring towns to share what they were learning. When Dembeli began a Theological Education By Extension (TEE) course, the Storyteller thought maybe things had become a little carried away. TEE is a program designed as a Bible study course to be used five days a week for ten weeks. Beginning with the first day, Dembeli drew stick figures to illustrate the main points of each day's lesson. It soon became apparent to all that he was not an artist, by any stretch of the imagination. Hearty laughter ensued as he tried to design enough variety in the stick figures and the activities they were doing to keep the men from getting mixed up as each figure represented a different principle Dembeli wanted to communicate.

Dembeli readily appreciated a culture where history, tradition, and learning is passed on orally. The oral historians in the area can go back generations and give an accurate history of their people. Some of them could name all the white men who had lived in their area of Kuranko land during the past five generations. He reasoned that they could use their incredible memories to associate stick figures with God's Word and then share it in their own way with their own people. Dembeli never realized that it would take him nine months to get through a ten-week course. Nor did he envision that at the end of the nine months the men would be able to look at the stick figures he had drawn for them and tell him the main points from each day's lesson, all the way through the course. Of course Finaba knew, but he had no way of stepping in and telling the young missionary, so he could only laugh when at the end of the nine months, Dembeli saw what the men could do and marveled at what God was doing. All Dembeli could say was, "Wow, you guys are good! Now it is time to take the pictures and share the story of salvation with your own people."

Dembeli noticed that in a remote area with no technical means of communication, the people were fantastic communicators. He realized that pictures could be used to enhance the stories of God's Word and would enable the Gospel Team members to share more consistently. Pictures that would communicate within the culture were hard to come by at first, and Dembeli knew that he would need more than his simple stick figures to adequately communicate as effectively as he desired.

Having pastored in America, Dembeli had some beautiful pictures he had used while teaching a Sunday school class. He spent weeks teaching the Bible story to the Team members using the American pictures that depicted Bible scenes in great detail. Dembeli encouraged them to do some role playing and they practiced showing the pictures to each other. The day came when the men on the Team were ready and confident enough to show the pictures and tell the Bible story in a nearby town. The service went great until it was time to show the pictures and tell the story. The words were right, but somehow the picture idea did not work so well. Finaba laughed as the men told their stories, but Dembeli could not understand why the men showed some of the pictures upside down. After watching the same thing happen in several different towns, it finally dawned on him that it was usually the same pictures that were being shown upside down. He reasoned that those pictures must not mean anything to them, or simply that they could not see past all the detail so that the picture was not even really seen. Dembeli began to scrap the pictures that the men consistently showed upside down, and soon he was left with only a couple of pictures.

Finaba sensed a little frustration in Dembeli with one of the men on the Gospel Team named Senke. Dembeli spent extra time with him because Senke seemed slow to pick up on the stories and to relate the picture with the part of the story he was telling. Sometimes he would hold up one picture and tell half the story, forgetting to show the other pictures as he went along. At other times he would show the wrong picture. Dembeli worked patiently with Senke. He had Senke role play with the other Gospel Team members until he knew that Senke could show the pictures in the right order and that he could tell the story with the right picture at the right time. He then invited Senke to show the pictures to the children and young men who came out to Dembeli's house every afternoon to play soccer with Dembeli and his children. Dembeli and Faith had been showing the picture stories to the children, but it seemed a good place for the Gospel Team to start honing their skills. At the time Dembeli could not have even dreamed of the impact that this practice would have on the lives of the children and young men in the town who were such good listeners. Gospel Team members began to take turns as they practiced their newfound skills on the children. Then one Christmas, nine of the young men who were part of the group, were baptized as a public witness of their faith in Christ. Most of them went on to become pastors or teachers and today are leaders in the Church throughout the area. Over the years others followed their example.

One evening Dembeli walked with the Team to a little town a couple miles out of Heredugu, and it was decided that Senke was ready to give the picture sermon that night. Showing pictures to adults in a nearby village was certainly different then showing pictures to the young men and children out on the miniature soccer field near Dembeli's house. Under pressure that evening, Senke forgot about half the story. He mixed up the pictures, and he showed some of the pictures up side down. He must have reached the decision that he was not doing so good so he shifted gears and just shared about how he had met Jesus. Dembeli sat quietly through the whole service wondering what on earth he could do to improve Senke's presentation the next time. Finaba knew that mentally he was criticizing himself and Senke for a job not well done.

Following the service, the Gospel Team spent time greeting the people and then slowly made their way out of town and down the path toward home. In the light of the kerosene lamp, Dembeli counted the men and noticed that one was missing, so he called for the Team to wait for the last man to arrive. They walked a little farther and then stopped under a tree as if everything was pre-arranged and they were to meet somebody there. Finaba was the only one who sensed Dembeli's frustration as he asked the rest of the men where Senke was. When they responded that Senke was coming, it did not entirely appease his irritation with how the evening had gone.

Then in the dark Dembeli heard several voices and realized that Senke was coming, but he was not alone. Senke stopped before reaching the Team, still talking with others out in the darkness. Dembeli waited with the little group of men that seemed totally relaxed as they waited for the last member of the Team to join them. When Senke joined the group, Dembeli found out the rest of the story.

Apparently two of the men at the service that night saw a whole lot more than Dembeli did. Dembeli saw a lousy job of picture-showing and storytelling. The two men saw a changed life. After the service they told Senke that they knew that he had been a Muslim, but tonight they had seen that he had found forgiveness of his sins and peace of heart because of the Supreme Sacrifice for sin. They wanted what he had. As Dembeli and the team waited in the dark under the tree, Senke introduced his two friends to Jesus. The next few miles the Holy Spirit and Dembeli had a good talk about priorities on the Team. The stories and the pictures were still important, but they were not the priority. Senke had his priorities in order.

Dembeli wrote to missionaries in other countries asking if they had pictures that would communicate in the culture in which he was serving. He was unable to find what he was looking for. Still feeling that he needed pictures, Dembeli shared his idea with some missionaries who were artists. Two of them began to draw the pictures he was asking for. Using the pictures, Dembeli taught the Gospel Team the stories of The Lost Sheep, The Lost Coin, and The Lost Boy (The Prodigal Son). At first he had to show the pictures himself, but before long the Team members caught on to the idea and knew the stories well enough to show the pictures to help their people visualize what was happening as the truths of God's Word unfolded.

Dembeli listened carefully to the men as they told the Bible stories, and he discovered that they often emphasized different points of the story than he had when teaching them the stories from the Word. Finaba smiled as he listened in on the two-way radio conversations as Dembeli tried to explain to the artists miles away what new pictures he needed to be drawn so that the stories would become more meaningful to his people. On his next trip down-country, Dembeli would pick up the new pictures and add them to the ones he already had. Soon a set of pictures emerged that the men could use to clearly communicate the Bible stories which became stepping- stones for sharing the message of salvation.

Dembeli also found tracts with lots of pictures in them that became pocket-sized "picture sermons." He taught these to several of the gospel team members, and they in turn taught the others until they all knew *The Wordless Book*, *The Two Roads*, and several others. The men carried these "mini sermons" in their hunting bags, to their farms, to the market, and just about everywhere they went so they could share with their friends the wonderful truths of God's Word. They learned the first principle of discipleship. They learned to saturate their souls with the Word of God.

It was now time for the second principle of discipleship to be learned. As simple as the first, and just as deep, the second principle is *preach Jesus.* Jesus said, "If I be lifted up, I will draw all men unto myself." (John 12:32) Finaba laughed at the blank stares on the faces of the Gospel Team as Dembeli explained that this simply means *Preach Jesus! Preach Jesus! Preach Jesus! Preach Jesus!* Dembeli explained that there is no other reason to walk out into the hills or to neighboring towns except to *preach Jesus!* Actually he sounded like a beginning drummer who only knows one rhythm. Finaba marveled that at each session, the same theme was repeated over and over and over, again and again.

Dembeli explained that when going into an animistic town one may find a woman who had a sick child which she laid on the floor of her hut while she went out into the bush. There, at a designated spot in the forest, she sacrificed her last chicken, gave some rice, and possibly left some other gifts to the spirits in an attempt to appease them so they would leave her child alone and her child would be well. Leaving the gift in the forest, she returned to town feeling that she had appeased the evil spirits and they would leave her child alone. She believed that her child would recover because of her gift to the spirits. When she returned to town and found the baby dead, it does not help to ridicule the sacrifice. One must simply share with her the love of Jesus. *Preach Jesus! Preach Jesus! Preach Jesus!*

Dembeli explained that when meeting a man who is a Muslim and discovering that he went to the Muslim teacher wanting to know the future, one must listen. The teacher may have asked the Muslim for a sheep that was sacrificed. Then cola nuts were cast on the ground and the teacher observed how the nuts had landed and how the way that they lay predicted the future. The man waited for weeks, months, maybe a year for the prophecy to be fulfilled in his life and it was not. Now he is empty, and wondering what went wrong. It does no good to ridicule the sacrifice. One must simply p*reach Jesus! Preach Jesus! Preach Jesus!*

Finaba sensed Dembeli's doubts about his methods of trying to teach this principle that he felt was so crucial and so basic to the whole evangelistic program of the Gospel Team. He knew Dembeli was wondering if the men could understand what he was trying to communicate. Knowing that he could not step in and help cross the language and cultural barriers, the Storyteller had to stand aside and listen as Dembeli shared his struggles with the Lord in prayer.

One day the Team traveled in the truck as far as they could go along the road and left it in the care of a friend. The Team was prepared to walk several hours back into the hills for a series of services in a town that had just been reached with the Gospel. Food, picture sermons, and supplies for the weekend had been tied in bundles of about 50 pounds each before leaving home. Friendly banter and laughter were the order of the day, and Finaba watched as the Gospel Team members helped each other adjust the loads on their heads before starting down the path. Dembeli never learned to carry a load on his head like most of the people of West Africa do. He had his backpack shouldered and was ready to go. One Team member had rolled up a T-shirt into a donut shape to use as a cushion between his load and his head. Another Team member stepped over to help him pick up the load and place it on the "donut". After he lifted the load, the man asked his partner if he knew why they were walking almost five hours to the town way out in the bush.

Dembeli heard the question, too, and scurried around the back of the truck to hear the answer, because he really wanted to know what they thought was the real reason they were going through all this trouble. As the load settled gently down on the carrier's head, the helper put his finger right up to the carrier's face and said to his fellow teammate, "Bande, we are going there for one reason. We are going there to *Preach Jesus! Preach Jesus! Preach Jesus!*" Perhaps Finaba was the only one who heard the young missionary exclaim, "You got it buddy! That's what it's all about!" But he was not the only one who noticed that Dembeli's feet didn't touch the ground for the first three miles of the walk. Dembeli was flying high because he realized that he had communicated and that the second principle had been learned.

The third element of the discipleship program seemed even harder for the young missionary to communicate. Pastor Pita often asked Dembeli to speak to the Heredugu Church family in the Sunday services. The Storyteller listened attentively as the young missionary shared some of the same truths he was sharing with the Gospel Team in the discipleship sessions. From God's Word he explained that as Christians we need to be different from the world. We need to dance to the beat of a different drum. We need to be set apart. God's people are called to be holy. "We are a chosen people, a royal priesthood, a holy nation" (I Peter 2:9), and we are told to be holy even as Christ is holy (I Peter 1:16).

Dembeli shared shared all kinds of illustrations to point out that our lives should attract people to Jesus as we pattern them after the Master's life. Even Finaba had difficulty understanding the concept that we are Christians first and then we are Americans, or that we are Christians first and then we are Kurankos—that above all we are to be imitators of Christ.

As the days passed into weeks, Dembeli attempted a variety of methods to support the truth he was trying to teach the team. One evening after a service in a nearby town, one of the men on the team and Dembeli were taking a shortcut home. Dembeli was following Musa through the swamp when Musa stepped off the beaten trail and half disappeared. Dembeli helped him out, and pretty soon both men were covered with the mud and mire of the swamp. Reaching the bank, they looked at each other in the beam of the flashlight and both began to laugh. They both saw great humor in the whole incident, for even in the light it was hard to distinguish which of the two travelers was the white man.

Then the light of the flashlight caught the reflection of something out in the swamp, and Dembeli immediately pointed it out to his partner saying, "Hey, look at that." The immediate response was, "Yeah, it's a flower." But Dembeli wasn't satisfied, so he said, "Look at it again." The reply was equally quick in coming back: "Okay, it is a lily flower." By this time Dembeli knew he was onto something and there must have been something in his voice to catch the attention of his partner. Pausing in the task of cleaning the real estate off his clothes, Dembeli's partner stood staring off into the middle of the swamp at the tiny lily centered in the light at the end of the beam radiating from Dembeli's flashlight. Then Dembeli continued. "Yes, it is a lily. But look at us. One cannot tell who is the white man, and who is the Kuranko, because of all the swamp covering us. But that flower came up through the same muck, mire and mud that we did. Look at it! It is spotless! Don't you think that God can keep us that way among our own people? Don't you see that He can keep you clean in the midst of a people who have survived through generations of animism and Islam? He wants to live through us to reach this people for Himself. Our lives of holiness will attract people to our Master. That's what He means when His Word says that we are to 'be holy even as He is holy.'" Dembeli's partner nodded as if to ask, "Say what?" and went back to removing the mud from his hands and feet. The silent walk home was testimony to the fact that Dembeli knew he still had not communicated on the Kuranko wavelength of understanding.

The dry season came and the parched ground cried out for water because months had passed without a drop of rain. Dust rolled from the wheels of the vehicle, and soon the contents in the back of the truck as well as all the passengers were covered with a fine coating of dust that turned the sky dark red and made the missionaries look like they had a super tan. However, that tan was disappointing, because it would all wash off in the shower at the end of the journey. Plants beside the road were covered with the dusty film as the billowing cloud following the vehicle settled back down after the brief disturbance caused by its passing. But one plant seemed totally unaffected by the billowing cloud of dust that chased the vehicle down the road and then—because it could never hope to catch up—settled down with an ugly sort of contentment on all the other plants and bushes along the roadside. The Creator had covered the broad leaves of one plant with a waxy surface so that no matter how thick the dust, or how much dirt fell on it, the particles would slowly slither off onto the ground and the little plant always remained totally clean. Having observed this phenomenon in the past as merely a thing of interest, Dembeli suddenly saw it now as a beautiful lesson on holiness.

Stopping the truck, he called the men over and drew a little picture with his finger in the dust that covered several plants along the road. Faith, Toby, and Andy—Dembeli's children—joined in the fun and before long the little exercise became a game and laughter rolled along as the dust settled. Then came the "waxy plant." The Storyteller had suspected that something was up and had been watching Dembeli rather closely. He was not disappointed to see him call all the men together and ask them to draw a picture for him on the waxy plant. Of course no one could, for it was spotless in a world of plants that had been covered with the dust of months of dry season. Dembeli pointed out that like the lily, and the waxy plant, we can stay clean in the midst of a yucky world. That is what God wants to do in us. Perhaps Finaba was the only one who sensed Dembeli's disappointment as the men on the Team once again failed to grasp the truth of what he was trying to teach them in this third element of discipleship: pattern your lives after the Master's life—be holy as He is holy.

At best, cross-cultural communication is difficult. Finaba sensed that Dembeli was searching to find a way to share biblical truth in a cultural context so that it could be understood. The Storyteller remembered the time the Gospel Team visited in a town where the feet of white men had never before passed. Although Dembeli had greeted the people in their own language, and endeavored to talk to them, they could not seem to understand anything after his greetings and had turned to the Gospel Team members and asked that the white man's words be translated. Dembeli made some comment about his Kuranko being hard to understand, and the Team laughed and then willingly interpreted for him, even though he was already talking in Kuranko.

It wasn't until the second day in the village that some of the people began to accept the fact that Dembeli was talking to them in their language and they could understand. The barriers of communication began to crumble and some valuable one-on-one sharing took place with the stranger who spoke an even stranger brand of Kuranko. The barrier had been a mental block, for they had never seen a white man in their village, let alone one who spoke Kuranko. The reality of such a thing happening seemed a great improbability. Some of the older men shared about a former missionary, Jake Schierling, whom they had met years and years ago in Dugusigi when they had been called to a meeting by the Paramount Chief. He also spoke their language, and as a matter of fact he spoke it a whole lot better than this young missionary who now walked in their midst.

Dembeli and the Storyteller both had to laugh at that because they knew there were stages to the process of learning a language. Dembeli had encountered the first stage immediately upon arrival. As he learned the greetings, the Heredugu people congratulated him on his ability to speak Kuranko. Dembeli knew better than anyone else that the greeting contained his entire vocabulary at that point.

The second stage of language learning came after the language courses were completed, the books were set aside, and the young missionary went into town to talk. It may have appeared to an outsider that he could communicate very well at that point, but if the missionary began to sense any pride in his achievement, it was quickly shattered as he entered the second stage. The nationals began to correct the missionary's grammar, enunciation, and the use of the correct words in the right places at the right time with the right endings used in the right way. Oh, how many Kurankos offered to teach Kuranko to Dembeli at that stage of the game! Surely the professors were far more numerous than the students. A plateau of learning the language came at that point, followed by a deep sense of frustration at the possibility that an outsider would never learn to communicate adequately. But if the desire and the drive are there, one can overcome the barriers, and pretty soon he or she leaves the plateau and begins to communicate more effectively.

The third stage is when the Kuranko hears you speaking and really does understand, but then makes a comment about how well a missionary of the past spoke the language. The Storyteller often laughed when his people told Dembeli how well Pa Jake Schierling spoke the language, because Dembeli would jump into the conversation again and heartily agree with them while he made another language goof in describing how well Jake could communicate in Kuranko.

The fourth stage came when the young missionary stopped dreaming *about* the new language and started dreaming *in* the language he was learning. What an incredible difference! Others, however, did not notice this for they were excluded from the world of the dreams. The fifth stage is probably reached when nationals find themselves laughing at the jokes told by the missionary in their own language.

Better than the others, the Storyteller knew that his people were a people whose favorite past time has always been, and still is, communication. Through the ages story-telling has been one of the most powerful means of communicating truth, teaching morals and ethics, and passing on to the next generation the core values of a people. Finaba sensed that Dembeli was searching for an effective way to communicate the third principle of discipleship, but he knew that he could not step in and help, and that he would just have to wait and watch until the young missionary discovered a way to share that truth in a relevant way.

As the white man counts time, that answer seemed forever in coming, but to Finaba and his people it really was not that long, for the next dry season had hardly begun when Dembeli tried again to share the third principle. The rains were still a long way off when the answer came. But come it did, and in a very simple yet surprising way.

The Storyteller and several Gospel Team members were sitting on the veranda of a house swapping stories with Dembeli as they so often did. During a lull in the conversation, a pair of mud daubers made their presence known. Mud daubers could be described as giant, over-grown wasps. Now the mud daubers that live in northern Sierra Leone sound like miniature B-52 bombers when they fly over. Brrrrzzzz! Brrrrzzzz! Brrrrzzzz! As they circled overhead, one of the Gospel Team members asked Dembeli, "Do you know what those mud daubers are saying?"

Finaba almost laughed out loud when Dembeli answered that they really weren't saying anything, that the noise was just how they fly. The Storyteller knew better, and he also knew that the young white man was about to learn a valuable lesson. One of the men on the Gospel Team was quick to respond "Oh yes, those mud daubers are saying something. Do you see that cone up in the corner of your house, way up out of reach of people? That cone is the mud daubers' house. They build the cone out of mud, and then they leave a little hole in the top of it so they can go in and out of their house. Then they fly around the yard and they zap grasshoppers, bugs, beetles, and all other kinds of juicy insects and carry them back and stuff them into the cone. When the cone is full of all the dead bugs, beetles, grasshoppers and other insects that they can possibly get into it, they seal the top shut very lightly. Then for the next few weeks, they fly around calling Brrrrzzzz, Brrrrzzzz, Brrrrzzzz, which really means 'Be like me.' They call that back to the dead bugs, beetles and insects over and over and over again. 'Be like me, Brrrrzzzz Brrrrzzzz Brrrrzzzz. Be like me, Brrrrzzzz. Be like me, Brrrrzzzz. Be like me.'"

The story was interrupted by Dembeli, who chuckled as he said, "Wait a minute. Brrrrzzzz doesn't mean 'Be like me' in any body's language."

"Oh, but it does in mud dauber language" the man argued. "You see, they fly around calling to those dead bugs, beetles, and insects so long, 'Be like me! Be like me!' that after a couple of weeks, the dead bugs, beetles, and insects get so tired of hearing 'Be like me' that they turn themselves into mud daubers and burst out of the top of the cone in the newness of life—as mud daubers."

Finaba could hardly believe his ears when the young missionary burst out laughing, and then exclaimed, "You're not telling me that those dead bugs, beetles, and insects hear that noise so long that they turn themselves into mud daubers and come out of the cone as mud daubers are you?"

"Well, yes we are," responded the team member. "You see, that is why the mud daubers call that way. 'Brrrrrzzzz. Be like me.'"

Dembeli chuckled and then explained that really and truly, we all know that the parent mud daubers lay eggs in the bottom of the cone. After an incubation period, the eggs hatch and the little tiny, itty bitty mud daubers discover that there is food stored all around them. So they proceed with all diligence to gobble up all the bugs, beetles, and insects that the parent mud daubers so thoughtfully stuffed into their cone. As they eat, they grow, and by the time they have devoured all the food stored up for them in their little house, they are big enough and strong enough to burst forth out of the top of the cone and enter the great big world around them. He exclaimed, "You see, they were born mud daubers and that is why they burst out of the cone as mud daubers."

The debate that followed still makes the Storyteller chuckle, for he remembers how vehemently his people defended their theory against the new idea introduced by the missionary. He can still hear the immediate response to the tall tale told by the missionary of eggs laid, eggs hatched, born mud daubers: "No they weren't."

"Why yes they were. We all know they were." "Dead bugs don't turn into live mud daubers."

"Yes, they do."

"No, they don't!"

"They sure do!"

"Now wait a minute. I don't think so. Let me run it by you all again." And so the debate continued in good fun, with lots of laughter as each side defended their own opinion.

Then, in the midst of the discussion, one of the team members asked, "If they were born mud daubers, why did the mommy and daddy mud dauber have to fly around calling to them for so long, 'Be like me?'"

Finaba watched as the young missionary absorbed that thought. Finally Dembeli responded, "Maybe you are right after all. Yeah, why would they have to call 'Brrrrzzzz. Be like me?'" This was just the beginning of the stories told that dry season afternoon as the Team sat together in the shade away from the heat of the tropical sun.

A couple days later while Dembeli was having his devotions, Finaba saw the lights suddenly go on in the missionary's thinking. Leaning over Dembeli's shoulder and listening carefully as the missionary reread the verse that had suddenly been illuminated in his mind, The Storyteller heard him say out loud to himself... "Be holy even as I am holy" (I Peter 1:16). Finaba still did not understand as he followed the missionary down the road, across the little bridge to the place where the Gospel Team was meeting for their regular discipleship session. Songs were followed by testimonies of what God was doing in the various villages where the Team members had been the previous week. Problems were discussed. Questions they had been asked that they found hard to answer were shared for a group opinion, and time was spent in prayer. Then came the time for Bible study. Finaba waited in anticipation for he knew Dembeli had gained new insight into how to communicate the Biblical truth in a Kuranko context. Even so, he was surprised when he heard Dembeli ask, "Does anyone know what Jesus is saying to you, and to me—to His Church?" The silence that followed was interrupted when Dembeli continued, "You know what He is saying? Jesus is saying "Brrrrzzzz.""

Several responded as the team members broke out in laughter, "Oh yes, He is telling us to 'Be like me!' He is saying, 'Christian, be like me: Be holy even as I am holy.'" So the third principle of discipleship had now been taken off paper and driven home to the hearts and minds of men who were being discipled. Dembeli has often mused that that was the shortest Bible study or sermon he has ever taught or preached, yet it was one of the most effective.

Chapter 8: The Crucible of Kuranko Living

Brrrrzzzz carried with it some really tough implications. The Gospel Team had to learn that it applied to everyday living and not just to those times when they were on evangelism away from home or visiting in a nearby village. It was not something you wear, but something you are. This was brought home to them one day when Dembeli's family was preparing to go to Freetown for their semi-annual shopping trip.

As so often happened, they were delayed by a countless stream of visitors coming to the door. Some had letters they wanted delivered to friends or family members who lived in towns or cities closer to the coast. Others came with money to give Dembeli so he would buy a needed item for them down in the capital city. The family was also going to try to get in a few days vacation time on the beach, so they would not be home for about two weeks, and Dembeli was anxious to get going. Several of the Gospel Team members stopped by to help load the truck and do any last minute preparations that had to be done. Finaba wanted to jump in and tell Dembeli to slow down, that the road would not change, and the capital would not go anywhere, even if their departure was delayed a whole day, but Dembeli continued to rush around. Eventually the family was loaded into the truck, prayers were said, and the missionary family was headed out of town.

Road conditions had improved since the rains had stopped, but even so it would take Dembeli's family about eight hours to travel one hundred miles to Kurela, the home of the children's school, the Bible school, and several other missionary families. The last minute rush was soon behind them and the family settled in for a long drive. During a lull in the conversation the Holy Spirit spoke to Dembeli and told him that he had offended one of the Team members in the rush of getting ready to head out. Dembeli's response was a prayer that if God would bring him safely back to Heredugu and to the next Gospel Team meeting, he would make things right immediately. Frequently during the vacation and shopping trip the Lord reminded him of that promise, and Finaba wondered how it would go when they actually returned home.

The two weeks passed quickly and soon the Dembeli's family had loaded their truck with six months' supply of groceries and was ready for the journey home. It was a rather uneventful journey except that Dembeli was able to shoot a couple of monkeys to add to the cooking pot when they unpacked that evening. Knowing it would not be long before they would have a furlough, four-year-old Toby asked Dembeli if there were any monkeys in America where they would be going for a year. When he was told that there aren't any monkeys to shoot in Indiana, he became very concerned and asked, "Well, then, what are we going to eat for beef?"

The journey ended without any mishap, and the truck was unloaded while delicious rice and soup was prepared. Along the grapevine the news that the missionary family was back soon spread, and before long people arrived to get the responses to their messages sent, letters from down-country friends, and the items they had asked Dembeli to purchase. The Gospel Team knew that there would be a discipleship session as usual the next morning, and they gathered to welcome Dembeli and his family home and to hear the tales of the travels from the kids. It was an exciting time, but in the midst of the homecoming, the Holy Spirit reminded Dembeli that in the morning he would need to make things right with the Gospel Team member.

The next morning the singing seemed to last a little longer than usual, but the reports were just as exciting as ever. The Gospel Team had continued to function in the absence of the missionary and the truck. Then came the time for the Bible study. The Storyteller listened attentively with the rest of the team as Dembeli explained how the Holy Spirit had spoken to him and told him that he had offended a brother in Christ. He told them of the promise he had made, and he wanted to make things right. He explained the setting and shared with the Team the offense he had committed against the Team member. Then to Finaba's surprise, he knelt in Kuranko fashion and held the feet of the one he had offended and asked his forgiveness. The one offended quickly put his hand on Dembeli's shoulder, signifying that he was forgiven, and told him that he had forgotten the offense because it had not been serious and that all was forgiven anyway. The Team joined them both in praise and prayer and the meeting continued.

Dembeli realized that the ministry of the one discipled often looks very similar to the one who mentored him. This was brought out to him in a unique way when God blessed him with three of the greatest children in the world. Sometimes when the Team would speak in a town some distance from home, the chief or one of the elders, would present Dembeli with a chicken as a gift. Occasionally those chickens would be taken home and turned loose with the growing flock of chickens that Dembeli had originally brought up from the coast. When it was time for them to join the family meal, Dembeli would catch one, ring its neck, and send it to the "cookin' pot."

One day Dembeli was relaxing with a glass of iced tea when he heard a terrible racket out in the yard. Jumping up, he ran outside to see what was happening. There was four-year-old Toby pouncing on Dembeli's prize rooster. Toby grabbed it with both hands and tried to fling it around to wring its neck. The poor rooster would slip out of the two little hands that were not quite big enough to hold its weight and would try to escape. Having had its neck kinked by a four-year-old, it had trouble getting its bearing, so it could not make enough headway to completely escape its tormentor.

Dembeli quickly assessed the situation and went to the rescue of the rooster before Toby could inflict any more pain. Holding the rooster under his arm, he turned to his son and asked, "Toby, what do you think you are doing. You are going to kill my rooster. You'll break his neck."

A determined little guy answered, "But dad, you do it all the time."

Finaba wanted to laugh out loud, because Dembeli had just been reminded of the simple fact that the one discipled often imitates his mentor.

Time marched on as it always does, and Dembeli had the opportunity to invite the Schierlings back up to Heredugu for a visit. This was a special time for the missionary family because they did not get many visitors since they lived in such a remote area. Some who did come felt that Heredugu was at the end of the world. But to the Jake and Ruth Schierlings it was like home. They had a lot of friends in the area, and many whom they had led to Christ in the previous generation. Somehow it always seemed like they grew a little younger when they were able to visit Heredugu and see those they had led to Jesus so long ago still walking with the Lord, and now so ably filling roles as leaders in the church.

Since it was holiday season, a few days were set aside to fish and hunt. It was a great time for all the men, and their families rejoiced when the truck came home carrying a load of meat and a happy group of men who had shared so much together over the weekend. It seemed such a short visit, but the Schierling's returned to Kurela after encouraging the Church and the Gospel Team to be faithful in their walk with the Lord and to share His love all around.

The next morning the coffee was ready a little early for the Gospel Team meeting, for the men seemed excited to share what had taken place in the various villages over the weekend. It was an exciting time, but when it came time for the Bible study, Dembeli was interrupted. One of the Team members asked everyone to bear with him a minute while he said something very important. He told of a time while out fishing on the river when he had said something and acted towards Dembeli in a way that he should not have. He told how the Holy Spirit had come to him and "poked him in the heart" and told him that he had done wrong to Dembeli. He remembered how Dembeli had set the example months before after a trip to Freetown, when Dembeli had held his feet in an act of repentance, and now he felt that he too should make things right. He pointed out that if Dembeli as the leader and teacher could make restitution in an appropriate manner, that he as one being discipled should have the courage to do the same when it was necessary. With that he got up and walked over to hold Dembeli's feet, but he found an arm around him and the assurance of forgiveness already offered for an offense already forgiven. The Storyteller knew that in moments like this, living lessons were being learned. Here was a group of men who had heard the Master calling "Brrrrzzzz, " and they were taking Him seriously.

The Storyteller soon realized that it was not only the Gospel Team members who had learned from that experience. He was witnessing a group of men involved in a continual learning process. He often saw Dembeli sitting under the shade of a tree asking a pastor or church leader what a particular Bible passage meant to him. Sometimes he would read a verse or portion of Scripture and then ask the Kuranko beside him, "What did Jesus mean when He said that?" Or "What does God's Word mean when he wrote that to the Church? What does it mean to you? What does it mean to a Kuranko?" There, under the shade of a tree, or on a veranda to escape the heat of the tropical sun, real issues of life would be discussed in the light of God's Word. Similar questions would often come while traveling in the truck. After all, Dembeli had a captive audience as the vehicle "galloped" along the road to Kurela, a full day's journey away.

The principles Dembeli spoke of had to be fleshed out in the crucible of Kuranko living before a sense of ownership would claim them for the Kuranko people. Finaba remembers the time one of the Christians in the area came to Dembeli and explained that he felt that he should get rid of two of his three wives. When Dembeli asked "Why?" he responded that one of them was cursed of God because she was barren and could not have children. He said he would need to get rid of the second one, although she had several children, because he had been told that to be a real Christian he must have only one wife. As they walked along the path, Dembeli began to share God's Word with his friend. He asked him if the marriage was complete without children in light of the Scripture they had just considered. His friend acknowledged that children do not make a marriage, but that a man and women are complete, and one, before God even without children. The discussion came to a temporary conclusion when Dembeli covenanted to pray with his friend every day until God gave his friend an answer to his searching heart.

About two weeks later, the same man stopped by the mission to greet Dembeli. As usual, they talked about all kinds of events and issues before he expressed the real reason for his visit. He began by saying that after he had carefully considered God's Word, he had decided to keep all three of his wives. Finaba could not believe it when Dembeli turned to his friend and quietly asked, "What was it that made you decide that?" His friend explained first, that he had really married all three women by paying the required dowry for them, and so he was responsible for them. Second, he understood from God's Word that he has a responsibility to each of those women and to the children born in his marriage with them. He explained that he also understood from God's Word that even if a wife bore no children she was still a man's wife, so even the marriage with the one who had no children was a complete marriage. Third, if he sent the two back to their families, they would be married off to someone else. He said he knew that most likely they would never hear the Gospel again since they were both from animistic or Muslim homes far from where the Gospel is being taught. So he had decided to keep all three of them.

After praying with his friend, Dembeli encouraged him to be the spiritual head of the house and to teach all his wives and children all the material he was learning as a member of the Gospel Team. The man began using the picture Bible he used for evangelism as the basis for teaching his family about God each evening.

Dembeli noticed that the man encouraged his wives and children in the things of God, and within a year the two that he had thought about sending back to their families were baptized believers. The one who was barren was expecting her first child when she was baptized. Later she had a beautiful little girl that was given a Biblical name. When he was challenged why he took the stand he did in supporting his friend's decision, Dembeli just smiled and asked, "What can I say?" The Storyteller chuckled, for usually Dembeli had a lot to say. The man shared his faith consistently with his family and soon he had led all his wives and their children, and the grand children who were old enough to understand, to saving faith in his Savior and Lord.

Finaba was aware that the issue of polygamy had been debated for years among the missionaries who had come to serve his people. He was well aware of some of the vicious battles that had taken place in an effort to convince others to take the same stand the speaker took on such a major issue. He knew it had been a dividing issue that had polarized missionaries over the years. He now realized that Dembeli, like some who had gone before him, felt strongly that the Kuranko Church had to take God's Word and make it theirs, for God's Word transcends all cultures. Since he had seen the young missionary sitting so often asking questions to help him understand and gain insights into the hearts and lives of his people, Finaba was not surprised to see Dembeli ask the Church leaders where they stood on this issue as well. The Storyteller was almost afraid that a major battle would follow among his people, but as he watched them discuss the issue, he was pleased to see them reach an understanding.

After reading Paul's instruction to the Church in Corinth, they concluded that the Scriptures teach that a man can come to Christ in whatever condition, or station in life, he is in (I Cor. 7:17). They were aware that many of the leaders in their area already have more than one wife when they hear the Gospel for the first time. They decided that a man who accepts Christ as his personal Savior can be baptized even if he has more than one wife. However, they also concluded that if a man has one wife and becomes a Christian, he cannot take a second. If a man has two wives when he becomes a Christian, he may keep both of them, but he is not entitled to take any more, nor will he be permitted to be the pastor of a church. A man would be disciplined by the Church if he allowed his daughter to be given as a second wife. If a man is single he is encouraged to marry a wife with the understanding that she will be the only wife.

A little misunderstanding came when one of a man's four wives died in childbirth, and he felt that she could be replaced, so he married another to keep his total at four. Dembeli chuckled at the misunderstanding, but the Church elders soon explained to the man that what he did was not what the Scriptures or the church leaders meant, and they encouraged him to seek to lead all his wives and children to saving faith in Jesus Christ. What a joy it was to see them all walking with the Lord.

—

Dembeli tried to encourage the Church to meet daily for prayer and Bible study to help those who could not read gain a deeper understanding of God's Word. He taught them that they should read—or have someone from the literacy class read—a couple verses from the Word of God. Then he challenged them to answer three simple questions as they shared the truths of Word of God in the services or at home with their families— every time they taught from the Bible. The people needed to be able to understand the answers to the questions:

What does God's Word say?

What does God's Word mean?

How can I apply this truth from God's Word in my life today?

The Storyteller, like Dembeli, realized that these Biblical principles would have no value until they had been applied and found to hold true in Kuranko life. As they were encouraged to understand the stories and what they taught, the members of the Gospel Team discovered truths in God's Word that spanned time and generations and spoke to issues that they faced in daily living. The stories also became steppingstones for them to share their faith in Christ and what He meant to them. Yet there was still a little bit of hesitancy when it came to sharing with Muslim leaders.

This was clearly illustrated one evening when the Team walked to a nearby town. As usual, they divided into pairs to share the picture tract of their choice, and to personally invite anyone who would listen to come to the evening service, which would be held in front of the chief's house. The Storyteller followed Dembeli and his partner, for he realized that the missionary often chose as his partner the one that needed the most help with the pictures or the most encouragement. For some reason unknown to Finaba, on this particular evening Dembeli chose instead, one of the Team leaders as his partner. Seeing a group of men sitting in the shade of a tree, Dembeli suggested that they go there and share one of the picture tracts that they were carrying in their pockets. The immediate response from his partner was, "No, let's not go there. That is the Muslim teacher's house." Needless to say, his response started a lively discussion.

Dembeli: "Good, let's go there and show them the pictures."

Team member: "No, Let's not go there. That is the Muslim teacher's house."

Dembeli: "Well, our rules are that when we go into a town we will split up into pairs and each member of the pair will pick a house and show the picture tract. Then the second member of the pair will pick a home and share the Gospel with them. That way we all get to share our faith in Christ. I pick that house for the one where I will show the picture tract."

Team member: "You still don't understand. That is the Muslim teacher's house."

Dembeli: "Okay, I'll show the pictures."

Finaba followed reluctantly as they casually meandered over to the tree near the Muslim teacher's house. After asking for, and receiving permission to show the little picture tract, Dembeli proceeded to destroy the Kuranko language. Actually, he butchered it to the point of hilarity. When he was done, the Team member laughed and said, "Here, let me explain it to them." Needless to say, he did a beautiful job. Dembeli later expressed that no matter how well we, as missionaries, learn to speak the language, we still do not have the intuitive knowledge of the language that our host people have. He often marveled at his partner's ability to communicate through the medium of the story.

The Team member was only about halfway through when several more young men joined the group. As soon as he was done, they said, "We missed the first part of the story. Show that to us." So the Team member showed it again. Halfway through, several other people joined the gathering just to see what was going on. They also asked to see the first part after the presentation was complete. The Team member patiently showed the pictures again and again.

The beating of the chief's drum calling everyone to the area in front of his house ended the little session at the Muslim teacher's house. People quickly headed in the direction of the chief's compound so they would not miss an important meeting. When Dembeli and his partner arrived, one of the Team members led singing, another gave his testimony, yet another prayed, and more songs were sung. Finaba was pleased that the missionary had insisted that songs telling the Gospel be sung to local tunes. These were songs that the Team would teach the people when they went to the various villages. Like the missionary, he was not particularly interested in seeing hymns sung in a village where nobody knew the words, the tune, or even the rhythm of songs from a far-away land. They needed songs from the heart of the Kuranko Christians, and when a drum began to beat and the Team members began to clap their hands in time with the music and the leader began to sing, Finaba knew it would not be long before his people would be singing along with the Team. Indeed, it did not take long before the children had learned the songs, taught them to other children, and proudly joined the Team in singing songs of praise. In one town where the Team often went, they assumed that everyone would know who they were so they did not identify themselves by Church or denomination. When they arrived in a town, the word quickly spread from house to house, "The Praisers of God are here. Let's go join them and hear from God's Word." What a name for His people, "Praisers of God."

After the singing, the large picture sermons were brought out and the Team member who had been chosen to show the story gave his presentation. He walked around in front of the circle of people, making sure that each elder and those around him could clearly see the picture and that they understood the portion of the Scripture illustrated by that particular picture. After telling the story, the speaker for the evening would make an application or ask the team leader if he had anything to say. This was how Dembeli started the team out when they did not know the stories and he had to tell the stories himself. Following the telling of the story he would ask one of the Gospel Team members or the leader of the team to make the application of the story. It was often at this time in the visit to the town that the Kuranko views of the Scriptures were applied. Testimonies were given and the reality of salvation as it was lived out was shared with their own people.

As they were walking home, the Storyteller wondered what was going through Dembeli's thoughts as he mused about the events of the evening and the visit with the Muslim teacher. The beam of the flashlight pierced the darkness, but did not penetrate the silence, and Finaba had no way of knowing what was on his friend's mind. Then Dembeli's partner for the evening walked up beside him and opened the conversation with a simple statement that perked up the missionary's ears real quick: "I learned something tonight"

Dembeli quickly asked, "Oh, what did you learn?"

The Team member responded, "I learned never to be afraid to share the Gospel with any one, even with a Muslim teacher."

This response brought another quick question from Dembeli who asked, "Why?"

The team member's reply revealed to Dembeli that the man had a new vision of why Dembeli was asking them to go to all the nearby towns when he replied, "They listened because they need a Savior, too."

Dembeli remembered this conversation some time later when the Team walked back into the foothills of the mountains to hold a service in a different town. It had been a long walk and the Gospel Team members arrived thankful for the end of the journey. The chief quickly arranged housing for the Team, and the evening meal was cooked. As usual the Team paired off and walked through the town to visit friends and to share the real purpose of their trip. Pocket-sized picture tracts were shared with as many as possible, and all were invited to respond to the call of the chief's drum and join the Team for a service in front of the chief's house.

It had been a good service, although the prayer had ended very abruptly when a goat began bleating out of fear or pain, and it was discovered that a python had found its way to the edge of the village and satisfied its hunger by capturing, squeezing, and swallowing a young goat. The Team members and Dembeli joined in the search for the snake. The search was futile in the dark, and the owner of the goat resigned himself to accept his loss, so the Team headed back to their huts to sleep. As Dembeli stretched out in his sleeping bag, he heard one of the Team members talking in the hut nearby. By now he had learned enough Kuranko to understand that this was not a normal "end of the day conversation," but that one of the Team members was sharing the picture sermons with somebody. He drifted off to sleep praying for the sharer as well as the listener.

An excited Team member called at Dembeli's door shortly after dawn the next morning. After the greeting, the conversation took an interesting turn.

The team member simply stated, "Dembeli, You know Pa Mori."

Dembeli responded, "No, I don't know Pa Mori."

The team member explained, "He is the Muslim teacher in town."

Dembeli replied, "I don't know the Muslim teacher in this town."

The team member insisted, "Yes you do. He is the little old man with the big feet."

Suddenly Dembeli remembered the man and exclaimed, "Oh yes, I know him. What about him?"

The Team member started his story again. "He is the Muslim teacher here in town. Last night after the service he came and started asking me questions. I was not sure how to answer all his questions, so I just showed him all the picture sermons and Bible stories we have learned. A little after midnight, he accepted Christ as his Savior." This was the same Team member who, a few months before, had been afraid to share his faith with a Muslim teacher. Dembeli realized that God had shown him the need of the Muslim heart.

Finaba understood then that there are no words to express the joy one feels when he leads someone to Christ, or the incredible satisfaction one senses when he has spent days, weeks, or even months discipling someone and then sees that someone lead another person to Jesus. The Storyteller recalled an earlier visit to the same town. As Dembeli rolled his sleeping bag out on the mud floor everything looked cozy. It was not long until Finaba noticed that after everyone else had fallen asleep, Dembeli was still tossing and turning, trying to adjust his body around a rock buried in the mud floor that simply did not want to yield to the curves of an American body. Finaba only knew what happened then as he heard the prayers of the young missionary sharing with his heavenly Father the frustration of what he was experiencing. Hours of walking, carrying a heavy backpack through the heat of the day had taken him to this little town tucked away in the foothills of the mountains. A silly little obstacle like a rock, buried in the floor under his sleeping bag was preventing him from getting the much needed rest, but that was minor.

In the middle of the night, when a sleepless night looked like it would become a reality and the frustration was mounting, the devil whispered in a tiny voice, "What are you doing here anyway? You are hours' walk away from home. You are way out here in the middle of the bush and nobody really knows where you are, or even cares. Your family has not even been to this town so they do not have a clue where you are. Besides that, those people in the churches in America don't know where you are, and they couldn't care less anyway. Why are you here? Why not roll up your sleeping bag and walk home in the morning, drink a cold Pepsi, relax, and forget about it. Nobody cares that you are here miles and miles from anybody in the middle of nowhere."

Then in the stillness of his heart Dembeli heard the voice of his Savior and Lord saying, "But I know where you are, and I care." Now there was one who accepted Jesus because the Gospel Team had stayed that time, and had come again to share the glorious news of salvation—a message of love and forgiveness—through the simple means of storytelling and the example of lives that were being lived for the Master.

Chapter 9: A Strategy for Evangelism

Before the sun peeked over the hills in the morning, Dembeli and Barnabasi, the Gospel Team leader, joined a hunter from town and headed out into the hills to invite steaks, roasts, and hamburgers to join them for the evening meal. Dembeli and Barnabasi knew that while they were out hunting, the rest of the Gospel Team members would meander through the town sharing the pocket-sized picture sermons with anyone who would listen. Those pictures would become a stepping-stone for discussion and a take-off point for them to share their testimony about what Jesus had done for them. The pairs would explain how He was the Supreme Sacrifice that ended all sacrificing and that now we, by faith, can have our heads pulled, our feet planted on the road to an eternal refuge in heaven, and our hearts set on fire by the power of His Holy Spirit.

A bath in a cool stream nearby refreshed the hunters after a day in the hills, and then they too, walked through the town greeting old friends, making new ones, telling the thrills of the hunt, and sharing their faith in Christ. Sometimes the hunter who had been their guide would join them as they wandered through the village, although he had already seen the pictures. On this particular occasion, God had blessed their efforts and Dembeli had shot an animal big enough that the small party of three hunters could not carry "the beef" back to town by themselves. So one of the hunters had volunteered to go back to town and call other men to come and help them. While he was gone, several men from a nearby farm who had heard the shot joined the hunters as they relaxed in the shade of the trees waiting for more men from town to join them.

While they waited, the hunters swapped stories of past hunts, reliving the thrill of danger and sharing in the camaraderie of victory or in the memory of defeat. Had he been real, the Storyteller could have thrilled the hunters with the exploits of great hunts of by-gone days. Instead, he found himself listening as the hunters recalled the struggles of victory as they bore the heat of the day, the thirst of the dry season, and torrential storms during the rainy season, and yet conquered and marched into town carrying their portions of the animal that did not get away. He sensed the agony of defeat as the hunters shared among themselves the times they had lost their way in the vast African bush, or the time when they had skillfully followed a wounded animal for hours only to have the tracks washed away in a torrential downpour before they found their prey. He pictured the humility of defeat as the hunters quietly walked back into town empty-handed.

Somewhere along the line, one of the Gospel Team members would sense an opportunity to share an even greater story, and he would reach into his hunting bag and withdraw a pocket-sized picture sermon to lead the conversation in a new direction. By now the Storyteller had heard it many times, but somehow it still seemed new and fresh. It was the story of God, who loved so much that He became man and bore the agony of sins so that we might know the victory of eternal life. It is the story of grace and forgiveness, of lives being re-created by the power of the Holy Spirit. It is the story of Christ's victory over sin and death and hell. It is the story of a Jesus creating the road back to a right relationship with Creator God. It is a story with eternal values lived out among the Kuranko people. It is the story of faith and victory.

The animal was butchered and the hunters each carried a sizable portion back into town. Somehow the weight of the meat did not seem like a burden, and nobody seemed to mind the slower pace going up the hills. Silence was abandoned and laughter rang through the hills as the little line of hunters made their way joyfully back to the village. As they approached the town they could hear the sound of children playing, the roosters crowing, the women beating the rice to knock the hulls off so it could be winnowed, washed, and cooked for the evening meal. It was a comforting sound for the hunters at the end of the day, for it carried a universal message: "You're home now."

Following the evening meal, the chief's drum would sound a call for all to come to his compound, and contented tummies would find their way to a comfortable place where the owners could participate in the gathering. If it had been a dangerous animal, such as a cape buffalo, that had been killed, one of the hunters would be asked to relive the hunt for the benefit of the people who seemed more than willing to hear the story again. Then the Gospel Team would begin to share the real reason of why they had come. In all the fun, laughter, and singing, they knew that the preaching and teaching of God's Word was central and it was the only reason the Team had walked back into the hills: to *Preach Jesus! Preach Jesus! Preach Jesus!*

The service would often close with an invitation for anyone who wanted to know more to come and visit with a Team member who would help him, or her, pray and accept Jesus as Savior and Lord. The Storyteller followed Dembeli back to his hut at the end of a long, hard day, but one that had been so satisfying. Finaba was not surprised when the man who had lead the hunt called softly before entering the hut and joined Dembeli sitting on the floor. Dembeli was surprised that this great hunter had come to share the closing moments of the day with him. Custom dictated that since this hunter had led the hunt when Dembeli had killed his first dangerous animal, Dembeli would have to honor him as long as he was alive. This man had now become the young missionary's hunting mentor. They had experienced some difficulty communicating in the bush because the white man did not understand much of the Kuranko language, and the hunter did not know any English. Sitting together in the hut, the two hunters shared long periods of silence, but somehow—as the young missionary tried to share again his faith in Christ—a bond was formed that spanned the months until effective communication could take place. When that happened later, the hunter was able to understand and he accepted Christ. The two became brothers in Christ by faith, thus forming a bond that is much stronger than even the traditional bond of a hunter and his mentor.

The following day, the line of men walking single file along the foot path heading home were in great spirits in spite of the loads they carried on their heads. The Storyteller noticed Dembeli's backpack and laughed when he thought of how awkward that must be, for it is so much easier to carry a load on your head. He laughed about the fact that the white man with the backpack was also the only one who seemed to be in a hurry. Somehow he knew that in time that would change. And change it did! As the team entered each town along the path, they would set their loads down on a veranda or under a shade tree. Then they would mosey through the town greeting all their friends and relatives that they had not seen since they last met in the market or passed along this way. They all knew they would make it home before dark, and there was no hurry because word had already gone along the incredible African grapevine, telling their people back in Heredugu that an animal had been killed and the Team was on its way home. Finaba could never figure out why the young white man was in such a hurry. The loads did not get any lighter when you hurried. The path would not get any shorter. If you hurried you'd miss all the chatter that takes place as you meander along the winding trails. Besides that, it would not be acceptable to rush through a town without stopping to greet friends—or if you had none, to make some new friends in this town that was someone else's home.

Dembeli learned quickly that those passing through a town brought news from where they had been and picked up the news from various ones in town who wanted to send a message on down the route the travelers would pass that day. He soon discovered that this was just a small part of the incredible communications "grapevine." The Storyteller chuckled for he knew that it would not be long until Dembeli would learn these priorities in life and would come to enjoy those hours of walking and visiting, which somehow made the journey seem lighter.

Soon, Dembeli did learn this important lesson, and he was able to take it a step farther in the discipleship process. When sensing that one of the Team was struggling, he would often drop back a little bit from the rest of the group as they walked between towns and would ask about his friends' struggles. Sometimes, a Team member would suggest that they get away from town and the listening ears of children by going out to the farm or by going hunting. Later, while heading to the area they planned to hunt, the two men would talk, often scaring up game that could have easily been shot had the men been silent. But Dembeli had a dual purpose for this time together. He sensed that those he was seeking to disciple were struggling, and he wanted to understand and help carry the load if he could. So, walking through the hills or slogging through the swamps, the truths of the Word were taught. The Team members were told over and over that they were God's Church and that they could look to Him for all their needs. This time together also afforded Dembeli the opportunity to learn the customs, culture, and heartbeat of the people God had sent him to serve.

Dembeli wasn't sure that all of the men from the Church who accompanied the Team were really committed Christians, and he was concerned about them. Brodi, a man from another tribe who lived in town, was one of the men who often asked for work and on occasion would ask to accompany the Team as they went out to share the Gospel. One evening he was riding in the front of the truck with Dembeli, and Dembeli decided to ask him about his salvation. So Dembeli asked, "Brodi, how long have you been a Christian?"

Brodi expressed some surprise and responded with a question. "Dembeli, have you forgotten? Remember when I was so very sick and was dying? Every day you and the Gospel Team would come and check on me. You brought me medicine and you prayed for me. I saw the love of God for me in you and the Team, and I accepted Christ as my Savior and Lord."

Finaba recalled the blind man named Fiyon who used to visit Dembeli. He originally visited because he wanted Dembeli to give him something. Dembeli found work for him and paid him for the work so that he had a job and maintained his pride in his accomplishment. It was not every day, but it did help, and so the man would often come and sit and talk and then ask for odd jobs that he could do.

Dembeli began to talk to him about his blindness, and explained that there are two kinds of blindness. There is a physical blindness, which in this case was caused by a disease. But there is also a spiritual blindness because one does not accept the Light that God sent into the world. As time went on, Dembeli's friend decided that he did not want to be blind in two ways, and so he accepted Christ and experienced a new Light in his life.

When the Paramount chief asked Dembeli to build a major bridge and install steel tread ways instead of pouring a concrete decking, Dembeli knew he had a major task on his hands. The pins that were to secure the tread ways together had been lying around for nearly twenty years and were extremely rusty. Then the thought struck Dembeli that if he bought some sandpaper his blind friend named Fiyon, could sand off the four-foot long pins and prepare them to be used again. He asked Fiyon if he wanted a major job. Sure enough he did, and he went right to work.

A couple days later Dembeli and his friend Daudu were walking through town when one of the ladies approached Dembeli and asked him why he was making Fiyon, a blind man work so hard. Dembeli was surprised until he learned that the reason for her concern was that she had found the man working on sanding the steel pins during the night. Suddenly Dauda broke out in laughter as he explained to the lady that Fiyon could not tell whether it was day or night and he was just working whenever he wanted to. Finaba still chuckled when Dembeli went to Fiyon and asked him about it. He explained that he was awake and had taken a contract to smooth off the steel, and since he worked by feeling and not by sight, he just got up and went to work when he felt like it. When he got tired, day or night, he rested.

The one-on-one times were also valuable mentoring sessions, as Dembeli helped the men on the Gospel Team deal with how to live out Biblical principles in an animistic world. Sometimes those issues were complicated, but at other times they were fairly straight forward. On one occasion Dembeli and one of the men were traveling together, and Dembeli saw a man standing at the side of the road holding a chicken up in the air as an indication that he wanted to sell it. They stopped, and after bartering for a little bit Dembeli was able to buy the chicken for $5. A couple miles down the road they saw another man holding up his chicken for sale so they stopped for the second chicken. When Dembeli asked him how much he wanted for his chicken, he said that he would take $7. The Gospel Team member jumped in by declaring that we had just paid $3 for the chicken we had and it was bigger than the one being sold now. Dembeli knew right away that after he bought the second chicken he would need to talk to his friend about it.

The second chicken was purchased for a fair price, and Dembeli drove off. Then he asked Dauda why he had lied to the man about the price of the first chicken. Of course Dauda did not see it as a lie. He declared that it was acceptable because the man did not know how much they had paid for the first chicken and had no way of finding out where we got it. Finaba knew that Dembeli would not let that go, and he was right. The next few miles were spent in a discussion about truth and the fact that God knows even if the people around us are not aware of the truth. Since we are accountable to Him, we need to live and talk and walk in such a way that He is honored. We need to listen to Him saying "BRRRRZZZZZZZZZ".

Of course there are times truth does not win out immediately, or is not even discovered until years later. Dembeli and Dauda both laughed as they recalled an earlier trip when they had a Muslim friend traveling with them. The truck was loaded down, and there was little space for any extra passengers. A band of baboons ran across the road ahead of them, so Dembeli took the gun and went to invite one of them for supper. While following the baboon he met a warthog and invited it to dinner. The big hog did not drop in its tracks, but ran off, and so Dembeli asked his Muslim friend to go find it for him while he followed the baboons.

The baboons escaped and soon Dembeli turned around and went back to the truck where he met the other man. He asked about the wart hog and the man informed Dembeli that he had missed it. It was not until years later that his Muslim friend told Dembeli that he had not missed the wart hog, but that he had actually found it lying dead in the swamp. He reminded Dembeli that at that time he was a Muslim and he was not allowed to handle the warthog, so he had lied. Dembeli often had the opportunity to share the Gospel with this Muslim friend, and one day he asked him if he could go to his encampment and share the Gospel with his people.

A couple of days later the young man came back and said that the elders would not allow Dembeli to bring the picture sermons into the encampment and share the Gospel, but that he could come and listen to tapes out at Dembeli's house. So Dembeli found some tapes in his language. Each week the man came to market with a friend, and after he had finished his business in the market he would come out to visit Dembeli and listen to the Gospel message on tapes in his own language. His interest began to grow, and soon he asked for a Bible. Some of his friends also wanted Bibles, so Dembeli was able to share God's Word with them as well. His friendship served to remind Dembeli of the many people in the area who had not heard the Gospel, and Dembeli was concerned that somehow the Gospel Team would be able to reach those people for Christ.

At one of the Gospel Team meetings, Dembeli asked the Team members for a commitment. There are few roads in the area and so most of the towns had to be reached by walking. He wanted to know how many evenings a week the men could go out, and which towns they felt they could reach. The question opened a lengthy discussion, but in the end the men on the Team agreed that they could all come in from their farms early four evenings a week and walk to nearby towns to share the Gospel message. They named the towns that they felt they could reach in an evening. Dembeli marked them on a map and then realized that the Team felt they could walk out five miles, hold a service, and come back in the same evening. They were willing to do this four evenings a week. To reach more towns, the truck could be used to get to the towns along the few roads that did exist. It was agreed that the truck would carry the Team out along the road, dropping off a couple of men at each town they passed through. When they reached the farthest point, Dembeli and the two or three Team members left with him in the truck would hold a service in that town before turning around and picking up the other team members on their way home.

This plan worked well for a while, but soon other towns began to request that the Gospel Team share their stories and pictures with them, and it was difficult to decide which towns to go to. Dembeli felt it was time to plan a new strategy for evangelism in the area, so during one of the discipleship sessions the problem was discussed at great length. Some of the Team members felt that they should reach as many towns as possible. Others felt that the Team should view their ministry as a farm. Since all the farming is done by hand, it is extremely labor intensive. Machetes and axes are used to clear a section of forest for a farm. After the fallen trees are dry, they are set on fire. A short-handled hoe is used to dig up the earth, and then seed is scattered by hand. Birds have to be driven off the newly planted areas so the seed can take root. The weeds are pulled by hand, and then when harvest time comes a knife is used to cut the ripened grain. Dembeli often mused that farming in Kuranko land has to be one of the hardest ways imaginable to make a living.

The men on the Gospel Team reasoned that a man has to decide how big a farm he and his family can really take care of. If he makes it too big, he will never be able to chase away the birds that come to eat the newly-scattered seed. The farmer would never be able to scare away all the monkeys that somehow manage to steal more than their fair share of the crop. He would not be able to build a fence around the farm to keep out the rodents that will eventually destroy the rice. He would certainly never be able to get enough women to help him pull all the weeds if the farm was too big. So, if the farm is too big, the birds would eat most of the seed, the rodents would sneak through and destroy the young crop, and the weeds would choke out what remained. Very simply, the man with the farm too big to handle would end up without a harvest.

However, if a man concentrates on a portion of land that he can handle, he will be effective in his efforts to chase away the birds, and they will not be able to steal the seed rice when it is scattered. The woven grass fence will be strong and the traps in the fence will capture rodents, thus preventing the destruction of the crop. The traps will also provide meat for the cooking pot. The weeds will be pulled long before they can choke out the tender young rice plants. The man will rejoice in a harvest and be rewarded for his efforts and his family will have plenty to eat.

Similarly, the men reasoned that if the Gospel Team spread themselves too thin doing evangelism, they would not get a spiritual harvest of souls, nor would they be able to disciple the new believers. The devil would come in with temptations and false doctrines and lead them astray, and the spiritual harvest would fail. This line of reasoning reminded Dembeli of Jesus' parable of the Sower and the Seed (Luke 8:1-15). Dembeli saw the wisdom in this line of reasoning and agreed that the outreach evangelism program would be more effective if they would continue to go back to the same towns each week until they had groups of believers strong enough to stand on their own.

Only one main road ran through the area, and many times during the rainy season portions of the road became impassable. Sometimes the bridges were washed away in the floods, or portions of the roads disappeared under the rushing current. However, some of the towns that requested visits from the Team felt that if they could maintain a road, the Team would be able to come to their town as well. So, they sent a delegation to ask Dembeli and the Gospel Team to help them improve their section of the road. In some cases where there had never been a road, they asked Dembeli to help them build a road to reach their town. The Team was more than happy to comply with these requests when they saw the people from those towns getting serious about the work on the road. The mission provided some of the hand tools, and road construction became an important "bridge ministry" that enabled Dembeli to reach many of the people in the area.

Discipleship sessions each week were a highlight of the program. Obviously the Team leader and Dembeli were not able to be in all the towns on any given night of outreach, so they were thrilled to hear how the Lord was working in the various towns. Each session included a time of sharing the questions that the Team members had found difficult to answer, or the problems they had faced. Later, as the Team leader and Dembeli talked, it became increasingly apparent that ground rules had to be laid. After much discussion it was decided that the ground rules for Team members would have to be few and simple so that it would not become a long list of "do's" and " don'ts". With careful and prayerful consideration, it was decided that there would only be three basic rules.

The first one was, "If you cannot walk to the towns where the Team leader has asked you to walk, then you will not be privileged to ride in the truck on the nights it goes to towns along the road". As the driver of the vehicle, Dembeli would often be swamped with many, many, requests to carry people here and there en route to the various towns where services were planned. Relatives and friends of the Gospel Team members wanted to join the group of young men and ride along just for the fun of traveling in the open back of the truck as it sped along the roads or to visit friends for an evening in a town far away. So, this simple rule was enforced, and everyone had to check with the Team leader before jumping into the truck, a solution that saved Dembeli countless headaches.

The second rule was equally clear. "Any new Team member is to go as an observer until he has been discipled to the point where he understands the reason for evangelism". The Storyteller laughed when he heard this rule. He remembered the evening a well-meaning spokesman for the Team told the people that if they would let Dembeli come to their town with the Gospel Team and build a church, that a road would be built to their town. He went on to say that they would be given a school, and of course they would also have the benefits of a clinic and all the good things that the mission could provide. He recalled how Dembeli sat in the shadows that evening and chuckled at all the fantastic promises, and how in the next discipleship session the Team was taken back to "base one" in the discipleship training program: *Preach Jesus! Preach Jesus! Preach Jesus!* So the second rule was born.

The third rule was perhaps the easiest to understand: When out in a town away from home. "No member of the Gospel Team is to walk alone". Jesus had sent the disciples out two-by-two, and now a new generation of disciples had learned the value of that basic principle. Not only could they encourage one another in difficult times and support each other in hard situations, but the Team members often found themselves staying in the homes of people who had never heard the Gospel, or in towns where some people were not in favor of the Gospel being preached. It would be so easy to become discouraged, and easier still for someone in the town to begin a nasty rumor about one of the Christians that had come and "done bad" in their town. So, Team members out on evangelism were always seen in twos and threes or more. This arrangement gave the advantage of increasing the joys of the journey too, for experiences are so much more real when shared with a friend.

Even so, tough times could not be avoided. One Team member had to be asked to step down because he frequently became involved in some kind of conflict in various towns. Others on the Team felt that he was hurting the testimony they were trying to uphold. Apparently he wasn't hearing the Brrrrzzzz ("Be like Me") from Jesus as loud as he should have been. They endeavored to stay with him so that he would not be left alone, but he seemed to be able to slip away quietly and appear somewhere else in the middle of a conflict. For a time, he sat out and did not travel with the team. Later, after some growth in Christ, he was able to rejoin the Team in outreach and rejoiced with the rest of the Team when he could report at the discipleship session that there had been no conflicts between him and the town people where he had been.

Those who continued on the Team and adhered to the simple rules found great joy in sharing with others their faith in Christ. Although the area they traveled was fairly limited, they soon discovered that word moved along the African grapevine rather quickly. As requests for them to come and share their stories came from towns throughout the area, it became increasingly difficult to decide where to go and where not to go. In the process Dembeli spent a lot of time discussing various towns with the Team members so that they could evaluate where the most fertile, responsive soil was.

Many Christians walked though the foothills of the Konko Mountain range from the upper Kuranko area to the other side of the mountains where the "Forest Kuranko" lived. God had impressed Dembeli with a vision to reach the people in the towns in the foothills with the Gospel, and so he shared that vision with the Gospel Team. After much discussion, they decided that part of the Team should walk through the foothills sharing the Gospel in each of the towns along the way. When they returned they could encourage other Christians to follow the same route in hopes that there would be a consistent-enough witness throughout the year to encourage people in these remote towns to accept Christ. They could then form a group of believers and establish their own Church in each of the towns. Estimates of the distance between the upper Kuranko mission station in Heredugu and the mission station on the other side of the mountains ranged from forty five to well over sixty miles, so the Team knew that they were in for a long hike regardless of which path they took.

Having walked the path many times before, the Storyteller was able to recall the days when a man could walk all day through the forest and never be under the direct light of the sun. He pondered the changes that had taken place over the years as farmers cut down and burned off more and more of the beautiful tropical forest in their attempts to find suitable soil to plant their farms and grow their crops.

The rugged terrain held its own kind of beauty, and the walkers enjoyed themselves immensely the first day as stories and laughter rolled along the footpath right along with the team members. Finaba wished that he could join in the swapping of fables, but years of experience had taught him that he would always be just an invisible observer that nobody could hear anyway, so he remained locked in silence. Yet he enjoyed listening as Dembeli plied the Team with questions and watched them carefully in an attempt to learn more about the people he had come to serve. The Storyteller knew that Dembeli was aware of the fact that a man can say anything he wants to say, but if one watches him long enough, what the man really believes will be revealed. By asking the right questions and watching ever so carefully, Dembeli began to learn what really motivated the members of the Gospel Team and what their core values were. Finaba noticed that Dembeli would often ask searching questions and a Team member would respond with a story or a parable. A common response was that the Team member did what he did because his father had done things that way. Somehow Finaba knew, before it was ever voiced, that Dembeli would never be satisfied with an answer like that, and so he was not surprised when the young missionary asked his friend why his father had done it that way. The men on the team laughed as the response came back that the father had done things that way because the grandfather had done it that way. Without a moment's hesitation Dembeli would then ask, "Now why do you think your grandfather did it that way?"

The stage was set, and the discussion would go all the way back to the "beginning of time". Even the Storyteller could not remember that far back. Finaba had seen Dembeli ask such questions often enough that he knew the subject would be temporarily dropped, but on another day, in another town, perhaps with an older man, Dembeli would again ask his question. Finaba perceived that Dembeli was slowly piecing together a picture of what the Kurankos really believed in an effort to be more effective in evangelism and in discipling Team members to reach their own people with the Gospel.

Steep were the hills and hot was the sun that beat down upon the Team the second day of the journey. The loads on their heads seemed so very heavy and the end of the walk through the hills seemed so *terribly* far away. The beginning of the walk became more blurred in their memories as it was pushed aside in favor of the thought of the sweet rice and soup they would share together that evening, and of the hope that they would be able to feast and rest at the end of the trek. They were grateful that for once Dembeli was not chomping at the bit to pick up the pace. Finaba chuckled to himself as he recalled how often it had seemed that Dembeli was the only one in the world who was in a hurry to get wherever he was going. Apparently he was learning, for today even Dembeli seemed content to walk along at a slower pace. The loads, the heat, the hills, and the distance seemed to wear away at the Team, and as so often happens when a Team is ministering together under those conditions a spark of tension can light the flame of conflict. Soon the sense of unity begins to erode and the devil has an open door through which to pass as he tries to destroy the effectiveness of the Team's ministry. No physical conflict took place, but the undercurrent of irritation was still strong when the Team arrived at their designated stopover town for the night.

After greeting the chief and the elders, the weary travelers were shown their lodging places for the night. Conversation was not as lively as usual, and the Storyteller knew that Dembeli sensed that it was not just because of the long haul through the foothills of the mountains. In the typical tradition of Kuranko hospitality, the town chief sent a large pot of rice and soup to his visitors, and they quickly gathered to dip their hands into the common bowl. As they gathered around the evening meal, Dembeli asked the Team leader to lead in prayer, but the leader was interrupted before he could even get started. One of the men on the Team suggested that it would be more honoring to God for them to first sort out the conflict that had started a few miles back down the trail. He shared that he really did not feel that he could dip his hand into the bowl with a specific Team member and then take part in the service following if what was in his heart was not expressed and straightened out first. The moments that followed were a lesson to all as the Team worked together to resolve the conflict that had divided them. Dembeli watched and listened as other members of the Team stepped in as mediators to help the two men reach reconciliation.

Once the relationship was restored, prayers of thanksgiving were offered. No one seemed to mind that the soup had grown cold and the rice had turned to a sticky glob in a cold bowl. Broken relationships had been mended, and Dembeli rejoiced as side by side the men walked over to the chief's house where they would minister together, once again as a Team, to exalt Jesus Christ. Sitting in the shadows watching the people, Finaba mused that it was not only Dembeli watching the Kuranko people to learn their core values, but it was also the Kuranko people watching the Christians to see if what they said about love, peace, and joy was real in their lives. Tonight had been a living example of the healing power of forgiveness and grace, and the impact on the lives of the Team would be a lasting one.

Chapter 10: Facing Opposition

Dembeli knew that inter-team conflicts could be devastating to the ministry, but he was also concerned about the outside pressure that was beginning to come against the Team. The first hint of this was when he journeyed down-country and an older missionary challenged him concerning the whole concept of the Gospel Team. The senior missionary informed Dembeli that evangelism and church planting had never been done in Sierra Leone the way he was doing it with a Gospel Team. He stated that such a ministry style had never even been heard of before. Not knowing what to say, Dembeli responded that it would be heard of because God was working through the Team and they were winning people to Jesus. Another down-country missionary reminded Dembeli that his family had been on furlough when Dembeli had been stationed clear up in the remote Heredugu area alone, and that if they had been on the field, they would have opposed the decision, and it would never have happened. The Storyteller knew that the Dembeli felt strongly that God had led him to that area and that it was God who had given Dembeli the vision for the Gospel Team. It was God's team! It was God's Church! All God wanted Dembeli to do was to disciple believers to reach their own people. Dembeli reasoned that it was God's timing that had determined who was on the scene at the Annual Field Council when the missionaries decided to station him and his family in the Heredugu area in answer to God's call. It was God Who has sent illiterate men to him to be discipled in evangelism and church planting and so Dembeli reasoned that God certainly approved of the Gospel Team.

The gathering of all the missionaries for the next Annual Field Council meeting proved to be another time of testing for the whole concept of the Gospel Team. Finaba had often listened in on conversations when Dembeli had bounced his ideas off some of the senior missionaries whose experience far surpassed his own. Now he listened as each missionary gave a report of what was happening in his or her area of ministry. The opportunity came to discuss the Gospel Team from the Heredugu area and the methods being used in evangelism. Some council members immediately accepted the idea and proposed that the Gospel Team members be paid for their time as they walked out to the nearby towns. Finaba thought Dembeli would be excited about the proposal because it indicated that some of the others were willing to accept this new style of ministry. He was very surprised that Dembeli so vigorously opposed it.

Other missionaries from down-country pointed out how long and hard they had struggled to get individuals to go out and teach or preach. They reasoned that for an effective program to continue they needed to pay the workers because the Scripture declares that the "worker is worthy of his hire." They explained how some who were ministering down-country were receiving "benefits." The Storyteller listened patiently as Dembeli argued that paying the Gospel Team members would create dependency on himself and on the mission, and that was the last thing he felt he needed. Dembeli argued that if, as a mission, they began to pay men to witness, they would kill the Spirit of the witness. He expressed his opinion that if they were paid then men would begin to witness just for the job, and not because they are in love with Jesus.

Dembeli shared his dream of how the Team would be able to gather the believers in the various towns where they were ministering. The groups of believers would become Churches, and each of these Churches would start their own teams. He asked the council how many such Churches, and teams, they felt the mission could support. He reasoned that it would be better not to pay the Gospel Team members right from the beginning so that in the future, the mission would not have to tell them that they could not start any new teams to do evangelism because the mission did not have enough funds to support such a large ministry. He reasoned that if the mission never paid the Gospel Teams to begin with that the growth of the Church in the Heredugu area would not be governed by the size of the mission's pocketbook. He expressed the idea that the outreach should instead be a spontaneous response to the spiritual needs of the area, based on the ability of the national Church to respond to that need as God gave the necessary spiritual gifts.

When the issue finally came to a vote, it was decided to let the Gospel Team from the Heredugu area continue without financial assistance from the mission. Perhaps it was because Dembeli was so outspoken and passionate in his arguments, or maybe it was because the others felt that the Team was so far away that they really did not have to get involved, that they finally agreed to let Dembeli continue with the Gospel Team ministry he had begun. Some may have felt relieved that if they agreed with Dembeli the mission would not have to finance another program. It had been a long, hard-fought battle for Dembeli, but the Storyteller now understood why Dembeli so vigorously opposed the idea of tying the Team to the financial ability of the mission. Although it was not discussed with the Gospel Team, Finaba knew that Dembeli sensed they had passed a milestone in Church planting in the Heredugu area, and he was grateful for his missionary mentors who stood favorably with him in his endeavor to establish an indigenous Church.

For each one of the missionaries who opposed the idea, activity, and style of the Gospel Team, there seemed to be one who came alongside and added great encouragement to the concept. Their support and advice was valuable, and Dembeli soon found them to be reliable sounding boards for new ideas and endeavors that he wanted to put into practice

Unfortunately, opposition also came from other quarters. Some down-country leaders in the national church opposed the idea of the Gospel Team because it was something they were not used to, and because they had not been trained that way. Dembeli noticed that missionaries and pastors seemed to train others in the same way that they had been trained. Because of the nature of a new concept, they could not control it, govern it, or measure it. Some of the leaders insisted that an offering be taken in every village where the Team went for meetings, while others felt that a head count should be taken so accurate records could be kept as to how many were in attendance at each meeting. The Team was asked to submit the number of people who attended services in each of the towns, how many people they preached to, and how much was collected in offerings so that the program could be officially recognized. Dembeli argued that these were not the purpose of the Team. He pointed out that evangelism and discipleship were its priority.

Each pastor was required to stand before the National Church Conference and give a report of what was happening in his church. Since

Pastor Pita was the only pastor in the area he represented the whole of the Heredugu area. The National Church President tabled Pastor Pitas' report until he could come back with some numbers to present to the Conference. After a brief huddle, the Team decided that the only thing they could do was make an estimate. How do you count people when so many are sitting in the shadows of a hut or are outside the small circle of light cast by a kerosene lantern on a dark night? On several occasions the Gospel Team had tried to count the people. One time Dembeli had asked the men to count how many homes were in each town because he knew from the results of the national census approximately how many people lived in each hut. So they did know how many homes were in each town, and they could make a conservative estimate. They discussed it briefly and then sent their pastor back to the conference body. Dembeli and the Storyteller both chuckled when they saw the looks of amazement on the faces of the church leaders when Pastor Pita reported that the team was witnessing to a combined total of approximately one thousand people in the towns they were visiting.

Other leaders in the national church felt that the Team should not be allowed to function because most of them were illiterate. They felt that the Team needed to have proper training in an established institution, or at least some schooling, before they could evangelize and disciple people. They argued that the Team certainly could not plant churches without officially recognized training.

It was this last line of reasoning that prompted Dembeli to argue vigorously in favor of the Gospel Team. The Storyteller knew what was coming, for he had often heard Dembeli trying to encourage all of the men on the Team to enroll in the literacy class taught four or five evenings a week by Pastor Pita. He tried to hammer into their thinking that they could never have a strong Church until the believers could read God's Word for themselves. Finaba also knew the struggle and frustration Dembeli was experiencing as he tried to disciple men who could not read God's Word for themselves. But when the Team was put down because of their lack of education, Finaba knew, without a question, where the young missionary from the Heredugu area would stand, and stand he did.

Dembeli used the same line of reasoning he had used so often before in defense of the Team. He pointed out that in God's Word there are the *fixed* principles of the Word, and there are also the *flexible* principles of the Word. In this situation, the command of Jesus in the Great Commission provides us with the *fixed* principle: "Make disciples." The *flexible* principle is how this is to be done. Dembeli reasoned that the training could be done in an institution like a Bible school. He pointed out that he hoped that some of the men on the Team would learn to read and write, and that they would go on for further training in an established institution. That way they could come back as pastors in the Heredugu area, recognized and accepted by the national church leadership.

Dembeli pointed out that the second way to train was through Theological Education by Extension (TEE). He expressed great confidence in a practical "on-the-job training" that could be beneficial for new pastors and could serve as an advanced learning tool for men who have already graduated from Bible school.

Dembeli argued that the third option still existed as a *flexible* principle. That option was "on the job" discipleship training such as was being done with the Gospel Team in the Heredugu area, where men who are in love with Jesus are discipled and encouraged to share their faith in Christ with their own people. He explained that he believed that when they won someone to Christ they could disciple them and train them to win others. The new believers would then meet together, and this group of believers was part of the body of Christ which is the Church. He reasoned that this was Church planting in the rural areas. Many pastors in the national Church conference looked in favor on the Team and so for them the issue was settled and the Gospel Team was permitted to continue in ministry.

However, the debate with some of the national church leaders was not settled as easily as it had been with the missionaries. One of the teachers from the Bible school continued to look down on the Gospel Team members because of their lack of training, and he opposed what they were doing. He often reprimanded them for their illiteracy and asked what made them think they could be effective witnesses without proper training in a recognized or official institution. On one of his visits back to his home town of Heredugu, this teacher was particularly hard on the Gospel Team members and feelings were hurt. However, he felt that he had a cause to fight for and he wanted to win the battle, so he visited Dembeli who was really the one responsible for encouraging the illiterate and untrained men to perform far beyond their station in life.

Dembeli and the teacher from down-country took a walk together through the orchard, and the Storyteller tagged along unseen to observe what would happen. He heard the teacher scolding Dembeli in no uncertain terms for the lack of training in the ranks of the men he had recruited to do evangelism and Church planting. Finaba had seen Dembeli enthusiastically support the team in the face of this type of opposition already, and he thought he was going to hear it all over again. He was totally surprised when the young missionary agreed with the teacher that the men needed to learn to read and write. After all, he pointed out, he was encouraging them to do that himself. He reasoned that that was why he worked with the pastor to have a literacy class taught in the church several evenings each week. The teacher did not feel that a mere literacy class was adequate, and he reprimanded Dembeli for his stand in supporting unlearned and ignorant men in this type of outreach program.

What happened next became a turning point in the relationship of the teacher and the Gospel Team. Finaba watched as Dembeli stopped under one of the orange trees, and he heard him ask the teacher if the teacher preached to anyone when he came into the area, or if the other church leaders who opposed the Gospel Team held evangelistic services in the area. The Storyteller could see the glisten of tears in Dembeli's eyes as he turned to the teacher and quietly asked, "Teacher, if these men do not reach your people for Christ, then who will?"

Nobody needed to tell the teacher that there were over two hundred towns in the area, and only one church, and only one missionary helping the little church do evangelism. Nor did anyone have to remind him that there were only six schools in the entire area, and that fewer than a quarter of the towns could be reached by motorized vehicle, and that included motorcycles. It was not necessary to tell the teacher that most of the towns had never heard the Gospel, because he knew all those facts for it was his home, his area, and his people that were being discussed. It seemed to the Storyteller and to Dembeli, that the teacher's countenance suddenly changed as he confessed that he spent most of the year teaching in the city a full day's travel away. He was not able to come and hold meetings in his own area to share the Gospel with his own people. Then in a moment of total honesty, he acknowledged that he did not even hold a single meeting when he came home to visit, although on occasion he did share with various individuals or family members the glorious plan of salvation. Finaba still is not sure why Dembeli did not respond as he had to some others by saying that it was better to do evangelism the Gospel Team's way, even if it was done poorly, than to not do evangelism at all, which was the teacher's way. Maybe it was because Dembeli sensed that the Holy Spirit had stepped in and had taken over the conversation, and that it was not necessary for him to say anything more at all. The teacher would never again express negative opinions about the Gospel Team.

That evening the teacher met with the Gospel Team leader, and for the first time a national church leader encouraged the Team to share their faith, and to keep pressing on. The realization had dawned on him that these men were reaching his people with the Gospel and that they were accomplishing something that no one else was doing. From that day onward he became one of the Team's greatest supporters for outreach, and never again rallied against them due to their lack of education. God is so good that later on that same teacher had the privilege of teaching Bible school classes to some of the members of the Team who had learned to read and write and were able to go for advanced training.

The third source of opposition was even harder for the Team to handle because it came from their own people in their own town, often from their own families that they had to live with each day. They were ridiculed for their stand for Christ and for forsaking the practices of their forefathers. Christianity was seen as the "White Man's Religion," and Team members were mocked for coming in off their farms early several days a week to walk out and share the Gospel without pay or any other material benefit. In the heat of that battle, the Storyteller thought that maybe Dembeli would relent and agree to start paying the men. However, he discovered that the young missionary was going to stand by what he believed to be a principle of God's Word: the Kuranko Church was God's Church, with one Lord, one faith, one baptism, and that the Kuranko believer could be filled and directed by the Holy Spirit every bit as much as the white missionaries. He believed that they should look to their Lord and *not* to the missionaries to provide their needs as they shared the Gospel.

Chapter 11: Looking to God

About that time Pastor Pita recalled a time long before when the Heredugu Church was first planted. Pa Jake Schierling had told the church leaders that the Church would never go ahead until they "took their hands out of the missionaries' pockets". After confessing that the statement really offended him, Pastor Pita shared how he thought about it more and more and finally came to realize that Pa Schierling was challenging them with the same principle that Dembeli was putting before them now. Pastor Pita explained that he finally saw that this is a principle in God's Word and he challenged the Church in Heredugu to live by it. They were God's people and they needed to look to their Lord to meet their needs. The Team banded together in prayer, encouraged each other, and walked through another storm with their heads held high, unpaid by the mission, but totally in love with Jesus and confident that He was walking with them.

It seemed to Dembeli that this principle was often tested, and each time God showed Himself to be faithful. Dembeli often visited the Bible school, and occasionally was able to visit the station on the southern side of the mountain where the missionaries were working with what Dembeli's people referred to as the "Forest Kurankos." As a result he built solid friendships with some of the men from that area. Following graduation, one of the new pastors from there approached Dembeli about his need for a loan. After a few questions, Finaba knew what was coming and he almost chuckled when Dembeli asked the young pastor if he had prayed about his need and asked God to provide.

Pastor Yoni responded that he had not prayed about it, but that he had come to the missionary for assistance. When Dembeli assured Pastor Yoni that he would join him in prayer and ask God to provide the need, a very disappointed pastor left to continue his other business.

About three months later, Dembeli was at a meeting that Pastor Yoni also attended. During the break for lunch, Pastor Yoni sought out Dembeli and asked if he could talk to him. When they were alone together, Pastor Yoni asked Dembeli if he remembered his request for money. Dembeli responded that he did and that he had been praying daily that God would meet the need of the young pastor.

Pastor Yoni knelt in the grass under the shade of a tree and started counting out little piles of money. Then he looked up at Dembeli and said, "This amount comes from a man that I had loaned money to about two years ago. I forgot about it, but last week he came to me and paid me back in full. This second pile of money comes from a job that someone asked me to do, and they paid me more than I expected. This third pile of money comes from a friend who asked me to help him fix his house. I did not expect him to pay me anything, but he gave me a gift as a thank you for my work. This fourth pile was given to me here at the meeting from someone who was praying for me. While he was praying, God spoke to him and reminded him that the Lord had blessed him with unexpected funds and instructed him to give me a "blessing" because I was in financial need. He was obedient to God and he gave me this money. So God has answered my prayers and met my need."

Dembeli reached down and counted the money and discovered that it was almost fifty percent more than Pastor Yoni had asked him for a couple of months earlier. Then he looked up at Pastor Yoni and asked, "Do you realize that God gave you more than what you asked for?"

Grinning from ear to ear, Pastor Yoni responded, "Yes, had the missionary met my need I would have only the amount of the loan and still have a debt. But God did more than meet my need, and I don't have a debt to pay back to the missionary." Finaba knew that Dembeli left rejoicing in the way God teaches His children such valuable lessons.

Dembeli did not want Pastor Yoni to be in his debt. He had learned that those debts often spoil friendships, and so he tried to avoid putting his friends in that kind of relationship. Another principle involved was what caused Pastor Yoni to come to Dembeli in the first place. It came from the idea that the mission was a business and that the pastors worked for the mission and therefore it was the mission's responsibility to pay them.

Dembeli wanted to see an indigenous Church established. He came to the conclusion that there are two different kinds of paternalism. In the first, the mission pays the worker and the worker becomes dependent on the mission. The mission then feels that since they pay the fiddler they can call the tune, and so they keep the worker doing what they want done. The mission remains in control and the worker continues to be under the authority of the mission.

The second kind of paternalism is usually more hidden. In this case the mission, or the missionary, continues to control by making the decisions or seeing that his, or her, desires or ideas are implemented. The missionary may be behind the scene in this case, but his control is just as powerful. Dembeli suspected that deep under the surface the nationals felt a strong resentment over this type of leadership, even though it was not as open as the first type of paternalism. In either case the mission continues to remain in control, and a truly indigenous Church is not established. For these reasons, Dembeli refused to put the Gospel Team on salary, knowing that for some of them whose families felt that their position was a job, his stand would not be understood. Deeper still, Dembeli continued to believe that if the men were paid to share their faith in Christ, the salaries would kill the spirit of the witness.

The Storyteller knew that the Dembeli was well aware of the opposition the Team was facing from their own families, because they shared it in the prayer times during the discipleship sessions. Finaba also knew that Dembeli could not totally identify with the type of opposition that the Team members were facing. He saw Dembeli take the matter to the Lord in prayer and ask Him to help him understand. But as the Storyteller listened in on those prayer times, he began to sense that there was another realm of opposition the young missionary was facing.

In the daily Bible studies with various team members, Dembeli began to sense that there was a deeper battle going on in the lives of the believers. It came because of the chains that had bound the people through generations of animistic worship. During a study on the book of Luke, the concept of freedom in Christ was discussed. One of the older men shared with the group that he felt that their ancestors had ropes on them and that they were drawing the believers back and that those ropes had to be cut.

One of the young men on the team shared about his father being demonized. The Team stood beside him and supported him in the stand he felt he had to take as a young Christian. Dembeli gained insights into some of the battles the men were facing, and gained new insights as he studied the Scripture seeking answers to their questions.

—

When God calls one of His children to a place of service, He not only cares for them but He enables them to enjoy the place, and the people, where they serve in obedience to that calling. That does not always make it easy, but it does give a deep sense of peace that holds a missionary steady in the toughest times. Dembeli often acknowledged that the call of God on one's life is extremely important because when the chips are down and the going gets tough, that is the only thing that will keep the missionary in the trenches on the front lines of duty. Perhaps the hardest test comes when one of the children gets sick.

Finaba sensed that this was true when Toby took ill. He was just a little guy when the fever and chills and coughing hit. The medication available did not seem to do much for him, and a deep chest cough made it hard for him to breathe. Dembeli was extremely concerned, and during the family devotions extra time was spent in prayer for little Toby. At bedtime Toby fell into a troubled sleep, and his troubled breathing seemed to be getting worse. Shortly after midnight his harsh breathing woke Dembeli, who rushed to his room. Picking up the little boy and offering as much comfort as he could, Dembeli began to pace the floor and pray. After about an hour Toby fell back to sleep, but his breathing was still labored, and Dembeli was at his wit's end because he had no more medicine to give. Laying his son back in his bed, Dembeli left the room and continued pacing the living room floor as he prayed. After about an hour, an old song taken from one of Jesus' parables began to run through his mind. Suddenly he found himself changing the words a little bit and singing with his whole heart, "Lord, do not come to my house; I am unworthy. Speak and my son will be healed. For when the Word of Life is spoken, You will be revealed. You will be revealed."

The song echoed through the darkness. Heaven responded, and Dembeli sensed the Master had heard as a deep peace settled over him. Through his tears he knew that Toby was healed. And indeed he was!

Somehow kids have a way of pushing the limits—or is it just that they are so available for God to use to teach the adults things they need to learn? Sometime later Toby climbed up where kids are not supposed to be able to climb, and managed to get into the medicine cabinet which kids are not supposed to be able to open. He opened a new bottle of aspirin with a child proof lid on it. He discovered that the little tablets were orange flavored, and he liked them so much he ate the whole bottle of asprin by himself.

Dembeli was about four miles from home working on a bridge that day, so he was not around to try and make Toby vomit up the aspirin. When he returned home after a day of work on the road, he discovered that Toby had been fed raw eggs and other yucky "stuff" to get him to give back the aspirin. He could not believe that his little boy had not surrendered his trophy. Dembeli joined in prayer that God would step in and take over. Finaba listened as Dembeli and his family cried out to their heavenly Father on behalf of Toby. God not only helps His children enjoy where He has called them to serve; He takes care of them too. God stepped in. No, Toby did not "give back" the aspirin. God let him enjoy the orange flavored "treats," but somehow neutralized all negative effects of the medicine and Toby went on playing and having a grand time just as if nothing had ever happened. We serve an awesome God!

Dembeli didn't worry only about his own children, but also about some of his friends' children too. One afternoon a man brought his son to Dembeli for help. His two boys had been cutting firewood. One was holding the wood while the other split it with an ax. Needless to say, the situation was an accident waiting to happen and it did not wait long. The father's concern was evident when he called Dembeli and asked him to fix his son's index finger that had almost been severed by the blow. Finaba didn't even want to look at the injury.

Dembeli didn't really know what to do, but since they lived a day's travel from the closest hospital, he knew he had to do something. He disinfected the wound, smothered it in penicillin ointment, and wrapped it with a bandage. He knew he had to put a splint on the finger since the bone had been severed. As gently as he could, he put the wrapped finger in a used shotgun shell. Over the next few weeks the dressing was changed often and the process was repeated until the boy's finger began to heal nicely. Dembeli forgot about the incident until years later during the war. He was sitting in the shade of the veranda with some of his friends when a group of young men walked by on their way to the market in the town they had fled to in a neighboring country. Barnabasi asked Dembeli if he knew the fine young man in the middle of the group, and when Dembeli responded that he did not know the youth, Barnabasi called him over and told him to show Dembeli his finger. Suddenly Dembeli remembered a little boy, a serious injury, and a shotgun shell splint. The youth greeted Dembeli and praised the Lord who had healed the finger so completely that there was no loss of use in the hand and hardly a scar. Finaba chuckled because he knew Dembeli had used a shotgun shell as a splint for fingers more than once, but it was always God who brought the healing. He also knew that there were times that another kind of healing was needed, and that Dembeli had experienced that kind of healing too.

Before going on furlough, the Schierlings loaned Dembeli their washing machine and a small generator so that they would no longer have to use the "James Washer" to wash the clothes. The "James Washer" was a simple contraption that had an agitator fastened to a tub. The handle was worked back and forth by hand to move the clothes through the water in the tub. When the clothes were considered clean, or the arm moving the agitator grew weary, the clothes were sent through the ringer on the other end of the tub. The ringer consisted of two rollers with a handle attached to the top one so that when a corner of the article to be rinsed was stuck between the rollers and the handle was turned, the top roller turned, pulling the clothes between it and the bottom roller. The two rollers would squeeze the water out of the clothes so that they would be ready to be hung on the clothesline. Laundry was a chore that took a lot of time.

The vehicle that had been designated for the Reifel's use was in a sad state of repair. A new one, although budgeted for and ordered, had not yet arrived. Bottled gas for the stove, kerosene for the lamps, and fuel for the truck had to be picked up twice a month in Kurela, which was a day's travel away. Dembeli often made the two-day trip in one simply because he did not want to leave the family alone for an extended period of time.

After a great deal of work on the roads, the Gospel Team was still having to walk to most of the towns. It was important to keep the mechanical things running on the mission station so that time could be spent in evangelism. The problem was that Dembeli was not very mechanical.

Then it happened. The truck died. The lawn mower refused to start. The generator quit so water could not be pumped up to the tank that supplied water to the house. Without a generator, the washing machine could not be used. The water tank sprang a leak, and Dembeli's prize rooster died. Dembeli felt that there must have been a conference of all mechanical inventions on the station, and they decided to retire all at the same time. It was then that he understood the Kuranko proverb that says "When you see a turtle up a tree, you know there is trouble on the ground." When asked how he felt, Dembeli almost answered that he felt like a turtle up a tree because everything that could go wrong had gone wrong at the same time, and there was "trouble on the ground." Unfortunately, at the same time Dembeli got sick and developed a high fever.

The Storyteller watched as Dembeli took the regularly prescribed medications without any results. He listened in on the two-way radio as a nurse was contacted to see what he should do next. As instructed, the box of medication that the nurse had given them when the family moved into such a remote area was opened. The recommended medicine was found and taken, but even that medication did not touch Dembeli's fever. It kept climbing each day, and the young missionary was worse off than before. Again the radio was used to ask more questions, and another medication from the precious box of medicines was suggested and tried. It, too, failed.

After a couple more days, Dembeli announced that they were simply going to have to get the truck started and drive out to see the nurse, or if necessary, go all the way down country to a doctor. The family began packing. Dembeli asked some of the boys from town who were playing in the yard if they would walk into town and ask some of the men to come out and help push the truck to get it started. A whole troupe of willing men came, and they pushed the truck down the hill toward the town. When it failed to start, they pushed it back up the hill and tried again. This was repeated until they finally had to give up and admit that the truck simply was not going to start. The men were asked to come back in the morning and try again before they went to their farms. Dembeli was so weak he simply went back to bed and collapsed. True to their word, the men showed up the next morning with additional helpers, thinking that the extra muscle would make the truck go faster and would give Dembeli a better chance to get it started. But still the truck would not cooperate.

Pastor Pita assured Dembeli that the Church was praying earnestly for him. Although they had been praying fervently each day, Dembeli told his family that he felt that the rest of the day should be spent in prayer and fasting. Throughout the day they sought God's blessing and healing, but it seemed that there were no answers and the fever would not relent. About mid-afternoon they met together again to pray. After the prayer time together, Dembeli was left alone to rest, and he continued in prayer alone. Then the Lord ever so gently seemed to tap him on the shoulder and say, "My child, you have a root of bitterness springing up in your heart." Dembeli listened, and he knew exactly what the Lord was talking about.

Tears of repentance flowed as Dembeli confessed to his Lord that in truth he did have a root of bitterness hidden in his heart, and that God was right in touching this area of his life. Through the tears of repentance, he sensed anew the grace and forgiveness of a loving heavenly Father and the joy of a right relationship restored. Dembeli began to praise the Lord for Calvary and for the grace and love revealed there. When he got up from his knees, the fever was gone. Still weak, he went back to bed, but he knew he was healed. The next day found him up and around again. We serve such a wonderful Lord!

Chapter 12: Changed Lives

The Team however, was still battling tough times as they faced opposition from Muslim and animistic relatives and friends. Some of them were becoming discouraged. Dembeli traveled to Kurela twice a month to pick up the mail and to restock the fuel supply for the mission station. When they traveled as a family, they would often stay overnight and visit with other missionaries in the area. During the time when the Team seemed to be facing some of their greatest opposition, Dembeli had to travel to Kurela for their mail and fuel supplies. A day or so later he returned rejoicing over the news received from loved ones and friends back in the States. One letter in particular caused Dembeli great joy. The next morning at the Gospel Team meeting he shared it with the men. It was a typical letter from a little boy that Dembeli had been corresponding with for some time back in South Dakota. It was brief and to the point and said something like this: "Hi. How are you? I am fine. School is fine. I have lots of friends. Please write to me more about your work in Africa." The boy had added a brief "P.S." that forever remains imprinted in Dembeli's mind, and in the minds of some of the Gospel Team members. In neat child penmanship, the little boy had written the words that lifted the spirits of Dembeli and the whole Gospel Team: "I am praying for you because I believe in what you are doing."

Lives were being changed by the power of the Gospel, and the Church was growing. New believers were beginning to take their stand, and were publicly declaring their faith through baptism. Since there was only one Church in the whole area, it seemed that those desiring baptism should come to Kamaron and be baptized there, so special baptismal services were held. These special services usually took place during the a meeting which was called the "Institute" when all the believers from the area were gathered together. The three-day meeting usually ended with a baptismal service followed by communion and a feast. To begin the baptismal service, Christians would meet for a time of praise and worship in the church and then walk together—singing as they walked—the half mile down to the river where the baptismal service would take place.

Later on, Dembeli became convinced that the new believers should be baptized in their own towns, in front of their families and friends, so that it would be more of a public declaration of their faith in Christ. The testimonies would serve as a dynamic witness to what Christ had done in their lives. More than that, many of the people in the village would begin to ask questions about the purpose and the meaning of baptism, and that would open doors of opportunity to share the Gospel. So baptism services began to take place in many villages throughout the area as men and women took a stand for Christ. Believers were baptized in groups so that they would have a support group which could encourage each other.

As the Church grew, God called some to be pastors, and they often experienced great opposition from family members. One of the ladies in Heredugu who had several members of her family involved in the church seemed to take a hard negative attitude toward the Gospel and her brother who was a pastor. She would often publicly ridicule and oppose those who declared their faith in Christ. She caused them no end of trouble and heartache as she continually ridiculed them with her sharp tongue, sometimes even during the church services which she occasionally attended. Her motivation for attendance appeared to be her desire to hurt the cause even more. Dembeli once compared her to the little agitator somewhere in the middle of the washing machine that kept things consistently stirred up so the clothes would go wishy-washy, wishy-washy until they were clean. But unlike the clothes in the washing machine, things did not come clean when Duwa was around. She just simply agitated. Finaba recalled one day when Dembeli was tending the rose bushes he had imported. He had turned to a friend and made the comment that Duwa was so ornery that if she ever grew roses she would most likely be growing them for the thorns and not for the flowers. She seemed to thrive on making the Christians in her extended family miserable. It appeared that she felt it was her responsibility to keep things stirred up in the Church as well. It was her "gift," you know.

Then Duwa became sick. Hesitant and embarrassed about discussing her sickness with Dembeli, she sent one of her relatives to ask for medicine without really sharing the true nature of the illness. A couple of days later the relative returned to explain to Dembeli that the medication he had given Duwa had not helped her at all, and that—if anything—her condition had deteriorated. Sensing a deeper issue, Dembeli began to ask probing questions that led him to the conclusion that Duwa needed to see a real doctor. He instructed her family to discuss the necessity of sending Duwa to the hospital when he made his next mail trip to Kurela.

A couple of days later the family said she was ready, and Duwa, along with another family member, rode to the city with Dembeli and several other passengers. Minor surgery, weeks of treatment, and an uncountable number of pills confined Duwa to the hospital. She was a captive audience, and as she entertained visitors during that time, she was challenged to think about the message of love they brought to her as believers.

Weeks later a radio message informed Dembeli that if he had room in the vehicle on his next mail run, Duwa would be ready to return home with him. She rode home in nearly complete silence, but in great comfort as her illness had responded to the medication and her condition was greatly improved. Upon her arrival back in Heredugu, Duwa was welcomed home by Pastor Pita, church members, and her family. No mention was made of her unique ability to stir up heartache and trouble.

The following Sunday, the Church family was comfortably seated in church, singing had already begun, and the service was well under way when there was a stir in the back. Duwa had just come through the door. It seemed as though everyone in the church except Pastor Pita held their breath through the remainder of the service, for in the past it seemed that she had appeared in church only to ridicule and cause trouble. People expected that she was checking in after her lengthy absence, and that this visit would be no different than the previous ones.

At the close of the service, Pastor Pita gave an invitation for people who wanted to give their lives to Christ to step forward for prayer. A hushed expectancy settled over the Church family. It was at this point in the past that Duwa had found the freedom to express herself, and in the past she had not missed the opportunity to vehemently renounce all that she was opposed to. As she rose to her feet, the people braced themselves. However, today it was different! Duwa stood and asked for prayer. The Church never gave her a chance to get to the front. They simply started singing, one and all, the familiar Kuranko song: "Praise God, Praise God, Jesus is Lord."

The days that followed revealed the grace of God at work in the life of Duwa, a new creature in Christ. Dembeli, like so many others, was absolutely amazed at the change that took place in the former agitator. Bitterness, anger, resentment, and a harsh tongue were replaced with a smile and a gentle spirit. The transformation was almost unbelievable! It was as if a caterpillar had emerged from her cocoon as a beautiful butterfly. Her testimony ran along the grapevine, and others soon found out why there was such a dramatic and unbelievable change in Duwa. She had indeed become a new creation in Christ.

A few months later sickness and suffering returned, and Duwa once again asked to be taken back to the hospital. Dembeli arranged to take her to Kurela when he went on a mail trip. Some time later she was released, and everyone thought she had fully recovered. But shortly after her return home, Duwa died in the night.

Morning found a group of Church elders asking Dembeli how to conduct a Christian funeral. The Storyteller heard them explaining to Dembeli that the animists with whom Duwa had formerly identified herself would not have anything to do with her because of her testimony in the recent months. They explained that the Muslims would not have anything to do with the funeral because she had taken a strong stand for the Church. The Church had the funeral to themselves, and they did not know how to conduct a Christian funeral since none of them could remember having had one in the past. They were first-generation believers, and to their knowledge none of the believers had died.

As they sat together in the shade, Dembeli asked the pastor and Church leaders what they thought should be part of a Christian funeral. A brief discussion followed as the men expressed how it should really be a time of celebration and rejoicing for the one who had gone to heaven. They also felt that it should be a time of warning for those who did not know where they would spend eternity, and a time to express sorrow at the parting of a loved one or friend. They also saw that it should be an opportunity to express to others the hope the believer has that we will meet again in heaven.

The young men in the Church had finished digging the grave, and the body was ready to be carried to its final resting place. Tropical heat and the absence of embalming practices dictated that the funeral take place as soon as possible after a person had passed on. The youth who had come to summon Pastor Pita, the elders, and Dembeli led the way to the grave site. Word of the funeral spread quickly through town, and people gathered and joined in songs of praise that carried the theme of heaven. Someone shared how Duwa's life had been changed by the Master, and how she had become a new person in Christ. The songs and Scripture reading about heaven touched hearts. The prayers for the family and loved ones expressed the desire that God would walk with them through the valley of death. Dirt was then shoveled over the body, and in a moment that Finaba knew Dembeli would never forget, Duwa's two young children came forward. With their bare feet, they tamped down the fresh dirt on the top of their mother's grave as tears rolled unchecked down their cheeks.

Duwa had gone home to be with Jesus, and small group of Christians had publicly taken a stand to identify with her because of the miraculous change that had come about in her life when she had accepted Jesus Christ as the Supreme Sacrifice and had surrendered to Him as the Lord of her life.

Leaders in the Heredugu area decided that it would be a good idea to have a meeting of all those in the area who professed Christ as their personal Savior. In other districts such meetings were being held and people were calling them "Institutes." The Heredugu church decided to invite all the Christians in the area to come to their town for the special meeting. For lack of a better name, they chose to call their meeting an "Institute" as well. The Gospel Team shared the news in each of the towns where they held services each week and the Kuranko grapevine carried the news to Christians who had moved out of the area.

The program was planned with a lot of visiting time and plenty of good food. Plenty of time for relaxation was offered so that friendships could be developed that would encourage new believers. The highlight of the Institute came on the closing day, when the Christians walked together to the river, singing as they went to the baptismal service. Some people in town followed the "parade" just to see what was happening, and while observing they were privileged to hear the testimony of each baptismal candidate and they were challenged to give their lives to Christ, too.

The Institute was such a great success that they decided to hold another one at the beginning of the rainy season. At Easter time the Christians again walked to Heredugu for a time of fellowship, teaching, and encouragement. Some believers walked in from as far as fifteen miles away, and maybe more. The believers rejoiced to see the Church growing and to know that the family of God was bigger than just the Christians in their isolated town. They expressed how much they appreciated meeting with other believers, because in their isolation they sometimes felt that they were the only Christians in the area. The meeting with other believers strengthened their resolve to keep pressing on and encouraged them to share their faith with others.

The Paramount Chief gave the Church a cow for their meeting. The tangible gift carried with it deeper implications that Dembeli did not understand at first. In the coming days he began to realize that the chief's gift of a cow had affirmed Christianity as a viable option for the Kuranko people. Before there was only one road and that was the one of folk-Islam, a combination of Islam and animism. Now Christianity was a recognized and acceptable choice for his people. What a tremendous breakthrough that was for the new generation of Christians.

The Institutes at Christmas and Easter became highlights of the calendar year for the Heredugu District. When the Annual Missionary Council rolled around, a report of the Institutes in each area was given as part of each area missionary's report. It was only logical that the Institutes would be discussed by the council body. Ways to improve the Institutes and strengthen the Church in each area were discussed, with only one snag. All the other areas only had one Institute each year, and the missionaries picked up the pastors, delegates, and visitors in their vehicles and provided transportation for them to and from the Institute. When it was discovered that Dembeli did not do that in the Heredugu area—which had two Institutes instead of just one each year—and that the believers were expected to walk to the Institutes, the discussion took a different turn.

Once again the Storyteller saw Dembeli vigorously argue against creating dependency on the mission. In this case he argued that providing transportation was not logical because most of the towns in the Heredugu area did not have a road to their town. He reasoned that providing transportation would not only limit the size of the Institute to how many warm bodies he could carry in his vehicle, it would also dictate where the meetings could be held. It would mean that only the believers in towns along the road would be eligible to come to the Institute. Mission finances and the fact that Institutes were only held once a year in the other districts would dictate that the Heredugu area could only have one gathering of Christians per year. Dembeli felt strongly that the mission should not take such a step as the roads were difficult and time would limit how many trips he could make to haul people to the Institute. Therefore the number of people who could come would be greatly limited based on the size of the vehicle and the number of trips it would be possible to make in one day to transport them to the designated location. He reasoned that the down-country churches would appreciate the missionary hauling them around, but that in a remote area like Heredugu, the mission should let the church develop their own structure not governed by the technical or mechanical assistance the mission could provide. Long before Dembeli realized it, the Storyteller sensed that the young missionary and his mentors, would be voted down, and that the vehicle would be used for the coming Christmas Institute in the Heredugu area. And it was so.

When the time arrived, those who were able to ride to the Institute in Heredugu praised the mission and extended great words of appreciation for the vehicle that had picked them up. But when they all gathered, they discovered that many of their friends from the outlying villages had not been able to come. The attendance was limited to how many people the vehicle could carry. Although Dembeli spent all day making as many trips as possible to the various towns along the road, the attendance was only half of what the previous Institutes had been when everyone had walked to the meetings. They also discovered that they were now limited to one Institute a year instead of two, and although it was easier to come to the meeting and return home, they certainly felt the absence of those from remote villages, who would no longer be a part of the annual event.

The baptismal service remained a highlight of the Institutes, and it soon became a Christmas Day tradition for the Heredugu church. The Easter Institute became history. Dembeli wondered what effect this would have on the Church in the Heredugu area in the years to come. He recognized that someday the believers there might discover other options to strengthen their bonds of fellowship. But for now he had to accept the fact that the Missionary Council wanted to maintain a systematic pattern of operation throughout the country in all three tribes where they were ministering.

Chapter 13: New Leadership

Since Heredugu was the only Church in the area, it was part of the Northern District. The Northern District was composed of the Churches in the Yalunka tribe and the Heredugu Church. It was under the leadership of a Yalunka pastor who served as the District Superintendent. Although an exceptional pastor and a very capable leader, Pastor Bulus was unable to make frequent trips from his area up to Heredugu. Not only did he have pastoral and leadership duties among his own people, but he was also a key ingredient in the translation of the New Testament into his own language. He had more than enough to keep him busy in his own tribe without asking him to walk a couple of days over to Heredugu to supervise the work there.

By the time Dembeli moved into Heredugu, a long time had passed since the people had seen their District Superintendent. Dembeli was surprised one evening to see Pastor Pita and a delegation of Church leaders come to him asking that he help them straighten out a conflict concerning the Heredugu church finances. They arranged to meet the next day and discuss the case. Dembeli soon discovered, as the Storyteller knew he would, that this issue had tentacles that stretched way back. Without the advice and supervision of a District Superintendent, some financial practices had been allowed that cast doubt on the integrity of the pastor and the Church. As feelings became more and more involved, objectivity decreased and no one in the local Church seemed able to figure out the problem. Since the problem began before he had come to the area, Dembeli decided to stop in and talk to Pastor Bulus, the District Superintendent, on his next trip to Kurela. When they met, they decided that Pastor Bulus should travel up to Heredugu and spend some time helping the church work through the situation. He now had a motorcycle, and travel would not be as major a problem as it had been for him in the past few years.

Several days later Pastor Bulus arrived and was accorded all the honor and respect due to his position as the District Superintendent. Since most of the people had trouble pronouncing the English title of their leader, he was known as the "D. S." The following day Dembeli sat quietly in the church and watched the D.S., the pastor, and the church leaders sort out the financial situation. Knowing that the D.S. was coming, Dembeli had helped church leaders reconstruct three years of bookkeeping from the few records that they could find. Dembeli had quickly recognized that it was not a numerical problem, but rather an issue of feelings, and so he was extremely happy to have such a capable man as Pastor Bulus step in to help sort through the problem.

During the break for a meal, Pastor Bulus and Dembeli went through the books together again. Dembeli explained to Pastor Bulus what he had found as he analyzed the books. The Church gathered again that evening, and Pastor Bulus reported that the Church owed Pastor Pita about the same amount they felt Pastor Pita owed the Church. He purposed that they forgive each other the debts that they owed and that they start the bookkeeping process all over again with a zero balance in each account. A rather heated discussion followed as each party wanted the other party to pay up. With uncommon diplomacy, Pastor Bulus explained the advantage of what he was suggesting. He was finally able to persuade everyone involved that peace could come and that the Church could continue without the financial barriers of debt if they would each forgive what they felt the other party owed them. Dembeli marveled that such a simple thing could become such a major obstacle, and at times he wanted to step in and ask the people what they did not understand about getting along. The Storyteller knew the history of the case, and Pastor Bulus obviously understood some of the depth of the hurt feelings. With incredible patience he helped the Church walk through the first major struggle Dembeli had witnessed in the local body of Christ.

Pastor Bulus' proposal was finally accepted, and the next morning he left for the five-hour journey back home. His usual contacts with the Heredugu District came when there was a joint Institute, or a General Conference of the National Church, when pastors and delegates came from all three tribes in the area where the mission was ministering and met for a few days. At those times he was able to lend encouragement and advice to the Heredugu Church, but travel and other responsibilities made it extremely difficult for him to really fulfill the obligations of leadership to the Heredugu area.

Dembeli was a little surprised when the older missionary from the Yalunka area where Pastor Bulus was the District Superintendent suggested to Dembeli that the Northern District divide into two separate Districts. That way the Heredugu area could call their own shots and develop into a self-governing Church as it related to the national church. Being generations old and invisible, Finaba, the Storyteller, could recall some of the debates about the structure of the national church that had taken place among the missionaries in years past. The one side had declared that each tribe should be free to take ownership of the church among its people and that the missionaries should let Churches develop along ethnic lines. The other side strongly favored a unified Church where the three tribes met together as one in Christ around a central governing body designed to promote consistency throughout all areas of ministry within the country. Dembeli was not on the scene when that debate took place, and he did not have a clue that what he was about to suggest would re-open the discussion that many thought had been closed many years before.

The Storyteller was often on hand when the older missionary and Dembeli got together. Together they "ate, drank and dreamed missions." So when the senior missionary suggested that the area should be divided into two districts, Finaba was not surprised. The two men looked at the idea from all possible angles. They shot it down. They built it up. They tore it apart, and then they put it back together. They thought and prayed as they sought God's will and what was best for the Church. When they got together again a couple of weeks later when Dembeli stopped in Yalunka territory on his way home from a mail trip to Kurela, they discussed the issue again. They were trying to decide if what they were suggesting was really the right thing for the Churches in the district. After much prayer and lengthy discussion, they decided that Dembeli should suggest the idea to the Heredugu Church leaders and see what their response would be. The senior missionary would talk it over with Pastor Bulus and the leaders of the Yalunka District. If the Churches within the district were in favor of the idea, then the two missionaries together would suggest it to the Missionary Council at their next meeting.

The Heredugu Church strongly favored the idea. The Yalunka Church leaders thought it was a great idea too. So the two missionary friends presented the idea to the missionary body at the following Annual

Missionary Council. Some of the missionaries strongly opposed the idea. After all, they reasoned, why would you want a district with only one church in it? Geographically, the Konko Mountains separated the Heredugu area from the down-country Kurankos, so it was not practical for them to be in the same district with the other Kuranko Churches. They questioned why the two area missionaries in the upper District did not want to leave them as part of the Northern District. Having planted the Church in Heredugu years before, the Schierlings had a heart for the ministry in that area and had often visited Dembeli and the Church in Heredugu. They saw this as an opportunity for growth and eagerly lent their support to the idea presented by the older Yalunka area missionary with whom they had worked so closely for so many years, and Dembeli who was ministering in an area that they themselves had pioneered. Their knowledge of the area, the people, and the Church enabled them to challenge others to take a risk and let the Heredugu Church become a district so it could stand on its own. Their knowledge also enabled them to point out the need for each ethnic people group to take ownership of the Church in their area so that in this case it could truly become a Kuranko Church.

The missionary council knew that in a couple of weeks the Heredugu and Yalunka churches would be part of a bigger annual conference, for the up-country churches. The council of missionaries decided that if at that time the Heredugu and Yalunka churches requested that they be divided into two districts, the mission would support and encourage that action for the sake of growth.

When the issue was presented during the Institute, it was not as easily accepted by the National Church President as it had been at the Mission Council. The national church leader saw this as a step of division and strongly opposed it. However, the pastors and delegates from other up-country churches realized that the District Superintendent, the Heredugu Church, and all the Yalunka Churches supported the idea. They asked the national church leader to back down, and they voted to accept Heredugu as a full member district, even though there was only one Church in the whole area.

The full implication of that decision did not hit home for some time. One day, one of the Gospel Team members shared with the Heredugu Church a disadvantage of being their own district. He said that they could no longer look to the Yalunka Church, or the Yalunka District Superintendent, to come over and help win their people for Christ. The Heredugu Church now had the sole responsibility of reaching their people with the Gospel. They were the ones responsible to reach their area of over two hundred towns with the Gospel, and the Heredugu Church people would have to disciple the new believers and plant the new churches. A sense of ownership began to grow among the believers, and the idea that one must divide to grow took root. They sensed the prayers, support, and encouragement of the Yalunka Church as they began to plan for growth in their own district.

A district needs leadership, and so it was decided that an election should be held for district officers in the Heredugu area. The Storyteller wondered how that was going to work, but he soon realized that his fears were unfounded. The teacher from the Bible school in Kurela who had once so vigorously opposed the uneducated members of the Gospel team was visiting Heredugu the night of the election. When it was time for the election, several men stood declaring that they wanted to run for office and be the new District Superintendent for the Heredugu District. They were asked to be seated while the qualifications for the job were read from the By-Laws of the National Church. Dembeli was then asked to conduct the election. He stood in the light of the kerosene storm lantern and simply read God's Word concerning the qualifications of those who hold office in the Church. Immediately upon the completion of the reading of the Scripture, one of the nominees stood up and requested to withdraw his name. When Dembeli asked him why, he said that he did not meet the requirements of the Scripture because he had more than one wife. He already had several wives when he had accepted Christ as his personal Savior. A second stood and withdrew his name also, and then a third, for God's Word had spoken to them right where they were in life. When the election took place, Pastor Pita of Heredugu was chosen as the District Superintendent.

The teacher returned to Kurela a couple of days later with the report that in the Heredugu District they may not be educated, but the "The Word of God has power there, and they listen to it." Dembeli concluded that no District could ever ask for a higher commendation, or for a better way to start out on their own. The elected officers were approved by the National Church Conference Executive Committee, and the Heredugu District came into being. Pastor Pita held the office of District Superintendent for the next thirteen years.

The Storyteller often listened to the lengthy discussions on missions that Dembeli had when he met with some of the older missionaries he used as a sounding board for his ideas. Two of them in particular served as his mentors. Sometimes he was challenged to revamp his thinking or to hold off until he could find more answers in a deeper understanding of the culture. Often in their discussions Dembeli gained new insights. Sometimes he had to drop an idea altogether when he discovered that it had already been tried and that it had failed for a variety of reasons. But one idea kept cropping up over and over in his conversations with his mentors. How could the Heredugu District get some of its men to go on for further training at the Bible school in Kurela? He knew that as believers were discipled and baptized, there would soon be young churches in the new district that would need leadership and trained pastors. He strongly believed that those wanting to go to Bible school should function in the local church *before* going off to Bible school. This would give them an idea of what ministry was all about, and they would know what they would be getting themselves into when they returned after graduation.

It was with great joy that Dembeli watched three young men—the only ones on the Team who had any formal training in elementary school—as they sensed God's calling on their lives and headed for Bible school. At the time the Bible school was structured so that a student attended school in Kurela for two years and then went back to his home district for a year of practical training before returning for the last two years of Bible school education. Dauda and Yakubu, went to Kurela together and enrolled in the five-year program. Although neither of them completed the full program, they received a tremendous amount of blessing, encouragement, and training, and they were able to return to their home district as pastors. They continued their studies through Theological Education by Extension, and became effective in their ministries. Later four other men from the Heredugu area sensed God's call on their lives and joined the ranks of students who graduated from Bible school and returned to their home area to minister.

Chapter 14: Building Bridges

Torrential downpours caused rivers and swamps to flood. The floods often swept away the crude log bridges across the streams that bisected the roads. Those bridges were essential in keeping an open road for vehicles to bring market produce into the Heredugu area. The Storyteller always enjoyed the mass confusion that reigned when a vehicle from down-country coming to the market got stuck in one of the little streams. Sometimes slippery logs on a bridge would slide out from under the front tires of a truck rather than holding their place until the truck had passed over them. As the logs slid out of place, open holes would appear in the bridge and the vehicle would drop through the bridge instead of passing over, and the passengers would find themselves campers instead of travelers. Sometimes the weight of a heavily loaded vehicle would break the logs, and the vehicle would drop a couple tires through what had once been called a bridge. The vehicle that had seemed so powerful coming down the hill to the river would be sitting helplessly, suspended by the remaining logs on which the frame of the truck rested, while the wheels spun uselessly below the deck of the bridge.

Finaba enjoyed these times not because the people were experiencing difficulty, frustration, and delay, but because such incidents added the spice of life. He would add such events to his already bulging file of stories, which he would someday be able to relate to the next generation. Once Dembeli was established in the area, he discovered that he was often called upon to lend assistance to the unfortunate ones in these stories. He often helped those who had slid through the mud off the road into a ditch, or who found themselves trapped by a small bridge that could not support the great weight of their vehicles.

After a little experience, Dembeli discovered that freeing a truck from such a bridge was relatively simple. After the truck was unloaded, or partially so anyway, the vehicle would be jacked up and the bridge rebuilt underneath it with freshly cut logs. Usually the operation was completed within a few hours, and the truck could navigate the rest of the way across the bridge. On the other side, the truck driver could pick up the load that had previously been unloaded and carried to the shade of nearby trees, and the passengers could climb aboard and continue on their way.

On occasion, however, the floods were so fierce that the entire bridge would be washed away. One such time, Finaba and most of the Gospel Team members joined Dembeli to help a nearby town replace their bridge. One of the Team members was up in a tree cutting down a huge forked stick that was to be used as a brace under the larger logs that would serve as girders for the bridge. The town chief happened by and began to thank the Gospel Team member for his work and for coming out to help them rebuild their bridge. Dembeli stood quietly in the background, listening and watching as the Team member up in the tree stuck his ax in a branch before responding to the chief. He then shared how happy he was to be able to help, and how the whole town of Heredugu was glad that this town was fixing their bridge so that the market vehicles could get through to Heredugu on market day. Then he proceeded to explain very carefully that they really were not there just to build a bridge of logs and sticks, although they would help do that. The real purpose of their coming was to share with the village about a "Great Bridge" in life that spans from this world into eternity. He concluded by saying that the bridge he was talking about was the Supreme Sacrifice which makes all other sacrifices unnecessary. We can cross that Bridge by repentance and faith, and the Bridge of Truth will take us to heaven. He told the chief that the name of the real bridge about which we had come to share is Jesus, and that we would be willing to come and share more about Life's Bridge with him and the people of his town. It was no surprise to Dembeli that the Gospel Team soon received a request from that town asking them to come and share the story of the Gospel and their picture sermons with the people.

Often the bridge to be repaired became a site for sharing the Gospel. To the casual observer it might have looked like Dembeli had a pretty laid back crew who were not the least bit interested in the bridge. On a more careful examination, one would soon discover that the "Real Bridge" was just more important to them than the one they were building out of logs, sticks, stones, or concrete.

Sometimes when a vehicle fell through a bridge it was necessary to call all the men from the nearby towns to come and help. Dembeli discovered that sometimes even that was not enough, and this discovery motivated him to become involved in many construction projects over the years. The one that motivated him first was a bridge about four miles from home.

Dembeli and his family were traveling home from Kurela one evening and were almost home when some logs gave way and three wheels of the truck fell through the bridge they were crossing, leaving Dembeli and his family stranded until help could come. Soon the men from towns on each side of the river arrived, and tried to push, pull, or lift the truck out of the tangled mess of logs that it had fallen through. As men came by to help, they would take off their shoes and throw them in the truck. As they worked, one of the men climbed down into the river on the downriver side of the bridge. Soon Dembeli noticed him throwing one shoe after another into the truck. He could not figure out what was happening until he heard his three-year-old son, Toby, laughing. As the men took off their shoes to go work in the river they would put them in the truck. Toby would throw them out the window on the upriver side of the bridge so he could watch them float downstream, pass under the bridge, and come out on the other side. The man in the water on the downriver side did not know where all the shoes were coming from, so he just caught them and threw them back in the truck. Toby and his little brother, Andy, thought it was a great game. They would grab the shoes, hustle over to the open window on the other side of the truck, and send their little "boats" sailing back down the river again.

Unfortunately the men could not get Dembeli's truck off the bridge, and a storm was rolling in over the mountains. Dembeli and his family, along with several men from Heredugu, left the truck stranded in the middle of the broken bridge and walked the last four miles home. That night the storm hit, filled up the river, and shook the bridge, but the truck just settled deeper into the tangle of logs.

After that experience, Dembeli developed a deeper concern for bridges in the area. He and his kids counted the streams between home and the missionary children's school and discovered that in the one hundred miles there were twenty five streams that did not have bridges. Most of the streams were just little ones that would not cause hardship or delays, but some of them were major problems, and it was those bridges that opened Dembeli's eyes to the need for a bridge ministry.

To rebuild the bridge Dembeli's truck had fallen through took weeks of preparation. Men were needed to dig stone out of the hillsides and carry it down to the road so it could be hauled to the work site. More time was needed for the men sitting in the shade to break the stones with sledge hammers into usable-sized chunks that could be mixed with the cement. Finally, the forms were set and the concrete abutments were reconstructed. The Paramount Chief over the entire chiefdom had asked Dembeli to help rebuild the bridge and had summoned men from eleven towns to be on hand for the construction project. Upon the completion of the abutments, one of Dembeli's major concerns became a reality. He was concerned about lifting the steel girders up out of the mud and placing them on the abutments, because he did not have any of the necessary cranes, jacks, winches, or hoists needed for such an undertaking. The I-beams weighed four tons each, and there were two of them to be set in place.

Finaba laughed, almost out loud, when the Paramount Chief looked at Dembeli and said, "In the soup there is salt to make it sweet, and pepper. Don't you worry about setting the I-beams. You are the salt. You are to make the soup sweet because you provide the material and the know-how. I am the pepper. I will provide the manpower and we will lift the beams into place. The pepper makes the soup hot and strong."

Over the coming years, Dembeli heard that statement often. Whenever he had doubts about the manpower needed to accomplish a tough job on the road, the Team laughingly reminded him, that he was the "salt" and the Paramount Chief was the "pepper". Sure enough, when the day came for the beams to be hoisted into place, the Paramount Chief had men there from eleven towns in the area. Having cut short branches from trees along the river, the men stuck them under the I-beams with enough of the stick protruding from under the beam on each side for several men to take hold of it. Then they would move down the I-beam a step and repeat the procedure so that the men picking up on the front stick would not be in the way of those behind them. This was done the entire length of the I-beam.

Drums and balangi played the rhythm for work. (A "balangi" is a home made, portable xylophone used by Kuranko musicians.) When everybody was in place, the rhythm picked up and the men began to chant a cadence. The Paramount Chief gave a command, and in perfect unison hundreds of muscular arms began to strain, and the stout sticks under the beam began to bow as the steel girder was slowly picked up out of the mud and hoisted onto the concrete abutments. An invisible grin spread from ear to ear as the Storyteller watched amazement creep across Dembeli's face. The process was repeated for the second steel girder. Even though he has now seen the procedure repeated many times, Dembeli still marvels at what can be accomplished by a team of men unified with a common purpose and welded together in a loyalty that those who use machines will never know.

After the beams were in place, they were covered with a plank decking, and a usable bridge was put into service. There remained however, one major obstacle. At one end of the bridge a huge rock stuck out above the road surface and needed to be removed. Several of the Gospel Team were recruited to help remove the offending rock. Dembeli thought it might take a day or two to dig it out. He soon discovered that rocks, like icebergs, often have a larger portion out of sight below the surface than that which appears above ground.

After a few days of digging it became apparent that more help would be needed. In the town of Heredugu there was a young Muslim man who wanted work and asked if he could assist the Gospel Team in digging out the rock. Dembeli and the Team accepted his offer to help, and along with another young Muslim man they set out to remove the obstacle from the middle of the road. The rock turned out to be a piece of granite larger than the four-wheel drive truck that Dembeli drove, and the day of digging stretched into two and then three and then four. People walking by would laugh at the Team and tell them that three hundred men had tried to dig out that rock before, and there was no way that eight men could possibly remove the boulder from middle the road. What they did not know was that Dembeli had acquired some dynamite from a friend down-country, and he was planning on using it to get rid of the obstacle that blocked the way to the newly-built bridge.

When the digging was all done and the humongous rock stood alone in the bottom of a huge hole in the middle of the road, Dembeli, accompanied by the Team, went to the towns on either side of the river. They asked the town chiefs to have the town crier go through the town and warn the people that the next night, they should not be in the vicinity of the bridge because Dembeli was going to blow the stone out of the hole in the middle of the road. Dembeli and the Team went home in a spirit of anticipation. Dembeli could not tell you what the town criers actually said to the people that evening, but on the designated night the road was completely deserted.

With a couple of Gospel Team members and a friend who was visiting from the States, Dembeli drove out to the bridge site the following evening. Never having used dynamite before, Dembeli did not know where to place it. He reasoned that on TV when dynamite is used, things always blow upward. It seemed to him that the logical place to put the dynamite was under the rock. For that reason a small hole had been dug under the huge rock, with great effort on the part of those who dug it. Dembeli carefully set the dynamite in place in that small hole under the rock, fastened the detonators according to instructions, attached the fuses to the detonators, and then ran a wire up and out of the hole. With the help of his visiting American friend, he had gathered up all the old wire he could possibly find on the mission station. He had also borrowed some from other missionaries on his last mail trip down-country. With all that wire, they had enough to run the wire up out of the hole and over a small hill to a safe location behind some trees and another large rock some distance away. The truck was parked a long ways back down the road, and one of the Team had carried the battery to the safety zone over the hill among the trees.

It was a beautiful, full moon night when Dembeli and his friend crouched behind a huge rock just over the hill from where the granite bolder had been exposed. They could see the bridge down the road when the wires were touched to the terminals of the battery and the explosion erupted in the silence of that beautiful tropical evening.

Back at home, almost four miles away, people heard the thunder of the explosion. Looking out through the safety of the trees, Dembeli and his companions saw a beautiful cloud of smoke rise above the bridge and begin to mushroom out as it met a gentle tropical breeze. Higher and higher it rose into the clear moon-lit sky, and Dembeli and his friends sat in amazement as they watched the beauty of it unfold. They wondered how long it would be before they would be showered with rock fragments, or before the giant bolder itself would tumble down out of the sky. Minutes passed, and slowly the gentle breeze carried the mushroom cloud away. Finally the group ventured out of their hiding place, and Dembeli led the way down the hill to the site of the explosion.

It immediately became apparent that something had gone wrong. The bolder sat nestled in the bottom of the hole just as it had before, but possibly looking a little more comfortable and contented. Dembeli jumped down into the hole near the granite boulder. Dropping down on his knees, he proceeded to examine the place where he had so gently placed the dynamite. What he discovered was that he really had not known anything about dynamite, because instead of blowing the rock up, he had blown a huge hole in the ground below the boulder. The Storyteller and the others roared with laughter as they realized that it was back to the drawing board for Dembeli.

The next morning saw Dembeli and his crew heading back to the bridge site, only this time they traveled with axes instead of picks and shovels. People on each side of the river saw them heading to the work site and joined them to examine the results of the "mighty moonlight explosion" the night before. Laughter echoed much farther than the sound of the explosion, and again Dembeli was reminded that three hundred men had tried to move that rock, but could not do it. He was told that he should not presume that the eight of them could do the impossible.

As the day wore on, the laughter of passing people turned to amazement, for each man on Dembeli's crew was cutting down and hauling dried hardwood trees for a great bonfire that was roaring on top of the offending rock. All day long Dembeli drove the truck back and forth along the road, gathering up the piles of hardwood from the dead trees that the men were cutting down. Two men stayed and fed the hungry flames all night long. The next morning, more deadwood trees were gobbled up by the axes and the greedy fire. In the middle of the afternoon, the tired men stopped adding wood to the fire and sat around talking while the fire burned down to nothing but red-hot coals in the bottom of a huge hole around the foreboding granite giant.

Toward evening all the buckets that could be borrowed were put into service, and onlookers were asked to help as a bucket brigade formed from the river to the rock. As the cool water was poured onto the now overheated rock, a cloud of steam rose into the evening sky. Soon observers standing near the granite heard the cracking and popping of angry granite and saw the rock begin to split into pieces.

The next morning the procedure was repeated. The crew, a little more hopeful now, swung their axes with a new vengeance. All day long the fire on the rock raged. Then that evening, a Saturday, the rock was doused with water again. The Storyteller wondered if God chuckled a little bit and decided that Dembeli and his crew needed some help. That night the Creator sent a rain that was a little early for the season, and the cool rain accomplished what the tired bucket brigade could not finish.

Monday morning when the crew returned to examine the granite boulder, they discovered that they could pick it apart in manageable pieces. Some pieces were shifted around in the hole, others were thrown out, and the dirt that had been dug out to expose the rock was shoveled back on top of the whole project. By Monday afternoon the rock had disappeared, the road was level, and a triumphant Team was heading home claiming that they had accomplished what three hundred men could not do.

The real heart of the incident lies not in the dynamite, the removal of the boulder, or in the accomplishment of building a better road, but in the crew itself. The two young Muslim men who had needed work and had struggled right alongside the Gospel Team through the whole procedure had seen how the Team responded to the laughter and the kidding. The young Muslims saw them in the face of what had appeared to be a failure when the dynamite did not break up the rock, and they saw them tired, sweaty, and maybe a little discouraged. They had seen the hearts of the Gospel Team in a very down to earth, practical way. But more importantly, they had been there for the Bible study and prayer time that the Team shared together each day. They sat together in the shade of the trees during the heat of the day and saw the Gospel Team showing pocket-sized picture sermons to them and to any travelers who would take time to sit and chat before continuing on their journey to the next town. They saw the reality of the Gospel in the changed lives of the men from their hometown who were now being discipled to reach others with the incredible news of salvation. And they saw the joy and peace that the members of the Team exhibited.

At the next Gospel Team discipleship session, one of those young Muslim men showed up and declared that he had accepted Christ because of their lives and witness out at the boulder. He, too, wanted to be on the Gospel Team so that he could learn to share his new found faith with others just as they had done with him. Although he was never comfortable showing the pictures in a big public meeting, and to the author's knowledge never learned all the picture sermons, Hera became a real asset to the Team as a helper. He was not fluent in sharing his faith and tended to freeze up in front of a crowd. Yet he was a hard and willing worker with a ready smile who was always willing to carry his own load and often another person's load as well. He was always willing to go the extra mile. Incredible pressure from his family caused him for a time to turn back to the Islamic faith. After the evacuation of missionaries from the country years later, he died of an unknown illness. The author has not yet been able to discover if Hera re-affirmed his faith in Christ and took his stand for Jesus in front of his people before he died.

The second young man was probably the most physically powerful man that Dembeli or the Story Teller had ever met. His incredible strength was almost legendary in the area and certainly a cause for great amazement to Dembeli and his children. The Storyteller saw an example of this amazing strength one day while he was resting in the shade of a mango tree near the missionaries' workshop. The front end of a 6-cylinder gas engine, four-wheel-drive Toyota Landcruiser was jacked up with the wheel taken off because a strange noise was coming from inside the axle, caused by something or another rubbing against the whatchamacallit. For some unknown reason, the truck fell off the jack and the end of the axle came to rest in the hard gravel soil. Dembeli tried to dig a hole under the axle so he could set the jack back in place and lift the front end of the truck up for work on the vehicle to continue. It immediately became apparent that digging a hole in the gravel would be a monumental task because of the limited space under the front of the vehicle. Finaba almost jumped back when he saw the "lights come on" and realized that Dembeli had just been struck by a brilliant idea. Crawling out from under the truck, Dembeli called one of the little boys from town and asked him to go into town and call Mori to come and help.

In response to the call Mori meandered out to the mission compound and found Dembeli resting under the shade of the trees. When asked if he could lift the passenger side of the Toyota Landcruiser up so the jack could be put back in place, Mori simply smiled and walked over to the truck. Muscles bulged and a slight sweat began to creep to the surface of his brow through straining pores. Had it not been for the necessity of replacing the jack under the front axle of his truck, Dembeli would have been taking pictures for all to admire. All alone Mori lifted the front passenger side of the truck up off the hard ground and held it in place until Dembeli was satisfied that the jack would stand and hold the weight in its new position. As the truck settled back into place, Mori asked Dembeli if there was anything else he needed to do before he headed back into town. Other exploits followed this demonstration of strength during the year and a half that Mori worked with Dembeli in the Heredugu area.

It was a hard day for Dembeli when Mori announced that he had decided to take his wife and move down into another area so he could dig diamonds and discover his fortune. The Storyteller saw Dembeli's concern and sensed that he felt more than just the loss of a friend. It was not until the next day when Mori stopped by to bid Dembeli goodbye that Finaba really understood the concern he had seen on Dembeli's face the day before. Dembeli thanked Mori for all his work and for his friendship which had meant so very much to him during the time they had walked life's journey together. They stood in the shade of the little workshop down under the trees and swapped memories they had shared together. They recalled the fun and laughter of the good times. They remembered the struggles of unsuccessful hunts and the work, like the giant granite boulder that refused to be blown up.

Finally the Storyteller heard Dembeli asking Mori if he had ever accepted Jesus as the Supreme Sacrifice for his sins and as his personal Savior and Lord. Mori said that he had not, and Dembeli asked him if he really understood what had been read from God's Word and what had been said as the Gospel Team shared together in their Bible study and prayer time each morning before they went to work. Dembeli explained again how God had become man so that He could be our Sacrifice on the cross. He said that if we put our faith in Him our "heads would be pulled" and we would not have to stand before God in judgment, but would be welcomed into His presence and would live with Him forever in heaven. Mori said that he did understand all that, for he had been listening to the Bible studies each morning as they drank coffee and looked into God's Word together. He reminded Dembeli of the bridges he had helped build and how he had heard all the picture sermons. He declared that he understood, and that he knew that Dembeli and the Gospel Team were telling the truth. He even encouraged Dembeli not to give up but to keep teaching God's Word.

Mori understood what it meant to be "born from above," but he declared that he could not do that. When Dembeli asked why he could not accept Christ, Mori replied that his father and his grandfather had been Muslim teachers. He had inherited his name from them. He declared that he could not leave the way they had taught him. He graciously thanked Dembeli for all the work and the good times that they had shared and reminded him that he, Mori, would always be his friend. Then he turned and walked out of Dembeli's life.

The Storyteller saw the hurt and felt it even more deeply when he heard Dembeli tell his children that Mori had gone. Out of his life had walked the strongest man he had ever met, but one who did not have the spiritual strength to take his stand for what he knew to be the Truth. Mori had walked away to face life physically strong, but spiritually weak.

At about the same time one of the men on the Gospel Team gave in to the pressure from family and friends and chose to turn back to the road of his forefathers. Though this came as a setback, the Team was not discouraged and continued to go out as often as possible to share with others their faith in Christ. The morning prayer meeting and Scripture memory time was strengthening them in their faith and in their ability to share the Gospel. The local Church continued to encourage them and pray for them as they came in early off their farms and then went out to tell others about Jesus. They were asked to share their picture sermons at the area Institute when all the Christians who could get a ride gathered for a time of worship, teaching, and challenge. They rejoiced as more and more people followed the Lord in obedience and were baptized. They were aware that God was blessing, and they were excited about serving Him and sharing their faith with others.

When Dembeli was asked by the Paramount Chiefs to help with the construction of some of the bridges in the area, a whole new area of ministry opened up. Dembeli would take various Gospel Team members with him on every bridge project so they could mingle with the people and share their faith with them. Dembeli was to provide the expertise, and the chief provided the manpower. The chief would often call all the men from the surrounding villages to come and help break up stone, mix concrete, or build an approach to the bridge. Dembeli quickly saw the potential of the bridge ministry as he met men from many towns where the Gospel had never been shared.

On one occasion the Paramount Chief asked Dembeli to put a concrete decking on a major bridge that formerly had a plank decking. The planks had rotted and broken, and had been replaced with trees cut from the nearby forest. Dembeli took some Team members with him and over the next couple of months engineered the repair of the bridge. Stones were dug out of the hills and hauled to the site, where men with sledgehammers broke the rock into usable pieces. Other men cut the re-bar and wired it together. Lumber for the forms was purchased from a man who had a crew that split logs into boards using a two-man crosscut saw. Dembeli and his crew set the forms. When all was prepared, Dembeli informed the Paramount Chief that he was ready to pour the concrete. Surprisingly the chief responded that he did not want the bridge poured on different days and asked Dembeli how many men would be needed to mix the cement by hand and pour the whole decking in one day. Dembeli had no way of figuring how many men it would take, so off the top of his head he told the chief that he thought he would need two hundred men. The chief set the date for the work and sent runners out to spread the news throughout the surrounding villages.

On the designated day, Dembeli drove out to the bridge site to discover that men from all the villages around were ready to go to work. In all his regal formality, the Paramount Chief had the men line up to be counted. He called Dembeli and showed him over two hundred willing workers who wanted to see the bridge constructed so that their markets could stay open throughout the rainy season. The chief divided the men into groups so Dembeli could show each group their designated task, and then they started to work. The chief left for a few minutes. Little did Dembeli realize that the chief had killed a cow and had simply gone to check on the feast that he was preparing for the workmen. As he left, the musicians finished tuning their drums, the music started, and the work began.

The whole bridge was poured in one day, and the chief praised the men for their work. The men in turn acknowledged the chief's leadership and praised him for what he was doing for the development of their community. Dembeli watched the mutual praise session and rejoiced with the people for a task well done. Yet Dembeli had far more to rejoice over than just a bridge, for as in all major bridge projects, the Team had led several men to Jesus during the weeks of hard physical labor.

Barriers were constructed to prevent any vehicles from crossing the bridge while the cement cured. Since the closest town was a considerable distance away, the chief felt that several men should stay and guard the bridge to make sure that nobody came along and tore down the barriers too soon. A shelter was constructed for the men to live in for the month that they would be guarding the bridge. Turning to Dembeli, he asked if Dembeli could recommend two Christians for him as watchmen for the bridge. Later, when Dembeli was discussing the matter with the chief, he asked why the chief wanted Christians to guard the bridge for him when both men lived a day's walk away and there were many towns closer to the bridge. The chief replied simply, "I can trust them."

Dembeli discovered rather quickly that the two Paramount Chiefs in the area where he was ministering were two of the last great chiefs from the traditional role of a Paramount Chief. This was brought home to him when he was working on a bridge in the other chiefdom. When the project was completed and the bridge was completed, the two members of the Team who were responsible to keep track of the tools reported to Dembeli that he was missing two sledgehammers. Dembeli wanted to make sure the count was right, so he went with the men and carefully checked all his tools before saying anything to the chief.

When Dembeli mentioned to the chief that he was missing two hammers, the chief said that he could not believe anyone in his chiefdom would take a hammer from Dembeli. He asked that Dembeli recount all his tools again when he got home. About a week later Dembeli met with the chief again, and the chief asked him if he had found his hammers. When told that the two hammers were still missing, the chief simply stated that if the hammers were anywhere in his chiefdom, Dembeli would get them back. Driving home, Dembeli asked the Team members if they thought the hammers would ever show up considering that there were about one hundred twenty towns where they could be "hiding", and less than a quarter of those towns were reachable by vehicle. The men just chuckled and assured him that the hammers would find their way home.

The next week when Dembeli parked his truck in the shade and walked up to the chief's veranda, the chief stood to greet him. Unlike his usual greeting when he asked about the family, friends back in town, and the journey, the chief grinned and simply stated, "I have something to show you." He presented Dembeli with the two hammers which belonged to him. Dembeli understood then that the issue was not the hammers, but the power and authority of the chief. The missing hammers had challenged that authority, but now everything was in order and life could continue within the boundaries of a clearly defined power structure.

Finaba wondered why Dembeli would often stop on the bridge where the hammers had come up missing, but then he looked carefully and noticed that Dembeli was not looking at the bridge. He was looking at the sandbar over under the shade trees along the river. It was there that the first people in the newly established Church in the town near the bridge had been baptized. Once again God had used a bridge as a steppingstone to ministry.

Chapter 15: Standing on Their Own

Church attendance in the "mother church" continued to increase, and the faithful continued to reach out to the people in their town and throughout the area. One Sunday when Dembeli and some of the Gospel Team members were sharing in town away from home, Pastor Pita was preaching in Heredugu. The church has rafters but no ceiling, and birds would often build their nests in the rafters and hatch their eggs. On this particular Sunday morning, a snake had found the hidden treasure and was making its way along the beams from one nest to the next, checking out the menu. In the middle of Pastor Pita's sermon, the snake slipped and fell out of the rafters down onto the floor in the middle of the church. When Dembeli heard about the people jumping out the open windows and scurrying through the door, he commented that the rapture is the only thing that will ever empty the church faster than that snake did that Sunday morning.

During the next dry season Dembeli told the Gospel Team and the Church that it was time for him and his family to go on furlough, and that they would be gone for a year of "Home Ministry Assignment." He told them that as he traveled to the various churches, he would challenge people to pray for the Church there, the Gospel Team, and the Kurankos. They began to wonder aloud how they could carry on alone. They questioned how they would get to the various towns and who would help them when it came time to transport people to the Institute. Finaba knew the answer before Dembeli ever said a word, because he had been listening when Dembeli had told the men that a day would come when they would have to stand on their own. Dembeli had often reminded them that they were God's Church and that they could look to Him to help them through.

He reminded them again of all the towns they had walked to together and how they had shared the Gospel. He assured them that they could continue in ministry without a missionary there to help them. They expressed the sentiment that without the input and assistance of the missionary that they would falter. They feared that people would not believe their message, even though Dembeli continually reminded them that they serve one Lord and have one faith and one baptism. They had their doubts even though Dembeli had taught them that the same Holy Spirit that works in the life of a missionary can work in their lives as well, and just as powerfully.

Various Team members expressed concern about their ability to handle tough situations, discipline, or questions that came up. Dembeli reminded them of the structure of the Team and how when they came to him with problems, his first question was always, "Have you discussed this with your Team leader?" If the answer was, "no," Dembeli would send them back to the Team leader, or go with them to talk with him. He reminded them that many of the issues never came to him as the missionary because the Team had learned to deal with them so much more effectively on their own. He also reminded them that often the problems they faced were worked through together at Team meetings. There they had discussed the various towns and sought God's will in the face of difficulty, and they could continue to have the meetings even if he was gone. He reminded them that they were God's people, God's church, and God's Team and that he had done his best to disciple them as followers of the Way. He assured them that God would not forsake them in the absence of a resident missionary.

Toward the end of that dry season, Dembeli presented an idea to the Team leader and suggested that together they present the idea to the rest of the Team. At the next discipleship session he suggested that the Gospel Team divide up all the towns that they went to and that they go back to those towns without the missionary along. In each town they would ask the people who had accepted Christ to stand in front of their own people and be counted. Their names would then be written down and the Team could make sure they looked them up and encouraged them each time they went back to that particular town.

Finaba saw very quickly that the Gospel Team did not think this was such a good idea, even though they had often gone out to witness without

Dembeli along. Although their hearts were heavy, they agreed to go to each town where they had been sharing the Gospel and to count those who had the courage to stand up and ask that their names be written down.

A week later the men came to the discipleship session all excited. They had totaled the number of people in each town who had been willing to stand and have their names written down. They discovered in some towns that more people had showed up for the service than when Dembeli had accompanied them, and the people had listened attentively. What a joy they felt when they realized that in the three years they had been ministering as a Gospel Team that they had led one hundred and twenty people to faith in Jesus Christ.

Dembeli rejoiced because he suddenly realized that when the little Church in Heredugu had become its own district, the seeds of ownership had been planted. Now the people were beginning to reap the harvest and to see the blessing of the Lord on their ministry. They had begun to grasp the reality that they really are God's Church. They are His people. They are His Gospel Team. Dembeli had just been sent to disciple them. They came to realize that God will always honor His Word and that what Dembeli had been telling them was true. Their Savior and Lord could flow through their lives to reach others just as the Holy Spirit flowed through the lives of the missionaries who had reached them. It began to dawn on them that they could hold the ownership of the Church among their own people, for the Church belongs to God. He will be faithful and will never fail those who walk with Him.

The Storyteller could see some hard times ahead in the next year, but along with Dembeli he rejoiced because he knew that the Church was now prepared to handle those tough times. They had learned about the faithfulness of their God. The Storyteller also knew that this was only the beginning of a story that would be written in the hearts and lives of the Kuranko people who would come to know Jesus Christ before His return to take His Bride home.

Part 2: Two Roads

Chapter 16: The Two Road Map

During the beginning months of evangelism with the Gospel Team in the Heredugu area, Dembeli often had to show pictures and tell the Bible stories himself. Soon, however, he was able to tell the stories and then ask one of the men on the Team to give an application at the end of the story. This gave the men courage to step out and tell the stories themselves. It also gave Dembeli the opportunity to sit and listen, and see what parts of each story the men emphasized and what truths seemed to speak most clearly to them.

As time passed, Dembeli began to notice that although the men on the Gospel Team were being discipled in the Word and were able to share their faith through the medium of storytelling, the outreach program still had its weaknesses. As they met each week to discuss the towns in which they had ministered during the week, the shortcomings of the discipleship-training program became more and more apparent. Kurankos are master communicators, so story telling came naturally to most of the men on the team. Using the pictures as they had been taught, the men told the stories of Jesus and laid a foundation, which enabled them to give their own testimonies or to share a relevant application. However, the men were not teaching in any consecutive pattern, and were not taking advantage of the lessons from the stories of the week before.

The weekly lesson in any given town seemed to be on the basis of an isolated truth, with an emphasis on salvation. Dembeli strongly felt that the teaching in each town should be progressive and decided that a chronological approach to the Scriptures would alleviate the problem. With that in mind, Dembeli contacted various mission agencies around the world to see what they had available in the form of picture Bibles. He felt that if he had the Bible in pictures he could set up a chronological approach culminating in the purpose and victory of Christ's death and resurrection.

Dembeli struggled to find what he was looking for. Soon however, Dembeli's father, a missionary to Nigeria since 1945, was able to help him locate an organization that had the same vision for a picture Bible that he had. At the time they were in the early stages of doing the entire Bible in pictures and Dembeli was able to purchase from them the pictures he needed to correct this area of weakness in the Team's ministry. It was not long until the entire Bible was completed, and Dembeli rejoiced in the completion of a monumental task that enabled him to train the men in a chronological presentation of the Scriptures and later to correct other areas of weakness in the program. (*The Bible in Pictures* comes from Bible Visuals International, P.O. Box 153, Akron, Pennsylvania, Phone 717-859-1131).

Dembeli was thrilled with the new pictures which communicated so clearly, but he often chuckled when he recalled showing the new pictures to the Gospel Team for the first time. When they came to the life of Christ, Dembeli asked the men on the Gospel Team if they wanted him to color the picture of Jesus black so that it would communicate more clearly to the Kuranko people that He was their Jesus too.

One of the men on the team immediately answered, "No, you do not need to color Him black because we all know He was black anyway."

As Dembeli thought about that, he thought of Moses at the burning bush asking for the name of God, and God simply replying that He is "I AM." Dembeli thought about how in the deep jungles along the Amazon Jesus is seen as brown so that the little Indian boy can have a Jesus who understands and identifies with his way of life in the jungle. To the white boy in the cities of America he is white so that Jesus can understand his heartaches and concerns in the rush and hurry of the city. To the little black boy in Africa Jesus is black so he can identify with what it is like to live in the bush. The "I Am" is "everything we need. He still is the great "I AM" and Dembeli concluded that he would not have to color the pictures because they know that He is that everything they need. He is still the great "I Am" and that is beautiful!

Before long Dembeli was able to simply go along with the men and listen to them do the entire service. Sometimes they would ask him to take a turn and show the pictures, but more often than not he would be one of the spectators. The Team was divided into groups so that more than one town could be reached on any given evening. Each group would leave Heredugu, walk to the town they had been asked to reach, hold a service and then return that same evening. It was impossible for Dembeli to be in all the towns on the same evening, but as time progressed Dembeli was able to help build roads to several towns so the truck could be used to reach a number of towns in the area. This made it possible for Dembeli to take the truck two evenings a week. He would drop off several men in each of the towns they passed through until they came to their destination. There Dembeli and the few men that were left would hold a service before turning around and heading for home, picking up all the men they had dropped off on the way out.

Following each service the townspeople were encouraged to ask questions. If they had none, the men of the Gospel Team, or Dembeli, would ask them questions to learn more about their personal beliefs and to challenge them to think through the issues brought up in the Bible teachings. At each discipleship training session, each man was given the opportunity to share about his ministry in each of the towns they had been in since the last session. Often men would share questions they had been asked that they did not feel they had answered adequately. These questions usually focused on one of two aspects of their lives, which Dembeli realized had to be dealt with if the Gospel Team was going to be effective in sharing the Gospel among the Kuranko people. One aspect dealt with issues in the Quran and Islam itself. The other aspect dealt with animism and issues of spiritual warfare. Because of their background of animism and the powerful influence of Islam in their culture, the Kuranko people had developed their own brand of "Folk Islam" which synchronized the teaching of the forefathers (animism) with the teachings of the Quran (Islam).

Unfortunately, Dembeli felt a weakness in his own training that made it difficult for him to adequately deal with the major issues presented by this unique brand of Folk Islam. To compensate for this weakness, he began to read books dealing with folk Islam and animistic belief systems. He also picked the brains of anyone he could find that had more knowledge in these areas than he did. Often he relied on the expertise of his parents, whose forty plus years of ministry in Nigeria had given them vast knowledge and great insights into the African way of thinking. Dembeli also questioned former missionaries whose ministry God had blessed. Finding helpful answers to areas of need in his own life—and sometimes discovering through others' insights errors that he had made in his approach to the heart of the African people—helped Dembeli greatly. One of the men who had a great influence on Dembeli was Russell Sloat—a missionary to Nigeria for over fifty years — whose insights challenged Dembeli and motivated him to keep pressing on.

Dembeli spent countless hours asking Kuranko people of all ages about what they believed, why they believed what they did, and how they learned to apply their belief system. He searched the Scriptures and began to find deeper truths in God's Word. By his first furlough, Dembeli knew that he had to continue his education and sit at the feet of someone who was farther along the pathway than he was. He felt he needed someone to help him stay on the cutting edge of effective ministry. Dembeli continued this approach on each successive furlough.

An advanced degree was not the issue for Dembeli. Staying on the cutting edge of ministry was! He enrolled in a Master's program, taking classes from two different schools to learn everything he could about the realities of Kuranko beliefs. He spent as much time as possible with former missionaries to Africa that he met as he traveled to raise support. He was able to glean little bits of insight here and there that helped him not only in his classwork, but in his preparation to return to Heredugu. He focused primarily on the two areas that he felt weakest in: Islam and spiritual warfare.

Having completed the classes he was able to take, Dembeli purchased as many books as possible on the subjects he felt weakest in and packed them to send to Sierra Leone. Shortly after his return there another missionary couple joined the staff. Although Stan and Valli Yoder were working among the Yalunka people, for several years they were the closest white neighbors he had, and Dembeli soon discovered that Stan had interests in studies equal to his own. Together they hammered away at an approach to answer the questions of Islam. Quite frankly, Stan became the brains behind the project and Dembeli the feet. As soon as they came up with a new idea, Dembeli would bounce it off the Gospel Team members. If they responded positively, he would immediately try the new approach in the next town they ministered in.

Since the Yoders lived between Heredugu and the missionary children's school in Kurela, Dembeli often had the opportunity to see Stan, and together they would tangle with the issues that the Team faced when they presented a new approach. Stan, like Dembeli, had gone for further training during his first furlough and had taken a very aggressive program of studies in Islam. His insights were extremely valuable as Dembeli continued to work with the Gospel Team in establishing an even more effective ministry of evangelism.

Over the months that followed, a program emerged that has been effective because of God's blessing upon it. Taking some of the major characters in the Quran that are shared with the Scriptures, Stan and Dembeli put together the following outline for a simplified chronological approach to evangelism among the Folk Muslims of the area. As Dembeli field-tested it with the Gospel Teams that had been discipled in the Heredugu area, he further expanded it to deal more effectively with the issues of animism and Islam. A brief overview is presented in the following pages to share some of the truths the Gospel Teams discovered as they ministered. (See APPENDIX B for a diagram of the Two Road Map used by the Gospel Team.)

The men on the Gospel Team took special care with the picture Bible and stayed true to the Word of God as they taught about the Creator God. They realized that the Quran brought its own interpretation of may of the Biblical accounts. The story of Adam and Eve in the Garden is but one example. As an illiterate people they had over time formed their own ideas and had passed on their own teachings about the ancestors of all men. Because of those teachings, Dembeli spent extra time instructing the men on how to stay close to the Word when telling the story. Often at the close of a service when the creation story had been taught, the local Muslim Imam (teacher) would confirm publicly that what the men had presented was indeed the truth. This assurance was helpful to the people, but not necessarily an encouragement to the Gospel Team because the Muslim teacher would usually go on to explain that that the story showed how we are "all the same, worshiping one God, and finding our own road to heaven." At this point in the teaching of the Bible, the men would let such comments go, although at first Dembeli had to bite his tongue and try hard to sit still to keep from jumping up and saying, "Wait a minute. There are some major differences! There is the issue of who Jesus is, redemption, the resurrection, and eternal life." He learned to wait for an appropriate time and setting to present these truths.

Most of the Kuranko people are a little familiar with Noah and have some vague understanding of the story of the flood. They missed the purpose of the flood and why God wiped people out because of sin, but they did appreciate the promise that such a flood would not take place again, and seemed interested in the rainbow as a sign of God's promise.

The Team was able to explain God's unfolding plan of salvation and the importance of doing things God's way.

Dembeli was a little surprised at the interest the people expressed in the story of the Tower of Babel. The story seemed to answer so many questions that the people had about how various tribes began and why people were scattered all over the earth. It also was a powerful time of teaching on the sovereignty of God and that He is the final judge for all people.

Abraham was one of the most familiar characters to most of the people but they struggled with the idea that it was Isaac, the "son of promise," who was offered on the altar of sacrifice and not Ishmael, the "son of the bond servant," as they had been taught by their Muslim teachers. Dembeli had to encourage the Team to stick with the Word of God, and not to argue but to simply present the truths of the Bible and let the Holy Spirit be faithful in opening the minds and the hearts of the hearers of that truth. The basic principle was to *preach Jesus*, not to win an argument.

As the story of God's plan for the nations and the salvation of every individual unfolded, the people in each town were encouraged to ask questions. If they had just finished the story of Abraham, for example, the Gospel Team would answer any questions they could about Creation or any of the stories or characters, up to Abraham. If a question came up about David, or Jesus, the Team would ask the people to wait and assure them that question would be answered later. They would show them the *Two Road Map* and point out that they would be telling the story about that person later and the question would be in its proper place then. This did away with many issues that could possibly cause conflict, because the focus remained on the teaching that had already taken place. By focusing on one character at a time, the Team helped people focus on what they understood and not on the differences.

When the people in the town were done asking questions, or if they did not have any to ask, the Gospel Team members would then ask them a few questions. This was done with two purposes in mind. Dembeli quickly discovered that many of the people did not have a real grasp of the teachings of Islam and the Quran because the area is primarily illiterate and as a result, their knowledge was extremely limited. He soon learned that he had to be careful not to teach the people more about the Quran than they already knew, and in some situations this was hard to avoid since they did not have qualified teachers and their theological background was so negligible. During the discipleship sessions the Team looked at each reference to Jesus in the Quran, so they would know how to answer questions about Christ. They were taught to be very careful not to quote the Quran, and not to refer to it as a source of truth when sharing the Gospel.

Each of the men on the Gospel Team had their own area of giftedness, and although storytelling is the oldest and most powerful form of communication, some were simply better storytellers than others. The character being studied seemed to come alive in the hands of some of the men, while for others it was simply a matter of relating the facts as recorded in the Word of God.

One evening one of the men was expounding on the life of Jacob and how Jacob must have felt on the morning after his marriage when he discovered that his father-in-law, Laban, had deceived him and given him Leah as his wife instead of Rachael--whom he loved (Gen. 29:15-30). He wondered how deep Jacob's love for Rachel must have been to cause him to work for seven years as her dowry payment. His audience understood paying dowry and the problems that come from having more than one wife, so they easily identified with the story he was telling. Jacob's love for Rachael was so great that the Word of God declares that those seven years passed as quickly for him as a few days. Then Jacob woke up on his first morning of married life and discovered that he was married to the wrong woman. His new bride was Leah.

The man telling the story wanted to describe Leah in such a way that everyone would feel Jacobs' disappointment and anger along with him, but Dembeli could not keep a straight face when the young man declared, "Leah was so ugly! Why, she was as ugly as an old used truck tire!" Now that is getting pretty bad! But he had his audience in the palm of his hand as he continued to unravel the mystery of God's plan of salvation for His people through faith. He explained that the law had not yet been given, and the saints of old, like Abraham, were justified by faith and not by the law.

Shortly after that the Team began to teach on the great songwriter and prophet King David. They would tell the people that at the end of the series they would be asking them which of the Two Roads they were walking on. As they approached the time of Christ, the people were encouraged to carefully consider who Jesus is and how they are going to respond to Him. By the time they came to the stories on the life of Christ, the people were prepared to make some kind of declaration about which road they were walking on.

At the close of the resurrection story, people often asked a lot of questions. When the townspeople were done asking their questions, the Gospel Team would begin to gently ask them about who Jesus really was. Often the people would call their Imam to answer such deep questions for them. Like so many others, the Imam was willing to talk about Allah (God), but was hesitant to talk about Isa (Jesus). Many who are religious talk about God, but when confronted with the reality of who Jesus is, they are hesitant to talk about a personal relationship with the Savior and Lord. The name of Jesus "draws a line in the sand" and polarizes people. Jesus Himself said that "He is the way, the Truth, and the Life and no one comes to the Father accept through Him" (John 14:6). The apostles taught that "salvation is found in no one else, for there is no other name under heaven given to men by which we must be saved" (Acts 4:12).

One either accepts Him for who He said He was, or they reject Him as a liar. In many of the towns, the Muslim teacher would not miss the services the Team held because he did not want to miss out on what the people were being taught. Dembeli also suspected that there was often a strong ulterior motive for the Muslim teacher showing up at all the services: the Imam wanted to be able to refute the teaching of the "white man's religion" after the Gospel Team left town. That way he had a couple days, or maybe even a week, before the Team came back during which he could teach them the ways of the Quran.

After the powerful story of the crucifixion and resurrection of Christ had been taught, the Team would ask the people who Jesus was and the Imam would invariably answer that Jesus was a great teacher and healer. The Team would heartily agree and then ask about some of the miracles. For example, they would ask, "Who can just speak the word and a blind man is healed, by the power of His word alone?"

The people in town would answer, "Nobody but God has that power!"

"Well, who can just speak a word and a leper is healed, and his hands and feet become new?"

"Nobody but God can do that."

"Who can call a dead man from the grave and he comes out alive?"

"Nobody but God can do that. God alone has that power."

"Well then, if nobody but God can heal the sick, make the blind to see, help the lame to walk, make the cripple whole, restore the leper, and raise the dead, how did Jesus do all those miracles? He must be God!"

Usually about this time the Imam would have his say. Frequently he would say something like, "No, you don't understand. He was a great miracle worker and teacher. He was a great prophet." Then he would quote the Quran "Isa (Jesus) is the Word of Allah (God)."

It sounds a lot like the Gospel of John: "And the Word became flesh and dwelt among us and we have seen His glory, the glory of the only begotten of the Father, full of grace and truth" (John 1:14).

On this powerful truth, tucked away in the secret places of the Quran, the Gospel Team would now pounce. "That is true. Isa (Yesu) is the Word. If you have me, you have my word. If you have my word, you have me. Me and my word are one and the same. If a person is the same as his word, and his word is the same as a person, and Jesus is the Word of God, then Jesus must be God! Can one be separated from his word when the word and the person are one?"

At this point there would often be some kind of response that would indicate that the teacher did not agree that Isa (Jesus) was actually Allah (God), although he would concede that Jesus was indeed the "Word of Allah, and because of that He had great power as a prophet".

Usually another member of the Team would step into the discussion at this point with another line of reasoning. He would ask the people if they believed that men had the power to turn themselves into animals. They would readily declare that this is not only a possibility, but also a reality among the Kuranko people. When Dembeli first arrived in the country, missionaries were quick to tell him about this "superstition," as they called it. Many were quick to ridicule it, and brush it off as meaningless. Dembeli felt that there had to be more to this than just a "figment of the people's imagination," so as usual he asked questions to learn more about the belief system of the people God had called him to serve. He soon discovered that what he learned was not readily accepted by most of the other missionaries, so he kept the information he gained pretty much to himself. He shared it with a carefully selected few that he could use as sounding boards to get feedback.

Dembeli began to piece together a belief system concerning the world of the demonic that left him with a whole new series of questions and nowhere to get answers that satisfied him. Because he did not ridicule this belief, he soon gained the confidence of many who held to traditional animistic beliefs. Before long he began to put together a list of the demonic powers whose presence was acknowledged among the people of the area.

Confident that Dembeli would not ridicule or mock their beliefs, the men began to share deeper insights into their world view, and Dembeli soon had a list of the spirits that the "forefathers" believed in. He continued to gather information until he had a list of what powers those spirits had, what sacrifices were necessary to procure their services, and what the payoff was for the one who called upon them for help. In the course of time, Dembeli came to the conclusion that a Gospel must be presented that deals with those issues, or it would fall far short in reaching the real heart of the people. The Kuranko people need a Jesus who can deliver them from the bondage of the spirit world and set them free in the power of the Holy Spirit so they can experience the truth of Jesus' words, "If the Son shall set you free you shall be free indeed" (John 8:36). Otherwise Jesus is not real in the crucible of Kuranko living. When the pressure is on, and the going gets tough, believers who have not found the answer to these issues in Christ will turn back, possibly secretly, to the world of the demonic because "that is where the power is."

As Dembeli gained insights into this aspect of the Kuranko belief system, he noticed some Christians who continued to wear the fetish charms. Others would turn back to this world of darkness when their property was stolen so that a person with "spirit powers" could show them who the thief was. Before long, Dembeli realized that if the Church of Jesus Christ did not deal with this realm of Kuranko beliefs, we would end up with a church that was a mile wide and only an eighth of an inch deep. There can be no real spiritual depth if the Gospel is simply synchronized with animism even in the secret places of the heart as had been done with Islam.

Dembeli knew that many of the people held to the animistic belief system of the forefathers. They believed that the good spirits—as opposed to evil spirits—hold the world in balance, but that since the good spirits will not harm them, they do not have to worry about them. Yet fear griped their hearts as they tried to appease the evil spirits that held sway over the territory. Some evil spirits had the power of sickness, tragedy, and even of life and death. The bondage was incredible, and far beyond the understanding of most western minds. Because they could not grasp it, many missionaries simply dismissed this world view as superstition and were never able to help the people come to grips with these issues that troubled them so deeply. Dembeli did find another missionary who was tangling with the same issues, and later in his studies in America he found some who were much farther along the journey of probing into this world view and belief system. He was able to "sit at their feet" and learn truths in the Scriptures that helped answer some of his many questions. He also was led to books, articles, and other individuals that dealt with these issues in a Biblical manner, and he was able to begin to piece together a theology that responds to these deep issues of the Kuranko heart.

Into this animistic world of darkness the devil brought Islam. The people bought into the teaching of the "law of Mohamed the prophet," for they thought this would surely please God. It also gave them a measuring standard of works so they could measure their progress in a tangible way. Unfortunately, what Islam did was to further blind the hearts and minds of the people (Matt. 23:15). They synchronized their own belief system with that of Islam, while still maintaining their own concept of the world of the demonic.

As the men realized that Dembeli would not attack their view, they exposed more and more of their beliefs to him. Sometimes they would point out a person to him and quietly tell him that that particular person had the power to change into an animal and was a hyena, a leopard, a bush cat, or some other animal or bird. This was pretty well held in secret until after the war broke out in 1992, and then the people began to expose and talk about such individuals publicly. The reason was very simple. The military had not been able to put down rebel forces, and "traditional methods" were called upon for help. For a while, rebel activity was held in check, and the hunters with supernatural powers were acclaimed heroes. One friend Dembeli and his boys hunted with shared with them that he is so powerful that he has the choice of being different animals. He explained that this power was why he was such a success as a hunter, and it is the reason others in the town feared him.

Chapter 17: Jesus the Mediator

Since Dembeli had explored some of the ideas of their animistic beliefs he knew that those core issues would have to be addressed. This took place after the teaching on the life of Christ. When the appropriate time came one of the Gospel Team members would ask the people if they believed that one of them could change themselves into an animal. They would declare emphatically that this was indeed possible. Before the war they would laugh—it seemed to Dembeli a little nervously—and indicate a person who had the power to change into a leopard or a hyena, or another specific creature of the bush.

"Yes," they would say, "Men have that power."

Then one of the Gospel Team members would ask if the devil had the power to change himself into an animal. The response was always immediate, "Of course he can. Why he changed into a snake to tempt Grandpa Adam and Grandma Eve and they spoiled God's laws."

"Does God have the power to change Himself into an animal?" the Gospel Team members asked.

Invariably, the response would be that God could not do that and so the Gospel Team would proceed with their line of reasoning: "If man has the power to change himself into an animal, and the devil has the power to change himself into an animal, why does not Creator God who is all powerful have the power to do the same? He does! He can! He did! We call Him Emmanuel. The real meaning of this name is "God with us." God did not change Himself into an animal, but into a mortal man so that He could show us the way to heaven. He came so that He could die for us on the cross and be our Supreme Sacrifice to end all sacrifices. Then He rose from the dead to show us His power over death, and assure us that if we would only believe and accept Him as our Supreme Sacrifice that we too would have everlasting life through Him."

This was a new concept to the people in the village, and they would often tell the Team that they needed to come back and teach them more about this Truth. Some of them would openly admit that the Team was teaching them the truth and that they wanted the Team to come and teach their children, so their children could come to know God. They expressed their feeling that it was too late for them and that they could not leave the road they were walking on.

The Team would then refer again to the Two-Road Map and ask where the road ended. The people would often defer to their Muslim teacher, if he was present and he would respond that the road of Islam goes to the judgment. Sometimes the teacher would add that in judgment, God, as a blindfolded Judge, would weigh our good deeds on a scale against our bad deeds and that if our bad deeds are heavier (more plentiful), then we would be sent to hell. If our good deeds are heavier (more plentiful), then God can peek under the blindfold and see whether or not He wants us in heaven. If He does not, then we do not go in. But if He does like us, He allows us to enter heaven.

The bottom line for the Kuranko is that there is no assurance of sins forgiven or of salvation, and there is no real hope of heaven. Even after one has done everything he has been taught to do, there is no assurance that God will accept him into heaven. The Folk Islam of the Kuranko people does not offer a mediator between God and man, and so man has to stand alone in judgment before God. They are scared to death to stand alone before a Holy God, for they are afraid that they will be ashamed on that day.

Dembeli learned something of the importance of the role of a mediator in the culture as he watched the people. He observed that when a child is born and it is time to name it, a mediator must be present to represent the child and the family to the spirit world. He noticed that when a young man is ready to get married that he has to have a mediator who will negotiate the bride price and make the arrangements for him with the bride's family. If an argument takes place in the home or among friends—even if the oldest person in the village is involved—there must be a mediator to make peace. But the role of the mediator within the culture never really hit home until one day Dembeli found himself in a situation where he desperately needed one.

Dembeli had noticed several rocks in the area that had a very unique shape, something that reminded him of a liberty bell. When he asked about the rocks, he was told that they were meteorites and that they had fallen down from heaven. On closer inspection he came to his own conclusion that they were probably volcanic and they took their shape as they cooled off on their way back to earth following the eruption that sent them airborne. Either way, the rocks interested him, and he continued to ask about them. One of the men volunteered the fact that one of the stones Dembeli was interested in had fallen on the area of ground that was part of the town chief's farm. Dembeli wondered if he could go get it. Men on the Gospel Team told him that he would have to ask the chief for it because it would not be right just to go take the rock off the chief's farm without first asking permission. That sounded pretty reasonable, so Dembeli continued with his plans to take a trip to visit a pastor a day's travel away and told the men he would talk to the chief about the rock later. He reasoned that the rock would still be there when he returned in a couple of days.

Those traveling with Dembeli piled into the truck, and they headed out of town anticipating a great day encouraging other believers in a town not too far away. As they were leaving Heredugu they met the town chief walking into town from his farm. After the proper greetings had been completed, Dembeli asked him about the stone that had fallen from the sky. The chief responded that it would be fine for Dembeli to have the stone if he would first give him a gift. Dembeli immediately offered about a day's wages as an appropriate gift. The chief chuckled and said that that really was not enough of a gift for a stone that had fallen from the heavens onto his property. It had fallen generations before, and of course nobody had seen it fall. Dembeli asked why he should give more than a days wages and wondered if it was really the chief's stone if it had fallen from the sky. Well, that is what he meant to ask, and that is what he thought he asked.

The question was no sooner out of his mouth than the Gospel Team members accompanying him burst out in peals of laughter. Dembeli had never seen them laugh so hard. He asked what was so funny, but by then they were laughing so hard they could not talk. Some were rolling with laughter in the back of the truck and could hardly contain themselves. The chief himself joined in the laughter, and only Dembeli missed the humor—whatever it was. Soon one of the men stopped laughing long enough to gasp for a breath of fresh air and Dembeli asked him again what was so funny. With tears of laughter streaming down his cheeks he explained that Dembeli had just cursed the chief. It took awhile, but during each gasp for breath that caused a pause in the laughter, Dembeli was able to draw out of the men the linguistic error he had made and what he had really said. Indeed he had cursed the chief, and what he said is not printable.

Realizing that if he left on his journey without making amends, his error would be seen as a major offense, Dembeli endeavored to penetrate their laughter long enough to ask what he needed to do to correct the situation. The men told him that he would need to take a gift and go see the town elders. He would need to have them beg the chief's forgiveness so that people would not feel that he had purposely cursed their chief. Turning the truck around, Dembeli headed back to his house on the other side of town and picked up a sizable gift before heading back into town to see the elders.

The Gospel Team, still rolling with laughter, informed him that he could not go to the elders and the chief directly, but that he needed a mediator to talk on his behalf in such a serious case as this. Sitting quietly in the truck with laughter all around, Dembeli asked the men who he could get to be his mediator. One of the men, Yakubu, volunteered.

Dembeli said, "Look, you can't even sit up straight you are laughing so hard. How can you go and talk to the elders on my behalf?"

The response came through more waves of laughter, "Oh, I will be serious when we stand before the elders."

For lack of anyone else to speak on his behalf, Dembeli agreed and stepped out of the truck. Yakubu also got out, and they stepped across the ditch which marked the edge of the road and the boundary of the chief's property. A loud shuffling behind him caused Dembeli to turn in time to see all the rest of the Team members piling out of the truck. He stopped and asked what they were doing. On behalf of the whole group, one of them answered, "Our missionary just cursed our chief. Now they are going to talk the case. We would not miss this for anything!"

Since he knew that he could not restrain them, Dembeli decided that he had to allow his friends to join him and his mediator. After all, he might need someone else to help explain that he had not cursed the chief on purpose. However bad the curse was, he had simply made a language error, and they were all familiar with his language errors. Some of them had often corrected him in the past, and many of them had been of real assistance to him as instructors in the language learning process.

Stepping across the ditch somehow transformed the Team's laughter into inner rumblings as they headed for the chief's house where the elders had already started to gather. It does not take long among the Kuranko people to gather a crowd when a serious case is in the making. Nobody wants to miss out on the action.

After all the necessary greetings had been offered, Yakubu, who was representing Dembeli, turned to the elders and began to explain what had happened. Dembeli noticed that the corners of the chief's mouth were still twitching with laughter and his eyes were sparkling with humor. Somehow, in the brief walk from the truck to the chief's house, the Team had been able to get themselves under control, and they listened quietly as Yakubu explained the situation and begged the elders to stand with him in interceding with the chief to forgive the guilty party, in this case Dembeli. They listened carefully and then joined him in presenting good reasoning for pardoning the guilty and dismissing the case.

The details of their response are not important, nor is their reasoning an issue. But the conclusion is of uttermost importance. As the elders finished expressing their support of Dembeli's mediator, the chief responded in typical Kuranko fashion. As usual, the guilty party kneels in the dirt and holds the feet of the party he has offended. The offended puts his hand on the guilty one's shoulder and offers forgiveness and pardon. In this case, as in so many others that Dembeli later listened to, the chief made a powerful statement that gave Dembeli deep insights into Kuranko thinking.

Putting his hand on Dembeli's shoulder the chief declared, "On behalf of your mediator, you are forgiven." That is huge! What an incredible redemptive analogy of Christ our Mediator who forgives our sins, cleanses us, and sets us free because of who He is and what He did for us on Calvary.

Now nobody is ever allowed to bring up Dembeli's offense again. Sitting around the fire during the cold season, or while just taking a break in shade, the men will often bring up grammatical errors that their friends have made while learning English, or that some of the missionaries have made while learning Kuranko. If Dembeli should happen to mention the day he cursed the chief all will roar with laughter, but no one else is ever allowed to recall that incident to memory because it was forgiven and canceled on behalf of Dembeli's mediator.

Chapter 18: Which Road?

Dembeli's mind often went back to that event as the Gospel Team shared with the people the importance of Christ's death and resurrection. He listened to the Team as they reasoned with the townspeople following the story of the resurrection of Christ, and he was fully aware of the need for a mediator in their lives. His own experience had born out that need. He also knew that the people around him were scared to death to face God in judgment alone without someone to speak on their behalf. In their belief system they were taught to do good deeds to "cover their sins," but deep inside their hearts they know that no one can hide anything from Creator God, and that they will one day stand before Him in judgment. They have a deep fear that they will be shamed that day when He uncovers their sin for all to see, and then they will be sent to hell. Throughout their lives they have relied on a mediator to intercede on their behalf, for a name when born, for a wife when ready to be married, for peace when troubles come, and so on. The thought of facing a holy God in judgment, without a mediator, is a fearful concept. Many long to find someone who will intercede on their behalf. So when the Team shares that Jesus rose from the dead to be the Mediator for those who accept Him as Savior and Lord, it is indeed a powerful, new concept worth considering.

Often, at this point in the discussion, one of the elders, or perhaps the Imam (Muslim teacher) himself, would remind the people that the Gospel Team was presenting "the white man's religion" and will emphatically declare that this is "the white man's road." Gospel Team members having discussed with Dembeli at length an adequate answer to this issue, would then share gently the background of the Two Roads which were being discussed. Turning again to the picture of the *Two Road Map* that had been shown so often throughout the presentation of the picture Bible, one of the Team would again briefly explain how the Arab nations came from Ishmael, son of Abraham, and that Mohammed came from the Arab nations. He would ask the people who brought them the teaching of the Quran and of the prophet Mohammed. He would ask who brought this road to them. Some of the older ones would explain how the Fullah nomadic cow herders and traders, coming down from the north, had brought this teaching to them as they traded their goods. They might even explain how it had first gained power in the courts and then it had eventually permeated all of their lives until they had the Folk Islam that they have today. Actually, it did not seem to take very long from the coming of those first traders until the culture was saturated with Islam, and Dembeli marveled at how quickly that change had taken place. Although that had taken place several generations before, when challenged by the Gospel Team, the people declared that they all understood and agreed that they had indeed received this teaching from "outsiders".

Then the Gospel Team would ask them who brought the teaching of Christianity. Well, that was easy to answer, for many of the people present had been alive when the Schierlings had come into the area and settled down to teach the people this new way. Sometimes some of the people would laugh and be a little embarrassed as they shared how Dembeli, sitting right there in their midst, was the one who brought the Gospel to their town, and he obviously is a white man. They reasoned that the obvious conclusion was that qualified the road of Christianity as "the white man's road" because they were obviously the only ones who brought it to them.

It was like a bomb when one of the members of the Gospel Team took them one step farther along their own road of reasoning and asked a powerful question. "If this is the white man's road because the white man brought it to you, then Islam must be the road of the Fullahs, or the Arabs, because they brought it to you. Where is the Kuranko man's road?"

In the silence that usually follows this question, the little wheels of minds and hearts begin to turn. Sometimes some of the people would respond defensively saying that "all roads are the same, for they all go to Allah." For them, that statement seems to sweep away the issue. But for many hungry hearts this answer does not satisfy, and they would probe deeper for truth as they discussed this new concept. In many towns the people came to the conclusion that it is true that neither of the roads originated with the Kuranko, but to them that means that the Kuranko is free to choose which of the roads he wants to walk on. At this point the Gospel Team would remind them that each individual needs to choose carefully what road they will follow because although both roads lead to judgment, only the road of Jesus provides a Redeemer/Mediator. The Team then reminds the people that the time has come for them to declare which road they are walking on.

Usually the Team would let people know that they would be back in a week at their usual time, and that they would be asking the people to tell them at that time what road they have chosen as their own road to follow.

The response varied from town to town. In the little town of Mesene, all the adult men except the town chief, who felt he was too old to accept a new way, decided that they needed to choose and walk on the Jesus Road. A little round church was built as a house of worship. A literacy class was started, and the Gospel Team began to disciple those who made the commitment to walk the "Jesus Road" in an endeavor to help them learn to pass on their newfound faith in Christ.

In the town of Folote, the town chief presented three young men to the Gospel Team at the close of the service. The chief declared that these three young men no longer wanted to walk the road of Islam but that they wanted to walk the road of Jesus, and so the town was giving them to the Team and asking the Team to "take them and make them followers of the Way." What a commission the Gospel Team received from the town of Folote that night!

Dembeli observed that there was no altar service and very few individual responses to change roads, but a lot of groups that responded had decided together to change roads. He had read enough books on missionary practice to be aware of the debate about such patterns, but he came to the conclusion that God sees the heart, and he encouraged the Gospel Team to be faithful in discipling those who made the decision together. As already mentioned, the first baptismal services were held in Heredugu at the annual Institute when all the Christians from the area gathered. As the Team found more and more people in the nearby villages who wanted to make the choice of walking on the Jesus Road, it was decided that they should be baptized in their own towns as a witness to their own people of the choice they had made. Because baptisms usually included a group of people, the numbers helped to strengthen the truth that the Team was not presenting a "White man's religion" but that Kurankos have a choice, and they can choose which road they want to walk on. Also by coming as a group to be baptized, new believers could encourage each other in their walk when opposition got tough for them, for they would not be walking alone, but they would have a support group who would be walking with them.

As more and more people made the decision to declare that they were walking on the Jesus Road, it became apparent that the Gospel Team needed to spread out more. New believers shared their faith with family and friends in other towns, and more requests kept coming to the Gospel Team to go to towns where they had never been to teach the people about the "new road" that the Kurankos could choose to walk. Sometimes Dembeli and several Team members would walk hours back into the hills and share the Gospel with the people in the "new town" to check it out and see how serious they were and how willing they would be to listen to God's Word. So many requests came that they knew they would not be able to respond to all of them immediately.

Limited time, personnel, and the difficulty in travel meant that the Gospel Team had to learn to process these requests from the various towns and pick the ones that seemed to be "fertile soil." This process of evaluation was a hard one for the men to grasp, and it took several years of teaching before Dembeli was able to get the men to analyze the town's spiritual temperature rather than just the food, lodging, and welcome they received while they shared the Good News. One of the central themes in the culture is to avoid "spoiling the name of another person or town," so it was very difficult for the men to expose the elements, attitudes, or beliefs that would hinder a spiritual harvest in a given town. This was especially true if they had family or friends in that particular town. How could they skip over the town where their family and friends were and go to another town that was more responsive to the Gospel? Yet they were quick to recognize that they could not reach all the towns. In the course of time they got better at analyzing the towns while still endeavoring to give everyone an equal opportunity to hear the Gospel. This enabled Dembeli and the Team to invest more time with responsive towns.

Dembeli was excited when he returned from furlough one year to discover new believers that he had never met in a town he had never before been to, a town where the Team had found fertile soil and decided to "go for the harvest." The Team had reached new towns and discipled new believers there even though missionaries had never presented the Gospel to those particular people. The Team was eager to share the joy of the harvest with Dembeli, and insisted that he go to the new town with them right away so he could meet the believers that had been baptized there in his absence. The rain that soaked the men as they walked home that night could not dampen their spirits. They realized in a new way the truth of the Psalmist's words when he said that those who sow in tears will indeed come again with rejoicing bringing a harvest with them (Ps. 126:5-6).

The original picture Bible that Dembeli assembled stopped after the resurrection and ascension of Christ. The series ended on the powerful note that because He lives we can live also. Because Christ triumphed over the grave we have eternal life with Him in heaven. The truth that He is now our mediator and intercedes on our behalf left the new believer with a real sense of victory.

Initially Dembeli had taught only about the characters who were common to both the Scriptures and the Quran, but as he evaluated the growing Church among the Kuranko people, he began to realize that he needed to add the Book of Acts. Although the book of Acts is not part of the Scriptures recognized by the Quran, it holds powerful teachings and is a great encouragement for believers in their walk with the Lord. It gives us examples of how believers, empowered by the Holy Spirit, stood up under the pressure of persecution and how God honored His Word, as people remained faithful to it. It also gives a pattern for church planting and teaches a lot of practical truths about how the Church should function, not only as it relates to the world and evangelism, but as it relates to believers within the body and their relationships with each other. It shows what the Church of Jesus Christ should look like.

Each furlough Dembeli continued with his training. Not only did he take classes to help keep him on the cutting edge of missions, but he also attended seminars that challenged him and gave him new ideas. Those classes and seminars afforded him the opportunity to learn from others around the world and to keep in touch with what God is doing as He builds His Church.

Dembeli was privileged to be in a small group of missionaries for a special training program in Pasadena, California, where he sat under the instruction of leaders on the cutting edge of world evangelism. One of those leaders, Dr. George Patterson, challenged him to teach the new believers not to follow the traditions of the church but to obey the commands of Christ. As a result of that challenge, Dembeli added a new section to the picture Bibles that the Gospel Teams use in their evangelism and discipleship program. Although Dr. Patterson lists only seven commands of Christ, Dembeli felt that another one (worship) is also necessary and he included it in his training program.

Using pictures to illustrate the truths, the direct commands of Christ are taught so that new believers know what the Church of Jesus Christ is supposed to look like. These basic commands of Christ are:

1. Repent, believe, be filled with the Holy Spirit (Mark 1:15)
2. Be baptized and continue in the new life it initiates (Matthew 28:18-20; Acts 2:38; Romans 6:1-11)
3. Love God and your neighbor in a practical way (Matthew 22:37-40)
4. Celebrate the Lord's Supper (Luke 22:17-20)
5. Pray (Matthew 6:5-15)
6. Give (Matthew 6:19-21; Luke 6:38)
7. Worship (John 4:24)
8. Disciple others (Matthew 28:18-20)

As Dembeli went through these principles with the pastors and the Gospel Team members, he learned their perspectives on how these various commands should be implemented. Once again he was reminded that this is God's Church and that the Kuranko Church is not going to look like the Church in England, America, or possibly other areas of Africa. He affirmed that the fixed principle is not *how* we obey these commands, but that we *do* obey them.

Since grapes are not indigenous to this area of the world, the "cup" during communion has been passed around with a variety of juices that come from local fruit. It may vary from one service to another depending on the fruit in season at the time. The Church decided that the important issue is that we celebrate the Lord's Supper and honor His sacrifice. They felt that the important thing is that the juice be taken "in remembrance of Him."

The discipling sessions on worship were of particular interest to Dembeli. The men discussed what should be different about a gathering of believers in worship and a gathering of the town people for a festive or political occasion. The bottom line was the issue of what worship is. Dembeli mused that the Kuranko perspective was a whole lot different from that of the people of the mid western United States where he usually spends his year of "Home Ministry Assignment". Biblical guidelines were discussed, and the church leaders expressed the sentiment that real worship, though it may take a different form than the tribes around them, needs to come from the heart, and that the individual needs to learn both private and corporate worship.

It was not hard for the Team to catch the concept of discipleship. They had been discipled in a very practical "hands on" way, and many of the men in the group had their own apprentices that they were discipling at the time. Some of the older men who are mentoring others cannot read or write, yet they are encouraging their apprentices to join the literacy classes and learn as much as they can from God's Word. They concluded that the important thing is that they pass on their faith in Christ and that they teach others to be obedient to His commands. How they do that will vary because of background, training, and skills, but their own obedience to Christ's commands will set an example to the new believers. It also demonstrates to the nonbeliever that followers of Christ have heard Him say "Brzzzzzzz" and they do "march to the beat of a different drummer" than those who walk in road of traditional African religions of of "Folk Islam".

As the men discipled others, it soon became apparent that there were some who would excel. Everyone was to be discipled, so the men taught the new believers Scripture verses using the same pictures that still prompt their own memories. The daily prayer meeting almost became a non-negotiable practice in each of the churches the men planted. As the new believers saturated their souls with the Word of God, they soon grew hungry to learn more. Team members and pastors would take those who were interested and begin to teach them the picture Bible. When they learned the entire Bible in pictures, each apprentice would be given a picture Bible of his own. Some of the men gathered their families around each evening and shared the Bible stories with them. As a result, many of the men have led their entire families to the Lord.

There was a hunger for more knowledge in the hearts of some of the young men, so they approached their pastor and asked him if there was any way they could learn more. Each church established a literacy class to respond to those needs, and young men and women learned to read God's Word for themselves. As they learned to read, it seemed that they yearned to be taught, so pastors would take apprentices and teach them Theological Education by Extension (TEE) classes just as Dembeli was teaching them. Often a pastor found that he was only one course ahead of his apprentice. He discovered that he had to be pretty serious in continuing his education so that he could pass it on to the eager young Christians he was training.

A few of the men in the TEE courses set their goals higher and began to seek an opportunity to study in an institution. As the Church watched them grow spiritually, church leaders evaluated their lives and then recommended them to the Bible Training School in Kurela. Dembeli was thrilled to see men from the area go to Bible school and sit under the teaching of Jake and Ruth Schierling, who had planted the first church in the area so many years before. He also suspected that the Schierlings were just as thrilled to see the men coming from that area that had been unreached with the Gospel for so many generations.

As time passed, several of the men from the area set their sights on a higher education that offered a degree and recognition from their government. One chose to go for further theological training where he became the first Christian from the area to be awarded a BA Degree. Not all of them chose Bible training. Some chose to be teachers, and others nurses. It really encouraged the church leaders when the teachers and nurses caught a vision for their home area and returned to train children in community schools. Some of the teachers also became church planters in the towns where they were stationed to teach. Interestingly enough, they began to disciple new believers just as they had been discipled, and they were soon asking for picture Bibles to teach to their apprentices how to share their faith with others.

Dembeli encouraged all the men who wanted to go to Bible school to function in the church first. Usually they would join the Gospel Team and be discipled in evangelism before they were recommended by their local church, or the District, to go to Bible school. Dembeli was pleased that when the men came out of Bible school, they had an attitude of ministry that was a life-style of evangelism and that it was not hard for them to reach to the towns around where the District stationed them.

The goal of training pastors continues to be a priority need of the Church. One of the most powerful missionary speakers that Dembeli ever met was a leader who came to visit Nigeria when he was growing up. He remembers that leader saying that we should "Train nationals not just to be leaders in the church, but to be the missionaries leaders as well." Dembeli often shared with the men that there will come a day that the men who are in training now will be leaders in a true partnership of ministry and they will be the leaders for the missionaries as well as for the national church.

The bottom line is that we walk in obedience to Christ's commands so that Christ will be glorified in our lives and in His Church.

Part 3: Church Planting

Chapter 19: Changing Times

Following a year on Home Ministry Assignment, Dembeli and his family returned to the Heredugu area. Dembeli became even more aware that unless one has experienced the process of leaving family and friends in America while looking forward to renewing relationships with loved ones in Africa, one can never identify with the kaleidoscope of feelings that a missionary family will experience. That kaleidoscope is the bitter-sweet feeling of saying good bye to loved ones on one side of the ocean while looking forward with anticipation to the ministry God has given you on the other side among people you love. It is the tears of parting and the sense of having your heart torn in two as you anticipate returning to an adopted land while leaving family and loved ones behind. It is the sorrow of parting with dear ones you may never see again this side of heaven, mixed with the excitement of seeing those who have come to mean so much to you through years of struggles as the miracle of Church planting blossoms among an unreached people.

After spending a few days in the capital to purchase basic items for the next six months of up-country living, Dembeli and his family were ready to travel. Since it was time for the missionary children's school to open for the new year, they were able to arrange to travel as part of the caravan heading north. Morning stars were still glowing when the long journey up-country began. The excitement of the travelers was contagious. At various points along the way the caravan would stop and pick up missionary kids who were also heading up to the school. As the kids met more of their friends and began to catch up on what they had missed while on furlough for a year back in the States, the anticipation of another year at the boarding

159

school grew. They renewed old acquaintances and made plans for events that would brighten their days at school. Dembeli realized, as he had many times before, that missionary children are a unique blend. Kids of all ages from different denominations and backgrounds blend into one big family, forming ties that last a lifetime, bonding a unique mixture of Africa and America into a tribe that has been called Third Culture Kids (TCK). Other kids, totally unrelated, became their "brothers and sisters," and the adults at the school were referred to as "Aunt" or "Uncle." Often a loyalty develops that only those who have experienced it can understand.

Once they reached the school at Kurela, Dembeli and the kids jumped right into the task of unloading the truck. Trunks were carried into the dorm, where mothers sorted and stashed the clothes that had all been carefully marked with name tags sewn in place so that the kids would not get their things mixed up. Last-minute instructions were given, and kids settled into their dorm rooms and rediscovered the favorite playing areas of the compound where forts could be built and games could be played.

As the mothers unpacked the belongings and put them in the dresser drawers, the fathers would often head to downtown Kurela to pick up items that had been missed or left behind in Freetown. This time, Dembeli parked his truck near the square in the middle of town and headed over to a store owned by a Lebanese family that had been friends since the Dembeli's first days on the mission field. Dembeli paused to look around for his buddy Sayon. The Storyteller smiled to himself as he thought of the unique relationship these two had developed over the years. Dembeli lived a full day's drive up country, but came down to Kurela to see the kids and to pick up the mail, supplies, and fuel twice a month. It was in Kurela that Dembeli first met Sayon. A dreaded disease had left him severely handicapped, and the years following had not been kind. Sayon's body was distorted all out of shape and he could no longer speak, although he could still make a lot of noise. His twisted limbs and distorted body made it impossible for him to work. In a culture that depends so much on one's physical strength, his only option was to resort to a lifestyle of begging.

For some reason Sayon had declared himself the personal guardian of Dembeli's vehicle whenever it pulled into town. He would find the truck and stand guard while Dembeli visited friends, shopped, or took care of business. In his own way he would offer help, and would often stand with spit drooling down his chin, patiently guarding the vehicle while Dembeli was gone. Sayon could, and would, make a terrible racket if anyone approached to close to the truck driven by his friend. The racket would draw the attention of others, and Sayon would have lots of help chasing away any potential thieves.

Over the years Dembeli developed a unique relationship with Sayon. Sayon would stand silently at his side listening intently while Dembeli shared his love for Jesus. Sometimes Dembeli would pray with Sayon. One day it dawned on Finaba that Dembeli was functioning on the belief that although Sayon could not communicate verbally, locked inside that twisted form was a person who could still understand, and still had the same needs and emotions as everyone else. The friendship had deepened over the years, and Finaba knew that when Dembeli paused in the middle of town he was looking for his friend and wondering if he was still around, or if he had passed away during the year of Dembeli's Home Ministry Assignment.

Not seeing the guardian of his truck, Dembeli continued his walk to the Lebanese store only to discover that the elite of the town had decided to gather in the store on that particular day and at that particular time. The doctor, the chief of police, the District officer, and many important business men were standing around casually sipping the strong black coffee served to them in a Lebanese demitasse (a very small, fancy cup). Dembeli had often declared that the coffee in a demitasse is so strong that one must bite off a chunk and chew it while smiling pleasantly, all the while waiting for barbed wire to sprout on your chin. Though very strong, it is not an unpleasant drink. Sometimes, as on this occasion, a sweet custard pudding is served along with the coffee, possibly to give balance to what otherwise might be a rather potent dose of caffeine.

Dembeli was invited to join the circle of friends and was given his little cup of coffee. He "bit off a chunk" and smiled graciously while "chewing" it and trying to fit into the conversation. He looked around the circle and noticed that almost everyone of great social status was in the store on that day, doing the same thing. Then, from across the town square there came a terrible racket. Sayon had spotted the familiar vehicle and realized that his friend from up country who had gone to America for a year, was in the store. In a stumbling shuffle he headed across the intervening space of the town square as fast as his distorted limbs could carry him and clambered up the stairs into the shop. Right there in front of God and everybody, with a big grin of welcome wrapped around his head and spit running down his chin, Sayon threw his arms around Dembeli, and in his own special way welcomed his friend back to Sierra Leone.

The Storyteller pressed a little closer so he could hear what Dembeli was whispering in Sayon's ear, for he knew that Sayon had taught Dembeli some very important truths about friendship. Dembeli responded immediately to Sayon's bear hug and then, so no one except Sayon and Finaba could hear, he said, "Sayon, Jesus loves you, and I love you, and I am on my way to heaven and I really want to take you along." Finaba knew that to Dembeli that is the bottom line of missions. When it is all said and done, the very purpose of our existence is to bring glory to God by sharing his plan of salvation with others so they too can share with us in His glory.

That evening Dembeli was informed that there was to be a joint committee meeting with the missionary and National Church leaders in the morning. Dembeli was also informed that he was part of the committee that was to represent the mission at this meeting with the National Church Executive committee. He was briefed on what were some pretty serious "requests" that the church leaders were making of the mission, and was informed that they might have to deal with those requests through the newly elected officers of the National Church.

The meeting went fairly well until about noon, when the president of the National Church had the secretary of the church read a letter stating that they felt that the mission had not responded favorably to the request of the national church for a vehicle for the president to use in his ministry. The letter further stated that the officers of the National Church were all resigning from the mission until the situation could be worked out to the satisfaction of the National Church leadership. The National Church treasurer would be the only one left in office, apparently so that he could be the recipient of any and all funds which the mission would give to the National Church during the time when the National Church would no longer have any officers who would be available to minister alongside the mission. This state of affairs would continue until an agreement that would satisfy the president and his committee, could be reached.

Needless to say, it was a devastating blow to the missionaries. As they took a lunch break following the announcement, few felt like eating. Instead, they spent time in prayer and discussion as they prepared to return to the afternoon session. A few, Dembeli among them, felt that a vehicle was not the real issue, but that it was a spiritual issue and should be handled as such. Others felt that it was a sign of the times and the changing attitude of leadership. They felt that the mission could reason with the leadership and a resolution could be reached.

Typical of what so often happens in missions, the National Church had elected as their first president years before, a man who had worked closely with the missionaries over the years as a pastor and as a leader.

When they first formed their own conference, he was the logical choice for the National Church because he had been trained by the missionaries in mission schools since the beginning, had come through the institutions established by the mission, and all the missionaries knew and respected him. As a pastor of the largest church in the denomination within the country, he had seemed like the logical choice from the viewpoint of both missionaries and nationals.

Now a younger, more aggressive leader had risen in the ranks. He was not afraid to make demands of the mission, or of the individual missionaries. He boldly declared that it was time to take a stand for what they as a National Church wanted, rather than just quietly sitting back and letting the mission continue in the same way it had over the years. His boldness had attracted enough support that he had been chosen to replace the first National Church President. Many of the missionaries thought at first that his leadership would be a breath of fresh air that was needed to get the work in the country on solid indigenous footing. The missionaries wanted to see a National Church that was self-governing, self-supporting, and self-propagating. However, it seemed that as soon as he gained position and found that he had authority, the new president of the National Church began to carry his requests into the realm of demands, and tensions began to mount between church and mission.

The Storyteller sat quietly and listened to the debate among the missionaries as to how they should respond to the demands of the new leader. Having watched Dembeli for so many years and knowing him like he did, Finaba could sense the mounting frustration in the next couple hours as the discussion continued. Dembeli asked questions about some of the events that had transpired while he had been on Home Ministry Assignment and began piecing together the new information with what he had already heard through letters and conversations that took place shortly after his return.

By the end of the day it seemed that the missionaries had split right down the middle into two camps of thought. Those who felt it was a spiritual issue disagreed with those who felt that the problem was a physical vehicle and that things would settle down once the National Church leadership discovered that the mission did not have the finances to provide a vehicle for the president. The marks of delineation were to become clearer and clearer as time rolled on. One segment felt very strongly that if the mission would lay low, in time the problem would work itself out. The other group of missionaries felt equally as strongly that it was a spiritual problem that should be tackled head on before the sin contaminated the attitude of the Church as they looked to the almighty dollar to meet their needs instead of to the power of God through the Holy Spirit.

Needless to say, the meeting did not end on a joyful note. The president of the National Church remained adamant in his stand that the church leadership had resigned, and would stay resigned if their demand for a vehicle was not met. It was unclear to Dembeli how the mission could accept the resignation of the National Church president when he had been elected by the National Church conference and really did not have any direct relationship, accountability, or responsibility to the mission. It seemed to Dembeli that the officers should have been resigning from the National Church conference that elected them, and not from the mission, but he reasoned that maybe he was missing something since he had been gone for a year. Dembeli's uneasiness continued in the closing session when the mission leaders returned to the meeting and quietly accepted the resignation of the committee, leaving Dembeli and several other missionaries with the feeling that the mission leaders had simply ignored the problem in hopes that it would go away.

This historical meeting took place the first week of Dembeli's return up country to begin his second term of service in Sierra Leone, and it set the stage for a conflict that took months to resolve. Being from a remote area, the ripple effect of the meeting did not hit Dembeli, or the Gospel Team as quickly as it did some of the down-country areas. It did, however, catch up with the Heredugu area since the National Church president had been born in the Heredugu District and grew up there before he began his training and ministry with the mission.

Early in the morning after the historic meeting Dembeli and several passengers began their long journey back to Heredugu. Tearful good-byes had been said to the children who stayed behind at the boarding school, and Dembeli was not the only one of the adults who felt his heart torn apart as they returned to ministry in the outlying areas. Other parents heading down country were not as fortunate as Dembeli who would return to Kurela for fuel supplies and mail a couple times a month. Most down-country parents would not see their children again until "Visiting Weekend," about halfway through the semester, when all the parents came to the school to share a few days of fun and relaxation together with the children.

Since Dembeli had been raised in a similar situation as missionary kid in Nigeria, he could identify with his own children and he knew how much they enjoyed their friendships in the missionary children's school. They were building memories and friendships that would last a lifetime, just as he had done growing up in Nigeria. He knew that his children had a positive attitude about the school, and even in the heartache of separation he recalled how Andy, the youngest of the three, had informed the house parents on the first day of school that they did not have anything to worry about because the kids were "good little rascals."

He also remembered the time that all the first, second and third grade boys got into a serious rumble. The cause of the disagreement has long since been forgotten, but whatever it was at the time, it was important enough in the minds of the boys to cause a serious fight. The house parents broke up the squabble and took the group of offenders to a "counsel meeting" under a nearby tree and tried to help them work through the issues and restore peace. When it looked like things were all straightened out, the house parent asked, "Alright boys, are you satisfied now?"

Without a moment's hesitation Andy responded, "We may be satisfied, but we are not happy." Dembeli often reflected on the incredible insight and honesty of that statement made by his youngest son. Finaba heard him wonder aloud how often adults come through a battle with the same sentiment, but are not open enough to express it. As he traveled north to reopen the station, Dembeli was already looking forward to his trip back to the city to see the kids in just a couple weeks.

Heredugu station had been vacant for a year and Dembeli knew that his family would have a few days work reclaiming the house from the ants, bugs, spiders and other critters that had taken up residence in their absence. They reminisced about the horrendous undertaking they had experienced a few short years earlier when they had moved to Heredugu after the absence of missionaries for many years. The elephant grass had grown almost twenty feet tall right to the edge of the orchard, and the compound had shrunk in size due to the increasing bush around it. The bush has always continued to march into any and all uncared-for land. During the years when the station was not occupied by missionaries only a small area around the house had been kept clear. This time during their absence another missionary couple had gone up to Heredugu several times to check on the property. A very dependable watchman had taken care of the grounds so Dembeli knew that it would not be a repeat of the battle they had fought with the creeping, crawling critters several years earlier when they reclaimed the land after years of nobody being stationed there.

.

The old planks on the Ruwa Bridge a half mile outside of town rattled their welcome as the vehicle crept over the bridge. Dembeli knew that the sound carried for well over a mile so all the people in the town were immediately aware of their arrival. As they rounded the corner in the road and headed down the little hill and across the log bridge into town, children were shouting as men strode forward and women grinned a welcome. Cries of joy welcomed the missionaries back as their vehicle headed to the Chief's compound. Dembeli was driving a new vehicle, and he wanted to show it to the chief and the town leaders even before he drove out to see the condition of the mission house. Dembeli had barely gotten the door open and his feet on the ground before the exuberance of the crowd took over and shouting friends welcomed him back. There were hugs, cheers, and welcomes as only the Kuranko people can give, and the Storyteller knew that Dembeli had been welcomed home in a manner that made the conflict in the city the day before seem like an abstract memory.

Townspeople rallied around to unload the truck, help clean the house, and move their missionary family back in. The evening meal was provided by loving hands, as joy and laughter echoed again in the house. Dembeli listened attentively as events of the past year were shared far into the night. He was saddened to hear of those who had passed away during the year he had been absent, and he was amazed at how soon the people had adjusted. Then he recalled how the people in the bush seem to live closer to life and death than his own people do, and so they seem to be able to make that kind of adjustment sooner. He often wondered if part of the reason for their resiliency is the reality that land has to be cleared, farms have to be put in, and days are taken up in just living as the demands of life keep on marching on.

Morning found the missionaries "up and at 'em" with the cleaning, eager to reclaim the house from all the creepy crawlers. Dembeli was anxious to settle into ministry again. Once the sounds of the town indicated that everyone was up and about their daily activities, Finaba accompanied Dembeli into town for a stroll along the paths to greet friends and offer sympathy for those whose family members had passed on during the past year. Warm words of welcome were offered. and the familiar sights, sounds, and smells of the village said in their own way that it was good to be together again.

As Dembeli prepared to make a trip back to the city for additional supplies, he was not surprised to see some of the elders from the church coming to greet him. He figured that they had been a long time without a good means of transportation down to the city and were probably coming to ask him for a ride. He was surprised when they came just to talk to him and to tell him that while he had been in America the town had opened a market. It was a good market and drew people from all over the area, but with the good people there also came some people who lacked integrity. They said that this had caused a little bit of change in the atmosphere of the town. They knew that when Dembeli left for the city he often did not leave a watchman at the mission. One of the men would go out and check on his place twice a day and feed the dog, but there had been no need for anyone to stay out at the mission house when it was only Heredugu people around. However, they concluded that times had changed and that now Dembeli would need to leave someone to guard the place at night, especially during the market time.

Dembeli knew that in years gone by none of the homes in town were locked. A door composed of sticks and reeds was hung over the doorway to each hut with a charm hanging on it. Some of the men had told him that in years past nobody would mess with the door that had such a charm hanging on it because they were afraid of the power, or possibly the curse, that charm represented.

A young man who had gone to the coast for schooling came home for the holidays, and while chatting with some of his friends he began to mock the power of the charm hanging over a neighbor's door. He told them that he was now educated and that his powers were great enough that such things would not affect him. They challenged him to prove that what he was saying was true, so he went over, pushed the reed door aside and walked around inside the neighbors hut. When nothing happened and he returned to his friends waiting outside, they accepted what he said as truth. Dembeli sadly listened to the men as they concluded that that incident had brought a change in the town and now everybody had to have their doors locked.

Dembeli knew that this kind of thinking was an ongoing struggle with the people. He recalled one town that the Gospel Team had visited some time before. Following the service, the men sat around the fire and chatted long into the night. As Dembeli sat and listened to the discussion, he noticed an old man who was not saying very much. The subject of thieves came up, and various individuals became rather heated as they denounced people of another tribe who were living among them as great thieves. They began to give examples and to imply that everything that was being stolen was taken by people of that tribe. The old man finally interrupted to make a very simple comment. He adequately reminded them that before those people moved into the area things were being stolen. The group had to acknowledge the truth of his statement, but it saddened Dembeli to see the effect that the change was making on the town in which he lived.

Dembeli asked the elders to recommend a man to watch the place for him, and arrangements were quickly made to secure the place while he was gone for supplies.

Chapter 20: A Real Partnership

The Storyteller sensed the excitement of the Gospel Team as they met for a feast to celebrate the return of their missionary. Dembeli asked them to tell him all that had happened during the year that he had been absent, and the meeting soon turned into a time of praise and thanksgiving for what God had done. The Team had reached a couple of new towns that had never heard the Gospel before, sharing with them from God's Word through the picture Bibles. Several had accepted Christ as their personal Savior and Lord as a result.

Plans were made to visit each of the towns where the Team had ministered during the year when there had been no area missionary to help them reach out. For the next couple of weeks various members of the Gospel Team accompanied Dembeli as he greeted old friends in familiar towns and went to the new towns that they had reached while he was on furlough. Finaba soon put together what Dembeli was trying to do as he asked a multitude of questions of Gospel Team members, literacy teachers, and the Christians from the various towns. Dembeli was soon able to formulate some of his evaluations, and his heart overflowed with joy for what God was doing. He was able to discover what aspects of the evangelistic and discipleship programs the Christians had maintained and why. He analyzed which activities or programs they had dropped to help him understand their reasoning. The time without a resident missionary gave an opportunity for a realistic evaluation of the ministry that had taken place when he had been there. It enabled Dembeli to discover and evaluate what was really important to the believers in the Heredugu area. He observed that some of the programs that the mission thought were the most important and the best, were the very programs that were dropped when the missionary, or his finances, were gone. Because Dembeli was the only missionary in the area, there was no one to buoy up the programs during the year that he was gone, and so what continued in his absence was the real heart of the outreach program in evangelism, discipleship, and church planting.

Since Dembeli's priority was to establish an indigenous Church, he did not want to institute programs that could not be carried on without mission personnel or finances. The year of furlough gave ample opportunity to evaluate how the evangelism and discipleship program was working. True, the Gospel Team did not reach as many towns without the assistance of the vehicle driven by the missionary. However, they had continued walking to the various towns that they were able to reach, and had ministered faithfully in a five-mile radius around their home town just as they had committed themselves to do. On several occasions they had taken a few days and walked to towns much farther away. The vehicle extended the area of ministry when it was available, but the ministry of consistently reaching the nearby towns and teaching the Word of God had been carried on without it. That was the exciting thing for the Church and for Dembeli. Dembeli's evaluation confirmed that the Kuranko Christians were on the right track and that the local Church could reach people in their area with the Gospel, with or without a missionary. The big task now was to begin forming the new believers in each of the towns into growing, reproducing bodies of believers called a Church. His evaluation also convinced Dembeli that he would need to plan some absences in the future so that he would have opportunities to evaluate the effectiveness and growth of the Church and the development of its leaders.

After each trip Dembeli took down country, he returned home with a growing concern about the tensions that seemed to be mounting with the National Church leadership. Contrary to the hopes of some of the missionaries, the National Church president did not simply dismiss the demand for a vehicle when he discovered that the mission did not have funds to comply with his demand. Instead he came out with a statement that the whole of the National Church in the denomination should cease working directly with the mission and the missionaries on any and all joint projects until the mission met the requirements of his committee which had resigned from the mission. The same committee still claimed their leadership positions in relation to the National Church that had elected them. As a result of the National Church president's demands, all monthly pastors meetings, joint committee meetings, district church meetings, and local Institutes were canceled. The Institutes were canceled since they were seen as a gathering of all the Christians in the area, including the missionaries who often participated in the teaching and planning of the ministry in their particular areas. Since this was seen as a "joint ministry" of church and mission, the president canceled them until he gave further notice. Tensions were mounting and the heartaches and frustrations were increasing. Ministry in the Heredugu area continued in spite of the demands. Being in a very remote area afforded Dembeli the opportunity to continue ministering with the Gospel Team in evangelism and discipleship as he had always done. Plans for the Institute in Heredugu proceeded without being hampered by direct involvement of the leadership in the city. But word travels quickly along the "African grapevine," a unique but fairly effective means of transferring information without the use of telephones, radio, or other means of modern technology.

The National Church president sent one of his close friends up to the Heredugu area to keep track of what was happening since the church there was continuing to work with Dembeli and the Gospel Team was continuing to function as if there had been no statement made by the president. Several of the leaders of the Heredugu Church made Dembeli aware of the situation and encouraged him to keep working with them. He agreed with them, and the Gospel Team and Dembeli continued to go out in evangelism four evenings each week.

Walking from town out to the mission compound with the Gospel Team one bright morning, Finaba sensed that the hearts of the Team members were very sad. It was a beautiful morning. The birds were singing and the little critters in the swamp were still chirping away with the gusto of happiness in their own little world. Usually Dembeli could hear the Gospel Team approaching from about a quarter of a mile before they arrived for the discipleship session. Their stories and laughter echoed across the little valley and reached the house long before they made their appearance. Today, the Gospel Team members were silent as they headed to a meeting that had been called to discuss how they were going to respond to the demands of their National Church president. Those demands related to the mission and now apparently to Dembeli in particular. The president's messenger declared that Dembeli was ignoring the president's demands, and that he was the only one continuing to work directly with the National Church as if the resignation of the National Church committee had not taken place. The representative from the National Church president joined the group en route to the meeting and his presence caused increased tension. Although the representative had grown up in Heredugu he had moved away a long time before and was a pastor in another district. The fact that he was not highly respected by the people in the town did not help the situation in any way.

As usual, the meeting began with prayer, but the lightheartedness was missing. Following the time in prayer, the position of the National Church president was briefly outlined, and then, not so briefly, various members of the Gospel Team expressed their perspective on the history of the situation as it led up to the point where they now found themselves. The representative from the National Church President sat silently and listened, making very few interruptions and not giving any advice. Dembeli and the Gospel Team had the feeling that he was there more, or less, to report how the meeting went more than to try and persuade anyone into thinking or acting in a given manner.

Finally Dembeli outlined what he perceived to be the heart of the problem. He stated that he believed that the whole issue was a spiritual one and that the men had to decide if they were going to serve God and continue the ministry as they felt God had called and gifted them to do, or if they were going to go along with man and stop reaching their own people with the Gospel until they had material possessions, in this case a vehicle for their president. The issue of whether or not the vehicle was a necessity was not even discussed. The Storyteller and the Gospel Team members were surprised when Dembeli praised the National Church president for his leadership ability and his charisma, but pointed out that the bottom line was still a spiritual issue of whether or not they were going to obey God and continue to *"Preach Jesus! Preach Jesus! Preach Jesus!"* or if they were going to obey man and stop ministering until the demands of the leadership were met. About that time, the tape recorder sitting in the window shut off with a loud click. Finaba and Gospel Team were suddenly aware of the fact that the man sent to them by the president was going to have to be pretty accurate in his tale of woe because there was no way that the tape recorder that Dembeli had placed nearby would change the message of what had been spoken that day. For some reason the loud click of a simple tape recorder when it reached the end of the tape relieved the tension, and a ripple of chuckles swept through the group, stopping only when it reached the man sent from the National Church president.

Finaba already had a pretty good idea what the Gospel Team members and local church leaders were going to decide because he had heard them talking in town, on the road to the market, and out on their farms. He knew that for the past few years the Team had walked the hills together with Dembeli, had shared the same cooking pot, had slept on the same mud floors in a variety of huts tucked away in obscure villages throughout the area. What was even more important was that they had seen what the Gospel could do when various individuals in those towns had accepted Christ, and had had their lives changed by *God's* transforming love. It was this more than anything else that caused the Gospel Team to unanimously decide to keep reaching out, to keep the Team intact, and to continue to evangelize and disciple their own people for Christ.

Although Dembeli was not in town that evening, the men on the Gospel Team met informally and made a second momentous decision he soon heard about. They were going to go ahead with the Institute even though Institutes had been canceled in all the other districts throughout the denomination. In the morning a delegation of church leaders met with Dembeli and informed him of their decision. They asked him to make the vehicle available to bring Christians in to Heredugu from all the nearby towns. They agreed to arrange with the believers to walk out to towns along the road so that Dembeli could meet them and bring them to the Institute in Heredugu the following week. Without a moment's hesitation, Dembeli agreed to continue with the plan and assured them of his total support in their decision to continue with the program which had been planned for so long.

A trip to Kurela was planned a couple days later. Dembeli needed to pick up fuel to make the necessary trips with the truck to bring the believers in from the nearby towns, and additional supplies could be purchased in the Kurela market for the use of the cooking crew during the Institute. Although Dembeli had spent much of his time listening during these first few weeks back on their second term of service, he now proceeded to share with another missionary couple in Kurela about the progress of the ministry in the Heredugu area. They expressed their tremendous frustration about what was taking place on the National Church leadership level. They lived in the same town as the National Church president and were unable to avoid the conflict that raged with increasing tension. The Storyteller noticed that at first Dembeli listened to the account of the mounting tensions, but soon he relaxed, and in an endeavor to encourage them began to share with them the recent decision of the Gospel Team and the Heredugu church leaders to go ahead with the Institute in their area. He shared the last bit of information in confidence asking them to pray with him for the outcome of the Institute so that it might be a real encouragement to all the believers in the area.

After loading the vehicle with the needed supplies, Dembeli and his passengers who had come to purchase materials for the Institute returned to Heredugu. When the weekend of the Institute rolled around, Dembeli and one of the leaders chosen by the church began their journey to the designated villages to bring in the Christians from all over the area. They left Heredugu early and spent the whole day bouncing back and forth over the rough roads carrying people to the Institute. As they drove into town that evening with the last load of happy worshipers, they were anticipating a grand feast at the end of the day that would unite all those who had come. It had been a long, hard day for the traveling crew, and they were eager to settle down with a big pot of rice and the laughter of friends when they were not being bounced around over the rough roads.

Dembeli sensed that things were not quite right when he drove into town. The church was dark, and there were no friendly little groups of people meeting around as usually happened just prior to the opening service of an Institute. As the last load of people piled out of the truck, they were met by a solemn group of men who asked Dembeli to join them for a brief meeting. The Storyteller saw, and felt, the frustration that hit Dembeli when he was told that there was not going to be a meeting because the president and his man had finally been able to put a stop to it when he had found out what was happening. Dembeli walked over to the home of the man who had been sent by the president and confronted him on the issue and asked how he could stop a meeting of believers in the area. It was then that he discovered that after he left Kurela, the missionary he had shared with had become involved in a confrontation with the president, and had told him about the plans of the Heredugu Church to go ahead with the Institute.

Having worked so hard to help the leaders in the local church bring the delegates from all over the area, and then to have the meeting canceled at night when all the believers were already present, frustrated Dembeli. Added to that was the additional trip to Kurela to get the fuel necessary for the endeavor, and the frustration that came from the feeling of having been betrayed by a fellow missionary who should not have said anything about the Institute to the president. Then there was the fact that Dembeli was angry with himself for having shared that information which should not have been shared until after the fact. Dembeli's frustration turned to anger as he struggled with the issue that anyone could stop a gathering of

God's people when the intention was to worship the Lord, to learn from His Word, and to honor Him. The Institute had nothing to do with the vehicle that the president of the National Church wanted. The work of God was being stopped, and that was more than Dembeli wanted to handle at the end of a long hard day of travel over roads that to most would be considered off-road logging trails fit only for 4 X 4 contests.

Unfortunately, Dembeli expressed his anger to the man sent by the National Church president to stop the meeting. Several months later when another joint committee meeting was called, the president confronted Dembeli on his approach to the man. That night however, Finaba was well aware of the fact that it was an angry young missionary who headed home, knowing that he would have to hit the road again early in the morning to take all the people back to their villages because there was not going to be a meeting. Dembeli knew he would have to spend the whole of a second day bouncing over the roads, through no fault of his own or of the church leaders who had called the meeting. But what hurt him worse than that was that the believers would not have their annual Institute that was so important to the growth and development of the Church in the Heredugu area. Later, Finaba heard Dembeli share with another missionary about how he handled the conflict that night. Dembeli stated that he had been so "absolutely right in what he said and the stand he had taken, but so desperately wrong in how he said it and in how he had handled the situation."

As he was taking the people home the next day, Dembeli recalled the parable some of the church leaders had shared with him when they were trying to tell him that the president had sent a man into the area to stop the Institute. They said that when someone puts a rock in an orange and throws it at you, it is not the sweetness of the orange that catches your attention, and it is not the orange that hurts you. It is the rock inside that gets your attention and hurts you. They explained that the one sent by the National Church President to destroy their plans was the rock inside the orange and by the end of the second day of hard travel, Dembeli had to agree with them that, that was where the hurt came from.

For a period of about six months the conflict continued to increase. The Gospel Team stood true to their decision and continued to minister right along with Dembeli. Going out four nights a week, they refused to stop when told to do so by the men who had stopped the Institute. Other messengers were sent from the president himself, but the Gospel Team had made a choice and did not listen to them, even when they were told that they were the only ones defying the National Church president's orders. God continued to bless their ministry, and during the time of the conflict several new believers were baptized. It was becoming increasingly apparent to the members of the Church in Heredugu that another church would have to be planted, so in the midst of the conflict they set about planning to start the first daughter church.

Meanwhile, the battle over a vehicle for the National Church President raged. Finally, about six months after the resignation of the officers of the national church, the issue came to a head, and each church was asked to send representatives to a meeting in Kurela where an agreement would be worked out so that ministry could resume.

Church leaders from the Heredugu area joined Dembeli on the journey and headed for Kurela with heavy hearts. Unfortunately, the first hours of the meeting were taken up by the National Church President denouncing various missionaries for their mistakes, and the mission in general for its lack of love, which, he stated, was revealed in a negative response to his request for a vehicle. It was during that session that Dembeli was publicly put in the frying pan for the anger he had verbalized over the closing of the Institute in the Heredugu area, as well as for the defiance he had exhibited in not obeying the president's orders to stop all joint endeavors between the church and the mission. Finaba noticed that Dembeli was pretty much alone in the griddle for about an hour until the National Church president started in on a second young missionary. Company in the griddle was a little comforting, but it did not resolve the issues. Soon, however, the griddle was full as others were chucked in with the two young missionaries. Even some of the older missionaries who had given advice to Dembeli and the other young missionary found themselves being scorched as the president took over the meeting and expressed his views. It was not a happy, or healthy situation, as, one by one, missionaries and mission programs and activities were publicly "fried."

Dembeli did not help matters in the least when, after a couple hours of listening to the rampage, he told the president that it was time that he "closed his mouth and opened his ears to listen to others." That brought on a new tirade, and a well-deserved one at that. Some thoughts are better left unexpressed! Dembeli immediately saw the error of his ways and apologized, asking the National Church President's forgiveness for such a statement because he was aware of the fact that the purpose of the meeting was reconciliation and not battle. Still, Finaba mused, the statement did carry the sting of truth.

The second day, the mission field director presented the idea that the church and mission could work together and that a document could be drawn up that would define the areas of ministry and clarify what both the church and the mission's responsibilities would be to be able to function peacefully. After much debate and hours upon hours of discussion, it was decided that a committee composed of designated national church leaders and missionaries would meet and begin to draw up the document that would be called a "Working Agreement" between the mission and the church.

Over the next year and a half the committee met frequently to hammer out the issues and the wording of that agreement. Countless hours of ministry were lost as national church committee members and missionaries left their stations to go to the various meetings in an endeavor to put together a mutually acceptable document that would serve as a guideline for both church and mission. Dembeli saw the necessity of the process, but regretted the time it took him away from village evangelism.

At the end of the year and a half of negotiation, the American-based overseas director of the mission was scheduled for a trip to Africa. His journey would take him to Kurela, and a special service was designated for the signing of the "Working Agreement" which had been born out of conflict. For the next five years, the term set as the duration of the agreement, the "Working Agreement" ruled. The document served either to confine, or to clout activities, depending on the circumstances. The important thing was that the agreement enabled ministry to resume, even though a vehicle had not been purchased for the National Church president. During all this time that the conflict raged, the outreach ministry of the Gospel Team continued in the Heredugu area.

Before the "Working Agreement" expired at the end of five years, new leadership was in place for both the church and the mission. Peace had been achieved and the Church was growing, so it was decided that a small committee, composed of two nationals and two missionaries should go through the document and update it. The document was to be reviewed by the Executive Committees of both groups before being presented to the Missionary Council and the National Church conference for a vote of acceptance. The field director and Dembeli represented the mission, and the newly elected National Church president and vice president represented the church.

Unlike the "Working Agreement" which had taken a year and a half to draw up, the second agreement went smoothly and was readily accepted as a "Partnership Agreement." The interesting thing for Dembeli was not so much the name change, but the attitude that was reflected in the whole procedure. In the months prior to meeting to form the new agreement, Dembeli had sensed that during his personal devotions the Lord seemed to emphasize the prayers of the prophets as they confessed their sins, the sins of their nation, and the sins of their forefathers. Dembeli thought about the concept of accepting responsibility and repenting for sins of the forefathers that the prophet himself had never been involved in. One day as he was discussing missions with the field director, he asked him what he thought about the issue, and this opened the door to a whole new aspect of missions. The subject came up often in their ensuing conversations and prayers as they prepared the New Agreement proposal.

Several weeks later they traveled together to meet with the representatives from the National Church who would form the other half of the committee. On the way to the meeting they discussed what their response should be in relation to the National Church as they considered the prophets' approach to a positive relationship with a holy God. The results of their decision impacted the other two members of the committee in a powerful way. After spending time together in prayer, the four men felt prepared to begin work on the new agreement proposal. But the mission field director asked the men to wait, and he shared with them the issue of repentance that he and Dembeli had been discussing for the past several weeks. Then he said that on behalf of the mission he was asking the representatives of the Church to forgive the present missionaries and their forefathers for the wrongs committed knowing and unknowingly, willfully or out of ignorance, against the Church. Together the mission field director and Dembeli shared with them how they were aware of how at times the missionaries, past and present, had wronged the nationals, sometimes in culturally inappropriate ways that they were not even aware of, sometimes because of their lack of understanding, and sometimes because of pride or because they saw things only through the grid of their own culture. They asked the two nationals, as representatives of the National Church, to forgive and to accept the missionary staff as men and women who loved Jesus and loved His Church and loved the African people, but who had so often been wrong.

The two African Church leaders were so taken aback by such a repentant attitude that their initial response of was one total silence. Then the love of Jesus flowed through them to embrace the two missionaries as they extended forgiveness to them on behalf of their African brothers.

Having taken care of the main issue, the meeting could proceed, but Dembeli wondered later if the change in attitude was one of the reasons why the proposal did not meet any resistance and if that was why it became a "Partnership Agreement" rather than a mere "Working Agreement".

Ministry between the church and the mission began again, and God began to pour out His blessing in new areas as partnership became a reality. Things did not change much for the Gospel Team and Dembeli as they continued to minister just as they had before except that Dembeli was not called away to meetings as often as he had been during the days of the Working Agreement. Pastor Pita saw it as an opportunity to have Dembeli speak at the "mother church" in Heredugu, and asked him to step in and do some teaching. Sensing that the Lord was leading him in a different direction than usual, Dembeli decided to spend the time teaching on spiritual warfare. He went through God's Word and chose many portions of Scripture that talked about the issues of spiritism, the demonic, and spiritual warfare. Dembeli explained that he did not understand all the implications of what God's Word was saying to the Kuranko culture so he was just going to read the Word and explain as simply as he could what it said and then let the Holy Spirit speak to His people. The people asked that he continue the series in the evening and so once again Dembeli opened God's Word.

During the following week several individuals came to Dembeli with questions, and they began to face issues in their lives that they had not tangled with before. Some went to Pastor Pita and asked if Dembeli could continue walking through the Word with them so that they could gain a new understanding of what God had to say to them about some of the things their forefathers had taught them. So the series continued. Dembeli learned more and more about their beliefs as various ones came to seek God's answers to issues they had never dealt with before. Some in the church found new freedom in Christ and discovered that Jesus' love is much more powerful than they had ever imagined. They came to the realization that they could be truly free in Christ and that the "spirits of their ancestors" could no longer tie them down.

A General Conference of the National Church was coming up in a few months, and Dembeli was asked to present the same teaching to the conference that he had just presented to the local church. Interestingly enough, at the close of the second service Dembeli felt that the Holy Spirit was leading him to ask forgiveness for the sins of missionary forefathers just as he and the mission field director had done some time before with the two members of the Partnership Agreement Committee. When Dembeli obeyed the Lord and asked the Conference which was composed of pastors and delegates from most of the Churches in three different linguistic areas to forgive the offenses of past and present missionary staff, one of the pastors immediately rose to his feet and responded with words of forgiveness, love and encouragement to the missionaries. He thanked the missionaries for bringing God's Word, and for the sacrifices they had made to reach his people for Jesus. In a sensitive and understanding way he extended forgiveness on behalf of the Church, and barriers came down. A sense of unity and love prevailed for those who were willing to stand together at the foot of the cross. It was a unique experience for all present. When Dembeli shared the experience with the mission field director who had not been able to attend the conference, he was not the least bit surprised at the response of the Church, for he had been praying that God would move in a fantastic way to unite the hearts of His children from all the ethnic groups that were meeting at the conference. The Partnership Agreement was taken off paper and became a reality as pastors and delegates prepared to return to their homes to reach their people for Christ while ministering with a new spirit of oneness.

Chapter 21: Letting Go

As Dembeli was working to teach the men on the Gospel Team to analyze the spiritual atmosphere of a town, his focus was on how the people responded to the message of the Gospel. One of the towns where this first became a reality was the town of Dansoya. Dembeli and several team members had visited the town of Dansoya on several occasions, and Dembeli had built a solid relationship with one of the hunters there.

The Team usually stayed in one of the huts owned by the town chief, so they were not surprised when they arrived in town and he immediately indicated where they were to stay. Rather than have them stay in a hut as usual, the chief indicated that a three-room, grass-thatched house very close to his would serve as their temporary home while they were in town. The Team quickly settled in and then walked through the town greeting all their friends from previous visits.

Following the evening service, the Team visited with friends late into the night and then went to settle in for the night. There were no ceilings in the house, and sound carried fairly well throughout the whole house. Dembeli was a little concerned because there seemed to be a very lengthy conversation going on in one of the other rooms. The men told him not to worry about it, and explained that a man was dying and he had already called in the family and given his will orally, but now he and his wife were discussing their lives together. They were clearing their hearts of all "bad" that had ever passed between them so that when the time came for him to pass into eternity that he would not have to carry any evil load with him. Dembeli drifted off to sleep as the background conversation became more intense.

At about 2:30 AM a gun was fired just outside the door of the house where the Team was staying. That woke everybody up in a hurry, and the echo had not even died away when a man began to beat the chief's drum. Finaba had to chuckle at Dembeli's reaction when the two sounds merged into one. Dembeli had been asleep on the floor with his head close to the mud wall, and the huge drum was hanging on the other side of the wall—probably only about two feet from his head—so he got the full impact of its sound. He almost levitated from his position on the floor where he had been sleeping over to the edge of the bed where several Gospel Team members were stretched out, trying to go back to sleep. They assured him that everything was quite normal. An important man had died, and so the gun was fired. The drum was beating to announce to the people in the town that the man had gone into eternity. A few minutes later the death wail erupted, announcing to the town that the man's family was mourning his absence for he had gone into eternity, and they did not know where he was.

The noise was more than adequate to keep Dembeli awake the rest of the night, but it was the cry of the drum and the death wail that soaked into his being and challenged him that so many were going into eternity and had never heard that they could have their heads pulled, their feet planted on a path to an eternal refuge, and their hearts filled with the light of the Holy Spirit which would guide them to Heaven. The drum cried the rest of the night, and Dembeli knew it was a message that he would never be able to forget. The situation helped the Team realize the importance of what they were doing as they walked to towns throughout the whole area. It opened their eyes to the need to see beyond just the physical and to look at the spiritual needs of their people.

—

Looking down from his perch in the mango tree where he sat contentedly munching on a sweet juicy mango, the Storyteller observed a most interesting drama. Dembeli was teaching his sons to ride a two-wheeled bicycle. Their older sister, Faith, encouraged them and never seemed to tire in demonstrating how easy it is to ride a bike and the tremendous advantages of the mobility it offered. They were jealous of her skill, and each day their desire and determination to ride seemed to grow more intense.

For days Dembeli had been running along behind the bike, stooped slightly over so he could hold it steady with a firm grip on the back of the seat while the little guys pedaled for all they were worth. Sometimes the boys would wonder out loud if they would ever be able to ride their bikes. Dembeli and Faith would assure them that they would soon learn and that the frustration was all part of the learning experience. Dembeli shared with them about his experience when he was a kid learning to ride a bicycle. He recalled how he did well as long as he could go in a straight line. But for some odd reason roads have curves and bends, and there are corners to turn. Once as he pedaled his unsteady way along, he discovered that he was going too fast to make a crucial corner. Unable to balance through the turn, Dembeli piled his bike and himself into the middle of a thorny lemon tree. While telling the story, he chuckled as he recalled that at that time there was a popular song about the lemon tree: "Lemon tree very pretty, and the lemon flower is sweet, but the fruit of the poor lemon is impossible to eat." The kids laughed as Dembeli told them that the writer of the song had written from outside the tree, whereas he had discovered the lemon tree from the inside, and what he found was not very pretty. The cuts, scrapes, and bruises were all part of the process of learning to ride a bike, but once you have it mastered, it becomes pretty natural and you never seem to forget how to ride.

Once while the "bike training" was going on, Barnabasi, the Gospel Team leader, came by to add encouragement, and rightly so, for he was the first person ever to bring a bicycle into the town of Heredugu and had become a legend in his own right. He had also been the first to ever bring a transistor radio into town, and his name had gone down in oral tradition as a real innovator. Finaba just sat up in the tree and watched. Being invisible he was able to see things from a different perspective than those who were sweating in their attempt to learn to ride a bike. He saw the sweat streaming down Dembeli's face as he ran alongside the bicycle giving words of encouragement, challenge, and instruction. The Storyteller noticed that Dembeli would occasionally take his hands off the bike and let the boys pedal a few paces alone, but he kept running along with the bike so they would think he was still holding on. As soon as they started to lose their balance he was there to grab hold of the bike and to encourage them on their way again.

Soon Dembeli would let go and just run alongside the bike. Finally the day came when the boys realized that he was no longer holding on and so they took their bikes, jumped on, and took off –*alone!* Their joy was full, and their exuberance demonstrated their pride in their accomplishment.

The Storyteller watched Dembeli closely as his eyes followed the three kids racing their bikes, fancy free, around the yard, through the orchard, and down the hill to the river. Finaba saw the hint of longing in Dembeli's eyes, and suddenly it dawned on him why. As Dembeli watched his kids riding alone, he knew that they would never again need him to hang on to the bicycle seat, running alongside, offering encouraging words. They were on their own now and he had let them go. There would be bumps and bruises as they developed new skills, and there would be the triumph of new achievements as they experimented and learned techniques that Dembeli himself had never mastered. Finaba sensed that sometimes it is easier to hang on and run alongside, than it is to let go, because while holding on, you are needed.

It was not long until a motorcycle came into the lives of Dembeli's three kids. During their second Home Ministry Assignment, the children negotiated with Dembeli, and he paid half the price of a new motorcycle. The kids split the other half between the three of them, working to earn enough to cover their share. The motorcycle was even tougher on Dembeli's parental love than the bikes, because the stakes were higher. Dembeli had a motorcycle and he had talked to many others who also rode them along the rough trails. He had come to the conclusion that if someone told you that they had never fallen with their motorcycle then they probably had not ridden one very much. The Storyteller watched one day as Dembeli sent each of the kids in turn to a different town with a message for the pastor, a member of a TEE class, or the chief of the town. They never knew his anxiety when they did not return on time. Dembeli knew how long it would take the kids to accomplish their mission, for he had ridden those same roads himself, but he continued his work around the compound while he waited for their return. It was only the Storyteller who noticed the worry on Dembeli's face as he mentally took the journey in his mind to try and figure out what could have happened to his young messenger.

Meanwhile, the messengers thrilled with the ride and the new responsibility. They exalted in the honor of being trusted, and accepted each new challenge of off-road riding as only youthful hearts can imagine. Finaba still watched Dembeli carefully and he could sense the concern as the time passed. He also caught the silent sigh of relief when Dembeli's head would pop up at the sound of a little motorcycle coming over the hill way off in the distance. It seemed that Dembeli always heard it before anybody else, and he knew that little cycle was wound out to the maximum RPM's as his trusty messenger flew towards home. A couple minutes later, others would hear the bike and tell Dembeli a fact he already knew. The message had been delivered successfully. The Storyteller wondered how it is that parental love always seems to sharpen the hearing.

A few minutes later the little motorcycle, carrying its precious cargo, would come flying down the last hill toward home in a cloud of dust. Usually a victory lap around the compound, or at least through the orchard and around the soccer field, was in order. Then the messenger would come to a halt under the shade of the trees and relate the thrill of the ride into the town where he, or she, had been sent. The kids quickly learned to jump the bike, cross log bridges, sail through rivers without any bridges, and do just about anything one can imagine doing on two rolling wheels. They ran over snakes (live ones), hit chickens (live before the meeting), dodged goats, sheep, and cattle. They outran dogs, and even ran over rabbits at night so they could bring home something for the cooking pot. They rode through the rain and hail of the rainy season, and the dust and heat of the dry season, and in each season, came home covered with mud or bathed in dust. Although the dust gave them the appearance of having beautiful tans that would later be washed off, they wore it with pride as a trophy of their ride, and somehow managed to keep it long enough to brighten their dreams before taking a shower.

As they grew bigger, their rides took them farther and farther from home. They became living legends as they rode into towns where wheeled vehicles had never been. They served as front runners for Dembeli as he sent them to measure rivers that needed bridges for a road the Paramount Chief planned to build and wanted Dembeli's help. They were exuberant in the ride and built their own repertoire of stories that stand second to none in excitement and adventure. Dembeli thrilled in their accomplishments: after all, he had taught them to ride. But Dembeli was always concerned about their safety.

As Dembeli's children grew into faithful messengers, the risks increased and letting go became ever harder. After all, a cycle moves faster, jumps higher, goes a lot farther, and has more potential things to go wrong than a bicycle. And as the children outgrew the little motorcycle, a larger one was purchased to accommodate their size. The new and bigger cycle brought new challenges. It helped develop an independent spirit in each of Dembeli's children, and it also helped them learn about taking responsibility as they helped to maintain the cycle and keep it roadworthy under the most severe conditions.

One day the Storyteller noticed a group of men coming down the path toward the mission and recognized them as church leaders, so he jumped down out of his perch in the mango tree and joined Dembeli who was walking to meet them. After the greetings had been completed and the light talk was finished, the spokesman of the group presented their problem to Dembeli, asking for his advice. The Storyteller watched carefully, for this was not an easy problem. To Finaba's surprise he saw the same fleeting look in Dembeli's eyes as he had seen on his face when he was running alongside the bicycle encouraging the kids. Could it be that Dembeli was weighing the risks of letting go? Finaba's heart skipped a beat as he watched and wondered if Dembeli would accept the risk, or if he would opt for the easier route and hang on?

In his typical fashion, Dembeli began to ask questions to gain a better understanding of the situation. As usual in the Kuranko culture, everyone gave their perspective and had their say, but all looked to the opinion leader with respect as he explained the history of the problem and shared the present entanglements. Finaba watched carefully and saw the same look of determination on Dembeli's face as when he released the bicycle and he understood that Dembeli was going to take the risk of letting go. He would still be there to pray and to cry and to rejoice with the church leaders who were now beginning to take ownership of the Church, but he was going to set them free to go this one alone.

Finaba recalled times Dembeli had cried out to God on behalf of his children, wondering if he had done the right thing in letting them go in some tough situations, when it would have been so much easier to hang on just a little longer. Now as the pieces fell together, the Storyteller began to see that there would be times in the future Dembeli would face issues in the Church that would cause him again to pace the floor, pray, and cry, and wonder if maybe he should have held on just a little bit longer. Then his mind went back to that night so long ago when the Gospel Team had first gone out and he saw Dembeli crying out to God in prayer and was reminded that God had said, "This is my people. This is my Church. This is my Gospel Team. All I want you to do is disciple them." Now Finaba understood that discipleship involves risks for both parties and he knew what Dembeli would do.

Suddenly, in the midst of the conversation, Dembeli's head popped up and he cocked it to one side listening. A faint smile spread across his face, and though the rest of the group did not know what that meant and probably had not even noticed, Finaba knew that love heard a little motorcycle fully cranked out, climbing a hill outside of town, and he knew that a messenger was on the way home. Sure enough, a few minutes later others heard it too. Then, in a cloud of dust, with the horn blowing, there appeared a flashy little red motorcycle that did a victory lap around the soccer field and buzzed through the orchard. Dembeli chuckled as he watched, realizing that he no longer worried about the skill of the youthful riders as the little cycle went airborne over an ant hill and bounced its way to the shade of the trees. The rider had a scraped knee and mud from head to foot, but the most obvious feature was the grin that stretched from ear to ear—a look that told the world that the journey had been completed and the joy was full. Dembeli's confidence had not been in vain. The message had been delivered.

The victory lap completed, the messenger came to greet the elders. Finaba's attention was still focused on Dembeli, and he thought he saw a faraway look that seemed to focus on something in the future. It seemed to say, "Like the skinned knees and the mud splattered kids, this Church is going to experience some of the hardships, heartaches, and tough times, but they will come through it with the thrill of victory, and someday in heaven this Church will take a victory lap, and all the risks of having let go will be worthwhile."

Finaba watched in silence as Dembeli turned to the elders and encouraged them to take a step of faith and to make a decision. He assured them of his support and prayers. After all, Dembeli reasoned, what is the ride worth if someone is always hanging on and you never get to take a victory lap? Finaba watched as this principle was worked out in the following months and years of church planting.

Chapter 22: A Church for Dutsikoro

Several years before Dembeli arrived in Heredugu, a building had been built on the edge of town that was intended to be used as a clinic. For a brief period of time, two nurses had labored there in a ministry of healing. Although there was not a man on the station to help them follow up with evangelism and church planting, taking advantage of the medical ministry as a bridge to reach the people, it was a ministry that the people respected and appreciated greatly. The building, although it had been put into service, had never been completed. The Gospel Team acquired permission from the town leaders and the mission authorities and turned the now-empty building into a meetinghouse for their discipleship program. There they stored their materials and met to sing, pray, and practice their storytelling with picture sermons. However, the building stood as a constant reminder of their needs for a nurse in the area. Each Institute, and every Conference, the representatives from the Heredugu District would put into their report a major appeal to the mission for a nurse to come and minister among them again.

The Gospel Team would often discuss with Dembeli the need for a nurse, and it came up over and over again in a general way. At one particular session of the Gospel Team, several men made an extremely strong appeal to Dembeli for a nurse to come from America to help them, and they asked that he present their needs again to the mission at their council.

The Storyteller was not surprised that the subject of a nurse had come up again. But he was surprised when Dembeli asked the men how they could expect a nurse to leave her family far away in America and come to Heredugu and be separated from her loved ones and friends for three or four years at a time when they themselves would not move to a town a couple miles away. The Storyteller, along with everyone else on the team, was aware of the fact that Dembeli had been talking to several young men on the Gospel Team about moving to a nearby town in answer to the new believers' request for a pastor. None of the men wanted to go. They did not want to leave their family, their homes, and their farms and start over in a new community. Dembeli pointed out that they could walk back to Heredugu each week for the market and see their family and friends. He challenged them to consider the fairness of their request, and asked them if they could really ask God to answer their request for a nurse willing to sacrifice so much when they themselves were not willing to move even a little way from home and give up the convenience of living in the town they had grown up in all their lives.

Dembeli began to respond to their request with the same question each time they brought up the issue. Several towns in the area that the Gospel Team went to were asking for a pastor, and none of the men in Heredugu would leave their home town and go settle down in a nearby town because they did not want to move. It soon became obvious that it was going to be a real struggle to get the first one to move out. It was almost as if a mother had carried a child until the time of birth had come, and now she refused to give up her burden and bring a new being into the world. The mother church had done all the evangelism and now a daughter church was to be born and the Team members seemed so unwilling to let it happen.

God has His own way of working, and in His faithfulness he never gave up. He took the question concerning the medical need, and challenged the young man who asked most often about a nurse coming from America. God began to work in his heart about the fact that he had received some Bible school training and he was capable of leading a church, but he remained so unwilling to move out of his comfort zone to help establish a new church and reach a new area with the Gospel.

Dembeli often shared with the men some of his early experiences in the pastorate in a small, growing church in Michigan. He reminded them that the call had to come from God, because when the going gets tough, it is the call of God on your life that keeps you faithful in your place of service. The going will sometimes get tough, no matter who we are or where we are in life. Over the coming months, God began to work in the heart of Yakubu, who often came and asked Dembeli for work so that he could support his new wife, Pastor Pita's eldest daughter. Dembeli spent time with Yakubu one on one, just as he did with other Gospel Team members. Sometimes it was working on a project together, and sometimes it was hunting. Dembeli began to sense that God was dealing with Yakubu in a unique way, and so he watched to see what would happen.

Dembeli was not surprised when, at one of the Gospel Team discipleship meeting a few weeks later, Yakubu stated a call to ministry, saying that God was asking him to help out in one of the new church plants. Yakubu had been the first one in the church to have a Christian wedding when he married Musu the beautiful daughter of Pastor Pita. Musu, a vibrant Christian, was more than willing to go with her husband to plant a daughter church somewhere in the Heredugu District.

At the next Institute Yakubu stated his call to ministry. After some discussion, which involved Christians from the entire Heredugu District, he was asked to plant a church in Dutsikoro, a town fifteen miles away from Heredugu. The Gospel Team and Dembeli had gone there often and knew that there was a good core of believers there. The Team and Dembeli helped the District leaders negotiate with the Paramount Chief for a home in the town with a large veranda where the church could hold services. The Paramount Chief had often requested a pastor because in the one hundred twenty towns in his chiefdom there was not one church, pastor, or missionary. He wanted all three. He assured the church leaders from Heredugu that he would make sure that the pastor was cared for the first year. He promised that Pastor Yakubu would be given land so he could put in a farm and feed his family the second year. He assured the new pastor that the people would help make the farm due to the fact that they did not have money to pay a salary. Yakubu and the church leaders in Heredugu felt very comfortable with the arrangement ,and along with Dembeli they moved Yakubu into his new home in Dutsikoro.

It soon became apparent that the growing group of believers in Dutsikoro needed their own church building. They presented the need to the Paramount Chief and he gave them a nice plot of ground not far from his house. Some funds were available from the mission for a church building, so Dembeli and Yakubu met with the church leaders to design a building that would serve as a church as well as a parsonage. The Pastor and his wife would live in one half of the building, and the opposite end, which was just a big open veranda, would serve as the church building. Both were under the same galvanized metal roof, but a person had to step outside and around a wall to come into the church from the pastor's living quarters. So in a sense, the church and pastor's house were separate.

It seemed a pretty ideal situation, and Dembeli and the Gospel Team got behind the project. With the help of various men and children in the town, they were able to put up the structure the next dry season.

The dedication service was a tremendous witness to the people in the town of what God can do. They had already seen His blessing on the new pastor and his wife. Musu was already known as an outstanding woman of integrity in the town and was also known as one of the hardest workers among the women. The growth of the church and the number of new believers was a real encouragement to the mother church of Heredugu. Like the mother church, the believers in Dutsikoro met every morning just after daylight for a time of Bible study and prayer. The picture memory program which had been such a vital part of Yakubu's own training became an essential part of the ministry he led each morning to help get new believers established in God's Word. Musu's outgoing personality and commitment to Christ enabled her to teach a literacy class each evening and to minister to women in the town so that they could see the love of God revealed in a Christian family.

Dembeli and the Gospel Team made frequent trips to Dutsikoro to encourage Yakubu and Musu and the new believers. Better than any of the others on those journeys, Finaba knew the difficult times that Yakubu and Musu were facing as they struggled to make ends meet in a newly planted church without any financial backing from the District or from the mother church. The agreement had been that the Chief and the believers in the town would help feed the pastor and his family until the harvest, and then a swamp would be given to to the pastor and the church would help plant rice which would provide sustenance for the coming year. True to his word, the Paramount Chief gave Pastor Yakubu a nearby swamp. Dembeli and the others rejoiced with Yakubu to see the generosity of the people, but there were still difficult times ahead.

An additional piece of ground was acquired so that Yakubu and Musu could have a dry land rice farm as well. People helped Yakubu clear the forest and then the undergrowth was left to dry for a few days before he set fire to it to burn it off and clear the land for plowing and planting. This practice is referred to as the "slash and burn" method of farming. A section of forest is chosen as the site for the farm, and then the undergrowth is cut down using machetes. When it has dried adequately, it is set on fire so that the area around the trees is cleared. Most of the trees are then cut down with an ax made by the blacksmith out of scrap metal, usually a broken leaf spring from a truck. The smaller branches are then cut off, piled up, and burned. The bigger branches are carried to town to be used as firewood for cooking meals. The process is repeated each year, and thousands of acres of forest are cut down annually to make it possible for the people to feed their families. Once the land is cleared hoes are used to dig up the ground by hand. Swamps on the other hand, are replanted each year so there is not the devastation to the land that the dry, or up-land, farming method causes. However, the swamp still needs to be dug up, by hand, and planted. Dembeli often stated that he could not think of a harder way to provide for his family or to make a living.

Yakubu had two years of Bible School training in Kurela and was continuing his education by studying a Theological Education by Extension (TEE) course. Dembeli met with him every week to give instruction and direction. Dembeli became aware of some of the struggles the new pastor was having. Various members of the Gospel Team often joined him when he went to teach the class and they were aware of some of the difficult times that Yakubu and Musu were facing in the new venture and so they often went to encourage them. One Sunday morning they arrived just in time for the service and joined in the vigorous singing led by the pastor. One of the favorite songs of the new believers was a song of praise. The leader would sing a statement which would then be repeated by the group. This would be done twice, and then the leader and the "echo" would join together in singing the refrain. As the pastor told the story of the life of Christ in song, the congregation responded in a hearty echo. Only as the closing strains of the songs died away did Dembeli and the Gospel Team realize just how hard the week had been for the church planter in Dutsikoro. The refrain was still echoing when the Paramount Chief made up a new verse to the song as he took over the lead from the Pastor. The Paramount Chief sang, "The Pastor set the town on fire, let us not praise him." The echo followed, "Oh the pastor set the town on fire, let us not praise him."

Apparently, when Pastor Yakubu started the fire to burn the underbrush that the people had helped him cut down a few days before, the wind direction changed and carried the flames across the hills to the town. It burned several gardens and plots of banana plants, but fortunately did not catch any houses on fire. As the refrain died down the people cheered, the Paramount Chief grinned, and everyone knew that forgiveness had been extended and made public in a spontaneous and very original manner. Dembeli gained a new insight into leadership among the Kuranko people and their whole concept of forgiveness.

When the National Church of Sierra Leone received a grant from an organization outside the Church, the leaders decided to divide it by districts to allow the various areas the opportunity to use it as they saw fit, with no strings attached except that they give a report to the National Church Conference about how they used the money. The Heredugu District decided to invest their money in soap, an important commodity that was in short supply in the local market at that time.

The Heredugu church leaders brought their portion of the money to Dembeli and asked him to buy soap for them on his next trip to the coast. The cases of soap were then turned over to the Gospel Team leader, who happened to be a business man with a small shop of his own so there was ready access to the market built into their thinking. They discussed the situation with Dembeli about how much they should charge for the soap. He told them that if they sold the soap by piece for the regular market rate that it would take them too long to sell it, and suggested that they sell it for less. He said that he felt that they would then have a faster turnover which would enable them to re-invest their profits more quickly. They decided to sell it by the case for a little less, hoping that traders from other villages would buy it and still make a profit. As Dembeli had predicted it sold surprisingly fast, and the profits were quickly invested in more soap. Soon they had a real corner on the market, and they discovered that by keeping the price a little lower they were indeed able to sell a whole case to someone from an outlying village who would carry it back home, sell it for the regular market price, and still make a profit. The church, on the other hand, would be able to quickly reinvest their money and soon they were able to build up a savings account.

Dembeli had not been very excited when they had first approached him with the whole soap idea. As requested, he had given them some "marketing advice" since he was the one who would buy the soap for them when he went down country for supplies. The bookkeeping for the project was very simple. As the soap was sold, Barnabasi would deposit the money in a special bag for soap money which he kept in his little store. At the end of the month he would bring the bag to the pastor's meeting, and in front of everyone the bag would be emptied and the money counted. There were no written records and the District leaders and the Team did not expect them. When they had asked Barnabasi to keep the money, they knew he could not read or write, so they were trusting his integrity. Each month he would show up with the bag and they would count out the money in piles, each pile representing a case of soap sold. It was a very simple system since everyone knew how many cases of soap had been purchased on each trip down country. Over the years it proved to be a very reliable system and there were never any complaints about mismanagement of their funds. The District leaders would then ask Dembeli how many cases of soap he could buy for them on his next trip down country and they would give him enough money to fill that space in his truck. The rest of the money would be put back in the bag.

The reason Dembeli did not initially approve of the project was that he felt that the Church is not about making money. He felt that the Church should do stronger teaching on tithing and stewardship, and that the tithes and offerings which would come to the Church as a result, would be sufficient to meet the needs. The time came when the leaders began to realize that they were buying as much soap as could be conveniently handled on each trip Dembeli took down country, and a great discussion arose as to what could and should be done with the profits. They unanimously agreed that the profits should go to help the pastors and the new churches. They immediately reached into the fund and took out enough money to buy a bag of rice for Pastor Yakubu and Musu as a tangible expression of their awareness of the difficulty facing the young couple, and as an expression of the support of the District.

Over the years the soap fund was used to help all the pastors in new churches planted in the area, and sometimes it financed projects in established churches as well. It also paid for kerosene to put in the lamps for the evening literacy classes being taught in each of the churches.

—

Pastor Yakubu would often walk in from Dutsikoro, fifteen miles each direction, to Heredugu so that he could be part of the Gospel Team training session. He came in every other week, and the weeks in between Dembeli and the Team would visit him in Dutsikoro. Dembeli instructed him in a TEE class so that he could continue his training.

Sometimes a bridge would be washed out and Dembeli would find himself walking through the foothills of the Konko Mountains to Dutsikoro to keep the appointment with Yakubu and the members of the TEE class. On one particular visit back to Heredugu, Yakubu had a serious conflict with several men on the Gospel Team that did not end in town, but spilled over into the Team discipleship meeting. During the discussion, one of the men turned to Dembeli and asked him to intervene. As usual, Dembeli asked if the situation had been presented to the Team leader first.

When assured that it had been, he paused to listen more intently to the discussion. In the course of the heated debate that followed, Dembeli and Barnabasi, the Gospel Team leader, both intervened. Both men sensed that Yakubu was out of line in his action but that it was a situation which could be worked through if all involved were willing to communicate and let the love of Jesus overrule. Unfortunately Pastor Yakubu was very upset, and though he remained for the rest of the Team meeting, he left town without having resolved the conflict with his companions.

Finaba sensed the concern Dembeli and Barnabasi had for all involved as they discussed and prayed for the situation. They even debated taking a trip into Dutsikoro to resolve it. Both men knew Yakubu well, having hunted and worked with him in a variety of situations. They knew that there are times when God needs strong-willed people in the ministry to plant churches in difficult places where a man of lesser tensile strength would fold up and call it quits. So rather than go after Yakubu and call him back, or make a special trip, they chose to let the strong-willed church planter walk the fifteen miles back home all alone, knowing that they would not see him for another week when they were scheduled to go to Dutsikoro for Dembeli to teach him the next TEE class. Finaba sensed that it was not easy for Dembeli and Barnabasi to let Yakubu go, for he saw the heartache and the tears, but he also sensed that they felt God was still in control, for after all, it is His Church and it is His people.

A few days later, vigorous singing could be heard all through the town as the Gospel Team met to share the exciting events of the past week of ministry. There was laughter and some friendly joking, and then Pastor Yakubu walked in. Several on the Team had been planning to go to Dutsikoro with Dembeli the next day when he went for the TEE class, and they did not expect Yakubu to appear at all. Unresolved conflict still lay beneath the surface, so there was a subtle change in the atmosphere when he entered the room.

The meeting progressed well until it was time for Dembeli to lead the discipleship training segment of the meeting. Pastor Yakubu interrupted Dembeli and asked if he could say a few words first. He told how he had walked home after the last Team meeting and how he had studied in preparation for the sermon he was to preach Sunday. It seemed to him that God gave him the right message to share with his people. He was not scheduled to return to Heredugu for two weeks, but as he studied God's Word in preparation for the message he felt he was to share, God preached the message to him and told him that he had offended his Christian brothers back in Heredugu. He felt God telling him that he was wrong in what he had said and done, and that he needed to walk back through the hills and make things right, in front of the Gospel Team, with the brother he had offended.

In obedience to the Lord, Yakubu had preached the message to himself in front of the believers in Dutsikoro, and then the next morning he hiked back over the hills fifteen miles to Heredugu to be in the next discipleship session so he could get things cleared up between himself, his Lord, and his Christian brother. He had left early enough to walk that fifteen miles so that he arrived just a few minutes after 8:00 AM when the Team started the meeting. He asked the Team to mediate between him and the one he had offended. Dembeli felt that was more than adequate demonstration that his heart was in the right place. But Yakubu was not finished yet. In traditional Kuranko manner he walked over to the one he had offended and knelt in front of him to hold his feet and ask forgiveness. Before the task was ever completed, even before he could get to his knees, his brother offered forgiveness and restoration took place.

As Finaba looked over at Dembeli and saw the tears of joy in his eyes, he reached up and dried his own tears. Even a Storyteller can cry. What the Gospel Team leader, the missionary, and several elders from town had not been able to accomplish with sound advice, God had accomplished in a moment through the power of His Word. Restitution had taken place, relationships were restored, and nobody needed to tell Dembeli that the Discipleship Training session was over for the day. God had stepped in and taken over the training session with a living example of His power and His faithfulness.

As time passed, the work in Dutsikoro continued to grow, and God blessed Yakubu and Musu. They had a good harvest of rice and their home knew the happiness of a special little bundle of joy as their little family began to grow. As the Church grew, God gave Yakubu a heart to reach out to nearby towns, and he began to walk to other towns sharing the stories and picture sermons as he had been taught. Interestingly enough, it seems that we train others in the same way as we ourselves were trained. Yakubu had been trained in a very practical, "hands on" style of evangelism and discipleship, so he ventured out to share as others had shared with him. He took the picture memory verse program, led in morning prayers, and shared pocket-sized picture tracts with anyone who would listen. He taught others the wordless books, just he had been taught, and gave them a copy of their own to share with others once they were able to use it to explain the plan of salvation back to him. The picture Bible was his constant traveling companion, even though he himself could read both English and Kuranko.

Pastor Yakubu invited Dembeli and the Gospel Team members to assist him in some of his outreach, and Dembeli had the privilege of witnessing what God was doing through a blacksmith/hunter who had turned church planter. He watched Pastor Yakubu and the Team reach into new towns in a new territory and he saw the Gospel take root.

—

Thunder warned of a coming storm as the clouds began to roll in, carrying with them the rains that would end the dry season. A meeting was being held down country that had been scheduled to deal with a storm of a different kind, and Dembeli had the truck almost ready to go when a small delegation came to tell him about a new struggle that had developed in the fledgling Church in Dutsikoro. After some discussion it was decided to meet again in the morning before Dembeli and his family would head down country.

During his devotional time God spoke to Dembeli, but the Storyteller and the others did not have any way of realizing it until they met in the morning just prior to Dembeli's departure. The Gospel Team and church leaders saw the situation in Dutsikoro as priority, taking precedence over the meeting down country, and so they more or less assumed that Dembeli would take them in the truck to Dutsikoro, take care of the situation, return home and then head for the meeting down country a day late. Dembeli thought and planned that too, until God spoke to him that morning and plans were changed.

Finaba chuckled as the protests gained momentum when Dembeli shared his idea. You see, he was telling the men on the Gospel Team that they could go to Dutsikoro in his place and take care of the situation. He was instructing them to take God's Word and stand on it. He declared that God would honor His Word and they could go and adequately resolve the most difficult situation, if they would go in faith and not handle it as a cultural situation but deal with it as a spiritual issue.

Finaba suspected that Dembeli was letting go of the bicycle again and that he was trusting them to learn to ride by the power of the Holy Spirit, rather than by dependence on the one who ran alongside. What God had reminded Dembeli of that morning was that Paul sent Timothy to a daughter church with a message that Timothy's coming was every bit as good as if Paul himself were there. They would both have the same words to speak, for Paul had discipled and mentored Timothy, and they were both directed by the same Holy Spirit.

The Storyteller watched as Dembeli encouraged and assured the men that God could work in and through them every bit as much as He could through a missionary. They all knew he was willing to go, but somehow it seemed that God had timed it so Dembeli had good reason not to be present and he was opting out. He reasoned with them that he had been discipling them for several years and that they had a knowledge of the language and the culture that far surpassed his own. He assured them that the Lord would be faithful and give them the wisdom and discernment that they needed, even if Dembeli, as the discipler, was not there. After all, he reasoned, the ultimate purpose of the mentor is to turn disciples loose so that he does not have to be around all the time anyway, and those discipled must disciple others.

Two men were chosen to go to Dutsikoro. Dembeli and his family piled into the truck to head down country as the Gospel Team leader and his companion packed their own bags and began the fifteen mile hike through the hills to Dutsikoro. They were not at all confident in what they were doing, and not sure that they even wanted to do it, but they left knowing that it had to be done.

As usual, Finanba followed Dembeli down country. As the truck galloped along over the rocky road, and in places slogged through the mud caused by the recent rain, the Storyteller sensed that Dembeli was beginning to wonder if he had heard the Lord right that morning, or if he had been wrong in opting out of a tough situation. After all, God's voice had not been an audible voice. How could one be assured that the Team would hear His voice even if God did speak to them, and how could one know that the Team would maintain the purity of the teachings of God's Word if the situation slid into a totally cultural context? The Storyteller recalled hearing Dembeli tell the men many, many times in the past that we are first of all Christians, then we are Americans or Kurankos. He would tell them that he was a Christian American, because his loyalty was first of all to Christ and then to his heritage. He often challenged them that they should be Christian Kurankos for the same reason.

As the miles rolled by, carrying him in the opposite direction of where he really wanted to be, Dembeli felt again that affirmation from the Lord that it really is His people, His Church, His Gospel Team, and He is Lord of all.

The trip down country was great, but Finaba sensed that Dembeli longed for a phone, a two way radio, or some form of contact with the Gospel Team to assure him that all was well back in the foothills of the Konko Mountains. Dembeli probably "pedaled" the truck a little faster than usual on the way home even though he knew that the situation had either been resolved or destroyed already. He still could hardly contain his curiosity as to what had transpired, and he knew that he would find out all about it at the Gospel Team meeting in the morning.

As Dembeli pulled into town, the word spread quickly that he was back from down country. As fascinating as it may seem to an outsider, the communication system of the rural areas of Africa continues to be one step ahead of what anyone outside the culture can believe possible. Dembeli had seen the efficiency of the system often enough not to doubt its effectiveness. When he arrived in town the evening before a Gospel Team meeting, without any modern technology or communication system to inform them, the Gospel Team would all know Dembeli had returned home. They all knew that the discipleship training session would take place in the morning as usual, and they would all be there early the next morning.

Several men and boys followed the truck out to the mission compound to help Dembeli and his sons unload the truck and get resettled. The Storyteller saw them coming first and watched Dembeli carefully to see what his reaction would be to the two messengers he had asked to go to Dutsikoro in his place. They had already heard the truck from a long way off and knew that he was back. Apparently they could not contain themselves any better than he could, so instead of waiting until morning, they came that evening and shared with him how they had handled the situation. They rejoiced that everything had worked out wonderfully. The situation had been resolved. Peace had been restored. Most important of all, God had been glorified. Dembeli picked up a little bit of the sense of awe that the men felt when they realized that God had used them in a very special way to bring peace in an extremely difficult situation.

A couple days later Dembeli went to Dutsikoro to teach the T.E.E. class and discovered, not at all to his surprise, that the situation had been handled better than he could have handled it himself. Time proved that his analysis of the solution was accurate, for once the problem was resolved it became a stepping stone for growth for the Dutsikoro Church and for those involved. This was affirmed in Yakubu's personal ministry as well, as the Church grew and began to reach out to neighboring towns.

Chapter 23: Obedie and Tomala

The Storyteller often heard Dembeli recall some of the first trips he made with the Gospel Team into the little town of Tomala, eight miles out of Heredugu. There were only two Christians there who could read, so the others just sat and listened intently as God's Word was read and explained to them. One young man there, severely challenged by the dreaded disease of leprosy, had had some formal schooling before spending several years in the Leprosy Hospital down country. The disease was arrested, but left Obedie seriously challenged to support his family. Obedie, however, was a committed Christian, and with encouragement from Dembeli, the Gospel Team, and Pastor Pita, Obedie began to teach a literacy class every evening on the veranda of his home. Since Obedie could not attend the Bible school, Dembeli offered to teach him a Theological Education by Extension (TEE) course. He also encouraged him to lead the people in a prayer meeting each day so that they could use the picture association memory program that was being used in Heredugu. He pointed out that they too could hide God's Word in their hearts, even if there were only a few believers.

Over the months that followed, Dembeli sought to help others establish literacy classes in their towns because he felt that a church can never be strong if the believers cannot read God's Word for themselves. The literacy class in Heredugu, the mother church, needed to set an example for the other towns even if they did not have established churches due to the lack of pastoral leadership. Some of the Gospel Team members joined those literacy classes and learned to read. This enabled them to become even more effective in their outreach ministry.

The Gospel Team continued to go to Tomala as it did the other towns in the area, and it became increasingly apparent that God had given Obedie a special ability to lead the Christians through his giftedness in teaching literacy. Several young men learned to read very quickly, and soon when Dembeli, or one of the Team members, would refer to God's Word there would be the sweet rustle of pages as they located the portion of Scripture being read so they could follow along. Once they found the Scripture reading, they were asked to read it out loud for everyone. Often Dembeli would wait until everyone had found the passage in their Bibles before proceeding, and sometimes this meant a delay in the service as Obedie, Dembeli, or one of the better readers walked around helping others find the passage of Scripture. No one minded the delay, and everyone rejoiced in the fact that there were now those in Tomala who could read God's Word for themselves. Soon most of the men in the Church and a few of the women could read.

Pastor Pita and Dembeli made special efforts to spend extra time with Obedie and to encourage him. It was not long until Pastor Pita, with the support of the leaders back in Heredugu, approached Obedie and asked him to be the pastor at Tomala. Obedie was hesitant to accept such a position since he felt that he was untrained. Then Dembeli reminded him of the TEE course he had just finished and pointed out that he could teach the believers what he had learned. Dembeli also mentioned that he could continue to come to Tomala every week and help him with the next TEE course. That way Obedie would be able to stay one course ahead of what he was teaching the new believers, and they would all continue to grow together.

So a new church came into being in the Heredugu area, and all this happened while the conflict raged over the "Working Agreement". At the following Institute, Obedie was officially recognized as the pastor of the Church, and the Tomala people rejoiced that their request for a leader had been granted and that they could now have a church of their own.

The Tomala leadership felt that they needed a church building, so they designated several days for the people of the town to make mud blocks. Then they sent word to Pastor Pita, the District Superintendent, asking if other Christians would be interested in helping them put up the building. The Gospel Team and other believers from Heredugu, joined them to help put up the walls of their new church. Dembeli couldn't help build the church because at that time a work team from America was in Heredugu to help build a new home for Dembeli's family. Termites had built their own homes in the mud walls of the mission house and had tunneled out through the floors, window sills, and door jambs, practically eating the place up. When the old house was torn down, there was enough lumber salvaged to build one door frame and one window frame for the new house. So the termites had had their say, but a new house rose in the place of the old one.

Various business men and traders in the area asked if they could purchase the galvanized roofing pan off the old mission house when it was torn down because they wanted to build a new shop or extend an existing one. Others wanted to purchase the pan to build a new home for themselves. Dembeli discovered that he had a pretty hot item on his hands in the form of used roofing pans. One afternoon several Church leaders from Tomala arrived and asked Dembeli if they could have the pan for the new church building so that they would have a more permanent building than the grass thatched roof they had originally planned. When Dembeli presented the idea to the mission, the committee agreed to the request from Tomala, and Dembeli hauled the pan to Tomala in his truck. Even though Dembeli was not available to help them put on their "new" roof, they rejoiced in their good fortune. Dembeli did not even have a house to live in at the time since his old one was torn down and the new one was not built yet, so they did not mind at all that he could not help them. The Storyteller was there, and he witnessed the great rejoicing of the Tomala people when the pan arrived and they could complete their structure in style.

At the dedication service for the new church building, Dembeli was probably the only one that noticed that the walls bowed a little bit, that the rafters constructed out of saplings which had been cut down and carried in from a nearby forest were a little far apart, and that there were a few other structural problems. Finaba smiled to himself when he saw that Dembeli was not telling anyone, and he knew that Dembeli was proud of this church, built by the Tomala people. It was truly a church owned by the people of the town. Other than the used roofing pan from the mission house, no mission funds or financial assistance went into the building, and the people were also proud that it was their church—in spite of the bowed walls and the construction problems which they had overcome in their own unique way.

It was God's House, a place of worship and learning, and it was theirs by virtue of the fact that they had been the ones to design and build it. It consisted of four mud walls that were never plastered, openings for windows that never had a window or shutters, and a doorway that never knew the luxury of a door. Homemade benches and a couple of tables served the needs of the literacy classes and the morning prayers, and more benches were brought in by worshipers each Sunday. Now Tomala had a church and Obedie was their recognized leader. Heredugu also experienced a sense of pride: as a mother Church they had now given birth to two daughter Churches, and they could sense the satisfaction of a growing ministry in the area. There was tremendous rejoicing at the feast in Tomala on Dedication Day and no one needed to remind Dembeli that there was even greater rejoicing in heaven.

As he had done with Dutsikoro, and was to do with all the Churches that started up in the area, Dembeli met with the entire Church and discussed with them their responsibilities as a Church. Obedie continued his TEE classes so he could keep one step ahead of his people, and over the following years he continued to be the most productive literacy teacher in the area. The believers met each evening for a time of Scripture memory and prayer before they began their literacy class. Dembeli and Obedie challenged them to reach the rest of their town with the Gospel.

Dembeli also shared with them the vision to reach the towns around them. He reminded them that "sheep bear sheep" so they needed to win others to Jesus and reproduce, for that is the natural way to grow. But as "sheep bear sheep" so "shepherds need to bear shepherds." That meant that Obedie needed to reproduce leaders, and so from the little group of believers Obedie began to disciple apprentices who could lead a Gospel Team. They were challenged by the Heredugu Gospel Team to reach every town within five miles of Tomala, just as the Heredugu Team was doing from their town. They were also reminded that Tomala is eight miles away from Heredugu, and so if the Heredugu Church, through the Gospel Team, could plant a new Church in Tomala, surely Tomala could "bear some sheep" in the towns in their area.

Everyone recognized that Obedie's condition hindered him from being able to walk with a Gospel Team to the nearby towns. So several men from the Heredugu team offered to walk with the men from Tomala if Obedie would help train them. Obedie and the Tomala Church accepted the challenge, and the "sheep" began to reproduce "sheep". The shepherd took apprentices and turned them into shepherds. Interestingly enough, four of those apprentices went on to Bible School in Kurela and ended up returning to the area to pastor the new churches. God blessed Obedie's ministry in an abundant way, and the Tomala Church became a mother Church as well.

After Obedie had been pastoring the Tomala Church for eleven years, his brother died suddenly from an unknown disease and Obedie inherited his brother's wife and child. The Storyteller sensed Dembeli's heartache when Obedie sent word to him that he needed to talk with him. Finaba watched as the two men who had been companions in ministry for so long walked quietly out of town and paused under the shade of the trees. Obedie explained the situation surrounding his brother's death and the fact that with two wives he could no longer be a pastor. He was sending a letter of resignation to Pastor Pita, the District Superintendent, asking for understanding and continual prayer, for he realized the added weight of this new responsibility.

Dembeli expressed his appreciation to Obedie for his openness and honesty, and talked to him about his relationship with the Lord and his responsibility to lead the second wife to faith in Christ. Obedie gave affirmation to vibrant current faith in his walk with the Lord and rejoiced in the companionship and Dembeli's confidence in him. The presence of the Lord was very real as the two friends bowed together in prayer alone out under the huge trees that guard the little town of Tomala. Finaba sensed Dembeli's heartache when he expressed to Obedie his regrets that the District would be losing a good pastor and leader.

As they walked back into town, Dembeli asked Obedie how his business was going. Several years before, Dembeli had noticed how Obedie was struggling because of his condition and had challenged Obedie to create another source of income. As a result Obedie had invested in trade goods and had set up a little store on his veranda where people could purchase basic necessities. He also bought a few goats and ducks that provided a fine income for him when the young ones were sold in the nearby market at Heredugu. But perhaps the most beneficial investment was the plantation of coffee and cola nuts that Dembeli had encouraged him to plant. There was no school in town and so Obedie, as the literacy teacher, held a very important position. His young students helped him plant the seedlings and later were able to help him harvest the crops that provided for his growing family.

Obedie continued in his role as a literacy teacher and still carries great influence in the Church as he shares his faith and mentors younger men. His resignation affected his role as a designated leader, but did not hinder his desire to walk with God or to help train the next generation of leaders. Today the Tomala Church is full of men and women who can read God's Word for themselves largely due to the continuing efforts of Obedie.

Dembeli has often expressed joy when he has been asked to speak in this church. After announcing the Scripture reading, pages begin to rustle as believers find the right chapter and verse so they can follow along with the one Dembeli or the pastor has asked to read. Because people are learning to read, the Church has grown stronger because they can now read God's Word for themselves.

Dembeli has often thanked Obedie for his incredible contribution to the growth and development of the believers. He has often marveled that most of our pastors who have gone to Bible School have come out of this little town that was once well known for its powers in the demonic world. Now spiritual leadership has emerged, and the Church is taking a stand and leading the way as they present the truth of God's Word.

Chapter 24: Church Discipline

Pastor Yakubu continued as the pastor in Dutsikoro, and his wife, Musu, taught the literacy classes as he trained apprentices. Like the others, Dembeli taught him that "sheep need to bear sheep" and "shepherds need to bear shepherds". Yakubu began to walk to Dafeya, twelve miles away, where there was a big market on the tribal border of Kuranko and Sundan territories. Soon he was asking the Gospel Team to help him by going with him to encourage the one or two new believers in that town.

With the vision of a church planter and the stubborn heart of a man who knows what God wants him to do and simply will not give up, Yakubu began to make consistent trips covering that twelve miles either on foot or with a bicycle. On many occasions Dembeli and the Gospel Team were right there with him, but more often, he walked the lonely road to Dafeya alone. God was there and men began to respond and to be discipled as Yakubu himself had been discipled, and they began to gather regularly for prayer and worship. It was not long until they asked the Heredugu District to recognize them as a Church and send them a pastor.

As men and women gathered for a celebration service in Dafeya followed by a feast, Yakubu had the best seat in the crowd. He was home with the Lord by then, and would never again tread the paths through the hills. As God smiled on the celebration service, Dembeli imagined that He called Yakubu over and pointed down to a little town in the foothills of the Konko Mountains, reminding Yakubu that he had had a part in planting that Church. The lonely, dusty miles he had walked, the hunger he had endured, and the heartache he had known was worth it all, for there were people down there who had never heard the name of Jesus until one big brawny blacksmith/hunter, motivated by the Holy Spirit, began to walk through the hills sharing his faith in Jesus.

As the celebration worship service continued, there was no trouble hearing people praising the name of Jesus, their King of Kings. Someday they will stand with Yakubu in heaven and praise the Lamb they accepted as their Supreme Sacrifice because Yakubu had been willing to pay the price to carry the message of redemption through the hills in obedience to his Lord. Now they too had their feet planted on a road to an eternal refuge, because their heads had been pulled and they are His people, and His Church. Dembeli watched and wondered if maybe, as the day came to a close, Jesus didn't just slip his arm around the broad, powerful shoulders of that blacksmith/hunter and whisper, "Yakubu, well done." Dembeli knew that if that is what happened that day, in that glorious moment Yakubu truly knew that it was worth it all!

Back down in Dafeya, Dembeli and the Gospel Team had a tough time answering the questions and trying to explain to a new Church in Dutsikoro, and an even newer Church in Dafeya, why God had permitted an unknown, undiagnosed disease to take away the burly blacksmith/ hunter who had been their pastor, leader, and friend. Pastor Pita, Yakubu's father-in-law, probably explained it best when in his own simple way He said that God had finished building Yakubu' new home in heaven and so it was time for Yakubu to go and live there and leave the work among his people to those Yakubu had led to Jesus. He challenged the people that they needed to be as committed to the Lord as Yakubu had been.

Following the celebration of their new church, the believers in Dafeya sent another plea to the District for a pastor to teach them and to pick up the training that was incomplete when Yakubu went home to glory. A new church/pastor's house combination was constructed, following the pattern of the building in Dutsikoro. After much discussion and prayer, the District asked Pastor Pita, the District Superintendent, if he would be willing to move to Dafeya. Sensing God's call, Pastor Pita assured the District that he would move there with his family and pick up where Yakubu had left off.

The Heredugu Church and the District had no way of knowing that the National Church leadership down country would be upset with such a move. The National Church president argued that young men graduating from the Bible Training School should go to the new work that would require the pastor to put in a farm and work with the vigor of youth to make it big enough to support a family. The District stood strong in their resolve that that the more experienced pastor should go to the new work. They reasoned that the younger men should pastor closer to the mother Church so that experienced leaders could advise and help them until they were established and confident in the ministry. The Heredugu District leaders once again found themselves in opposition to the National Church President, but they stuck together. The Church leaders and Dembeli went ahead with their plans and moved Pastor Pita and his family down to Dafeya and helped them settle in to the newest Church in the District.

In cooperation with the Paramount Chief, Dembeli helped construct several bridges along the only road running through the entire area. The road needed to be open to vehicle travel year around, rather than just during the dry season months, so that basic necessities could be brought to the area markets each week. Dembeli may have had secondary motives for helping build the bridges, because if the road was passable Dembeli could drive the Toyota 4x4 down to Dafeya, and it would save several days of walking. This would free Dembeli and the Gospel Team up to invest time in some of the other Churches that were being planted in the area. Even with the bridges, in extreme rains the road was impassible and the Gospel Team and Dembeli found themselves walking the same road Yakubu had walked in establishing the Church.

Yakubu's passing left a big vacancy in Dutsikoro, but God is faithful, and he had another young man off-stage preparing for the ministry. As Obedie trained his apprentices, it was not surprising that some of them felt God calling them into the ministry. God is always one step ahead of us and a couple years before He had called a young man named Mansa into the ministry. Mansa, approached the mother Church at Heredugu about the possibility of going to Kurela as a student at the Bible school. After much prayer and discussion, the leaders felt that Mansa really did not know a whole lot about what he was getting himself into. Dembeli had taught them that anyone that they recommended for Bible school training should function in the Church before going to Bible school so that the student would know what ministry was all about. For this reason, they asked Mansa to come and be part of the Gospel Team for six months before taking off for Bible school. He consented to do that, and since he was still single he was able to move to Heredugu where he received valuable training in evangelism and outreach. Following six months training with the Gospel Team the District sent Mansa to Bible School in Kurela.

His years at the Bible School in Kurela were not always easy for Mansa, but the joy of finding a wife was one of the bright spots during those years of training. Then along the African grapevine there filtered the news that Mansa was not behaving himself at Bible School. District leaders heard that he was conducting himself in a manner that was not appropriate for a Christian. Several of the leaders approached Dembeli and asked him to take one of the men, whom they would chose, down to Kurela so that man could talk to Mansa and find out what was really going on. Dembeli agreed, and the designated member of the District committee joined Dembeli the next time he went on a mail and supply trip to Kurela.

While there, Dembeli also picked up the vibes that something was amiss. The messenger from the district found out some reliable information about Mansa's behavior, and the evening Dembeli and the other man returned to Heredugu, they held a brief meeting about how it should be handled. Again the District leaders came to Dembeli and asked for his assistance. They wanted to go with him on the next trip to Kurela and talk to Mansa and see if they could get the situation straightened out. Dembeli asked them what they would do if Mansa would not listen to them. They responded that they would pull him out of the Bible School because they had recommended him and he was spoiling their good name by the way he was behaving.

The Storyteller saw the look of doubt on Dembeli's face and realized that Dembeli did not really believe they would do such a thing. However, as the discussion progressed, Dembeli became convinced that these men really would bring Mansa home if he did not shape up. Then he recalled that in the past generation the Heredugu church had been the first Church in the denomination in Sierra Leone that had disciplined a man without calling in the National Church Executive Committee in to help make the decision. He also recalled that once they had become a District themselves, they had become the first District to discipline a man without calling in the National Church Executive Committee for advice or assistance.

Dembeli sat quietly and mentally walked back through the years to the crises that could have proved a turning point for the District. He remembered how Pastor Pita had come to him and asked how to handle a situation in which a Christian was living in sin that was known to the people in town. Dembeli asked what had been done about it already. Pastor Pita shared that he had approached the man on the subject, but that to his great disappointment, the man had simply denied everything. Now, as the man's pastor, he was coming to Dembeli for advice on how to handle the situation.

Dembeli recalled how he had told Pastor Pita that he could help him if the pastor and the Church would stand on God's Word, but that if it became a cultural issue he really did not have any advice for them. When assured that they would go God's way, Dembeli took the Scriptures, and the two men began to check it out. There under the shade trees they looked at God's pattern for discipline and affirmed that the purpose of discipline is always redemption. They discussed the Matthew 18 principle of confrontation in the Church. Since Pastor Pita had already confronted the man one on one, it was decided that he should take another man with him and ask the man again about the situation, not in an accusing way, but simply asking for truth. Pastor Pita asked Dembeli to go with him as the second person. After spending time in prayer, they walked in to town together to confront the man. The man denied all the accusations that were being made against him by people in the town.

As the two friends left the man's place, Pastor Pita expressed his confusion because just a few days earlier the court had found the man guilty, and he had been fined for the wrong doing. He was amazed that the man could deny it to Church leaders. He suspected that the man was denying it because he was a teacher employed to teach in a mission school and he was afraid of losing his job if he confessed that he was guilty. So the two men went back to God's Word and agreed that the next step was to be confrontation by a group of elders.

Pastor Pita went to the elders of the Church and the teacher was asked to meet with them. To Dembeli's surprise, the teacher once again denied everything, and the elders decided that they really needed to take the issue to the whole Church. Sunday evening the situation was presented before the body of Christ. Dembeli watched as Pastor Pita explained the Biblical purpose of discipline and how it should be handled because the goal of discipline is always redemption. Pastor Pita shared with the Church people the steps that had been taken to try and follow a Biblical pattern so that discipline would not be necessary. Several elders who had been in on the meeting with the teacher, confirmed what their pastor was saying and gave their view on what had taken place. Dembeli was amazed that the teacher sat and listened through all that transpired. Then Pastor Pita turned to the teacher and stated very simply that because the Church loved him they needed to discipline him. Silence.

That silence was finally broken when the teacher, now contrite, asked the Church to pray for him. He stood and confessed that for the past six months God had not been answering his prayers and he wanted God to listen to him again. This was the very same teacher whose pompous attitude in the past had offended many because he made them feel that they were not as good as he was because he was educated and they were not. Now he stood and humbly asked those very people he had looked down upon, to pray for him.

Redemption! As Dembeli sat musing, he recalled the months that followed that act of discipline in the Church. The teacher had submitted to the authority of the Church, but those in authority over him in the school system transferred him out of the area. After a couple years in another area, he came home to Heredugu and again took up the responsibility of teaching the children of his hometown once again.. The second time however, something was different in his attitude, for he had seen tough love demonstrated, and he had become an active part of the Body of Christ.

The Storyteller chuckled when Pastor Pita had to call Dembeli several times to bring him from memory lane back to the present. The present issue concerned a young man in training to be a pastor. The elders in the District wanted Dembeli to accompany them to go talk to Mansa at the Bible School in Kurela, and they wanted Dembeli to have a place in the truck to bring Mansa home if that proved to be necessary. After spending time in prayer for the situation, and praying that it would not be necessary to bring their student home from Bible school, the elders and Dembeli each went back to their homes.

A full moon smiled on the group of Kurankos that sat on the steps of the chapel at the Bible School compound just outside Kurela, but there were no smiles in the group. In the course of the discussion, the elders each shared with Mansa what they had heard and what had been confirmed to them by trustworthy witnesses. They reminded him that they had recommended him to the Bible school, that he represented his own Church, the mother Church, the Heredugu District, and that they would not have their name spoiled by a man who was walking in disobedience to God. They spoke of his inappropriate and shameful behavior and asked him to make a choice—shape up, or pack your things and return home. They asked Dembeli if he could wait an extra day to give Mansa time to pack up his belongings for the trip home. As Dembeli assured them that he would stay if necessary, he mentally reprimanded himself for ever doubting that the leaders of the District would take such a strong stand.

What followed was almost a repeat of the disciplining of the teacher a couple years before. Mansa humbled himself before God and the Church leaders and together they prayed. Dembeli watched as the Church leaders let God's grace just slosh all over them and the student, and unify their hearts in Christ.

In the days that followed, Mansa's attitude radically changed. After his graduation, the District asked him to step in and fill Yakubu's place as the pastor in Dutsikoro. A few short years later he was elected District Superintendent, a position that he held until the war in Sierra Leone drove many of the Kurankos from the Heredugu area across the border into the neighboring country. Rebels broke his arm and destroyed his property, but Mansa never again left his priorities and stands today as a witness to others of what God's mercy and protection can do for a man who is totally committed to Him.

Hardships faced during the war claimed the lives of many of the older generation who no longer had the physical stamina to endure the struggle and disease that accompanies such destruction and devastation. The section chief and the town chief from the Tomala area both passed away as a result, and new leadership needed to be set in place once peace resumed. Mansa' family asked him to represent them and stand for election as the section chief. Although much younger than the other candidates, Mansa was elected to the position of Section Chief and today serves in a position where he leads his people in establishing priorities to redevelop the area following the devastation of war. Under his leadership a school has been built in several towns in his section, and several new churches have been established. Among other programs, he continues to encourage pastors and teachers to educate the youth of the towns in the area, and he has become a key to development in his area.

Chapter 25: Growing Pains

Pastors could not be trained quickly enough in the institutional Bible School to meet all the demands of the towns asking for churches. This situation caused the Gospel Team to seriously consider again how far they could reach out and what their responsibilities should be. Towns far beyond the area the Heredugu Gospel Team had designated as reachable heard about what they were doing and began to send requests asking them to come and teach them as well. The Storyteller watched Dembeli struggle each time another genuine call would come, and he heard the discussion within the Gospel Team about how they could not spread themselves any thinner. Dembeli and Barnabasi, the Team leader, spent a lot of time together discussing the situation and finally decided that they had to maintain their resolve in order to be effective. The illustration of the farm used in the earlier days of the Team's ministry was often referred to. Everyone recognized that if the farm was too big they would not be able to care for it adequately, and the second state of the towns involved would be worse than the first.

It was decided that in addition to reaching their usual towns that the Team should help the pastors in the newly planted churches. When Dembeli and some of the Team members were gone to help a pastor for special meetings, the Gospel Team members left in Heredugu would divide the responsibility of reaching the towns so that each of the men would know where they needed to walk to while the vehicle was being used elsewhere. They always went out in pairs or in a small group, but their willingness to take on the added responsibility made it possible for a couple of men to travel with Dembeli to help the new Teams in the new Churches such as Tomala and Dutsikoro.

The little town of Mesenya was only about three miles away from Heredugu. The seeds of the Gospel had been planted there a generation before, during the ministry of Jake and Ruth Schierling, but those seeds had not taken root. The Gospel Team caught a vision for the town and began to go there consistently. When Dembeli was gone to help in another area, some of the men from the Heredugu team would walk to Mesenya to keep the promise they had made that somebody would be there each week to share the story of the Gospel with them. As they went through the picture Bible, the Gospel Team would remind the people that one day at the end of the teaching, they would ask them which road they were walking on. The people felt that there were only two roads to choose from: Islam and the Way of Jesus. The Gospel Team carefully shared and listened and answered questions. They went through the Picture Bible several times teaching deeper truths each time. When they felt that the people were ready to make a decision they told them that when the teaching came to the death and resurrection of Jesus, they would ask the people to let them know which road they were walking on.

When the people of Mesenya had gone through the whole series of picture sermons, probably for third time, they felt they were ready to make a decision. Every adult male, with the exception of the town chief, responded that he was going to walk the Jesus Road. The town chief had given his approval when the Gospel Team first asked to share the Gospel in his town. The Team sought out the opinion leader so that he would be well informed about what they were doing. But when the time came to decide, the town chief felt that he was too old to change from the ways of his forefathers. Although he gave his approval for the others to follow the Jesus Way, he decided that he would stay on the way of "those who had gone before".

On the designated day, the Gospel Team joined the people from the town and began the construction of their church building. They had been meeting outside in front of the chief's house, but with the rainy season coming on they needed a better place to meet. A building of their own would also provide a positive identity for them as a Church. Some of the men mixed the mortar while other shaped the mud blocks. Digging a big hole in the ground, they poured water in it and then covered it with straw. After a sufficient time had lapsed, the men stomped around in it until the mud and straw were mixed to the right consistency for bricks. The mud, with the straw mixed into it, was then taken over to the second group of workers who dumped it into wooden forms that had been soaked with water saturated with certain leaves that kept the water slimy to prevent the mud from sticking to the wooden frame. A bucket of the slimy water was kept on hand to wash the mud out of the frame after each brick was made.

A few days later, while the brick continued to "bake" in the hot tropical sun, the men from Mesenya and the Gospel Team from Heredugu headed off into the bush to cut young saplings and vines to build the framework for the roof. Others went to cut grass that would be used for the thatch. Bamboo poles were also cut to be used for benches. These poles were later tied in place above forked sticks that had been placed strategically to serve as legs for benches. Once the bamboo was tied in place with the vines, the benches were ready for the worshipers.

The next building day was designated as the day that the church was to be constructed. The Storyteller wished he could step into reality and join in the fun as the bricks, now dried in the hot tropical sun, were laid row upon row to form the walls. They had decided to make the walls less than three feet tall so that they could also be used as benches. The women prepared a feast, and the town resounded with joy and laughter as the church building took shape.

When the walls reached about three feet high, forked sticks were stuck in the ground so that they could bear the weight of the roof. The space between the walls and the roof was left open for the breeze, and then the thatched roof was constructed to keep the rain out. Rejoicing was the order of the day as tired bodies piled into the truck and the Gospel Team and Dembeli headed for home.

Little did they imagine that in a few short months they would be called before the conference delegates by the National Church president and reprimanded because they had built a round, grass-thatched church instead of one constructed according to the plan that the church leaders and the missionaries had in mind when they outlined a program for financial assistance from the mission some years earlier. Dembeli found himself in the frying pan again, but this time it was rather short-lived because the mission had run out of funds that had been available for the building of church buildings that year. Besides that, Dembeli was in total agreement with the Heredugu District for having built the little grass thatched church in the first place. After all, he had helped build it. He reasoned that the Church in the area should build the first church in a town up country. Then it would be their church, and it would stand as a monument to the fact that they wanted a church. He felt that this would encourage ownership in the Church, and he reasoned that if it fell down it was their loss and they would know how to handle it. If they outgrew it and the mission had funds to help them enlarge it, that was fine, but why not build a round church where the devil couldn't corner the people anyway?

Later, the Mesenya congregation did outgrow their little round church. The Storyteller observed that the frying pan must not have been too hot the first time because when the people of the town asked for help building their new church, Dembeli and the Gospel Team took a few more days to help. During the next few weeks they were able to build another mud block church. This one also had a grass-thatched roof, but it was square and seated about twice as many people as the first one had.

When the square church fell down a couple years later, the mission did have finances available. Mesenya made an appeal for help and the mission, under a new matching grant program that had just gone into effect, was able to provide enough galvanized metal to put a more permanent roof over the new structure they had built. The inside of the church has not changed much over the years. The bamboo seats still hold the people, and boards roughly hewn with ax and adz to form a crude pulpit still hold the sacred Word as the pastor preaches.

Even more important, the people's hearts have not given in to the demands for material comfort and they still gather to worship the same risen Lord that motivated them to build their church in the first place. Before the war the church stood as the only building in town that had a pan roof. Lacking in paint, windows, or finery, the little church blended in with its surrounding and stood as a quiet testimony to all who passed by that this was a Kuranko church. It is in a Kuranko town, where Kurankos worship and serve a risen Lord. Dembeli concluded that our heart attitude is what the gospel is all about, and the attitude demonstrated in worship in this little mud church was beautiful.

Pastor Pita, after getting the Dafeya church established and training lay leaders after Yakubu had gone to heaven, found that he was ready to retire. He returned to Heredugu, but the people at the mother Church asked him if he would help them by pastoring the Mesenya church. He ministered there until God called him home just prior to the war in Sierra Leone. His faithfulness stands as a challenge to the younger men, who, at times, may have seen the struggle as a burden too great to bear until they considered his life and testimony and were encouraged to hang in there a little longer. No matter how tough things got or where he was, Pastor Pita could always be counted on to preach the Word.

The Storyteller heard Dembeli comment many times that he was so thankful that Pastor Pita had accepted Christ when he was young and that he was among those who formed the first group of believers in the Heredugu area because Pastor Pita was a rut person par excellence, a plodder of the first degree. As the leader of the district that had some serious conflicts with the National Church president, as well as some personal clashes with the president, Pastor Pita was never ordained this side of glory. Yet in the midst of even the greatest difficulties, he never used the pulpit as a platform to air his views or to degrade the leadership that disagreed with him so strongly. On occasion his heart would be so heavy that he had a tough time preaching. At those times Dembeli marveled at the simplicity of the message Pastor Pita would present. He would simply take God's Word and read it to his people, then he would explain in his own words what it meant. He would paraphrase it so they could understand it more easily, and then he would read the Word again before closing in prayer. He wanted his people to be saturated with the Word. He often would sit down by someone else who was hurting and simply love them to Jesus. There are many in the heavenly kingdom today because the plodder of all plodders kept on plodding for Jesus.

—

For some time, the Gospel Team and the pastors had been discussing the possibility of reaching the largest town in the area, in spite of it being far beyond the five mile radius to which the team had committed themselves. Due to the fact that Dembeli had a vehicle and Dugusigi was on the road to Kurela, they felt that they could easily schedule consistent services there and use the vehicle to enable them to accomplish their goal of planting a church in the town where the Paramount Chief lived. As they discussed the towns that had sent requests for them to come and share their stories of Jesus, the decision was made that they should work to plant a church in Dugusigi. It was the largest population center in the area, and it had the potential of playing a key role in opening the area to the Gospel. Several elders in the church suggested that since there were not many pastors in the District with Bible school training, that it might be wise to request a pastor from another area to come and help the Gospel Team. He could live in Dugusigi so that there would be a resident example there. The Gospel Team could work with him to help him reach the town and realize the full potential of the opportunities there.

The elders reminded Dembeli that the first missionaries in their area had been stationed in Dugusigi long ago and that the house they had built there was still standing. The Storyteller could have given a pretty accurate history of the events of that time had he been able to verbalize it. Jake Schierling had pointed out the property to Dembeli on one of those first trips when Jake brought Dembeli into the area to visit. Dembeli had noticed that the fruit trees the early missionaries had planted were still standing and bearing fruit. Sadly enough, the efforts of those early missionaries had not taken permanent root like the trees they had planted, and as a result there was no Church in the town that had been the home of missionaries for such a brief period of time so long ago.

As usual, Dembeli began to ask questions, and he soon discovered that there had been some resistance to the missionaries' attempts to plant a Church in Dugusigi. Another organization had come in with an offer to build a school and a clinic, so it seemed that the mission was slowly pushed aside. The Storyteller mused that it had not been done in a harsh manner, but just in a subtle change in attitude that hinted that the missionaries could move on and that everyone would be just as happy. There was no open conflict, but then there were not many results of ministry either. The mission had decided to move on. They selected the town of Heredugu, seventeen miles further down the road in the next chiefdom, where they built a house on the hill near the edge of town. Little did they know that in a few short years the British would combine five chiefdoms in the area, and they would find themselves under the leadership of the Paramount Chief in Dugusigi once again. After a year or two in their house on the hill near Heredugu, the missionaries changed their location to a site just across the little creek outside of town where they built a more permanent dwelling.

The Chief in Heredugu accepted the missionaries and did not have a problem with them moving across the creek. He leased land to them for a mission station. After all, Heredugu had once been located on a hill in the opposite direction of the present location of the town, but sickness and other problems had struck. They felt that the spirits were not happy with them living there so they, as a whole town, moved about half a mile to the present location where they found water even more accessible, and the spirits kind to their endeavors. Why should not the missionaries move a little bit until they found a place to their liking?

A new generation was on the scene now and it seemed that it was time to try again to plant a Church in Dugusigi, especially since some of the people there were requesting it. The pastors and delegates went to conference with the hopes that someone would come and help them in their efforts to reach Dugusigi with the Gospel. The president of the National Church had been born and raised in Dugusigi, so when the suggestion was made he supported the idea and was instrumental in stationing one of the new graduates from the Bible school in the town. He went so far as to let the young man and his wife live in his house next to his mother's home in Dugusigi. For many it seemed an ideal arrangement, since the young man was also going to receive a salary from the National Church Conference. The Heredugu District accepted the approach, hoping that a new Church could be planted in a way new to the District. The District leaders soon discovered that the undercurrents of conflict that permeated the president's leadership would find their way into this most recent endeavor as well. The National Church President felt that the best way to plant a new church was to station a man there and pay him to do the job. He reasoned that if the new pastor was on an adequate salary he could accomplish the task without other distractions. The President got behind his own idea and told the Heredugu Church and District to help with the salary because it was extremely important that he, as the president, see to it that there was a church in his hometown.

Dembeli could only sit and watch events develop, and along with many others he hoped that the outcome would be positive for the Church. Dembeli and the Gospel Team rejoiced as they moved Hiram and his young wife into the little house on the outskirts of Dugusigi. The Gospel Team had led several people to Christ and were already holding regular services in Dugusigi. They had laid the groundwork with the Paramount Chief and the people in the town so Pastor Hiram had some believers right from the beginning who would stand with him as a core group for the new Church. Pastor Hiram joined the Gospel Team in some of their outreach so that he could gain a thorough knowledge of their ministry in the area and how it worked. As a result he built a solid friendship with the men who would be coming to help him in Dugusigi.

The Gospel Team traveled frequently to Dugusigi and helped Hiram with the services. They spent time walking through the town with him, sharing their faith in Christ with anyone who would listen, just as they did in the other towns they were witnessing in. Soon, the small group of Christians had grown and they needed a bigger meeting place than the tiny veranda on the front of the house where Hiram was living. On one particular visit, the elders of Heredugu Church, Dembeli, and the Gospel Team went with Hiram to meet the Paramount Chief with the request for a bigger meeting place for the growing number of believers coming to the worship services. The Chief offered one of his houses that had a large veranda and pointed out that he would soon be building a large meeting place where his court would be in session during the week. The facility would not be used on the weekends, and the church would be free to meet in the new courthouse building on Sundays. The regular daily prayers and the literacy classes could continue to meet on the veranda.

It was a time of great rejoicing for the church in the District, but the undercurrents with the National Church president put a little bit of a damper on their enthusiasm. There seemed to be a constant conflict over housing between the pastor's family and the National Church President's family. There was also the apparent attitude on the part of the President that, because of his position, and the fact that he had found a man to be a church planter in Dugusigi, he would be the one to give direction to the work there. At first, the conflicts seemed trivial in light of what was taking place. Even though the National Church president seemed to want to call all the shots in relation to the Dugusigi church, it seemed like a side issue in light of the growth of the church in Dugusigi. The district leaders continued to add encouragement and give direction to the ministry, often ignoring the National Church President's dictates when they did not fit in with what was happening on the scene.

Pastor Hiram and his wife caught the vision of teaching the people in the new church how to read, and started literacy classes for young people who could not attend the local school. Women who had never been given an opportunity to learn made up the class that Hiram's wife taught. Once a week Dembeli traveled to Dugusigi to meet with Hiram and instruct him in a TEE class one on one. As soon as the first course was completed, Dembeli encouraged Hiram to teach it to some of the young men in the town while he continued on in the second course himself. Dembeli reasoned that Hiram could stay one step ahead of those he was teaching by continuing in TEE himself, thus building a solid foundation of Biblical knowledge in the church.

Hiram said that he would consider and pray about the idea and talk to some of the men in town to see if he could even find enough interested who could already read and would be willing to make the commitment to meet with him as a class once a week. The next week when Dembeli visited

Dugusigi, he met an excited pastor. He had visited with his friends in town and discovered that several schoolteachers and the head nurse from the clinic were eager to take him up on the offer. They wanted to know when they could get their books and start their first TEE class.

In the following months rains sometimes flooded the road or a bridge was washed out and caused Dembeli's regular visits to Dugusigi to be delayed. But the new pastor continued to meet with his class even as he waited for Dembeli to show up for his own class. He found himself being stretched in his effort to keep one step ahead of his own students, but it was a growing time and the Church was progressing. People were learning to tithe, and the even bigger veranda on the house offered by the Chief was beginning to prove too small. Now there were enough people who could read among the worshipers that songbooks and Bibles were purchased with the money collected in tithes and offerings, and distributed to those who could benefit most from them. It seemed that the hopes for a church in Dugusigi were finally becoming a reality.

The Paramount Chief was well aware of what was taking place in his whole chiefdom, and he certainly did not miss the fact that the Church, although still small, was sending it roots deep into the hearts and lives of some of the people in his town. He could hardly miss the fact that the Church was faithfully meeting because the rim from a seven-ton truck tire had been hung by a wire from the low hanging branch of a tree near the house he had offered as a meeting place. When that rim was struck with a piece of iron, it became a church bell that called people from all over town to come and worship.

Sometimes the Chief himself would join in the services just to see the progress and to gain a better understanding of what was taking place in his town and throughout his chiefdom. Following the service one Sunday morning, he took Dembeli and some of the Gospel Team members and the pastor aside and shared with them his vision to someday have a small hospital in his town. This was a dire necessity since the closest government hospital was a full day's travel away in Kurela, and his people were struggling without proper medical facilities. He asked Dembeli if there was any possibility that their mission could provide the personnel to operate the clinic if he and his people would build the facilities. He offered to build a residence for a missionary family right alongside the new clinic.

It was an offer unlike any that Dembeli had ever faced before, and the elders in the Heredugu Church encouraged him to see if there was any possibility of such a thing ever happening. They reminded Dembeli that they had been making requests to the mission for a nurse to come and live in Heredugu for many years. They said that if the mission would send a nurse or a doctor to Dugusigi, it would meet the needs of the area and they would be satisfied even if the doctor did not live in their town. The Storyteller chuckled to himself as the Gospel Team members spoke their piece, for he sensed that Dembeli knew that they were ganging up on him with an idea that he knew he could do nothing about personally other than to present it to the leaders of the mission. He assured the Paramount Chief and all the others involved that he had heard their request and that he would present the idea to the overseas director who would soon be coming to visit Sierra Leone.

The conflict over housing for the pastor seemed to be coming to a head as the National Church president continued to dictate his own agenda to Pastor Hiram. The situation was complicated since Hiram and his family were living in the National Church president's house. Hiram came to Heredugu to share the situation with Dembeli and the church leaders, and said that he was going to have to move. God was blessing his ministry but he felt that he could no longer handle the tension and his wife was to the point that she did not even want to deal with the issue any more. She was ready to move back home to the district on the southern side of the Konko Mountains. The Team and the leaders in the District agreed to try again to help. This time they decided that it was necessary to help Hiram find a different home in Dugusigi and assured him of their support and of their appreciation for the tremendous ministry he was having there.

In the meantime, the Overseas Director from America arrived in Sierra Leone for a brief visit on his way to Nigeria. When the idea of a small clinic in Dugusigi was presented to him, he explained that it would not be possible for the mission to become involved in such a program. Dembeli had discovered, in further talks with the Paramount Chief, that a cabinet member in the Sierra Leone government who had been born and raised in the chiefdom, had gone to England for advanced training. He had returned to Sierra Leone and was presently holding office in the capital. Because of the contacts he had made while obtaining his doctorate degree in England, he had been able to acquire funds from a firm there that would donate thousands of dollars worth of equipment for the clinic, provided there were personnel to run it. There was a fear in the mission that even a small hospital would become "the tail that wags the dog." So, the Overseas Department in America was not interested in becoming involved

222

in the project, even if the facilities were constructed and the equipment was provided. The recruitment of trained personnel was never easy, and they did not have anyone in the process who would fill the needed role in such a hospital or clinic. The Overseas Director felt that institutions have a way of becoming a priority over other ministries, and that the recruitment of personnel to run an institution and the finances to maintain it would be a drain to the other programs. If a clinic were started, the mission would be committed to its continual operation and would not be permitted to come up short staffed or short on finances to keep it going. He reasoned that an institution is a long-term commitment, and often staff from other ministries would have to be taken out of their positions to keep it going.

The Storyteller saw the disappointment in Dembeli's eyes, but he also sensed that Dembeli knew that what the director was saying was true for he was speaking from a much broader perspective than just the one hospital or clinic. It did seem however, that a golden opportunity was slipping through the hands of the mission, and Dembeli knew that if the mission did not capitalize on this opportunity, someone else would. He reasoned that there still was the church, and it was doing well in spite of the conflicts with the National Church president.

Several weeks after the Overseas Director left, Dembeli was walking through the Heredugu market, greeting friends from many towns in the area who had come to buy, sell or trade their wares. He saw Pastor Hiram and wondered what had brought him to the market. He soon discovered that the National Church president had paid another visit to his hometown, and a serious conflict had developed between Hiram's family and the family of the president. A brief meeting was called with the elders of the District, and Pastor Hiram shared that he felt that he would have to move immediately. The elders assured him that they had already talked to the Paramount Chief and that a new home was available to him. Finaba was the only one who picked up the feeling of utter devastation in Dembeli's heart when Hiram informed the church leaders that he did not mean that he needed to move to another house in Dugusigi, but that he meant that he was going back to his home in the southern District on the other side of the Konko Mountains. His home District had recommended him to the Bible school, but now his wife could no longer tolerate the constant conflicts with the president and they needed to move on because they could see no resolution to the conflict. They felt that their home district would have a place for them to minister.

Dembeli and the Church leaders tried to encourage Hiram. Dembeli began to ask questions to find out more about the deeper currents that were running below the surface. Hiram shared that his wife had already taken public transportation and was headed home to Feyan. He was left alone to pack up and then join her back in their hometown on the other side of the mountains that separated the two districts of the Church among the Kuranko people. Dembeli and Hiram realized that there were a lot more pieces to pick up than just the material belongings that his wife had left scattered around the house when she left.

Without leadership, the Church in Dugusigi dwindled. The TEE class Pastor Hiram had taught melted into oblivion. The literacy classes taught by the pastor and his wife were soon forgotten. The conflict had scattered "pieces" all over, and no one was there who could pick them up. Sadly, the Church began to die.

Oh, the courthouse was still there. The truck tire rim still hung from the same branch of the mango tree, but it no longer sounded out a cheerful call to prayer and worship each day. The Bibles and the hymnbooks were stored away in hopes that someone else would be found to pick up where Hiram had left off. But the conflict had sent its ugly tentacles around the new church and slowly choked out its vitality. It was left without anyone willing, or strong enough, to take hold of the leadership role, tangle with the issues, and come out on top, so it died a slow, but natural death without leadership.

Having sensed that the mission was not going to be able to respond to his request for personnel to staff the clinic, the Paramount Chief approached another organization and put the request before them. Interestingly enough, it was the same one that, a generation earlier, had made the promises that had been instrumental in directing the missionaries out of Dugusigi and into the Heredugu Chiefdom in the first place. Unlike the mission, they took up the offer, recruited nurses with midwife training, and sent them to live in Dugusigi in the house built for them by the Paramount Chief and his people. As promised, the new facilities were well-equipped for service and large enough so that the government dispenser could move into one wing of the clinic and set up for treatment to handle those that the midwife wing was not equipped to handle.

Several years later the Storyteller enjoyed an interesting development in Heredugu when George, a resident of Elkhart, Indiana, arrived to help Dembeli set up a solar system in their home. The system included solar lights, a fridge, and fans to make life a little more comfortable. It also included a great way to keep batteries charged so that radio contact could be maintained with the other stations around the country. This had been especially important when the next closest missionaries lived a four-to six-hour drive away, depending on the season of the year. Now with the clinic in Dugusigi, there were two European nurses who often came to visit Dembeli's family. A great camaraderie developed with them in ministry. Dembeli was often called to take patients to them, and on many occasions they were able to save the lives of mother and child as they ministered in the midwife clinic. They also trained traditional birth attendants in various villages throughout the chiefdom so that a network of medical service was beginning to take shape.

While George was in Heredugu helping Dembeli install the solar equipment, the nurses from Dugusigi were invited over for an evening of food and games. Several months before, Dembeli had mentioned to them that George would be coming to help install a solar system in their home in Heredugu, and they had shared with him the fact that their organization was also sending them solar equipment, but unfortunately they did not have anyone to install it. During the evening one of the nurses explained that the solar system for the clinic had arrived but that all the instruction were written in Italian. Neither of them felt they could assemble the system with directions they could not understand, let alone in a language they did not feel comfortable reading. They asked if Dembeli and George could help them. After a brief discussion it was decided that the two men would go over to Dugusigi and take a look at the foreign equipment.

One glance confirmed that the instructions were indeed in Italian. Dembeli and the nurses joined in laughter when George wondered out loud who needed instructions anyway. Dembeli knew that he would need understandable directions and some diagrams, but George was different. In this case he had the technical knowledge and the expertise to assemble the system. He gave instructions to Dembeli so that he could pass them on to the Gospel Team members who had come along to help.

Although the system was different than the one George had assembled in Heredugu, after just a couple of days lights were shining in the nurses' home and the clinic glowed in the night. The fridge purred contentedly with a belly full of medication, and the clinic had lights in an emergency room in case it was needed. Later, other lights were added throughout the entire clinic and waiting area. The vision of the Paramount Chief had become a reality. His dream that his people would have a small hospital with outstanding medical care was fulfilled.

The relationship between the other organization and Dembeli continued to grow. The nurses were replaced every two years with a new team of volunteers. Finaba noticed that Dembeli's home often became an oasis for the nurses as they shared meals, played games, and enjoyed the traditional holiday seasons together. Dembeli's home became a stopping point for refreshment as the nurses traveled to various towns in the area to push the children's inoculations programs further into the frontier. The nurses' home became a place to relax for a little while for Dembeli and his family as they traveled back and forth to Kurela. A spirit of cooperation united the nurses and Dembeli's efforts to better serve the Kuranko people among whom they had been called to minister. On one occasion as Dembeli was passing through Dugusigi, he stopped to ask the nurses for some medication. They checked him, sent him right to bed, treated him for severe dehydration and malaria, and would not let him continue his journey until he regained his strength. Dembeli, like so many others in the area who had benefited from the little hospital, confirmed the appreciation that was often expressed to the nurses. It was good to have highly-trained medical personnel in the area.

Over the next few years, Dembeli was often called by the families of women in labor to bring a vehicle to the remotest parts in the chiefdom so that he could transport a patient to the clinic where the mother's life, and possibly the life of her little one, could be saved. Sometimes the clinic did not have all the facilities or equipment needed in a difficult birthing, and the nurses would have to take the patient on down to the hospital in Kurela, which was another six hours' drive away. Dembeli had the privilege of helping the Paramount Chief put in a new road that cut off several hours of travel to the nearest hospital. As Finaba and the people watched the relationship develop between Dembeli and the clinic, they sensed that the ministry of healing was important, and that the nurses and Dembeli really did care for the Kuranko people.

Two Catholic nurses discovered the remnants of the Church that had been planted several years before and began to encourage the believers. They talked to their priest down country and shared a little about their situation with him. Soon a catechist was sent to Dugusigi. The Bibles were found, the hymnbooks were pulled out, and the old tire rim once again began to sound out a call to worship. The believers gathered, and with the realization that the conflict with the former National Church President was no longer able to reach them, they began to share their faith with others.

Before long, a beautiful Church was under construction. A new nurses' residence was also built by the Catholic mission. Dembeli was invited to participate in the dedication service of the new Church, but he was down country in meetings at the time and was unable to attend. When he returned, he joined them in several services, and although he never said anything to those leading the service, Finaba noticed that when he looked around he recognized many of the believers that the Gospel Team and Hiram had lead to Jesus years before. He also saw some that had learned to read at those early literacy classes, and others who had been discipled through TEE. Now, outside the conflict, they had become the core group for this new Church under a new name. The Storyteller mused that it was a bittersweet situation for the Gospel Team and Dembeli, for they had, for a brief period of time, poured their hearts into a church plant, only to see it die in bitterness. Now it had come to life again as a Catholic Church—same hymn books, same Bibles, same church bell, and many of the same people. Dembeli pointed out that God is bigger than the conflict, and He will always have His people. Years later, the war that devastated Sierra Leone destroyed Dugusigi, but the church was quickly rebuilt and continues to stand as a house of worship.

Chapter 26: Eleven Men and a Miracle

The Storyteller tagged along at the end of the line of men heading for the river. He walked, unseen, at Dembeli's side, and like Dembeli, his thoughts played tag in his mind as he watched the long line of people ahead of him. Dembeli had learned to enjoy the meandering pace of the Kuranko people as they chattered noisily on their way to wherever they were going along the paths through the bush. Gone were the days when he would try to get them to speed up to arrive at their destination in less time. When he traveled the hills alone he would still set a good pace and enjoy it. He knew that it had not taken the African grapevine long to spread the word that he actually was in such a hurry to get no where that he went out and ran almost every day, working up a tremendous sweat to go no where in particular, except to get back where he had started from.

Finaba remembers the time that Dembeli was jogging along and as he came around a corner he met a lady carrying a load on her head. It scared her so much to see a white man running that she dropped her load and took off into the bush to hide. Although Dembeli called and told her that everything was fine and that there was no need to fear, she would not come out to pick up her load until he was long gone. When she reached town and reported what she had just witnessed and declared that something really bad must have happened to make a white man run like that, the others just laughed. The Gospel Team and townspeople had learned to accept Dembeli's funny ways. They also realized that he had learned to be very comfortable at their pace as they talked their way through the hills. Little did they realize that one of the reasons Dembeli ran almost every day was because he had come to the conclusion that if one is in halfway decent shape he could enjoy, rather than just endure, the last five miles of the walk through the hills to the next town. Like his friends, Dembeli had come to the realization that the towns were not going anywhere, so they would still be there a couple hours later when everyone arrived together.

Finaba observed that it was sometimes hard for Dembeli to catch all the conversation that bounced back and forth along the trail. When he walked in the middle of the line, there would sometimes be several different conversations going on in different segments of the line. He would hear parts of the conversation of those walking in front of him, and parts of the conversation of those walking behind him, and he would often miss major parts of both. He learned to settle in to a comfortable pace at the back of the line, and if he lost the train of thought as it traveled out of hearing distance he would be entertained by his own thoughts until he could pick up the thread of Kuranko conversation again. There is seldom silence when a group of Kurankos walk the paths of their nation. They are master communicators, and this is evidenced in every aspect of their lives.

On one particular day, Dembeli did not even seem to be interested in the many conversations going on along the trail, for he was totally lost in his own little world of thought. As the Storyteller watched him, he noticed Dembeli looking down the line of men walking ahead of him and he began to wonder if Dembeli was reviewing the recent past of each of the eleven men who were leading the procession. Today, along with a large group of observers, those eleven men were walking half an hour each direction to the river to be baptized. Each of them came with a unique story and some with a personal history that stretched way back. They were the first men to be baptized in the town of Yidafa, and of the eleven men, nine of them were past middle age. Dembeli marveled again, and rejoiced in the awesome grace of God as he thought about these men and their testimonies.

Finaba wished again that he could step into the world of people and tell Dembeli about the lives of the two elders who were near the front of the line. They were mere toddlers when the first missionaries had passed through their town on their way to the interior of Africa several generations ago, and their lives had not been impacted by the missionary who had been a resident of their town for a brief period of time so many years ago. Only one or two of the really old people in the town even remembered that missionary and the fact that he had tried to build a stone house in Yidafa. He had not been around long enough to complete the task, and that generation, like the ones before it, had passed into eternity without a consistent Christian witness. The elders did remember some missionaries who had walked through their town a couple of times a generation before on their way to Guinea, and they had paused long enough to share the Gospel. But there had been no consistent witness for Christ in their remote village in the foothills of the Konko Mountains until the Gospel Team and Dembeli started to come and share the picture sermons with them.

Then there was Danso. He was a big part of the reason that the Gospel Team had been so consistent in coming to his town. The town chief and elders of the town had welcomed Dembeli and the Gospel Team into Yidafa and had given their approval to have the Gospel shared with the people. When Danso, one of the opinion leaders of his clan, discovered that Dembeli and Barnabasi, the Gospel Team leader were hunters, he invited them to walk the hills with him. Over the years they built a solid relationship. Using the thrills and trials of the African bush as a bridge ministry, Dembeli and Barnabasi began to share with Danso the deeper reason for their willingness to come so far to build a relationship.

The Holy Spirit awakened in Danso a keen interest in the things of God. Today he was following some of his elders to the river to be baptized as a public witness that he had accepted Jesus not only as Savior, but as Lord of his life. Finaba watched Dembeli's face and could almost see the pictures that flashed through his mind as he recalled the victories and defeats of the hunts they had shared with the men of Yidafa. They were just the threads in the tapestry of the bigger picture that was now being revealed. Finaba saw a tear of joy in Dembeli's eye, and realized that the Master Artist had given Dembeli a brief glimpse of the masterpiece of the Church He was weaving as He brought the threads of these lives together for His glory. Dembeli felt humbled, and privileged, that God had allowed him to be a small part of what He was doing.

Segments of the lives of others in the group flashed through Dembeli's mind as he stood on the bank of the river and watched the Gospel Team baptize these men that they had led to faith in Christ. Joy and laughter were evident as they gave their testimonies and recalled how they had come to know Jesus. For years the Gospel Team had walked through the hills to reach Yidafa, but then the men of the town decided that they should build a road so trucks could come to their town. This would enable them to have a market, and it would qualify them to have wells dug in their town so they would have a source of pure water to drink. Pure drinking water would cut down on the disease in their homes.

Two of the men reminded the Gospel Team and Dembeli of the days they had worked together building a road from the main road six miles away to reach their town. They laughed again at how Dembeli had "buried" his 4 X 4 truck in the swamp he was helping them fill with stone that would serve as a bridge across the soggy mixture. How could anyone predict that when the truck got out to the middle of the stone "bridge" that all the stones would decide to settle deeper into the muck and that the truck would be "fastened" there under the shade of the trees, so comfortable in the cool mire around it.

There was also the hill that was so steep that one day a different truck Dembeli was driving could not even make it up the hill. There were trees to be cut down, huge rocks to be moved, and rivers to be crossed. Each barrier was overcome with a tremendous amount of determination and cooperation. Relationships had been built that became a bridge of sharing as Dembeli and the Gospel Team told the men of Yidafa about the road to heaven that Jesus had built by His death and resurrection.

Serious moments came for the men to as they recalled Fina, a little girl who was both deaf and mute. Fina had built a solid relationship with Dembeli's daughter, Faith. The men had seen love in action as Faith reached out in a special little girl's way, and loved one who was so physically challenged.

Through all the memories, the hand of God had been moving to build His Church, and today at the river eleven men were baptized. A church was born. Dembeli wondered if God opened the window of heaven one more time and let that early missionary peek down and catch just a brief glimpse of what He was doing in the town where the stone house had never been completed. Were there not two white men with tears of joy in their eyes that day? One, Dembeli, was standing on the sandy banks of a river in a remote area of the foothills of the Konko Mountains, and another was looking down from heaven, rejoicing because his investment had not been in vain.

Danso, the hunter, learned to read, and as a progressive young man, he tried to teach others to read as well. This created a new awareness of need in the town, and soon a young man moved to Yidafa to start a school. The District leaders asked him if he would help the Church by teaching a literacy class. Since he was a Christian, he was also asked to conduct the morning prayer time every day just like in the other churches that were active in the District. He did not feel competent to pastor the church since he was a new Christian himself, so the District leaders asked him just to teach the people the Scripture memory verses and have prayer with them every day. They assured him that the Gospel Team would come in for special services and additional teaching.

The teacher responded that he would be willing to do what the District leaders were asking him to do, but that he wanted to be one of the men who would be taught TEE so that he could continue to learn and improve himself. The Heredugu Church and the Dutsikoro Church had worked together to reach this town, so Yidafa became the first church planted as a granddaughter church of the mother church in Heredugu. Heredugu had planted the Dutsikoro Church, and now the Dutsikoro Church helped to reach Yidafa. Dembeli knew then that the chain of church planting would be able to continue. He rejoiced in the confirmation that healthy "sheep will born sheep" and that the "shepherds will born shepherds".

A little further back in the line walked another man who was a reminder of a miracle in the town. One day Danso sent a runner to Dembeli and Baranabasi bearing a message that made Dembeli feel that someone needed to go to Yidafa and encourage the believers. The Gospel Team had planned to be gone in the opposite direction for a weekend, and only a few of the men on the Team would be left in town to maintain the schedule of services where they usually went during the week. Then Musa, who had moved down country, showed up unexpectedly to visit his family. As a former Gospel Team member he knew all the stories in the picture Bible. After ministering on the Team for a couple of years he had spent two years at Bible school training for the ministry. When the opportunity to attend the top-ranked secondary school in the country presented itself he had jumped at it, and had received training that would later set him in good standing to attend college.

When Barnabasi and Dembeli heard the message from Yidafa, they decided that someone needed to go to encourage the believers and help with the literacy class as well. Musa was asked to go, and another Team member named Fara volunteered to go along with him since no one on the Team ever ministered alone. The two men walked to Yidafa to spend a couple days in meetings while the other members of the Team held special services in a different town.

Fortunately, Dembeli and his group returned to Heredugu a day or two before Musa and Fara were scheduled to return from Yidafa. After spending a couple days with the town Chief's family, Musa and Fara had decided that they really ought to contribute to the cooking pot, so they borrowed a gun and headed out looking for steaks, roasts, and hamburger which they could invite to the family table. A hunting accident in which Fara was shot with buckshot resulted, and Musa headed for town to call for help. The men immediately responded and carried Fara to town. When they saw how seriously he was injured, they knew that they could not keep him there and let him die, so Musa offered to walk the thirteen miles through the hills to Heredugu to call Dembeli if they would put Fara in a hammock and carry him out to the main road. This would save Dembeli a lot of travel time, and enable him to get Fara to the hospital much quicker.

Musa arrived in Heredugu after dark—brokenhearted, and desperate to find help for his dying friend. It did not take long for Dembeli and the Gospel Team to respond. Soon they were driving off into the night to see if they could get Fara and take him to a hospital down country where he would be able to receive adequate medical treatment. Finaba recalled the frustration that Dembeli felt when he discovered that before they could head out to a hospital they would first have to take Fara to the Paramount Chief in Dutsikoro and report a gun accident. Dutsikoro was over an hour's drive past the Yidafa junction and in the opposite direction of the hospital, which meant they would lose a lot of precious time.

The headlights of the truck picked up a small group of men, and it did not take long for anyone to see the forlorn looks on their faces and the burden of Fara in the hammock. The hammock was attached to a pole and resting on the shoulders of two men who walked as fast as they could with the hammock swinging from the pole suspended between them. When they tired of the load they were quickly relieved of their burden by two other men. The hammock was not the only burden they bore. Following Musa's request to carry Fara as far as they could, the men had set out in the night to meet Dembeli's truck in the hope that it would arrive before Fara died and their town had to bear the burden of having someone killed in a hunting accident.

Now they stood in a small, dejected group, talking to the Gospel Team while Dembeli hurried to the hammock to see Fara and try to evaluate the situation. Fara was still alive, although in desperate condition. Dembeli sensed that Fara was at death's door so his first question was not about what happened or about the pain, but his first concern was verbalized when he asked Fara about his current relationship with Jesus. Fara affirmed his faith in Christ and let Dembeli know that he was ready to go home to heaven. Then through his pain, he added that he wanted everyone to know that it really was an accident that he had been shot. The Team gathered around one of their members and earnestly, yet very briefly, they offered their prayers to a miracle-working God, asking that He would step in and touch one of their hurting members.

Precious hours were taken in the trip to Dutsikoro to see the Paramount Chief, but his response was immediate and definite. He called one of his chiefdom police and sent him along with Dembeli and Fara to assure that any legal action concerning the accident would be handled properly through his chiefdom.

An all-night drive ended just after daylight when Fara was checked into the government hospital at Kurela. A police report at the central District police office for the northern territory was filled out, and then the Team waited through the incredible delays in an endeavor to obtain medication. Fortunately Fara was still alive and conscious, and was able to testify to the police that it was indeed an accident. Unable to treat Fara's wounds adequately, the hospital staff decided to send Fara to the hospital in the capital city of the country. Meanwhile, one of the Gospel Team members who had some medical experience due to his prolonged stay in Magagiya Leprosy Hospital volunteered to clean the wounds and help prepare Fara for the trip. In a ministry of compassion, with a gentleness that will never be forgotten, Mr. Tenne set about cleaning the wounds of his friend and prepared him for the trip down country.

In the weeks that followed, Fara experienced extended stays in several different hospitals. These included the eye hospital in Magagiya where the eye Fara lost was replaced with an artificial eye. It also included time at a mission hospital, where some of the buckshot was removed and he was given treatment he so desperately needed.

Months later, Fara was able to return to Heredugu and give his testimony in church. At the close of the service he asked Dembeli and the Gospel Team if they would escort him back to Yidafa so he could share the miracle of healing with the people who had heard that he was alive but were totally unable to believe it.

The Team quickly made arrangements and headed out for a couple of days in Yidafa. Fara thanked the people there for their role in helping him as much as they possibly could. Then he shared with them how God had touched and healed him. The Gospel Team leader pointed out that Fara was really a walking miracle, for no one expected him to live through the night, and even those who saw that he had did not really expect to ever see him back in town alive. He became a living testimony to the power of prayer. In line to the river that day to be baptized, were men that had been impacted in a powerful way by the healing touch in the life and testimony of one they thought they would never see alive again.

All these thoughts and many more tumbled through Dembeli's mind as he watched the baptism service take place. He heard the testimonies and then watched as two men from the Gospel Team stepped into the water and called the new believers one by one to identify with their Lord in the public act of baptism.

The constitution of the Church in Sierra Leone said that an ordained minister had to do the baptizing, or at least give consent to have someone who was not ordained baptize new believers. Dembeli had coached the Gospel Team, and now he stood on the banks of the river and rejoiced as the Team members, now experienced "baptizers," took over. He sometimes compared it to soccer. Like Dembeli, his children learned to play soccer as soon as they were big enough to kick a ball. In the early years in Heredugu when his kids saw their team losing, they would call a time out and say to Dembeli, "Dad, you are not going to let them beat us are you?" Challenged by his children, Dembeli would take the ball down and score. It was a thrill to win another game, and a strong sense of unity developed between children and father who played many winning seasons on the rugged turf of a child-sized soccer field in the front yard of the mission station at Heredugu.

Time and years change things, and soon the kids grew and began to score themselves. Dembeli's joy at their goals scored was greater than when he scored a goal, and he often helped them relive those moments of victory as they told the stories over and over again. Then came the day when their team was losing again. Only this time it was Dembeli who called the time out and he turned to his sons and said, "Boys, you are not going to let them beat us are you?" Challenged by the one who had coached them for so many years, the boys blazed a trail down the field and chalked up another victory.

Other victories were won on that little soccer field too, more affectionately known by Dembeli and his children as "Skin Your Knees Stadium." Faith would often join in the soccer game, and then at the end of the game she would show the children a story from the picture Bible, just like the Gospel Team did when they practiced on the children in preparation for showing the picture sermons in the nearby towns and villages. Dembeli remembered one Christmas Day when nine of those children, who had grown to be young men, went to the river and made a public witness of their faith in Christ as they were baptized. It was great to score a goal, but the real goal had always been to gain an eternal victory.

Now Dembeli stood on the sandy banks of a remote river in the middle of the African bush and saw another victory taking place. Men whom he had discipled were baptizing men they had led to Jesus. It was a greater victory than any soccer game, and the joy of seeing someone he had discipled winning others to Christ runs so much deeper and lasts so much longer because it has eternal value.

Chapter 27: The So Called "Doctor"

Along the incredible grapevine of the Kuranko communication system, a whispered word ran from village to village. The Storyteller, whose ear was tuned to the frequency, picked up the news that a lady was dying in childbirth in Folote. Having been in Heredugu less than a year, Dembeli's awareness of the grapevine was not as keen, and sometimes he wondered if maybe the vine did not stretch across the creek to his abode. In time it did, and he learned to take advantage of many of the benefits that it bore. On this particular occasion several men from the church came out to talk to Dembeli and to let him know that their friend's sister had died after four days of hard labor, but the child was still unborn. Dembeli asked if he could join the men as they walked in to Folote, about three and a half miles away, to express their sympathy to the family for the death of a loved one.

Arriving in the town, Dembeli noticed immediately that only the aged and the toddlers were present. Not being familiar with this particular town, he did not question the situation, figuring that maybe all the able-bodied people were out on their farms or that they had gone to the market in Lowrow. There seemed to be a spirit of depression as the elders huddled in groups, and as the grannies spoke in hushed tones about the tragedy of death that had crept into their town. The two elders from Heredugu and Dembeli moved from one group to another, and then finally settled down at the home of the friend whose sister had died.

The group, seated in the shade of a tree, began to discuss what a tragedy it was for a lady to die in childbirth. Knowing that Dembeli had just recently moved into the area, one of the elders turned to him and explained the situation to him. He shared how the Kurankos of their area believe that if a lady died in childbirth and the body of the mother and child were not separated and buried in separate graves, that evil spirits had the right to claim all others who reached that stage of pregnancy. In the future, mother and child would both die unless the spirits were appeased. Fearing the evil spirits that had caused this evil, all of those of childbearing age had fled from the village until the two bodies could be buried in separate graves. It was then that Dembeli understood what he had observed earlier, and now he had an explanation as to why he had met only the elderly and the very young when he first arrived in the town.

When Dembeli asked where the people had gone when they fled, he was informed that some of them had gone to their farms and were staying out in the bush. Others had quickly taken the road to other towns and would not return until the news that the situation had been dealt with reached them. Fear had settled over the town, and people were treading softly so that they would not further antagonize the spirit world. Dembeli asked what was being done about the situation, and it was then that he learned that a person designated as the "doctor" in the area would separate the two bodies, making it possible for them to be buried in different graves. That way the spirits would be appeased and their anger would not be focused on the next ones who became pregnant. One of the family members explained that two runners had been sent out to find the "doctor". The Storyteller saw the look of confusion on Dembeli's face and wished that he could step in and explain that the man was not really a "doctor". He had never had a day of medical training in his life, and his "skill" was not one that anyone else desired to possess. He was merely a person who was willing to do the task of separating the two bodies, and he had been given the position and title of "doctor". Dembeli suspected that he had been trained by the former such "doctor" just as a blacksmith was trained by the older tradesman in the clan. One of the elders explained that the "doctor" in this position could pretty well charge whatever he wanted to because the family of the departed would have to comply with his wishes or the spirits would not be appeased with a proper burial. He would not separate the bodies until he was satisfied that he would receive adequate compensation for his work. It took a whole series of questions for Dembeli to finally discover some of the deeper beliefs and customs surrounding the situation. As they sat together under the shade of the tree and waited for the runners to return with the "doctor", they had nothing else to do but talk. This gave Dembeli lots of time to formulate his questions so he would get answers that would help him understand the belief system of the people he had come to serve. Dembeli's heart ached for the people of the town as he learned more about the fear that bound them.

Finaba was the first to notice the stir among the elders sitting on the veranda of the chief's hut across the way. The news spread quickly that one of the messengers had returned and that he had been unable to locate the "doctor". Some speculated that the "doctor" had gone up into Guinea, the neighboring country, where he had family members, and that they would need to send another runner across the border to call him. It was decided that since they did not really know where the "doctor" was, it would be wiser to wait until the second runner returned before they made any decisions.

They did not have long to wait before the second messenger returned. He had discovered that the doctor had traveled south to the Sundan area and was about three days' travel away. Dembeli wondered what would happen now with the "doctor" so far away. He wondered how one could preserve a body in a mud hut in tropical Africa for almost a week until the proper steps for burial could be taken. He knew that a body was usually buried within a couple hours after death so that the heat and decay would not be a problem.

He did not have long to wonder. Some of his friends were called away by the elders of the town, so Dembeli sat alone wondering what would happen now. One friend soon returned and began to explain that the town now had a very, very serious problem on their hands. They explained the obvious. By the time a young man could be recruited to walk three days' journey to the Sundan area, locate the "doctor", and bring him the three days' trip back to the town, the body of the deceased would be in a sad state. The "doctor" would charge the family far beyond what they were able to pay. The town would have to step in and help pay so that the town itself would not suffer any longer from this terrible attack from the evil spirits. The town people had sent Dembeli's friends to him to ask him if he would be willing to be the "doctor" in this case.

By this time several more elders from the Heredugu church had arrived. After consulting with them, Dembeli agreed to the request of the Folote people on the condition that his wife be permitted to accompany him. The walk back to Heredugu did not seem to take very long, and soon various members of the Heredugu church had come out to Dembeli's house to offer assistance. One of them agreed to stay with Dembeli's three children while Dembeli and his wife walked back to Folote. Others offered to walk as far as Folote with them so that they would not be alone at night.

Dark was the night that tried to engulf the little group that walked back to Folote, a town already struggling under a cloud of depression. As the light of the kerosene lamp came bobbing into town, the elders quickly rallied around the home of the family who had lost their loved one. Within a few minutes they had wrapped the body in a sheet and hoisted it to their shoulders and were heading out of town. About half a mile out of town they turned off the path, and there under two large trees they laid the body on the ground. They untied the young saplings that had been tied along side of the body to serve as carrying poles in a crudely-fashioned homemade stretcher. Having accomplished their designated task they quickly withdrew, calling back to Dembeli that when the bodies were separate and re-wrapped, he should call them and they would come back to cover the graves.

Left alone with a kerosene lamp, a small sack of tools that he had taken from his shop back in Heredugu, and a wife who was wondering why she was there, Dembeli faced a task that no missions class had ever prepared him for. In the simple prayer that Dembeli offered before the "surgery", the Storyteller heard a plea that God would use even this most unique circumstance to build His kingdom and reach these people with His love. As his wife held the flashlight, Dembeli quickly performed the necessary procedure. When the task was completed, Dembeli and his wife wrapped the two bodies in separate sheets that they had brought along for that purpose. Then he called the elders to come and complete the burial.

Dembeli stood and watched as the graves were covered. Later the Storyteller heard him comment that he had never seen graves filled in faster, even with a backhoe. Dembeli however, was convinced that God brought him into the situation for a reason. Although he could not see the immediate results of his obedience to the Lord, he was confident that his directions from the Lord were confirmed by the leaders in the Heredugu church. He was satisfied in the assurance that he had been where God wanted him to be, when God had wanted him to be there, and he had confidence and peace that God would bring glory out of the chaos.

The call to Church sounded earlier than usual the next morning, so Dembeli hurried into town to see what had caused the time change. Although he had already learned that time is irrelevant to most of the residents of the town, he had an acute awareness that people and events are of prime importance, so he responded to the call wondering what the event would be. As he walked into church he was surprised to find it almost full, but discovered that there was not going to be a church service that morning. Pastor Pita was asking all the people to walk to Folote and be there when the people of child-bearing age returned to their homes from their places of hiding. Dembeli hurried back home to inform his family about the change in plans, and then joined the church family as they walked the three and a half miles back in to Folote.

As if by arrangement, the believers scattered through the town. Sitting on the verandas of the grass-thatched huts or under the shade of trees, the believers casually joined in the conversations of the town people. Some who had fled returned in the night, but most of them came back during those morning hours after the grapevine had communicated the information that the spirits had been appeased and Folote was free once again.

As they came back, the people who had known such fear found visitors sitting on their verandas chatting quietly with their friends. When asked the obvious question as to why they were there, the believers simply shared that they had come to express sympathy for the loss of a loved one. They had come to share that we do not need to fear death, or to appease the evil spirits because Christ came as our Supreme Sacrifice and He overcame sin, death, the evil spirits and hell so that we could know His love and peace instead of fear and bondage. They shared that Christ is all powerful and that through Him one can be set free from the bondage and oppression of the devil.

Several in the Church family were able to share their testimonies of how they had come to know Christ and His saving power. One fact stood out to all who heard them: the peace of Christ is a gift of God that the devil cannot destroy, and it is given freely to all who believe in Christ as their Savior and Lord. He overcame the devil through His death and resurrection, and because He lives, those who believe in Him will live with Him forever. Quietly, in a multitude of ways, the story was shared and people saw the real evidence of the peace of God in action in the midst of darkness and oppression.

A short time later, when the Gospel Team was formed, Folote became the first town they chose to go to, and over the years Folote became the learning ground for many of the new Gospel Team members. The tragic death of a friend's sister had opened the door of opportunity for the Church, and by God's grace they had marched right through that open door and had demonstrated His love in a culturally appropriate way to a town that was hurting and ready to listen.

Chapter 28: The Road to Folote

When the Gospel Team began their ministry, they walked in to Folote one evening each week to sing songs of praise, share their testimonies, and show the picture sermons explaining the plan of salvation. People would gather on the chief's veranda, sit on benches placed strategically around the front of the house, or sit on the stones used to sharpen tools—located in the shade of the orange trees within easy hearing distance of the chief's house. Almost everyone in town attended those meetings. Dembeli often wondered when more would take their stand for Christ in Folote, for only one man had responded, and he was one of the elders of the town who had many friends in Heredugu.

One day, while Dembeli was working around his house in Heredugu, he heard a delegation of people coming and looked up to see the Folote chief, his elders, and many of the young men from the town escorting them. Elders from Heredugu had apparently joined the delegation as they came through town, and children, not wanting to miss the excitement of whatever was going to take place, were tagging along. Dembeli often hunted with the Folote Chief and several of the elders from the town, and a strong bond of friendship had developed, creating an open atmosphere for humor as well as for honest discussion. Dembeli enjoyed the humor of the opening comments and reveled in the joy of being able to share in the conversations with friends that had come to mean so very much to him, even though most of the men in the group were Muslims bound by animistic traditions.

Once the greetings and the stories had subsided, the town chief came to the real reason that they had all walked in together from Folote. Having been born and raised in Africa, Dembeli understood full well that all that had transpired up to this point was merely setting the stage for what was now to come. The Storyteller once heard Dembeli musing that if the stage was not properly set, or the vibes that the nationals were picking up did not suit them, they would not come to the real issue, but would simply skirt around it and return on another day to deal with the real issues. Dembeli was satisfied to see that the vibes were positive and the town chief and his elders could now present the real reason for their walk from Folote.

The chief reminded Dembeli of a little talk they had had some months previously while hunting. It was in a remote corner of the bush that he had expressed his desire to Dembeli to have a road into his town so vehicles could reach there. Dembeli had recognized the leadership qualities of the chief, and knew that he was not only a designated leader, but was also an opinion leader of his people and his clan. He knew that a designated leader was not often the opinion leader too. He listened carefully as the chief expressed the needs of his people and explained that now they had come to ask Dembeli if he would help them construct a road to their town.

Finaba, the Storyteller, sat quietly under the shade of the trees along with the elders and young men and followed this latest development with great interest. The men reminded Dembeli that the Paramount Chief in Dugusigi had divided the road through the whole chiefdom into sections, and each town was responsible to maintain a given section of the road. They reminded him of the great difficulty they had in maintaining their section of the road through the hills to the next chiefdom. They expressed their frustration, not that the road did not go through their town, but that one rocky hill was really unfit for a road and that vehicles could not get through the hills during the rainy season. This hindered the development of markets in their area, and caused the people to walk much further to markets where vehicles could come.

Dembeli chuckled as one after another the elders expressed their reasons for wanting a road to their town. They promised they would all help build it if Dembeli would help them fill in the swamps with stones, which would serve as bridges through the mud, and construct the necessary bridges where they could not fill in the streams with stones. Finaba knew, better than any of the others in the gathering, how pleased and honored Dembeli would be to help. Since that day hunting when the chief shared his vision for a road, the idea had been tumbling around in Dembeli's head as he wandered how it could become a reality. He had mentally been trying to figure out how to build the necessary bridges. Before him stood the reality in the form of volunteer manpower.

Dembeli carefully explained to his friends that putting in a new road was not a simple task, nor was it a one-time obligation, but it was a long-term commitment. Once it had been constructed it would need to be maintained. That would mean time and energy invested every dry season to repair the damage the rains had done to the road and to keep it open year-round. He reminded them of the forest that would have to be cut down and the hills that would have to be dug up. He explained how the rains would wash away great sections of the road as the water carved out new paths to the bottoms of the hills each year. A new road would mean that if a vehicle got stuck, the men from the town would have to go, day or night, rain or shine, to help the vehicle out of the mud and back onto the road. Dembeli told them that it would mean commitment to an incredible amount of work and asked them if they still wanted a road.

The Storyteller knew that Dembeli was just making sure of their commitment, because they could not start a project of such magnitude and leave it unfinished. If they did that, it would stand as a monument to their failure. Dembeli also knew that if any town in the area could pull off the construction of a new road through the bush, Folote could. They had a spirit of unity seen in few towns anywhere; they had a grim determination that the road would be completed; and they understood the great benefit it would bring to them and their families.

The work on the road went well, as various towns in the area joined the people from Folote in making their dream become reality. Dembeli and the Gospel Team helped, and Dembeli learned to understand the people and the culture so much better as they overcame barriers to construction together.

Deafening cheers ascended as Dembeli, the town chief, and a group of elders drove the truck into Folote for the first time. The noise was incredible as the sounds of dancing and feasting echoed through the hills. To say that a grand victory celebration took place would be to put it mildly! No one had gone out to their farm for fear they would miss this wondrous occasion when the first motorized vehicle came into their town. It appeared that invitations to the grand occasion had been sent out along the grapevine, for people from surrounding towns and villages came to join in the celebration. Joy and gladness ruled. The efforts of the people had been rewarded, a road had been constructed, and Dembeli's truck sitting in their town was a tangible symbol of their accomplishment.

Had anyone been able to see the future that day, they would have seen the road being extended right on through Folote to the next town, by-passing the rocky hill that had caused them so much grief and frustration in the past. The Paramount Chief supported the project, and with Dembeli's help the bridges were built. The Paramount Chief called in manpower from the whole area to help with the next section of road, which put Folote on the main road that runs a circle through the northern part of the country. Perhaps the town chief was the only one who had a vision of a market in his town, and Dembeli may have been the only one who saw in his mind's eye a church standing among the grass-hut homes of those who were celebrating.

Dembeli was embarrassed by the honor bestowed upon him, as credits were piled high for the small part he had played in helping to construct the bridges and fill in the swamps. He accepted it as an element of their celebrations and rejoiced with them, letting the chief and the people know that it was really their road and that they deserved the honor for constructing it.

The years were kind to Folote, and the benefits of the road soon became a reality. Their town soon became a market town on the main road into the next chiefdom. Their road became the link that joined the road from the neighboring tribe, and made it possible to travel through the whole country. They paid a price the first year or two until the road was fully usable year-round. They sent to Heredugu many times for Dembeli to come with his 4 X 4 and use his winch and cables to pull out vehicles that got stuck between the hills or slid off the road that was not quite broken in yet. But soon the mud settled, the road hardened into a year round passage way, and their market was a success.

Led on by the vision of their town chief, the people of Folote also got involved in a United Nations project to dig wells in their town. Only towns that were accessible by road and could provide the manpower to dig the wells qualified for the project. The people of Folote had proved their willingness to work together, and two wells providing the town with clean pure water became a reality. Since many diseases are water-borne, the level of sickness sharply decreased when the townspeople had a source of pure drinking water, and once again Dembeli was asked to join the celebration when the new wells were opened.

Progress crept up on the little town of Folote, tucked away in the foothills of the mountains, and the Storyteller could report how they paid the price of progress with their labor and sweat. In the middle of all that was happening to them in the town, a deeper and more meaningful vision was becoming a reality. Consistently, week after week, rainy season and dry season, the Gospel Team continued to visit the town. When Dembeli was down country or in another area for services, the men on the Team would walk to Folote just as they had before the road was ever thought about. When Dembeli was home, the trip was so much easier using the truck and taking the new road to the little town.

Following each service was a time for discussion and questions. During these discussions the people were free to ask the Gospel Team questions. Then the Team would ask them questions in return, challenging the people to search for the Truth. Following the service one evening, there were not the usual questions or discussions. The town chief asked three young men to stand in the circle of light created by the kerosene storm lanterns that the Gospel Team carried with them. The three men stood in front of their chief, and he presented them to the Gospel Team saying that they had come to him expressing the desire that they no longer walk in the way of Folk Islam (animism and Islam combined). They wanted to be free to walk in the "Road of Jesus."

On behalf of the town, the town chief presented the three young men to the Gospel Team and told the Team that they were to take them as apprentices, train them as believers, and make them followers of Jesus. The Storyteller saw the joy on Dembeli's face, even in the shadows that could not be dispelled by the lanterns. The town had a vision of a road, a market, and a well, but Dembeli believed that Jesus had a vision of a church, and this glorious night was the beginning. The one elder who was a believer no longer stood alone, for now there were three young men to walk the Jesus Road with him.

Dembeli wanted to see how the Gospel Team would handle the situation. He noticed that at their next discipleship session, they spent extra time in prayer for the town of Folote and asked God how they should go about training their three new apprentices. One of the Team members, a former leprosy patient in a hospital down country, had moved into Heredugu when the disease had been arrested. He had met his wife, a patient in the same hospital, when he had been in training to treat other patients. Although they were from different tribes, they had been readily accepted in Heredugu because of his medical training. His wife, a Fulani by tribe, already spoke Kuranko, but Mr. Tenne, a member of a tribe farther south, had to learn the language.

The Storyteller recalled the day that Dembeli had asked Mr. Tenne why he had settled down in Heredugu when his tribe was located far to the south and his wife was from the Fulani people. He replied that his wife's people were wanderers in the Heredugu area and so he moved there and was learning the language so he could fit in and be one of the tribe. Mr. Tenne was already fluent in five languages when he came to Heredugu, so Dembeli felt he was a real asset. Then God asked him to be on the Gospel Team, even though walking was very difficult for him because he had lost most of his toes before the leprosy had been arrested. Dembeli never questioned his calling to the Team, because the man brought a real sense of commitment, a lot of experience, and a tremendous sense of humor. Although at times he had to remain behind when the Team walked to a village a great distance away, Mr. Tenne's dependability, humor, and Christian witness forever remained an incredible asset to the Team.

A couple weeks after the three young men had been presented as apprentices to the Gospel Team, God once again reached down into the heart of the Team and asked Mr. Tenne to be the one to disciple the three men from Folote. Dembeli had often challenged the churches with the fact that we cannot have a strong church until the people learn to read God's Word for themselves, so Mr. Tenne committed himself to teaching those three men how to read. Several evenings a week he would walk to Folote, three and a half miles each direction, carrying a lantern. Then he would sit down and spend the evening with the three young men and return home alone in the dark.

If the Team was out in the truck on an evening when Mr. Tenne was teaching in Folote, Dembeli would swing by and give him a ride home. Dembeli often marveled at the man's commitment. He did not have all his fingers and most of the front of each of his feet was missing because of the dreaded disease of leprosy. One evening a week Mr. Tenne would walk to Folote early and teach a literacy class which would end at the arrival of the rest of the Team for an evening service. In a surprisingly short time the three young men in Folote were reading God's Word for themselves. But more than teaching them to read, Mr. Tenne had imparted something of his sense of surrender and commitment to Christ and they saw Christian living and love demonstrated before their eyes. Soon they expressed a desire to be baptized so that all would know that they really are followers of Jesus and walking on His road.

Finaba sensed Dembeli's excitement when Mr. Tenne shared with him the desire of the three young men. What seemed to thrill him the most was the fact that the men were willing to be baptized in their own town rather than wait to be baptized at the annual Christmas Institute in Heredugu. Due to the devastation of leprosy, Mr. Tenne was unable to stand in the river or to hold onto the men to baptize them, but he marveled and rejoiced at God's goodness for having allowed him to play such an important part in planting the church in Folote. Pastor Pita and one of the Team members had the honor of baptizing those three young men as Mr. Tenne, Dembeli, the Gospel Team, and people from town stood on the banks of the little river and witnessed the ceremony. The Storyteller could not be sure who was rejoicing the loudest, Mr. Tenne or Dembeli, but he did know that their joy echoed through the halls of heaven as the angels looked on and joined in the victory chorus.

Now that there were baptized believers, it seemed to the mother Church in Heredugu that there ought to be a church in Folote. The Town Chief and the elders gave the Church a plot of ground at the edge of town and designated a day when everyone in town who so desired could help build the church. Dembeli often wondered why the Muslim teacher seldom missed a service when the Gospel Team shared the picture Bibles, but then he thought maybe it was so the teacher would know what the Team was teaching and he could express his own views after they left. Yet, when he showed up to help build the new church Dembeli began to question his own theory.

The men from the town made the mud blocks for the walls, and cut saplings and grass for the roof, and then days later actually did the building. Dembeli was amazed to see the town chief, the elders, and the Muslim teacher laboring with great diligence to help build the church building. A blackboard was constructed so the literacy class could be enlarged to include everyone who wanted to learn to read, in addition to the three men who had been baptized. The church was dedicated as a place of worship and learning, and God's Word was the central theme of it all. The dedication Sunday was a day of real rejoicing when the truck arrived for a celebration service in the town of Folote.

Some time later, the town chief and elders felt that a larger mosque was needed in their town, due in part to the newly established market that attracted people from all over the area. So they set about constructing a new mosque. The old mosque, located near the center of the town, was then offered to the Church since it was bigger and in a better location than the little church building on the edge of town. The mother Church at Heredugu discussed the situation at some length and decided that God had given them a tremendous opportunity since the building was much more suited to their purposes than the structure they had helped build a couple of years previously. Besides that, the original church building was no longer adequate to meet the needs of the growing group of believers in Folote.

It did not take the Folote Church long, with the help of the Gospel Team from Heredugu, to renovate the old mosque and turn it into a church. The day of the dedication service was another great day of rejoicing for the Church in the area, for they now had a new building that would stand as a monument to what God was doing in the area and in the town of Folote in particular. The day was chosen carefully so that church leaders from the neighboring tribe could be there to help dedicate the building on their way to an Institute in Dutsikoro where all the Christians would be gathering. The former District Superintendent was the guest speaker for the Institute and was invited to the dedication service.

Songs of praise, prayers of cleansing and commitment, and testimonies expressed the joy of everyone who had even had a remote part in planting the church, or in helping with the new building. The Storyteller watched Dembeli closely through most of the service, and may have been the only one who saw the tear trickle down Dembeli's cheek. He knew why, too: Mr. Tenne was not there to see what was happening, for he had gone home to glory. As Finaba watched, he noticed Dembeli's face change, or was it just his imagination that placed a smile beneath the tears? Did Dembeli see God open a little window in heaven, and just for a moment let Mr. Tenne look down? Did Dembeli sense the rejoicing that was taking place in heaven as Mr. Tenne, now completely healed of the devastation of leprosy, with new hands and new feet, led a celebration of victory and marched around the throne praising the name of Jesus who alone is worthy to receive all the glory, honor, and praise?

Chapter 29: Around the Area

The Gospel Team and Dembeli worked to reach as many towns as possible throughout the Heredugu District. As soon as a new church was formed Dembeli and the leaders from the mother church would sit down with the new believers and explain their responsibilities to them. Invariably the meeting would end up with several issues decided. The times of the regular services would be agreed upon. The daily prayers and scripture memory time would be set. A literacy class and teacher would be in place. The goal of reaching all the towns in the immediate area around their newly planted church would be clarified. Often this meant that, like the Heredugu Gospel Team, men would need to walk up to five miles each direction to hold services. These new teams also provided an opportunity for various members of the Heredugu Team to minister along side of the pastor to help him train Gospel Team members or apprentices. It also meant that if they were to respond to requests in their area, they would often have to walk much farther than five miles to share the Gospel with towns that had never been reached before.

One of those towns was Tetine. Before long, a very innovative young man, dubbed "Joe Cool" by Dembeli's three children because he always seemed to appear in a flashy shirt and sunglasses, started a literacy class to teach the new believers in his home town. He was enthusiastic about the world that reading opened up to him. He later moved down into Sundan country to dig diamonds, but while he was in Tetine he had a real impact on the town and a good ministry to some of the young people he taught to read. Following the war he returned home and became the pastor and literacy teacher in a growing church. A lasting friendship formed between

Dembeli and Samba, the Chief's son. Samba and Barnabasi were friends from way back since they had so much in common. Both had small shops where they sold things that helped the market in their towns, and both were hunters. When Dembeli came along it was only natural that the three of them would hunt together. Samba was an incredibly powerful young man who was able to handle a two hundred pound bag of rice like most men would a bushel of grain. Bigger than most Kurankos, he was still, for all his size, extremely quiet and skillful in the bush.

A church was not yet established when the rebels moved into the area. Using Heredugu as a base for destruction, they carried out their raids into the surrounding area, and one of the towns they struck was the little village of Tetine. The horror stories of war fill a dark page in the history of the little town in the foothills. Samba, along with one of the ladies and a number of children will never again laugh, play, work, or hunt, for their lives were snuffed out in the destruction of the town. Joe Cool has since returned, and the church has grown up out of the ashes, for God's grace is greater than the tragedy that took place in that once peaceful setting.

—

Tucked away in the foothills of the Konko Mountains, in a place few would pass unless they were going there on purpose, sits the little town of Konkokoro. Dembeli wanted to reach the people as close to the mountains as possible, so the Gospel Team joined him in an excursion to this town. As Dembeli entered the town and took up lodging, it seemed as though an oppressive spirit of darkness controlled the place. The Gospel Team sensed that they were not being effective in their ministry in this town, although they shared as many stories as earnestly as possible, and Dembeli and the Team spoke to the few people who gathered each evening. The Storyteller knew that Dembeli left with a heavy heart, for this was one of the towns for which he really had a vision. He wondered how one could start a Church in such an oppressive setting.

Over the years, the Gospel Team learned to evaluate the "soil" in each town. The towns that were not responsive were put on the prayer list and prayer partners in America were made aware of the barriers that the Gospel Team encountered. Resistance came both from Islam and animism. The visit to Konkokoro made Dembeli and the Team vitally aware that evangelism and church planting in an area that the devil has claimed for generations is not fun and games, but it is spiritual warfare.

Konkokoro was on the prayer list, and through the years that followed Dembeli and the Team continued to build relationships with various ones from the town. Dembeli used two very important skills that he had acquired as bridge ministries. Through his friendship with a hunter that Dembeli's sons dubbed "Robin Hood," he was able to build solid relationships with designated leaders in the town as well as with the "man of peace" (Luke 10:6). When the Paramount Chief eventually needed a road into that area, it was Dembeli he called to assist the people, and the town of Konkokoro sent men to help with the construction project.

By this time, open lines of communication existed between Dembeli and some of the leaders in the town, and the Gospel Team had built solid friendships with men in the town. Backed by prayer, the Team felt it was time to approach the town again in hopes that this time they would be willing to accept the message of salvation.

Although there had been numerous visits, there had not been another concentrated effort to present the town with the claims of Christ as there had been during that dry season years before. To Dembeli it seemed like they entered a different town this time. It was as if the darkness and oppression had been rolled back and the spiritual ears of the people were now ready to listen. What an incredible contrast to the response they had received during the series of services they had held years before. Now the people listened with the "ears of their hearts" and asked Dembeli and the Team to come consistently to their town to teach them the way to God. They requested that someone stay with them and help them know the way to heaven, or that a pastor be sent to live in their town until they too could become part of God's people.

Before the Team could arrange for a teacher, the war drove the Kuranko people up across the border into a neighboring country and the people were scattered all over. Yet the prayers of God's people followed the people from this town. Dembeli has commented many times that the positive difference in the response of the town can only be attributed to answered prayer. God changed the heart of a town!

—

Dembeli stood with a large group of believers on the sandy banks of the Ruwa River near his home in Heredugu and watched a scrawny, skinny, old man wade slowly out to where two men were waiting in deeper water. Standing between them, the man squared his shoulders and began to share how in recent months he had accepted Christ as his personal Savior as a result of the Team's ministry in the little town of Tonkelen where he served as the town chief. Unlike so many of the other towns where several accepted Christ together, he was the only one in his town who believed and accepted the message of salvation. In his testimony, he declared that although none of his people would follow him in his decision, he felt that he should walk to Heredugu and be baptized with other new believers so that there would be no doubt where he stood in his walk with God, or in his testimony.

As the old man shared his faith in Christ, Finaba looked over to see how Dembeli would react, for he knew that Dembeli really wanted to see several in each town accept Christ and be baptized at the same time. That way they could encourage each other in their walk with the Lord, especially if tough times or opposition came from others in the town. Dripping wet, yet with a smile as big as could be, the old chief walked confidently up out of the water to join other worshipers in praise of the Chief above all chiefs.

The town of Tonkelen did react to their chief's decision to "go it alone." They reminded him that he was a very old man and that soon he would die. They assured him that if he forsook the way of their forefathers, nobody would bury him and he would journey into the hereafter alone. They declared that they themselves would not even bury him, and he would be alone as he entered the spirit world. It saddened his heart but strengthened his resolve to stand firm for Christ in spite of the opposition, threats, and even curses that came his way. This is a huge issue among the Kuranko people so he shared his loneliness and concerns with the Gospel Team and the pastor in Heredugu, and they assured him that they would be there when he needed them. They reminded him that he was now part of the family of God and that his new family would stand by him and accept the responsibility of his burial. He stood unwavering in his newfound faith and continually tried to encourage others in his town to choose God's way.

The time did come when he went into eternity, and the message reached Heredugu via the incredible African grapevine of communication. Christians quickly gathered and walked to Tonkelen to perform the last rites of burial as they had promised. The people in the little town could not believe how many people showed up for their old chief's funeral. They could not understand the joy as songs of praise were sung and believers celebrated victory rather than defeat. The believers showed that because of Christ Christians are triumphant and that they knew where the chief had gone and could look forward to meeting him again. The town people marveled that in the sorrow of parting there could still be such a celebration of victory.

Although the chief wanted them to come, the Gospel Team had not been welcomed for services in the town during the closing days of the chief's life. But they continued to pray for the little town located just a couple miles away from them. Months passed following the funeral. Then one market day a delegation from Tonkelen arrived in Heredugu and asked the Team to start coming back to their town. Without condemnation or judgment, the Team reappeared in the little town on the day regularly scheduled for that area. They walked through the town greeting people and then met in front of the new chief's house just as if nothing had happened. After the testimonies and picture sermon were completed, the Team asked the people if they had any questions. It was then that they were told why the town had called them.

Several elders shared how they had watched the chief after his baptism. They saw something new in him, but they remained unconvinced until his funeral when so many Christians came to celebrate his home going. Then they remembered the Bible stories and began to put things together. They decided that they really needed to find out more about what had happened to their Chief that gave him such confidence and courage, so they had sent for the Gospel Team. They asked the Team to come back so they could again hear the message that had changed the life of their chief. Once again, the grace and mercy of a loving heavenly Father flowed over into a little town tucked away in the foothills of the Konko Mountains Leone. A mighty God revealed Himself through the power of His Word, the comfort of His Holy Spirit, and a life that was changed. What an awesome God!

Lowrow is a major market town for the Dugusigi chiefdom, and people walk from many miles to buy, sell, or trade one day each week. The market is not its only pride, for it was also the location of one of the few schools in the area.

Dembeli's first meaningful contact with the town came on one of his first trips into the area with Jake Schierling before he had even moved to Heredugu. Jake had planned the trip to introduce Dembeli to various people in Heredugu and to the Kuranko culture. Leaving Kurela shortly after midnight, Jake, his son Keith, and Dembeli entertained themselves in the front of the Toyota pickup truck with stories of ministry and hunting.

Just at daybreak, they came to a washed-out bridge and decided that they could go around it, through the little stream and up the slippery bank on the other side. Unfortunately nobody had asked the truck's opinion, and it settled rather comfortably into the cool mud at the bottom of the stream. Chimpanzees watched from their perches high in the forest downriver and screamed their anger at being disturbed so early in the morning. With the assistance of the passengers and a small hand winch, the truck was finally persuaded to climb out of the stream, and the group continued on its way.

It was still early in the morning when Jake, Keith and Dembeli parked their truck in the town of Lowrow and walked to another town. They walked all day and returned in the evening to continue their journey on to Heredugu where they planned to spend the weekend. When they arrived back at Lowrow, a trader who had agreed to let them park the truck near his little shop met them and gave them a bottle of warm orange soda pop. The long days' walk made it seem like the best soft drink Dembeli could remember, and it was accompanied by a meal of rice and soup. Dembeli got his first glimpse of the incredible hospitality that is one of the central themes of Kuranko culture.

Little did Dembeli realize that this first contact with Mr. Fanko would become the cornerstone in a relationship that would span over thirty years and innumerable experiences. The mutual respect that developed between these two friends was soon recognized by others in the area as unique. Being an opinion leader in the town of Lowrow, Mr. Fanko soon opened the doors for Dembeli and the Gospel Team to begin sharing the Gospel with his people. Before long a Church was started, which met on Mr. Fanko's veranda. Later it moved to the school, and finally in a meetinghouse built right in front of the chief's compound.

Mr. Tenne often accompanied Dembeli to the Sunday services and did the teaching. When a bridge was washed out between Lowrow and Heredugu, Dembeli stayed overnight with Mr. Fanko and once again enjoyed his hospitality. On another occasion when the same bridge washed out, Dembeli tried to go around it and found his truck buried to the running boards in the mud. With the help of a multitude of friends and a winch, he was able to pull himself through the swamp in five hours, and continue on his way to Heredugu. Yet when Sunday rolled around, Dembeli, Mr. Tenne, and a couple of believers traveled back to the broken-down bridge, parked the truck, and walked the rest of the way to Lowrow to hold a service. They wanted the people there to know that they could be counted on each Sunday to come and share the Gospel.

As they were walking back to the truck after the service one evening, Dembeli and Mr. Tenne met a small python in the road. Knowing that some of the kids in the missionary children's school down in Kurela were intrigued with such pets, Mr. Tenne tried to persuade Dembeli to pick it up, put it in his bag that he was carrying over his shoulder and keep it for the children. Finaba almost laughed out loud for he knew how Dembeli felt about snakes. Although they are non-poisonous, Dembeli could not handle the thought of carrying a snake next to his ribs as he walked a few miles walk through the African night. He suggested that maybe Mr. Tenne would carry it for him. Mr. Tenne, having lost his fingers and toes to leprosy, declared that without fingers he could not pick up a snake, and without toes he could not run away from it if it decided to come after him. He reasoned that the only logical thing for him to do was to leave the snake for Dembeli to carry. Needless to say, the snake went his way, and the two friends continued their journey into the night, back to the truck.

After Mr. Tenne's death, a Christian teacher was stationed at Lowrow and he became the leader of the Church there. For some reason, that teacher was singled out by the president of the National Church as a target for his anger against the District's system of Church planting. The president declared that a Church should be planted by stationing a pastor in the town and paying him a salary, and not by taking a teacher and allowing him to be a pastor too. The District and Dembeli supported the teacher and he stayed at Lowrow, was blessed of God, and the Church continued to grow with a by-vocational pastor. When the rebels came and drove the people up across the border into the neighboring country, most of the people from the town fled. Yet when peace came and the people returned, the teacher took up the leadership of the Church again. Interestingly enough, other Christian teachers were stationed there under the leadership of the one who served as the pastor. They stood with him in planting the church and became powerful witnesses in a town that needed the Gospel so desperately and had potential to influence many towns through their market and their school.

The conflict helped the Heredugu District see the value of taking ownership not only of the church, but also of the value of working with the schools and the Christian teachers in the area. At the time of the rebel war, many of the teachers in the area were Christians and were dynamic witnesses for Christ. They left an impact on each of the towns they were in because they often replaced Muslim or non-Christian teachers. Their attitudes, work ethic, and lives bore witness to the people in town that they were committed to more than teaching just reading, writing, and arithmetic. As refugees during the war, some of those same teachers worked alongside Gospel Team members to plant churches in an area of their tribe that had never before been reached with the Gospel.

—

Over the years the Gospel Team from Heredugu walked to many towns in the foothills of the mountains. Dembeli was the first to admit that he had a tough time remembering the names of people from so many different towns. When he met them in the market he could usually mentally place them in the right town, but he often failed to remember their names. He reasoned that tens of thousands of the Kurankos in the area knew the one white man that lived among them, but he simply could not be expected to remember the names of the thousands of people he was meeting as he walked from village to village. This was brought home to him in a rather humorous way one day when he was jogging.

As he came around a corner in the road, he met an elderly man that he knew was from the town of Bonkoro. Out of respect to the man he stopped to greet him. Dembeli asked the old man to "Greet the elders when you get back to your village."

The man responded, "I will do that for you."

Dembeli requested, "Please greet the blacksmith for me."

Again the answer came back, "He is my friend, and I will do that for you."

Then Dembeli said, "Do not forget to greet the chief for me."

The elderly man calmly replied, "I am the chief."

Sometimes the walk through the hills would take all day. The Team might stay for a couple of days and share the Gospel with as many as they could, or they might move on to another town and share with people there who had never heard either. As the years passed, at times in the heat of the dry season, or in the storms of the rainy season, it seemed to Dembeli that the mountains grew higher, the climb got a little steeper, and the footpaths got a little rougher. But the motivation remained, and along with the various Gospel Teams he continued to reach as many people he could with the glorious news of salvation.

The Storyteller watched Dembeli through the years as the Gospel Teams moved from town to town and as new Churches were planted.

He shared in the laughter, and the tears, as together they recounted the experiences God lead them through in their Church-planting endeavors. He witnessed the power of prayer as intercessors back in America stood with the Team and became a vital part of their efforts to claim the Kuranko people for Jesus. He saw the hurt and the agony of war, and he witnessed the triumph of victory as the love of Jesus continued to flow through the lives of believers to reach Kurankos for Him. He saw the joy as lives were transformed by the power of the Gospel and he marveled at the grace of the Supreme Sacrifice that the Team continued to share about.

Part 4: Evacuated

Chapter 30: The Turmoil

In the spring of 1992, Dembeli and some of the Gospel Team were working with the Paramount Chief on the construction of a bridge on the new road from Dugusigi to Kurela. More important to Dembeli than the bridge was the fact that the Gospel Team was holding services each night in the town of Ponkoe when the work on the bridge site was done for the day. Everything had to be done by hand so it took a long time to put in a bridge, even with all the manpower the chief provided from the villages in the area. Dembeli always took some of the men on the Gospel Team to help him when he worked on a bridge because they had been with him on other bridge building projects and they knew what needed to be done. Secondly, it gave the Gospel Team an opportunity to share their faith with men from a new area. Over the years Dembeli helped in many such projects and on every major bridge project God enable the Gospel Team to lead several to saving faith in Christ. Sometimes it would be a small group of men, at other times it would be the family that they were staying with. The Gospel Team joined Dembeli in the project, staying overnight several nights in a row and then traveling back to Heredugu, thirty some miles away, for a few days. That gave the men of the town an opportunity to get other things done besides just the construction of the bridge. Once they had completed their other tasks, they would be able to return for a few more days of work on the bridge the following week.

It was an exciting time for Dembeli and the Team as they built relationships with various men from the town and Dembeli became acquainted with people from a whole new area of the chiefdom. The devotional and prayer times that the Team has whenever they are out in a village were especially meaningful during the time in Ponkoe. Dembeli, as usual, enjoyed the time with the children, the hours of entertainment they offered, and the education he gained as he learned from them. Long ago he had learned that since children are totally uninhibited, they are a valuable source of information about the language and the culture. Everywhere he went he sought to cultivate a relationship with the children. They would laugh at his language errors, teach him how to say the words properly, and share all kinds of valuable information with him. They would sometimes instruct him in the things that one does or does not do in Kuranko land. Over the years they became a valuable source of instruction for Dembeli. After being in the culture for over thirty years, he has discovered that some of his best friends are those very children that were his "instructors" during the early years of his ministry in Kuranko land. He still finds them valuable sources of knowledge, for some of them are now leaders among their own people, and the relationships established years ago are paying great dividends.

Some of the young men shared with Dembeli the struggles they felt their nation was facing. As secondary school students in various cities down-country, they were beginning to pick up the vibes of discontent and the feeling that there needed to be a change in the political structure. They shared some of their concerns with Dembeli, knowing that he was in no way involved, nor would he become involved, for he had always taken a strong stand against getting involved in any political situation. Somehow the undercurrents were different this time than they had ever been in the past. Rebel activity had broken out in the neighboring country of Liberia. The men sharing their concerns with Dembeli felt there was a good possibility that it would affect the peace in their own country. None of them could have foreseen how soon that would happen, or the impact that it would have on future generations.

One afternoon while working on the bridge in Ponkoe, Dembeli shared with the men that he felt he needed to return to Heredugu. Feeling an unusual sense of urgency, Dembeli asked the men from the village to reach a good stopping point so the Heredugu men could take off early and surprise their families back home who were not expecting them for a couple days. Since they had put in some long, hard days on the bridge, it was not difficult to persuade the local men to quit early. Tools and supplies were put away in record time as Gospel Team members prepared to head home.

Arriving home to an empty house, Dembeli decided to turn on the two-way radio to see if anyone was on and to catch up on the news from down country. He tuned in the radio just in time to hear the American Embassy in the capital telling all the missionaries on the outstations to head to previously designated centers. There had been a military coup and the new government could not guarantee the safety of any foreigners. The instructions were repeated several times, so Dembeli was sure that he had not misunderstood. Since he had been gone the last few days he had missed the recent events that were so troubling. He was able to contact the field director immediately and ask for clarification of what had taken place during the days he was away from the radio. He learned that the coup had taken place just the day before and he was directed to head for Kurela, where he would meet others coming in from the various outstations. Further instructions would be given by the embassy over two-way radio in the morning.

As Dembeli walked through the house, he mentally checked what he would need in case of an evacuation. While quickly packing a carry-on with the most important items for survival in case he found himself stranded in a foreign airport, Dembeli sent word into town with a couple of the children playing soccer in the yard that he needed to see the pastor, the elders of the Church, and the Gospel Team. Dembeli seldom sent messengers to town to call someone, because he much preferred to go himself and honor the one he needed to talk to rather than communicating in a non-verbal way that he was the important one who sent for those he needed to see. When they received Dembeli's message they knew immediately that something important had happened to make Dembeli send for them, and the men responded right away and came out to the mission house to find Dembeli packing a box of study materials and things he could work on during his hopefully brief stay in Kurela. He explained to them that he was hoping that things would settle down quickly and that he would be able to return shortly.

Explaining the situation to the men and telling them about the radio message, Dembeli assured them that if at all possible he would return from Kurela as soon as things were clear. However, they also discussed the possibility of an evacuation and arranged what should happen with the property in case Dembeli would not be able to return. Details such as who would watch the station, what would be done with the fruit from the orchard, and how the bridge in Ponkoe would be completed were discussed. The heavier issues were issues that dealt with the Church and the Gospel Team. Dembeli reminded the men again that they were God's Church and He would lead them and guide them and give them wisdom just as He did for the missionary. He assured them that they are of one Lord, one faith, one baptism and they could be confident that the Lord would be with them. Dembeli had often told them that they needed to be prepared to take total ownership of the Church when missionaries could not return, and they had just as often responded that Dembeli should not say "when the missionaries cannot return" but "if" the missionaries cannot return, for they did not like the thought that the missionaries would ever have to leave. Now they sat quietly as Dembeli assured them that God was still in control and they could trust Him to lead them in the right direction. One of them mentioned the fact that it was no longer "if" the missionaries have to leave, but it was "now the missionaries are leaving".

Pastor Pita, the Church leaders, the Gospel Team, and Dembeli spent some time together in prayer. Then Dembeli showed Barnabasi how to keep the solar fridge going, figuring that he would be back in a couple days. The thermostat had quit working and a new one had not found its way across the Atlantic yet, so Dembeli had unhooked the defective part and bypassed it with a couple of short wires which he hooked together with two alligator clamps to complete the circuit. Every morning he would hook the clamps together, and then in the evening when the sun went down he unhooked them so the fridge would not run twenty four hours straight and drain the batteries, which were recharged by the solar panels. Now he found two long wires, connected them to the fridge, ran them under the door and out onto the veranda so Barnabasi would not have trouble figuring out which ones to connect together. Amidst laughter from all watching, Barnabasi practiced hooking and unhooking the two clamps together. He listened for the fridge to start, or stop, depending on the connection of the wires that he held in his hands.

Dembeli walked through the house one more time, checking to see if he had forgotten anything important. As he prayed about the situation, it seemed that the Lord brought a portion of Scripture alive to him in a new way. In response to Dembeli's concerns about the Church, the Lord reminded him that "Unless the Lord builds the house, its builders labor in vain" (Psalm 127:1). After all, the Church is His "house" and He is building it with the lively stones of man. Then Dembeli thought about the mission house and the fact that it contained just about everything his family owned. The Lord gently responded, "Unless the Lord watches over the city, the watchmen stand guard in vain" (Psalm 127:1). What an assurance it is to know that the Lord is sovereign and that He is in control!

Dembeli locked the door behind him and stepped out to bid goodbye to the men he had ministered with for so long. He reminded them that God was still in control. Then he told Barnabasi that should anything happen, he was not to endanger his life, or the lives of his family and friends, to protect any mission or personal property belonging to Dembeli or his family. He counseled the men to remember that if anything would happen that would keep him from returning and would prevent them from seeing each other this side of eternity, he would look for them in heaven. As he had done so often, he told the men again that whatever it cost they should not miss heaven, for it will be worth it all.

Two hours after receiving the radio message to travel to the designated centers, and still thinking that he would be back in a couple days, Dembeli piled into the truck with a couple of men the Church asked to send with him to greet the Paramount Chief. Dembeli had placed the mission property and all his personal belongings in their hands, and they wanted to go to the Chief and place everything in his hands and assure him that they would watch it for him. Somebody had suggested that the two men should go along to Kurela with Dembeli so that if by any chance the missionaries were evacuated, the two men could return to Heredugu with the news immediately. Dembeli was happy to have the company as he traveled through the night.

About an hour and a half after leaving home, Dembeli and the men traveling with him met the Paramount Chief on the road. He had gone to check the progress on the bridge and was just returning home, assured that work would proceed again in the morning. Since he had been traveling, he had not had the opportunity to listen to his transistor radio and was totally unaware of the recent developments in his country and of the coup that had taken place. The men turned the mission and Dembeli's property over to his care. The Paramount Chief responded by appointing the church leaders as the caretakers of the property, adding that if they had any problems they should contact him immediately. A solemn group gathered around their chief as Dembeli led in prayer for peace and the safety of those he had worked with for so long, and for the country itself. And then they continued on their way through the night.

Missionaries gathered in designated centers all over the country stayed glued to the two-way radios for the next couple of days. Nationals were no different. They too planned their days around the transistor radio broadcasts as British Broadcasting Center and Voice of America kept them abreast of the latest developments in their own country.

The American Embassy continued to negotiate with the new government, but still the safety of ex-patriots could not be guaranteed. Calling in assistance in the form of Marines, Air Force, and Army, the Embassy set up a mass exodus of all American citizens from the troubled country of Sierra Leone. In an efficient manner that was not life-threatening to anyone, they proceeded to airlift American citizens to safety. Convoys of up-country vehicles carried people to the safety and protection of a major hotel in the capital on the coast which had been designated as the meeting place by the United States Embassy. By the time missionaries arrived in the capital they knew they would soon be en route back to America.

A giant hovercraft carried groups of foreigners across five miles of ocean to the peninsula where the airport is located. Children found themselves thrilled with the ride and excited about the troop transport planes that landed one at a time to whisk their families off to safety. The skill, efficiency, kindness, and humor of the United States military from all three branches that were cooperating together to take them to safety caused many to appreciate their homeland and our young men in uniform in a new way. It made one proud to be an American!

Chapter 31: The Return

Sixteen months later Dembeli returned with other missionaries to resume ministry. Reports that had reached the missionaries while they were in America were either confirmed or set aside as rumors, but everyone recognized that the atmosphere of the country had changed and the country was not yet stable. All the down-country stations had been raided by rebels, or thieves, so Dembeli wandered what he would find when he returned to Heredugu.

Upon his arrival, Dembeli discovered that the rebels had indeed been there, but the people from the town had gone out to Dembeli's house to greet them. The rebels wanted the mission vehicle that had been left behind. But the people told the rebels that they could not have it until they sent for the Paramount Chief because everything had been turned over to him when Dembeli left. To assure that the rebels would not take the vehicle, the people sat around the compound while someone rode a bicycle to call the Paramount Chief living seventeen miles away.

Suspecting that the men wanting to take the mission vehicle were indeed rebels, the Paramount Chief called a contingent of border guards from out along the Guinea border and asked them to escort him to Heredugu to check out the situation there. When the chief arrived with a well-armed truckload of soldiers a couple hours later, he found the people sitting comfortably under the shade of the trees and the rebels trying to find a suitable place to sit. The chief confirmed the word of the people that nothing on the compound was to be taken, and he "escorted" the rebels back to the base where the border guards were staying. Thus when Dembeli returned he discovered that nothing had been taken from the station.

Barnabasi had faithfully connected the alligator clamps for the solar fridge each day, and then had unhooked them at night so the fridge had purred along regularly for sixteen months without even being opened. There was cold Pepsi in the fridge to welcome Dembeli back home.

The Lord had watched the house, and through the goodness of the town's people nothing had been taken. Even some of the equipment that was regularly kept outside was still in place and in use. With a heart full of gratitude to God, Dembeli asked some of the Church leaders how he could tell the people from the town thank you for protecting the property he had left behind. Things may not be important, but the Storyteller was not surprised to hear Dembeli explain that he was grateful that not one of the things he had left with the Church elders and the chief had been taken. In response to his question, the leaders told Dembeli that it was not really necessary to give a gift of appreciation to the townspeople. But they mentioned that during turmoil they had not been able to keep the market open and so there was very little salt in town. Someone else pointed out that the ropes on the wells had deteriorated, and that if he really felt he wanted to Dembeli could buy some bags of salt and some new ropes for the water wells since those were two important items that the people had trouble keeping on hand during the rebel uprising.

On his next trip to Kurela for fuel and supplies, Dembeli bought the items suggested and asked the Church leaders to go with him to the town chief and elders so he could express his gratitude to the people. The Church leaders served as the mediators for Dembeli and presented his gifts to the town chief and elders.

The response of the town chief and elders was gratifying. They confirmed what Dembeli's advisors had already told him: that it really was not necessary for Dembeli to give the town a gift. Then they proceeded to explain their reason for saying it wasn't necessary. They explained that the first word that spread along the grapevine when the Dembeli returned was that "their white man" had come back, and they rejoiced. Then the chief turned to Dembeli and said that he knew Dembeli loved Heredugu, and that the Kuranko people loved Heredugu, and the only difference is that Dembeli has a white body and the people in the town have black bodies. The third reason they gave surprised Dembeli a little bit, for the chief and the elders said that nobody from Heredugu would steal anything from Dembeli's place because they knew it was theirs anyway. Finaba, the Storyteller, watched Dembeli's reaction very closely as the leaders of the town shared how they knew that Dembeli was taking care of the things out at the mission, but that if at any time they needed it, he would share with them. Because of that, they were not about to let anyone steal what was theirs anyway until "their white man" could come back to take care of it for them again. They assured Dembeli that though the skin color was different that in their hearts they knew that Dembeli and the town people were all Kurankos.

The town chief and the elders gave several examples of Dembeli's generosity and reminded him of the day he came home with a new mission vehicle. He stopped in town to show the chief before he ever drove it out to his house on the other side of town. Dembeli was humbled by their response and their reasoning, but he knew the feeling was mutual for they had so often shared what they had with him and his family, and he was grateful for friends that stood with him in the tough times as well as in the good times.

A couple weeks later the relationship was confirmed again when a paralyzed man from one of the towns far away was brought to a town along the road. Someone was sent to ask Dembeli to take the man to the hospital for help. Knowing that a bridge was out, Dembeli found some boards and used them to reinforce the bridge so that he could get across to give help where it was needed. The Storyteller chuckled as he rode along, thinking that this again confirmed what the town people had been saying all along: the truck was theirs. Dembeli just took care of it.

The Gospel Team continued to function and the churches continued to grow. The months ahead were exciting ones for the Church, but the instability in the country continued to cause a growing concern for the missionaries. The general attitude of the up country people was that the unrest would not affect the people in the remote areas of northern Sierra Leone, so although they were concerned about their country, the local people did not feel too much apprehension about what would happen to them. As time passed, vehicles began to come through Heredugu carrying people from the gold and diamond digging areas of the country. They were trying to escape the rebels who were destroying and looting their homes and stores in the high tension area. This caused growing concern, but still the people felt that the trouble was far away and would not affect their lives. Their feeling of safety however was being shaken.

Tensions continued to mount until in July of 1994, Dembeli, along with other up-country missionary families, left Sierra Leone on commercial flights because leadership expressed fear for their safety. Within a few months down-country personnel also had to leave, and soon there were no missionaries left outside the capital. The capital still appeared to be safe, so one couple was able to return and maintain a presence there for a few months, before they had to leave as well.

Chapter 32: The Impact of War

For the next couple of years the rebels gained momentum and wreaked havoc and devastation throughout the entire country. The atrocities of war were far worse than can be written. The Storyteller knew that Dembeli would not try to describe what was taking place. Along with others, he did his best to stay in touch through various media resources as he wondered about the people he had left behind.

Rumors of the terrible atrocities began to leak out, and Dembeli became extremely concerned about the people from the Heredugu area. Although official news was sketchy, missionaries had heard that many of the people had fled across the border into the neighboring country. A Church in Indiana that had supported Dembeli since 1975, shared his concern and offered to help finance a trip back so he could check on the Christians from the Heredugu area. Arrangements were made, and with the support of the Church where he was pastoring, Dembeli returned to West Africa in January 1998, to see if he could find Kuranko believers.

Due to a communication problem, Dembeli's itinerary did not get through to the missionary staff so no one was at the airport to meet him. Dembeli arrived in the country bordering Sierra Leone without any contacts, and no clue of where he was to go. Fortunately he was able to find someone who spoke Hausa, a language he had learned growing up in Nigeria, and was able to find a missionary residence where some guests were staying who knew missionaries from the same organization that Dembeli was with. The missionaries were very understanding and extremely helpful, as they went out of their way to help Dembeli reach the area in which the Kuranko people had relocated. They escorted him to one of the major towns in the area before dropping him off and bidding him adieu. From there he walked to various villages along the border locating the people he was so concerned about.

The people from the Heredugu area who had fled to safety welcomed Dembeli with open arms. They invited him to stay with them in their town and offered to walk with him to other nearby towns to visit with friends from across the border. For the next couple of weeks Dembeli walked through towns along the Sierra Leone border and spent most of his time just listening to horrendous escape stories and descriptions of the atrocities of the war. Wanting to know the truth, he questioned many of the stories. Since he could not comprehend how anyone could possibly do such horrendous things to another individual, he often did not accept the stories until several others, often from other towns, had shared similar information with him. He did not challenge any individual's perception of what had taken place, and he soon discovered that everything he was hearing could be confirmed by a variety of individuals from various areas.

Days were spent sitting under the trees listening to a multitude of escape stories. It seemed that everyone Dembeli met had an escape story to tell him. The world has been shocked by the evils of war, and Sierra Leone had not been any different. However, the rebel activity in Sierra Leone was more gruesome than most because the rebels seemed to thrive on mutilating living bodies to establish a reign of terror. The mutilation of hands, arms, and feet appeared to be one of their favorite tactics to instill fear in the hearts of the living. Dembeli marveled that a person could live through such agony and pain as the cutting off of a limb. For those who have suffered such atrocities, their bodies and minds will carry the scars to their graves.

The Kuranko people driven from the Heredugu area across the border were left with nothing but their lives. Their homes had been burned to the ground. Their food supply for the coming year was stolen or destroyed. Even some of the bridges were torn apart so that peace-keeping forces could not pursue the rebels whose demands locally were met simply because they had far superior firepower and hearts intent on evil. For a time, a group of rebels lived in Heredugu. Some of them took up residence in Dembeli's house. From there they raided other towns, and as the conflict raged, the people in Heredugu fled up across the border and left everything behind. As Dembeli moved from town to town along the border, he discovered very quickly that he had more in his thirty five-pound backpack than many of the families who had escaped at night across the border had left to their names.

At one point during the war, there were more rebels living in Heredugu than there were citizens, and the rebels simply took over the homes at gunpoint and forced the people to serve them. Many of the rebels came to church and sang the songs and prayed. They asked the pastor to have a Bible study with them out where they were living in Dembeli's house, and they continued to assure the people that all was well.

Pastor Dauda and others noted that the very map Dembeli had so often used to plan Gospel Team outreach and ministry in the area was lying on the kitchen table and the rebels were using it to plot their raids on various towns in the area. Word of their plans quickly filtered along the African grapevine and it was not long before the people in Heredugu knew what was being planned. Many told Dembeli that this was the signal to them that they needed to flee across the border for safety. Knowing that the rebels were keeping track of them, the men decided to escort their families up towards the border at night and then quietly return and pretend that they had never left town. Often the rebels would corner them and ask where their wives and children were, and the men would report that they had stayed out on the farm. They knew this would only satisfy the rebels for a brief period of time, but they felt it would buy them enough time to know that their families were safe. Soon the men who still had the freedom to do so simply wandered out of town and fled up across the border themselves to rejoin their families. Some of the young men who were held captive by the rebels took a little longer to escape.

Upon their arrival in safety, the people from the Heredugu area began to compare notes. Some tried to return home when rumors said that the rebels had moved on, only to discover that their entire town had been burned down, the food supply that they had so carefully stored following the harvest was gone, and their community was destroyed. Many faced unspeakable horrors as they witnessed rebel activity that systematically destroyed the country and its people. Dembeli was appalled, and often wondered if he was hearing and understanding right.

Most of the people from the Heredugu area did not flee to refugee camps. Instead they built temporary homes in their new host country using elephant grass for the walls and thatching the roofs with a different kind of grass. Their hope was that the rebels would soon move out of the area and they would be able to return to their homeland and rebuild their homes. Hunger forced these refugees to forage back across the border to try and find food among the debris of their burned-out towns. For some this venture proved disastrous, because the rebels remained in the area and were eager to make an example of anyone they caught. Others were able to quietly sneak in and find a few pounds of rice, beans, or squash, bringing food and hope to their families for a few more days. Still others spent each day foraging for food in the bush.

Dembeli listened and was humbled by the courage of a people who had lost everything and still dared to hope for an opportunity to start life over when peace would come to their country. Although some had family and friends who let them move into a hut or share a room in their home, most of them were living in temporary homes built of grass walls with grass thatched roofs. One of the poorest nations on earth had been reduced to even less by the destruction and devastation of a war motivated by greed for the ownership of the diamond mines of the country.

Dembeli discovered that Christians from one area who had witnessed the horrors of the war began to ask, "Where is God in all this?" Some of them, in frustration, disappointment, and anger, turned back to the way of their forefathers simply because they could not understand how a God of love could allow the rebels to continue to oppress the people and destroy their nation. They fled across the border for safety and met Christians from some of the other towns back home who shared the same feelings. Some had been arrested at the border and accused of being rebels. Others had been arrested on the accusation that they were collaborators with the rebels. Friends and relatives came to their rescue by going to the authorities and giving testimony that they were simply escaping from the rebels. Usually within a few hours, or a couple days at most, they were released and freed to settle in and wait for peace to come to their homeland.

Many of the Christians took a careful look at their faith. They realized that everything they had pinned their hope on was gone. Those who were teachers saw their means of making a living and supporting their family disappear overnight as schools and government jobs were shut down. Many Christians suddenly realized that everything they had hoped for in a brighter tomorrow had disappeared and they had nothing left but their faith in Christ. Coming to the conclusion that everything one can hold in his hands, and all material possessions, can be destroyed, but what is in one's hearts cannot be taken away or touched, they fell in love with Jesus all over again. As they prayed for courage to face the war and the oppression, they found that Jesus is more than adequate to meet their needs. And their loving heavenly Father gave them a boldness to share their faith that Dembeli had never seen before. As a result, most of those who had wavered came back to Jesus. Others who had never heard the Gospel before saw that these people had something they did not have, and began to seek the peace and joy that can survive in the midst of the most adverse circumstances.

One evening Dembeli was amazed to hear a testimony service begin to take shape. What a humbling experience to hear people praise the Lord in the midst of such incredible adversity! But praise the Lord they did! Once again Dembeli listened as they told how cholera had spread through their town because of a terrible water supply in the town to which they had fled. The Christians simply went to God in prayer and asked him to help them. God heard. God answered. Not one Christian died of cholera. God is so awesome!

Then one of the young church planters told a remarkable story. He shared that when he came across the border he did not have any way to feed his family, so he found work on various farms, earning enough to provide one meal a day. As he was helping to clear land, he carried some brush to a fire they had going. On the way to the fire a viper wiggled out of the brush he was carrying and bit him on the hand. He felt the poison moving up his arm. Someone in the group disappeared into the bush and came back with "native medicine". Unfortunately it did not help in the least and the poison kept moving up his arm. About the time it started past his elbow, he sensed that he was going to die and he told the men on the farm that he was heading in to town. Once in town, he called his wife and told her what had happened, and instructed her to call the family so he could say his last goodbyes and declare his will. If there is an opportunity to do so, this is usually done in front of the whole family or witnesses, who then carry out the desire of the deceased.

Soon the young man's father, Barnabasi, the Gospel Team leader, arrived. The young church planter greeted his father and told him that the poison was now up to his armpit and that it was time for him to give his parting words to the family. His father stopped him and said, "You do not need to do that." The young man thought that maybe his father did not understand so he reminded his dad that he did not have long to live since the poison only had a little over a foot to travel to his heart. His father responded that it would not be necessary to declare his will because they had not prayed yet. Then Barnabasi led the family in prayer on behalf of his son. God heard and answered. The young church planter was immediately healed. What an awesome God!

Others shared how God had provided them a way to escape. Still others told of the peace their Lord had given them when they were arrested coming across the border. Once again laughter rang out as they shared how six of them were thrown in a cell together. One of them stretched out on the floor and was soon fast asleep. The others could not figure out how he could sleep in the midst of such a tense situation, and in their frustration, they woke him up. Once awake, Mumburu simply looked at the others and reminded them that they were not going anywhere and asked them to move over again so he could stretch out and go back to sleep. It was then that they remembered he had been arrested before, several times as a matter of fact, and had spent months unable to escape the prison bars. Later on he woke up, looked around the room full of his buddies, and simply declared, "One of us must sure be unlucky to get us all in here together." When released, they appreciated even more the spirit and attitude he shared that cheered them up, especially those who had been thrown in the "clinker" for the first time.

Then there were those who shared how God had given them courage in the darkest nights of rebel activity when everything seemed so hopeless. They praised God for the boldness to be able to witness for Him in the face of tremendous opposition. Thanksgiving was offered for their new grass homes and for the people who had welcomed them into their towns. They praised the Lord that they had been able to find land they could farm the coming year. Dembeli was humbled by the simplicity and courage of their faith. What a learning experience!

Dembeli asked how he could pray for them. Immediately, a young church planter responded that he really needed prayer because he had been married for almost eight years and his wife had not been able to have a child. The Kuranko people see this as a curse from God, and they soon began to tell the young couple that his God was not as great as he claimed Him to be since God could not even give them a child. Some of the young couples friends had suggested that even as a pastor he should take a second wife so that the family name could be continued. Others hinted that he really ought to get rid of the wife he had because she was cursed of God and could not bear children. The young church planter asked Dembeli and the others to pray for him so that they would have a child and show the people in their town that God is even greater than they had been telling the people. He shared that the bottom line was that they needed a child for the glory of God.

This young couple had lost everything. Their home was burned down. Their supply of food for the year had been confiscated. Most of their belongings had been destroyed; they even had to borrow pots from their neighbors to cook their food. They were reduced to nothing as far as the world is concerned, and yet their prayer was not for things, but for a child so that God might be glorified. Wow! When peace came Dembeli helped this young couple go to the capital for medical tests and treatment. Saddened by the results, they returned home without a child. Their Church and Dembeli's friends in America continued to pray, and a few years later, in the fall of 2005 God blessed them with a beautiful baby boy!

Others asked Dembeli to pray that they would have courage in the face of danger. Their prayer was that they would be able to stand strong for Christ in the face of opposition from the Muslims and animists in the area. They prayed that they might know the right things to say to help others come to know Jesus as their personal Savior. Everyone joined in prayer that peace would come to their homeland.

Again Dembeli was challenged and humbled because when he tried to put himself in their place he wondered what his requests would be. In all honesty he had to admit that his temptation would be to pray for things, or at least that he would be saved from trouble and persecution. Yet he sat and listened as his friends asked him to pray for the really important things in life, and he realized again that when it is all said and done, that when we pray according to the will of God, we really need to desire that He be glorified in everything. Prayers in the Scripture go more along the lines of the Kuranko's believers requests, and Dembeli was challenged to really seek the mind of Christ in his prayers for himself and his friends.

As they walked together from town to town, Dembeli would often ask questions so that the time became a continual learning experience for him. It also enabled him to disciple those he was with in the practical, everyday crucible of Kuranko living. After a prayer meeting in one town, the men offered to walk with Dembeli to another town only a couple miles away so that he could visit some of his Muslim friends who had escaped across the border. As they were walking along, Dembeli asked the men about their prayer for peace to return to their war-torn country and what they felt could be done to rebuild their community. They mentioned that they would need to have missionaries to help them. Dembeli asked them what kind of missionaries they would need. He explained that he did not mean what type of work would they do, but what would their hearts need to be like to help the people rebuild in the face of such incredible heartache.

The first response was obviously something well thought through. A young pastor told Dembeli he felt that any missionaries coming back to help them would need to understand forgiveness; not with their heads, he pointed out, but with their hearts. He said that it is easy to teach on forgiveness without really understanding it. He went on to explain that he felt that the missionaries who come in after the war would need to understand forgiveness experientially with their hearts, or they would never be able to identify with the people of Sierra Leone. When it is time for the evening meal and the pan of rice is placed on the ground and the men and boys gather around to eat, and you look across the pan to your son who has had his hand, leg, nose, or ears cut off, and the anger wells up within you, you need to have more than just teaching on forgiveness. Others jumped in the conversation and agreed that although you can say you have forgiven, you have to reaffirm that forgiveness in your heart every time you see your son struggling with the life-changing handicap imposed upon him by the rebels.

Dembeli sensed the truth of what they were saying because he had had to deal with his own anger at what had taken place before he could even begin to help the Church deal with the issue of forgiveness. Sitting under a mango tree in the next town, the group continued their discussion, and Dembeli pointed them to Jesus as our example of forgiveness and applied the principles seen in His life to the circumstances. The men agreed that if the country is to be rebuilt it will have to be on the basis of forgiveness, and the church will have to lead the way because non-believers certainly do not understand the mind of Christ or the heart of forgiveness.

Then one of the men who was really struggling with the terrible things he experienced opened his heart and shared how he woke up almost every night because of nightmares. He wondered if God could even forgive a rebel for the horrors the rebel had inflicted on other people. It might be easy to sit down in the safety of a neutral country and say that you forgive, but how does that forgiveness manifest itself when it takes on flesh and bones in the form of a rebel who has moved to live along side of you again? As the group looked to God's Word, they realized again that there is nothing we can ever do to make God stop loving us. They concluded that since His love is eternal, then His forgiveness knows no bounds either, and a rebel who genuinely repents can be forgiven because of the grace and mercy of Almighty God. They declared that Christians need to share His love and forgiveness with others just as Christ has forgiven them. Like the others in the group, Dembeli was keenly aware that this is easier in theory than in practice.

The training sessions Dembeli led each evening centered on prayer. In the open-air services, the Holy Spirit led the discussion in the direction of victory in the face of suffering. It was a real learning experience for all those involved as time was spent together in the Word. Portions of Scripture that had sometimes been lightly passed over took on new meaning in light of what had taken place. Dembeli challenged the believers to continue to live for Christ and to share their faith just as they had done on the other side of the border. He returned to his ministry in America with a new vision and compassion for his Kuranko brothers and sisters in Christ.

—

Since it is such a remote area and there are no missionaries, pastors, or churches in the area where the people from the Heredugu area fled, news from the believers was sketchy at best. However, what word did filter out confirmed that they took seriously their role as light, salt and witnesses for Christ. Having fallen in love with Jesus all over again, they began to share boldly and unashamedly about their Lord and Savior. Soon a letter from the Kurankos living along the Sierra Leone border arrived at the headquarters of the mission in America. One of their leaders had passed through the area en route to the capital. He became the mail man who helped them write the letter sharing how they had continued to lead people to Jesus. They also shared how they needed someone to come and help them in their church planting endeavors since there were no missionaries, pastors, or churches in the border area where they had fled. What they really needed was a "bush missionary."

Apparently, the sending agency for the mission could not find anyone more "bushy" than Dembeli, so they contacted him and asked him to consider being a "non-resident" missionary to the Kuranko people of West Africa. The director for Africa and the Arab world spent time with the Church board where Dembeli was pastoring, and Dembeli was released to return to Africa several times a year to help the Kuranko Church. The overseas director and the Africa regional director met with Dembeli and outlined what they wanted to see happen among the Kurankos, and it was summed up in one very simple sentence. They told Dembeli they wanted him to go back to Africa and do everything he could to see that a totally indigenous Kuranko Church was planted along the Sierra Leone border. Later on, in 1999, when he realized the extent of time this would mean away from the pastorate, Dembeli resigned as pastor of the Church so that he could invest himself full-time in ministry as a non-resident missionary to the Kuranko people.

Having spent twenty years ministering with the Kuranko people in the Heredugu area, Dembeli had a pretty good idea of what type of materials they would need, so he began to gather the necessary items for training. While in Africa, Dembeli had seldom ministered alone, and so as a pastor he felt that he really wanted to take someone from the local church along with him on each trip. After much prayer he decided to ask a good friend to go along with him. It was really hard for Dembeli because he knew that his friend would have to raise approximately $2000 and take his vacation time off work to accompany him. He did not know how he could possibly ask someone to do that when he did not know how he would do it himself if he were the one being asked. Yet he felt strong leading from the Lord and he asked the church to join him in prayer about the need.

Once again God revealed Himself as Provider and funds began to come in. Most of the money came from unexpected sources, and soon his friend not only had enough for the trip, but enough to take along to meet some vital needs of the Church. Our heavenly Father confirmed over and over again His choice of having someone accompany Dembeli and worked out even the smallest details in a very wonderful way.

Dembeli and his friend were dropped off in a town right along the Sierra Leone border. The African grapevine spread the word quickly that Dembeli had returned, and men began to arrive to welcome him and his friend from America. The Gospel Team and pastors showed up, and a seminar was born. Exciting reports revealed that God had indeed been at work among His people, that He had answered their prayers for courage in the face of opposition, and that he was still on the throne. When all the reports came in, Dembeli discovered that the Heredugu area Christians who had been driven across the border into an area totally unreached by the Gospel had already planted some new churches. Dembeli quickly grasped the fact that his role had changed again. He found himself in the role of a coach, helping to give direction, providing teaching material, and giving training and encouragement to church planters who were already leading new churches.

As a non-resident missionary he realized that his contact with many of the new believers would not be direct as it had been previously, but it would be through the pastors and Gospel Team members who were able to move freely back and forth across the border. He would have to help them train the future leadership for the new church plants on both side of the border. It was an exciting development and a very challenging one! It was far from a typical classroom setting where one can discuss theories and principles that someday will apply to ministry. It was an on-the-job, hands-on setting, where believers are more interested in what works than in some theory. The teachings of God's Word are not pious ideals, but power for living in the reality of the here and now and in the glorious hope of eternal life. Once again Dembeli and the Team found themselves back to teaching the basics in every Bible study and prayer meeting, as Dembeli challenged the men to answer three questions every time they taught from God's Word. The people need answers that work. As the men taught each day, they were instructed to answer three basic questions about the portion of God's Word they were reading:

- *What does God's Word say?*
- *What does God's Word mean?*
- *How do I apply God's Word to my life today?*

The teaching had to be Biblical. It had to be practical. It had to be real. And it had to work. Thank God it is! And it does!

Accompanied by pastors, Gospel Team members, or old friends, Dembeli and his friend visited various towns along the border in what they soon found out was considered the "frontier" or "war zone". They were made acutely aware of this in each town as they took time not only to greet the chiefs and the "big men," but also to check in with the border patrol, soldiers stationed along the border to keep it secure. They returned each night to the town they were using as their base, slept on the mud floor of one of the best homes in town, and enjoyed the typical hospitality of their Kuranko hosts.

Dembeli soon discovered that God had chosen an excellent traveling companion for him on this journey as a non-resident missionary. This was especially true when a couple weeks later his friend needed to return to his job in the States. Several members of the Gospel Team offered to escort the two men out to the market town along the main road where they were to be met by a short-term missionary named Max. Knowing that their destination was twenty five miles away, the group set out early, thinking that if all went well they would be in the market town by nightfall.

Halfway out to the market town there was a checkpoint, which was designed to control movement along the border and to protect against rebel invasion into the area. An official from the capital was there checking to make sure there was a clear understanding of all procedures being implemented at the check points. Upon demand, Dembeli produced the documents that he had acquired before coming into the area. He thought everything was in proper order, but immediately sensed that something was wrong. Sure enough, something was wrong. Dembeli and his American friend were put under house arrest. Further questioning on Dembeli's part revealed that two additional signatures were needed on the travel documents for Dembeli and his traveling companion to be in the war zone. Since those signatures were absent, Dembeli and his companion were "illegally" in the area and therefore were under arrest. Unfortunately, the missionaries ministering in a neighboring tribe who had helped Dembeli secure the travel documents had not been informed of all the necessary signatures and he had come into the area blissfully ignorant, thinking that he was totally prepared with all the necessary documents. The military leaders turned Dembeli and his American friend over to the Paramount Chief until they could decide what should be done with them.

The Paramount Chief told Dembeli that he had heard a lot about him even before the war and was glad to be able to meet him. People began questioning the chief, wondering why their missionary had been arrested and requesting the chief to do something about it. The Paramount Chief donned his official robes and went off to see the military officials who had made the arrest. The men accompanying Dembeli and his American friend began referring to them as Paul and Silas for they, like those saints so long ago, were under arrest and no longer able to move about freely.

Before long the Paramount Chief returned with the news that his prisoners were now free. He said that he would be honored if they would spend the night in his compound. Since it was getting late, the group thanked the chief for interceding on behalf of "Paul and Silas" and accepted his generous offer to stay overnight. The chief's son showed them to his hut next door to the chief where they could spend the night. Once settled in, they enjoyed their freedom and wandered around the town to greet the people. One of the more recent graduates from the Bible school in Sierra Leone had been ministering in the town and had told the people that the initial service of the new church would take place the following Sunday. The attention attracted by the arrest of Dembeli and his American friend caused him to re-evaluate the situation, and he quickly sent word out that the first public service would be that very evening.

As night fell, the Paramount Chief sent Dembeli and his friends a meal that far exceeded their expectations. Once again traditional Kuranko hospitality manifested itself. Following the meal, people gathered for their first open-air service, and the church was off to a good start. The situation brought in a lot of curious people, but they listened and heard God's Word. In a very real and powerful way God spoke that evening.

Morning found Dembeli's group ready to head on to the market town where Max was to meet them. After a couple of weeks out on the frontier without cold drinks, the Coca Cola found in the kerosene refrigerator in the market was a special treat, and Dembeli and his companion rediscovered the joy of a cool, refreshing drink. They wandered around the town locating some of Dembeli's old friends, but somehow always ended up back at the "Coca Cola store." Finally they stored their backpacks and settled in on a veranda to wait for Max to arrive so they would have a ride back to the nearest missionary colleagues who would be taking Dembeli's guest back down to the coast to catch his flight back to the States.

Relaxation suddenly ended when a police officer showed up and demanded that the entire group follow him. He escorted the believers to the police headquarters and into the small office of the Commissioner of Police where they were to be interviewed. The officers soon discovered that none of the group with Dembeli spoke the official language of the country, and so in order to intimidate, they refused to use a common denominator language to communicate with Dembeli. It soon became more than apparent that the entire group that had accompanied Dembeli was also being arrested.

While going through Dembeli's backpack an officer found a Wordless Book. Since it was made of cloth and had only a few pages in it and none of them contained writing, he was totally confused. He brought it into the interrogation room for an explanation. The officer handed the book to Dembeli and demanded that he tell them what it was all about. Now our Heavenly Father knew exactly what was going on, and right about then He must have started to chuckle.

Dembeli took the little cloth book, and starting with the first page he explained that the black represented darkness and sin and that all men have sinned and come short of the glory of God (Romans 3:23). The red page of the book reminds us of the blood of Christ that was shed on the cross for us so that He could be our Supreme Sacrifice and end all sacrifices. He died for us while we were sinners because He loved us so much (Romans 5:8). The white page declares that for those who believe, repent, and accept Jesus as their Supreme Sacrifice, God will forgive their sins and cleanse them from all unrighteousness and they will stand clean before Him (1 John 1:9). Once clean before God we know that we are on our way to heaven. The yellow page represents the streets of gold in heaven (John 14:1-6). Now heaven is a wonderful place that God has prepared for those who accept Jesus Christ as their personal Savior, and they will have eternal life there with Him. The green page reminds us of life with Him forever (Romans 6:23).

Once they had demanded that Dembeli explain the wordless book, they could not very well stop him so he had a captive audience. They thought Dembeli and his friends were the ones arrested. Since they had refused to speak a common denominator language, Dembeli's words were translated, and three languages were used, as he shared the Gospel message to a room full of police officers. It was not until after their release that Dembeli discovered that all the officers knew at least two of the languages being used, and some of the officers knew all languages that were being used in the translation. They got the Gospel more than once — once in every language they understood. Isn't God awesome!

While sitting in the police headquarters office, Dembeli realized how God was in total control of the situation. Had they been arrested on the way in, Dembeli and his friends would not have been able to deliver the Bibles and training material that were so important to the ministry. Instead, they had been arrested on their way out, and so the books were already safe in the hands of the Church leaders and would soon be dispersed to the churches were they were needed so desperately.

Without explanation the Commissioner of Police began to fill out forms. The silence was oppressive, and Dembeli and his friends waited to find out what was going on. The three nationals accompanying Dembeli, all Christians, were taken out of the room and locked in the jail adjacent to the officer's room. Dembeli was told that he and his American friend would be escorted back to the state capital and turned over to the proper authorities there. Dembeli suggested that it might be easier if they used the mission vehicle since they had someone who was coming to pick them up shortly. The commissioner jumped on that suggestion since he did not have a vehicle at his disposal anyway and would have had to rent one, a fee that would have been charged to the account of "Paul and Silas," who had once again appeared.

About that time the mission vehicle pulled up and parked near the police headquarters. The documents for the vehicle were immediately confiscated and other forms were filled out. The documents along with the new forms were handed over to an official who would escort Paul and

Silas to the authorities in the state capital. Dembeli was the last to leave the room. As he departed, his three friends called to him from behind the locked doors of their cell. The three captives pled with Dembeli to help them, but he had to tell them that he was under arrest too, and not in a position where he could help "Shadrack, Meshack, and Abednego." One can hardly imagine how hard it was for Dembeli when the officer told him he had to leave, get in the truck, and head for the capital leaving his three friends in jail.

Fortunately the mission vehicle was equipped with a two-way radio, and Max was able to call his brother, and other missionaries, to report on the situation long before the truck reached the capital. Unfortunately none of the missionary men contacted were available at that time. Dembeli's official escort wanted to see his own brother in the capital, so he agreed to let the missionaries sit in their vehicle in the market until one of the missionaries they had called could come and escort them to the authorities. Dembeli and his friend from Indiana had a good chuckle when their police escort left all the documents in the truck and took off into the market to find his brother. Several hours later the other missionaries and a national leader who was well known to the authorities in the area arrived on the scene. About that time the police escort returned with his brother in tow.

One of the missionaries who had several years of seniority ministering as a translator in a neighboring tribe, and a national Christian who was well known as a leader in the community, interceded on behalf of Dembeli and his friend. The Commissioner of Police carefully explained the whys and wherefores of the case, and finally agreed to release the visiting American so he could return to Indiana on his regularly scheduled flight. Since it was Saturday, he graciously released Dembeli to stay with his missionary friends in the area, but informed him that it would be necessary for him to come back to the office on Monday morning.

Max and Dembeli's guest headed to the coast and a flight back to the States as planned, right on schedule. On Monday Dembeli returned to the police headquarters in the state capital as he had been instructed. The morning was spent with a new official escort who took him around to all the offices and introduced him to the highest authorities responsible for the security of the border throughout the whole state. This included police, soldiers, border patrol, etc. All were extremely courteous and helpful to Dembeli. By the afternoon he was released and ready to head back to the town where he had been arrested.

Upon his arrival, Dembeli immediately checked on the whereabouts of "Shadrach, Meshach and Abednego." While in the state capital he had requested that his friends also be released. A phone call from the Chief of Police had taken care of that, so the three men, a little worse for the wear, were freed by the time Dembeli arrived back in town. It was a forlorn group that Dembeli met, but within a couple hours their incredible sense of humor took over and the stories of the cell began to be told amidst gales of laughter. They chuckled at the manner they had devised to get in touch with "Shadrach's" wife so she could cook and bring meals to them. They shared how "Shadrach" had been able to talk a guard into letting him out for a little walk so he could find someone to intercede for them. He went immediately to a leader from their area and asked for help, but the Muslim leader said that all three men left in the cell were Christians and he would not help them. "Shadrach" went on his way rejoicing in the fact that their lives were such a clear testimony for Christ.

After they got back together, Dembeli and his friends discussed what the next step should be. Two of the men were chosen to walk back out to the border and tell the church leaders from the Heredugu area what had taken place so that they would have the facts straight and not be overly concerned. It was decided that Dembeli and the other two should stay in town and wait to hear from the border before making any further plans. A pastor from another tribe had settled in the market town where Dembeli and his friends had been arrested and he offered to let the three vagabonds sleep in one of the rooms in his house. Dembeli and his two friends moved into the storeroom where Dembeli found enough room on the concrete floor to spread out his sleeping bag while the others shared a straw mattress on a rickety wooden bed frame. Although difficult, it was adequate housing while they waited to see what would transpire.

Waiting is often hard, especially when it carries so many uncertainties. It was particularly hard for Dembeli this time because he did not know what was happening out on the border and was not sure that the believers would even be able to make it through all the check points to join him for another time of training as had been planned. Although Dembeli often slept on the floor of a mud hut and was used to traveling without a bed, the concrete floor he found as his bed did nothing to encourage a sound sleep. The house was located by the main road, and large trucks laboring up the hill into town sounded like they were en route to the living room, and all three men found themselves waking up ready to jump and run out of harm's way before they realized that the truck was still on the road and safely headed into town.

Some things wake Dembeli up even quicker than a noisy truck. A cockroach wanting to share his sleeping bag is even more effective than an alarm clock when it comes to an instant wake-up call. Dembeli was immediately fully awake, and the roaches found themselves in instant trouble. Then Dembeli began to talk to the Lord about it. He wondered if maybe the Lord would consider giving him a little bit of a break after the arrest, the not-so-soft bed, and everything that had happened in recent days. The Lord needed to talk to Dembeli and once He had his attention, the Lord spoke through His Word and told Dembeli to hold steady and wait on Him, and His plans would be revealed. He assured Dembeli with promises from His Word. So Dembeli prepared to wait, settled back down, and went back to sleep.

Each day while waiting, Dembeli and his friends, escorted by their newfound pastor friend, began to make tours of the town. Word spreads quickly in an African village and sometimes it seems that there really are no secrets. Before long, Dembeli and his friends had made the acquaintance of all the important men in town. It seemed that they met all those who thought they were important, and all those who hope to be important someday, and many of those who wanted them to think they were important. Actually the arrest attracted enough attention that the Lord used it to open wide the doors for ministry.

This was demonstrated to Dembeli in a powerful way about a week later when the Paramount Chief who had housed them when they were under house arrest sent a runner twelve miles each way to visit Dembeli and to give him a very simple message. The runner reported, "Dembeli, the Paramount Chief says that we have now seen your heart. He wants you to know that you are welcome in any town in his chiefdom at anytime and you will always be considered the personal guest of the Paramount Chief." With that message, the whole chiefdom opened up to the presentation of the Gospel. What had originally been intended for bad, God had turned into good for His glory.

On Saturday evening, five days after he had returned to town, Dembeli and his friends heard a commotion and discovered that some of the Christians from out on the border had arrived in town. What a joyous reunion that was! After the evening meal, all gathered around under the orange tree in the back yard under a beautiful full tropical moon and began to praise God for what He had been doing in their lives. The testimonies rolled on and on as each took time to give God the glory due His name. Then they began to pray. It seemed that heaven opened, and a little bit of glory came down. There was no doubt that the group was standing on holy ground. There was no clock, nobody keeping time, no sense of urgency to get on with something else, just the glory of His presence and nothing more important to do than to worship Him together. It was a powerful prayer meeting. Because of His presence it was an awesome experience!

The following days were good ones as the pastors and Team members, made plans to continue reaching into the area with the Gospel. Everyone knew that soon Dembeli would have to return to the States and the believers would need to head back to their towns along the border. On the closing day, the prayer time was limited because several needed to go to a hospital and had to catch public transport for their journey. Dembeli suddenly realized that it was the first time during the seminar that a time limit had been put on the prayer time. He sensed the disappointment of the believers, but knew that they all understood that the public transport vehicles would not wait and so they reluctantly accepted the inevitable. Dembeli left to return to the States a couple days later, challenged with the simplicity of the faith of God's people and the marvelous grace He provides when it is needed most. How true it is that in our weakness He will reveal His strength, if we will let Him.

—

As a non-resident missionary to the Kuranko people, Dembeli scheduled his next trip to Africa with the intention of focusing on training the Sierra Leone Christians to disciple the new believers in their host country so that when peace came to Sierra Leone, and the refugees returned home, they would leave a strong Church behind them. When Dembeli arrived, word quickly spread along the fantastic African grapevine, and soon pastors, Gospel Team members, and other Christians began to show up to greet him. They suggested that he find a place to live in a town out on the main road. They went with him to some of the authorities and asked for advice about lodging. Some of the very men who had arrested Dembeli earlier now helped him find an area of the town where they felt he could rent a few rooms or even a house, and they proved to be very helpful. Once the arrangements were made, Dembeli settled into what became the base for his ministry in the area.

In proper Kuranko tradition, the leadership and elders of all the churches met to make all major decisions that would affect the churches in the area. Dembeli felt like he was at the Jerusalem Council in Acts 15 as he sat listening to them discussing how the church should work. As in the traditional system the people had worked with for generations, no major decision would be made until all the right people were at the meeting. Dembeli looked around the group of men and saw that among the leadership there were many young men who, as boys, used to play with his children. They learned a whole lot more than how to ride bikes and play soccer. Dembeli chuckled as he thought about those days back in Heredugu when each little boy who came out to play was allowed to have four oranges off the trees in the orchard. Some of the boys would try to take many times that many and sneak off with them back to town. But they soon learned that if they were caught, none of the boys would get any oranges for the next three days. Dembeli often talked to them about trust and pointed out to them if they could not be trusted in the little things in life there was no way that they could be trusted in the big issues of life. There were days when a soccer tournament would be held for the kids and the reward for the winning team would be a whole wheelbarrow full of oranges. The boys caught on, and soon Dembeli did not have to worry about how many oranges they would take as they ran to the orchard calling to each other "four four, four four!"

Now, as men, these same individuals were being entrusted with things much greater than oranges. They were discussing the leadership of the Church. They had learned to be trustworthy in little things and now they were able to deal with real issues of life. Relief funds, food, and other benefits, including training materials, were not divided or distributed until the Church council of elders could meet and represent the needs of their people. Dembeli watched as the spiritual gifts of leadership in the Body began to emerge, and he saw the wisdom of the Lord reveal itself as the elders sat together and discussed the various issues. As in traditional Kuranko society, votes were not taken. Discussion continued until a consensus was reached. The decision was then clearly stated by the opinion leader and clarified so that each of the elders could take back to their people a clear statement of what had been decided. Since there was more than one elder from each church, there was a natural system of checks and balances.

Sometimes Dembeli sat listening and felt that the decision could be reached in a lot less time, but then the Holy Spirit would remind him to be patient. As the Spirit moved, Dembeli learned more about the creativity of the Kuranko Church and the wisdom and power of the Holy Spirit as the spiritual gifts He gave became evident. Dembeli saw a truly Kuranko Church emerging, and he wanted to share what was happening with some of the early missionaries who had longed to see such a Church a generation ago. Dembeli's role had changed again. Finaba knew that he often recalled the first time the Team went out and God had reminded him about ownership. Dembeli remembered so clearly the Lord telling him, "This is My people. This is My Church. This is My Gospel Team. All I want you to do is to disciple them."

As he sat listening to the discussion, Dembeli realized that a discipline problem needed to be taken care of. He was concerned about it because he feared that because of the war the men would not be as willing to take a stand for what was right, but would give in to pressure to make it easier for one who was already having a tough time. When the men took an hour off for the morning meal, he asked a couple of the men about it. Their response was encouraging. They simply looked at Dembeli and said, "We will take care of this just like we did on the other side of the border. This really is not a problem to us."

Dembeli remembered the last time discipline was necessary. There were rumblings of the oncoming war, but the people in remote areas felt it would never reach them. Life was going on pretty much the same as it had for years. One of the men became involved in a situation that was not befitting for a Christian and Dembeli knew that the church would need to deal with it. After the service one evening Dembeli was walking through town with a couple of the men and the issue came up. Dembeli asked about it and one of the men replied, "Dembeli, you don't need to worry about this. We will take care of it. If you don't want to, you don't even have to come to the meeting." They did take care of it, and affirmed once again that the purpose of discipline is always redemptive.

Dembeli knew that the Church was like a bicycle. One of the pedals was the Church leadership and the other was the missionary. If the pedals stayed in the same position the bicycle would not go anywhere. He knew that there had been times in the past that the "missionary pedal" had been on top and had called the shots, but now the "church leadership pedal" was on top and the "bicycle of the Church," under the direction of the Holy Spirit, was moving along smoothly. Dembeli rejoiced to see what God was doing and was confident that the leadership would be able to face any of the tests ahead as they listened to the Holy Spirit directing their decisions.

The first test of the new structure and authority came when one of the young church planters asked about baptizing the people that he had lead to Jesus. All their Church denominational policy manuals and by-laws had been destroyed on the other side of the border. They did recall that the policy was that no one could baptize a new believer unless he was an ordained minister or had the permission of an ordained minister to do so. Others argued that they did not feel that ordination was necessary and recalled some of the baptism services in the Heredugu area where Dembeli, the only ordained minister in the area at that time, had allowed them to baptize while he stood on the bank of the river and encouraged them. They recalled how he had told them that as believers they had lead people to Jesus, and then when they had discipled the new believers, he felt the leaders could be the ones to baptize them. Two men baptized the new believers, and it was often the local pastor and the one who had discipled the new convert who had the honor.

Later a Kuranko pastor ordained by the National Church in Sierra Leone moved into the Heredugu area. Unfortunately, his life did not support his words as far as the churches in the area were concerned, and they would not allow him to pastor a church in their district even though he was the only ordained minister in Heredugu District. Now he had fled across the border with them and was expressing a strong opinion that non-ordained men should not be allowed to baptize the new believers. Since he was the only ordained Kuranko minister in the area, it created a rather serious problem for the Church.

Dembeli was a little concerned about Reverend Kelen's relationship to the church since he had noticed that people in the town where he was living referred to him as "Reverend Kelen." Dembeli took this opportunity to find out what the church council felt. They informed him, in a very matter-of-fact manner, that the man had been ordained and they could not take that away from him, but that they had the same relationship with him on the present side of the border that they had had on the other side of the border. They would not allow him to pastor a church. He was considered a retired pastor, just as he had been before. They assured Dembeli that they were handling the situation and that everything was under control.

That did not solve the issue of baptism, nor did it answer the young church planter's question about baptism, so the elders turned to Dembeli for advice. In response Dembeli took the book of Acts and began to read, without commentary, the various records of the baptisms in the early Church. About half way through the book, one of the men interrupted by saying, "They did not have a policy manual or by-laws, and I don't see that those men who baptized the believers were ordained." As they looked carefully at the Scriptures, they concluded that the Church has the authority to approve baptism, and so they decided that each Church could check out those who wanted to be baptized. Then two men recognized and approved by the Church council as their spiritual leaders could baptize the new converts. They all knew that this decision would be challenged by Reverend Kelen, but they felt that they were living in obedience to the authority of God's Word and made the decision to go ahead with a baptismal service.

The men agreed that all the candidates for baptism should have some teaching on the meaning of baptism before they were baptized. The group discussed the real essence and meaning of baptism and decided that each new believer should be taught the basics and the purpose of baptism so they could answer questions about baptism if their family and friends in the community should ask them about it. They looked to the Scriptures to answer such questions as, "What is the meaning of baptism?" "Why are we baptized?" and "What does it mean to be part of the body of Christ?"

On the other side of the border they had faced this same issue. In the early years in down-country churches a person could be baptized but not accepted as a church member until they had gone through a membership course. The Heredugu area churches had decided that should not be and they took a different stand. When the subject came up for discussion in a new setting, the Church Council of Elders, confirmed the decision taken in the Heredugu District years before and stated that it was wrong to delay membership in the church once a person was baptized. They reasoned that a person is baptized into the body of Christ and therefore there is no reason for telling them that they have to take a membership course before they can become members of the Church, which according to the Scriptures is the Body of Christ. Besides that fact, there was the simple reality that the membership lessons had been destroyed on the other side of the border and they did not have them to teach anyway. So upon a confession of faith and baptism, a person was immediately considered a member of the Church. They were baptized into the Body of Christ, not into a waiting period until they had been taught a certain course, or had proved that they were capable of being a good member.

Baptism, like it had been for them on the other side of the border, became the public indication that they were now Believers in Christ and therefore members of the Church. They reasoned that this was logical since that is how they had approached the issue on the other side of the border, and the geography does not change a Biblical pattern. They did feel however, that church members should be given a baptism certificate and a membership card immediately because these documents would help them in the identification process in their new country of residence, especially if they were arrested. They were also aware that once a person is baptized and has made a public confession of his or her faith in Christ, the opposition sets in. If they are part of the Church, they have a support group to stand with them and help them face the conflict.

The little border town of Mogodi challenged this idea. A small group of Christians fled there to find peace, but the opposition came against them in a surprising way. Land to make a farm was denied them, and they were asked to pay high rent for a room to live in although the landowners knew that they had no jobs and no income. The ridicule was hard for them to take, and the single men could not find anyone willing to cook food for them unless they joined in the prayers at the mosque with the rest of the men. They continued to struggle for some time, but finally the church in Mogodi was forced to pull out as the Christians moved to towns farther into the interior where there was not as much opposition.

Several years passed, and during that time Dembeli and some of the Christians helped the town fix up their road and put in a couple of bridges so that the market vehicles could come and take their produce to market. It saved them walking about twenty five miles each direction and the people were thankful, but they still did not invite the Christians back to live among them. Dembeli and the Gospel Team continued to share with the people the real reason they were helping them. One day Finaba watched as Dembeli talked to Keta about salvation. He started out with a very simple Wordless Book. Keta began to ask questions, and Dembeli noticed a small group of people standing around watching and listening. Dembeli asked one of the pastors to keep in touch with Keta and to encourage him while he returned to the States for about six weeks.

Six weeks later Dembeli returned from the States and, as usual, began visiting the towns where there were believers. He also responded to the request from the chiefs and the military to help the people in various towns who needed road repairs done. Sunday is market day, so Dembeli would usually walk through the market to greet people and then relax out under a tree near the house where he could watch the people and chat with those who had time to visit. It was in the middle of the afternoon when Officer Dansanda stopped by to chat. Finaba chuckled when Officer Dansanda pulled up on his bicycle because he had been the "body guard" that had been assigned to walk with Dembeli when he had visited believers all along the border along the edge of the war zone months earlier. During those days they had developed a friendly relationship and Officer Dansanda had listened often to the Gospel message and knew the real reason why Dembeli was in the area.

Officer Dansanda greeted Dembeli with a big smile that few people can match. They chatted awhile and then Officer Dansanda got real serious. He asked Dembeli to write his name down because he wanted Dembeli to record the fact that he had accepted Jesus as his Supreme Sacrifice. He wanted Dembeli to know that he was "now walking in the Jesus Road." He told Dembeli that there were four other men in town who had also decided to change roads, and that they would be very happy to have Dembeli come and visit them. Officer Dansanda jumped on his bicycle and pedaled back to the town that just a few short years before had forced all the Christians to leave. After he was gone, Dembeli found a couple of the Gospel Team members in town and one of the pastors, and shared with them about his conversation with Officer Dansanda. They told him that they had heard the same thing from some of the others, and that there were indeed five men in Mogodi that were taking their stand for Christ, and Officer Dansanda was one of them.

The border guards in Mogodi sent a runner to ask Dembeli if he could come and help them rebuild a bridge near their town. When they arrived in town Dembeli found the soldiers sitting under their little thatched roof relaxing. The fact that there were no walls allowed the officers to watch the road crossing the border and to keep track of the traffic on the footpaths that came from neighboring towns. It also provided the structure that allowed them to hang a hammock or two in the shade so the hot tropical sun would not beat down on them as they faithfully guarded their post.

Dembeli was given a seat of honor and the commanding officer provided him and the men with him a fine meal as they discussed road repairs. Soon the subject switched to other issues and Dembeli was surprised to hear a man in town being referred to as Pastor Keta. Dembeli was fully aware of the fact that there was not a trained pastor in town and that this very town had been a tough place for the church to get started. So he casually asked about the pastor and the believers. What he heard caused him to realize that he needed to take a walk in to town and meet Pastor Keta, who was now leading the group of five believers in daily prayers.

Dembeli went to meet Pastor Keta, and discovered that it was the man who had learned to share Dembeli's "wordless book" with others. He spent some time with Pastor Keta and was pleased to learn that Pastor Keta could read a little bit. He arranged to send material to Pastor Keta so that he would have something to teach his people. Soon Pastor Keta was teaching his people every morning using the Scripture memory program in pictures. Then Dembeli took the TEE book *Following Jesus* to him and explained carefully how he should take just a little section of it and teach it to his people every day. Dembeli arranged with one of the other pastors to visit Pastor Keta and encourage him and help him with the material that had been left with him.

Dembeli went back to America and encouraged people in the States to pray for the new Church and their leader, and six weeks later returned to Africa with a real anticipation to see what God had done in Mogodi while he was gone. What a joy it was to discover that on his return there were fourteen believers in the little Church along the border. Over the next two years the Church continued to grow, and soon there were twenty five believers in the little border town where just a few short years before the Christians had pulled out of because of the severe opposition that they had faced for taking their stand for Christ.

Encouraged by Dembeli to take an apprentice to train, Pastor Keta found a young man and began to teach him all the material and to give him responsibility in the church. Together they led the believers in daily prayer and Scripture memorization as they continued to reach out to the people in their town knowing that it would not be easy, but with the knowledge that they had found the Truth.

Dembeli recalled the time when Church membership had become an issue in the Heredugu Church many years before. Pastor Pita wanted the people to know how serious it was that they know what they believe and why they believe it. Since most of the people in the area were illiterate, it was hard for them to study God's Word for themselves and grow. He reasoned that it was necessary to refresh their memories every year so that they would be able to answer questions about their faith when they were asked.

At one point in the politics of the country, Parliament was "dissolved" so that elections could take place. Feeling that that was not such a bad idea, Pastor Pita "dissolved parliament" in the Church, and declared that there were no longer any members in the Heredugu Church. Anyone who wanted to be a member needed to attend a doctrinal course that would be taught in every service for the whole month of January. Surprisingly, the Church accepted his decision without debate or hard feelings. In the years that followed, the course was taught every January in each of the Churches throughout the whole district. However, it was decided that it would not be necessary to "dissolve parliament" every year.

Following the brief training session with the all those who wanted to be baptized, the elders of the Church would meet with them and talk to them about their commitment to Christ. The elders would then be satisfied that each of the candidates really understood what it meant to be a Christian. Dembeli remembered being in on some of these sessions on the other side of the border as the elders interviewed the new believers. He recalled one of the elders telling a new believer that the man had to be really serious about his commitment to Christ because the Church did not want to be embarrassed if his life did not show he was a Christian. They did not want to be shamed when the community pointed at one of their number and wondered why he was still sacrificing to idols or wearing amulets after his baptism. He went on to point out that it was not only the Church that would be hurt by such an action, but that Jesus would be hurt even more, and they did not want that to happen. He emphasized that the community would be looking at the Christians to see if they were different now that they had been "born anew" or "born from above." Each of the candidates was challenged to examine themselves to see if they were totally surrendered to Christ as Savior and Lord.

Dembeli sat in the session knowing that the leadership of the Church knew exactly what they were talking about because some of them were only one step removed from animism and Folk Islam themselves. They were also very much aware of the lives of the new believers they were talking to, and there are not too many real secrets in a Kuranko town. Yet, Dembeli was also aware that even with this teaching there would be resistance from Reverend Kelen who was adamant that the baptism should be done only be an ordained minister.

During the next couple of days, Dembeli spent time in prayer about this issue because he was fully aware of what a ruckus Reverend Kelen was capable of causing since in past years the Church had been in conflict with him on several issues on the other side of the border. Dembeli sensed the Holy Spirit telling him to talk to the elders about the possibility of giving Reverend Kelen the honor of being one of the men to baptize the first group of converts. A few days later, while talking with the opinion leader of the Church council, Dembeli asked him about it. The elder said that he felt the same way and had already discussed it with some of the others and they had approved. By asking Pastor Kelen to help, they would pull the rug of contention out from under him, and thus they would pour peace on what could otherwise turn into a potential conflict for the newly structured church. God was one step ahead of all of them.

Because of political tensions in the area, all the Christians could not gather in one large group. Such a gathering of so many refugees would be seen in a very poor light politically, so it was decided that two separate baptism services should be held in two towns some distance apart. Dembeli was present at the first baptismal service, and when the day of baptism arrived and the candidates came forward, who should be one of the first but Reverend Kelen's youngest son. He had escaped to a village some miles away from his father and was living in a town other than where the council had met. At the time of their meeting they were not aware of his desire to be baptized. When he stepped into the water and gave his testimony of God's saving grace in his life, Dembeli suddenly realized how completely God had neutralized a very touchy situation. Although Reverend Kelen was not in the meeting where his son was baptized, he was honored to be one of the baptizers in the other location. God apparently used the circumstances and his son's baptism, to lead him to such a radical attitude check that he became a supporter of the Biblical pattern of baptism as the Heredugu District interprets it.

After the baptismal services, Dembeli had another eye opener. As he listened to the men discussing this first baptismal service ever held among the Kuranko people in their host country, he discovered that the Church leaders had interviewed some of those requesting baptism and that the elders of the local churches had asked some of the candidates to wait because their lives were not testimonies of their profession of their faith in Christ. Unlike missionaries, they were fully aware that some of those who had newly declared themselves to be aligned with the Church still sacrificed to ancestral spirits when the going got tough. They also knew that several still wore the amulets, or magic charms, to ward off the evil spirits. The Church elders sat down with them and counseled them to make a total surrender to Jesus as Savior and Lord. They pointed out that Jesus is not just our Savior, but that He must be Lord of our lives, and that an individual was not really ready for baptism until they had come to complete surrender to Christ as Savior and Lord, and were ready to set aside their sacrifices and amulets. The elders asked for that commitment and invited those who could not make that break in the secret areas of their lives to the service, but informed them that they would not be baptized until they could make a total surrender to Jesus. So the number of those baptized was fewer than had been anticipated. Yet, in denying baptism to some who had requested it, the Kuranko Church made a statement that it costs something to be a Christian and that they take very seriously the matter of believer's baptism. Later, some of those denied baptism the first time around came to a deeper understanding of what it means to be a Christian and were able to make the commitment and surrender their lives to Christ. They were baptized in a service a few months later.

A second test of how the newly-formed Church was going to handle things came up at the first communion service in their new country. The young church planters asked Dembeli to help them learn how to do a communion service. At the close of the training session, believers in the area joined the Church Council and had a time of worship together. The meeting was held outdoors under a shade tree. People sat on crude stick benches or on rocks that had been moved into place to serve as benches.

After a time of worship and Scripture reading, hearts were prepared for communion. Just before communion was served, one of the young men interrupted the service by saying that he realized that for a long time his Christian friends had been praying for him to become a believer. He shared how his heart had been hardened as a Muslim, but that a short time ago he had accepted Christ and this would be his first communion service. He asked the Church to approve him for baptism because he wanted to make a public declaration of his faith in Christ. They stopped the service to sing a song of praise and to ask God's blessing on Bunduka as he sought to live every day for Jesus.

After reading the story of Jesus at the Last Supper and the advice given by the Holy Spirit through the Apostle Paul concerning communion, Dembeli asked one of the elders to pray. A loaf of bread was broken in half, and each half started around the circle of believers going in opposite directions. Dembeli was amazed to see one of the young church planters get up and walk across the circle to kneel in front of one of the participants who was just about to break off a piece of the bread. It seemed as though the young man shut out everybody else in the meeting. He quietly began to speak to the person holding the bread. He pointed out that the person should not take the bread because he had never accepted Jesus as his personal Savior. Then he explained again very simply what the bread and the cup of the Lord's Supper means to us as Christians. He concluded by advising the person not to take the bread and the cup lightly. He suggested that the bread should be passed on if Jesus had not been accepted as the Supreme Sacrifice in his life. Without breaking off a piece of bread, the person quietly passed the loaf to the next person. The young pastor went back and sat down and the service continued.

The person that the pastor had challenged to examine his life did exactly that. The young church planter was able to lead him to total surrender to the Lordship of Jesus Christ. When Dembeli returned three months later, he discovered that this person had started down the road of discipleship. Dembeli was overjoyed to stand on the banks of the river and watch that very person step into the water of baptism. Tears of joy welled up as he listened to a radiant testimony of what Christ had done in changing a life, and he rejoiced again in the faithfulness of the Holy Spirit who had given a young pastor courage to stand on the principles of God's Word even when it was not easy. Realizing that there was increased opposition coming from Islam now that the church was planted, he rejoiced to see another testimony of God continuing to build His Church even when it cost something to be a follower of Jesus Christ.

Following the seminar, the Church leaders each returned to their various villages, but arrangements were made for some to gather at the Sabola church for a baptism the following Sunday so that the new believers from both the Sigitini and Sabola church could be baptized. After the service one of the church planters, along with several others from another church, came to Dembeli with a question about what the Apostle Paul instructed the Corinthian church concerning communion (I Corinthians 11:1-35). Dembeli had often reminded the men to read the Word and then answer the three simple questions: What does it say? What does it mean? How do I apply it in my life today? The young church planter read verses 27-32 and explained to Dembeli what he thought it said. Then he asked, "Does it really mean what it says, or am I not understanding what it means? Is communion really to be taken this seriously? Are we to examine ourselves that carefully?" Together they discussed the portion of Scripture in question and concluded that the Scripture really does mean what it says, and that we *are* to take communion that seriously, even when we remember the Lord's Supper in an obscure village in the middle of the African countryside far away from any established churches. We are to apply God's Word to our lives as the Holy Spirit directs us and then to trust God for the results. Once the young man knew that he did indeed understand God's Word and he could take it for what it says, the simplicity of his faith took over and he returned to his town determined to teach his people more of the truth of God's Word.

—

When tensions let up along the border, Dembeli was able to visit all the newly established churches. He was thrilled to meet some of the leaders in training, but he realized that there was no longer a boundary in the minds and hearts of the believers who now saw the Kuranko nation as their territory to be reached for Jesus. As always, he walked the footpaths to the various towns with a group of friends and often took advantage of the time to ask questions and to learn more about the people that God has put upon his heart. The time came for Dembeli to return to the States and to leave the newly-founded church the opportunity to forge ahead alone for a couple of months.

During his time in the area Dembeli had visited four Muslims friends that he had built unique friendships with over the years he had been in Sierra Leone. His goal had been to lead all four men to saving faith in Jesus Christ, but as he drove out of town his heart began to break because not one of those four men had accepted Jesus as their Savior and Lord. As the miles rolled by, the burden increased. Dembeli came to the point that he wanted to turn around and go back to the various villages and sit down one more time with each of the men and individually ask them, "Is it my fault or yours, that you have not accepted Jesus? Is it because I did not explain it clear enough and you do not understand? Will you listen one more time? Or, is it your fault because you simply do not want to let go of the way of the forefathers, and so you refuse to accept Jesus as your Supreme Sacrifice?" Dembeli felt that if he could take just one or two more days to try one more time to lead his friends to Christ, it would be worth the hassle of rescheduling a flight. He pulled the truck to the side of the road and wept as he interceded for his friends. He felt assured that he had often explained the truth of the Gospel as best as he could, so he started up the truck and continued on down to the coast to catch his flight.

Three months later Dembeli returned to the area and asked about each of the four men. His heart almost broke when he learned that two of the men had gone into eternity while he was back in the States. To his knowledge they had not publicly accepted Christ as their Savior. In his mind Dembeli could almost hear and feel the thunder of the drum as it announced to the whole community that somebody had died and gone into eternity, and those left behind were not sure where their friend had gone. He pictured the women of the families as they walked though town with their hands on their heads weeping and wailing for the departed loved ones. He envisioned the men and boys as they sat talking quietly on the verandas of the homes of the deceased. As the drum cried out the message that someone had gone into eternity, they would be wondering where their friends had gone.

This thought stuck in Dembeli's mind and he made a special effort to contact the other two men repeatedly to share the Gospel with them. He continues to pray that they will come to know Christ before it is too late, but now there is a sense of urgency in his sharing with them. When they go into eternity and their bodies are carried by their friends to the grave, Dembeli wants them to be accompanied by the songs of the saints singing about heaven rather than the thundering cry of an empty drum.

—

The Church council and Dembeli considered how they could be most effective in establishing the church in their new host country.. Their first step was to designate a leader in each of the towns where they felt they had enough believers to form a Church. They immediately recognized that they would not be able to have a church in every town where there are Christians from across the border, but they felt that it was necessary to have churches established in the area. As a result, they "stationed" men in five towns. They asked Tela to move from his location to Sigitini so that he could lead the church there, and also so he could help maintain the house which was to become the base for each of Dembeli's future visits. Tela readily agreed to do this. As a former leprosy patient, Tela had gone through a rehabilitation program and learned tailoring. When the rebels destroyed his sewing machine he was devastated because that was his means of supporting his family. God had provided enough extra finances to cover the costs for a member of a work team that accompanied Dembeli, so before he left he was able to buy a sewing machine for Pastor Tela and give him back his livelihood. Now the church council was asking Tela to pastor in a bigger town that had a market, and he saw God's hand leading him in a very practical way.

Pastor Mika, also a former leprosy patient, had gone through the same rehab program at the Leprosy Hospital in Sierra Leone. Rebels had burned his sewing machine when they destroyed his home across the border. A small church in Indiana had provided him with a new machine and he was already set up in his new location as a pastor/tailor. He was able to sew clothes and with the profits pay people to help him put in a farm each year so he could feed his family, provided he had the seed to plant. His wife, also a former leprosy patient, was one of the most joyous Christians that Dembeli had ever met. Although she lacks fingers on either hand because of the disease, she is raising four of the most beautiful little children one could meet anywhere. When the sewing machine arrived, she was jubilant to the point of tears praising God that she had been "given back her life" because her husband could now earn a living again. The other men designated as church leaders were already settled into their towns and leading services.

Following the war, Pastor Mika and his wife were some of the first to move back to their homeland. He set up his tailor shop in a little town in the foothills of the Konko Mountain range and began to preach Jesus. A niece moved into the town with them to help take care of the children and to do the cooking because of the pastor's wife's disability. Dembeli has often marveled at how she got so much done with just a thumb on each hand. He concluded that it was because she had a positive attitude, a radiant smile, and a heart that was totally in love with Jesus.

Pastor Mika put in a rice farm, but his wife needed to put in a farm so that her harvest would help make the soup that goes over the rice each day. These farms are usually peanuts, cassava, or sweet potatoes. It was arranged that the ladies from the Church would help his wife put in a peanut farm. She expected about a dozen women to come and help her, so she cooked a meal that would be totally adequate for that number, and with the help of her niece carried the meal out to the farm about a mile out of town. To her surprise she met forty four women already hard at work. She simply did not know what to say. One of the women explained it best when she simply stated that they had seen so much of the love of Jesus in the pastor's wife that they just wanted to express their appreciation by helping her put in a farm. Many of the women who showed up to help were not Christians. Dembeli continues to marvel at the impact that Pastor Mika and his wife have on the towns in their area, and he marvels as each year the number of women who show up to help Pastor Mika's wife increases. The Pastors and his wife's love for Jesus and their sweet Christian Spirit has often challenged Dembeli.

The Church leaders asked Dembeli to help them with a Scripture memory program similar to what they used in Sierra Leone so that they could teach the new believers to hide God's Word in their hearts even if they were illiterate. In each church the verses are taught either in the morning or evening prayer meetings, and it is so encouraging to see the new believers memorizing God's Word. For some of the churches the prayer meetings each day are held in a home, and although very small, they are extremely beneficial. Other churches have designated meeting places and can accommodate larger crowds. In either case, the important issue is that the believers are getting together daily to encourage each other and to learn from God's Word.

The Gospel Team members stepped up and offered to help wherever they could to disciple new believers and plant churches. Their efforts on the other side of the border had been a key ingredient in evangelism and church planting. The war also brought about an increased sense of urgency and they have a greater vision to reach their area for Christ. Their renewed courage and boldness in witnessing never ceases to amaze and challenge Dembeli as he watches them grow in their walk with God.

As a non-resident missionary to the Kuranko people, Dembeli returned three or four times a year to encourage and to coach the Church leadership. Each trip was unique in its own way, and provided a great learning experience for both the Church leadership and for Dembeli personally. There have been delays due to a variety of reasons and tensions created by political unrest, which have caused anxiety for all. But through it all, God has lead His Church and they continue to grow stronger.

During each of his trips, Dembeli endeavored to keep the teaching of the word of God central in all the sessions. To set an example of consistency in building upon previous teaching, he often goes through a book of the Bible a few verses at a time. At other times he may deal with a theme that runs through the Scriptures. Dembeli has emphasized that if there is no trained pastor in a gathering, someone who can read can take a few verses each day and help the people discuss them so each individual can leave with positive teaching from God's Word to be applied to their lives throughout the day. This includes the morning and evening Bible study and prayer times in the local churches. In the seminars, various pastors share in the daily Bible studies and lead in the prayer meetings as they give instruction to their people that will help them face each new day.

On one occasion, in response to the question of how we can recognize the church, Dembeli felt the Lord leading him to teach again the ideas mentioned earlier in this book that he had picked up from a seminar he had been in with Dr. George Patterson while on furlough. Patterson puts great emphasis on "obedience oriented discipleship" which requires obeying the commands of Christ. He states that all the commands of Christ can be put into seven categories. They are laid out here more fully than earlier:

1. **Repent, Believe and Receive the Holy Spirit** (Mark 1:15; John 20:22)
   These go together and we cannot do one without the other.

2. **Be Baptized** (Matthew 18:19-20)
   This includes identification with Christ and living a holy life that such identification signifies.

3. **Love God, Family, Fellow Disciples, Neighbors, and Enemies in a practical way** (Luke 10:25-37; Matthew 5:44)
   This command teaches forgiveness.

4. **Celebrate the Lord's Supper** (Matthew 26:26-28)
   True celebration of the Lord's Supper includes communion with Christ and His people.

5. **Pray Daily** (Matthew 6:5-13; Luke 11:9)
   In a Muslim culture, the call to prayer sounds five times a day. Many of the faithful go to the mosque in response to that call several times a day. Dembeli discovered that he did a lot of teaching about prayer. During the war, the Holy Spirit moved in on His people and taught them to pray. Dembeli has often commented that some of the most powerful prayer meetings he has even been in came during those war years. Fortunately God's people did not forget the lesson He taught them when the war was over and peace returned.

6. **Give Generously** (Matthew 6:19-21; Luke 6:38)
   This teaching has been particularly hard for some to understand since they lost everything they had in the war and were driven from their homes. It is a learning process that many of the believers are still going through.

7. **Worship** (John 4:24)
   This is not included in Patterson's list, and in talking to him Dembeli sensed it is because Patterson feels that it is included in the fulfillment of some of the other commands. However, Dembeli separated it in his teaching on obedience to the commands of Christ because he feels that one of the marks of the believer is that we know how to worship. During the seminar Dembeli asked the men what worship is. He found the discussion very interesting as he listened to what the Kurankos felt constitutes worship. It was particularly noteworthy to see

that they equated being a "living sacrifice" with the act of worship. However they felt that the non-believer should also see the Christians worship together. For most of the people in the area their belief system requires prayer time at the Mosque five times a day, and they cannot understand why Christians do not gather as they do. They discussed personal worship as well as corporate worship. The men felt that there needs to be something about a gathering of believers that is different than a political meeting, a tribal council, or a secular celebration, and that difference is "worship."

When the pastors gathered to encourage one another and share times of teaching Dembeli often shared the same house/ hut with one of his favorite pastors. At times there has been only a mud wall between them, and a thatched roof over their heads. Invariably the first streaks of daylight will wake Pastor Luka from a good night's sleep. He doesn't care who is around him or where he is. He starts the day with worship. Dembeli has often been awakened as dawn streaks in through the gaps in doors, windows, ceilings or thatch as Pastor Luka begins to sing, "Good morning Jesus. Good morning Lord. I love you Jesus. I love you Lord …" Then he reads his Bible and begins to pray. Dembeli usually stays in bed and simply listens and learns, and Pastor Luka moves into the presence of his Lord. He prays Scripture moving fluently from Kuranko to Krio and back again. Finaba is the only one that has seen the tears in Dembeli's eyes as a simple pastor from the hills leads him to the throne of an awesome God. You see, Pastor Luka was captured by the rebels several times during the war. He was later arrested several more times and thrown in jail. All that does not matter to Pastor Luka when he worships because he has learned the beauty of a personal relationship with Jesus. Every time Dembeli is privileged to remain unseen and to listen in on the conversation, he is humbled. So Dembeli teaches eight, rather than seven, commands of Christ. He teaches the Kuranko believer that we need to worship—alone and together.

8. **Make Disciples** (Matthew 28:18-19; Luke 24:46-48)
A lot of time was spent on how we make disciples by passing on the teachings of our Lord. The picture memory program

has been a tool that God has blessed as His children memorize God's Word. Dembeli has been amazed to see Pastor Tela's wife teaching the wives of the Folk Muslims and animists in her neighborhood the meaning of the pictures and in doing so teaching them to memorize God's Word. Making disciples also includes discipling new believers as well as training the church leadership in evangelism and shepherding. The more experienced members on the Gospel Teams train the newer members.

As the Church considered the need to be obedient to the commands of Christ, the discussion turned to what their goal should be in the training of church leaders. This led to a question on what the qualifications of a church leader are. Once again Dembeli helped the men turn to the Scriptures for the answers and spent time considering God's list of qualities that He wants to see in a leader (1 Timothy 3:1-10; Titus 1:5-9). The men decided that they would need to maintain contact with the new churches even after they returned to Sierra Leone because they are planting Kuranko churches and the true Church has no country borders dividing it. A spirit of unity moved over the meeting, and the men sensed once again that the Body of Christ is a whole lot bigger than a local Church or even the Church within one country.

—

The privileges of living in a market town soon became obvious to Dembeli. Each Saturday evening people come to Sigitini. Those who live in towns near the road are sometimes able to get public transport to carry them to the market for a small fee. Others walk in from over forty miles to sell their produce in the market and then make the necessary purchases before starting home Sunday afternoon. People walking in from all over the area offered Dembeli a great opportunity to meet friends from the days before the war and to make new acquaintances. Market days are usually the highlight of each week as friends from various towns meet and exchange information and return home to pass along the latest news, which keeps the African grapevine going. A statement Sammy Tippit once made challenged Dembeli to pray for the people as he walked through the market where numerous tribes and nations are represented. Pressing through the throng of the market, one brushes shoulders with people from all walks of life. There are local and state officials, tribal leaders, rich and poor, educated and illiterate, but most of them have one thing in common;

they have never heard the Gospel of Jesus Christ. So as Dembeli walked, he began to pray for many of the individuals: an old granny selling fruit, a happy child skipping through the market not wanting to miss any of the excitement, a young mother with her baby tied securely on her back trying to press through the crowd, a group of old men sitting in the shade remembering the joys of yesterday, and many, many more who came to buy, sell or trade their wares. The Lord began to deal with Dembeli in a special way as he prayed his way through the throng.

On another market day as he was preparing to go on a similar prayer walk, he was disturbed to hear that due to problems that had developed in the area the market had been suddenly closed. People fled in fear trying to escape what past experience told them could be danger as soldiers appeared out of nowhere to try to keep a lid on things and maintain the peace. Dembeli's heart broke as he once again witnessed the fear and anxiety that seized his friends as memories of recent days hounded them. Since the church is on the edge of town, many of the people stopped by to chat before heading back to their villages. There was hope that the soldiers would be able to solve the problem, and that they would be able to return in a couple weeks to a normal market. In the meantime they hurriedly packed their things and headed out of town. Fortunately, their hopes were realized and two weeks later the market was reopened. For Dembeli it served as a grim reminder that his friends live in a different world than he was used to in the freedom of America, and it gave him a little insight into the fear that plagues their lives.

Another experience gave him even deeper insights into how the people feel. After being gone for some time, Dembeli returned from America for another visit. A storm hit just as he arrived, so there was a grand rush to help him unload his truck and get things moved into his room before everything was soaked. A friend had given Pastor Tela a table to keep for him while he returned to Sierra Leone to check on his hometown to see if it was safe enough to return. Pastor Tela already had a table, so he kindly lent it to Dembeli. Setting it by the window, Dembeli unloaded some of his stuff on it, unconcerned about its location because there were bars on the window to protect the contents of the room from thieves.

Dembeli soon realized that not all thieves are hindered by the presence of metal bars on the windows. As he looked out the window he saw some of his stuff disappearing in the hands of a thief. The case was turned over to the police, but the thieves were not apprehended. Dembeli struggled at first with his anger with himself for being so careless. When traveling in the area he travels light, and the fact that most of his valuables, a few items that helped to make life a little more enjoyable, had been stolen did not help the situation at all. But as time went on he realized that he was now able to identify so much more closely with how his friends felt. Unlike Dembeli who still had some things left, they had lost everything at the hands of the rebels. It was a great attitude check for one coming from a country where we have so much and so often take it all for granted. Dembeli had to take time to think how he would feel if there was not any possibility at all of being able to replace the stolen property. That would put him in the place of his friends who had lost everything and had no means by which they could replace what was lost. Dembeli let the Church council handle the case on his behalf, and they negotiated with the police and communicated with the neighbors.

Dembeli asked the Lord to help him find a way to help the community and the leaders to understand why he was really there. When asked why he was there, Dembeli would answer that he was a "Teacher of God's Word," rather than trying to explain what a missionary is since they do not have the word "missionary" in their language. He helped several towns repair broken bridges or bad places in the road near their villages. God used some of the believers to encourage the people in their town to extend the road to reach their village. With the help of Dembeli and his truck they were able to see a vehicle drive into their town for the first time.

Word spread that Dembeli would help with the roads, and soon various town leaders and the border patrol were asking for help. Such a ministry opened the door for Dembeli and the Christians to build relationships in the community. There was also the day that a big truck ran into a cow out on the highway a couple miles from the market. The cow was not killed, but was seriously injured. The owners were extremely worried about their financial losses if she would die out in the bush. Somehow they got the idea that Dembeli could help them get their cow back to town, so they came and asked for assistance. Having spent some time working on a dairy farm while on furlough in Michigan, Dembeli understood and was able to help them with their cow. They loaded the cow into his truck and got her back to town safely. But Dembeli felt that he needed something more than injured cows and broken down bridges to help him connect with the community, so he asked the Lord to help him find a way to communicate the real reason he was there.

On one journey Dembeli arrived at the town where he set up his base on a Friday evening. Neighbors were gathering in a compound nearby, and

Dembeli soon discovered that it was because one of the trainees for the military who lived in the compound had suddenly taken sick and died. The Christians and Dembeli went to greet the family and found out that the concern was more than just the death of the young man. He had been living with his friends, but he was actually from a town in the war zone and they were unable to find a vehicle that would carry the body back to his home. After consulting with the Church leaders, Dembeli offered to take the body back to the young man's village the next morning. This greatly encouraged the family, but they soon discovered that Dembeli's truck was really too small for what they needed. However, the fact that he was willing to help gave the arguments they needed to persuade the owner of a large truck to let them charter his vehicle and hire his driver for the next day.

The following morning Dembeli and some of the Christian men drove over to the neighbor's compound to help load the body. Police, military men, and town officials had come to escort the body back to the young man's village. It was decided that Dembeli should carry the important men in his truck and that the body and the rest of the mourners, including the family he had lived with and his friends, should ride together in the back of the seven-ton truck.

The drive to the funeral in the frontier war zone was an all-day affair. Before their arrival, the family there was not aware that the young man had died. An elder of the village brought out the chief's drum and began to beat the rhythm that announced death as family members began to gather. The women in the family threw themselves on the ground and wailed their agony as the thunder of the drum announced that someone had gone into eternity and they did not know where he was.

As he watched the scene unfold, Dembeli prayed that God would empower His Church to reach these people with the message of hope in Christ so that they would come to know Him and accept His offer of eternal life. Then they would know for certain that they could, and would, spend eternity with Him in heaven if they would only accept Jesus as their Supreme Sacrifice for their sins. The African grapevine remains active in peace or in war, and this day was no exception. Before the day was done, word had traveled through the area that the Christians really do care and can be counted on to help in a crisis. God took the situation and turned it into a means of glorifying His name and adding credibility to the witness of His people. We serve an awesome God!

Tensions were such in the community that believers constantly had to deal with oppression, either as a result of rebel activity across the border or from those who opposed the Church. At this point in time "frontier" and "war zone" were used interchangeably to describe the area right along the border of the two countries. Dembeli found himself waiting for tensions to subside so that he could journey into the frontier and visit pastors and Churches. As his delay lengthened, he decided that he could share the Wordless Book with some of the neighborhood children. Children gather immediately whenever he would step out of the house, so it was not hard for him to find someone to listen.

The children listened carefully as Dembeli explained the Gospel with the little cloth book, and then they asked if they could have a book for themselves. Dembeli assured them that if they would learn to "read" it, he would give them a book. So they listened again and again until they were able to tell the story of the book for themselves.

Each day, and sometimes several times a day, the children would come back and ask Dembeli if he would teach them to read the little cloth book. One afternoon while they were sitting on the steps together, a new little boy joined the group. With his parents and other villagers he had run away from his village in Sierra Leone to the safety across the border. Apparently a white person had never been in his town so he had never seen one before. When a new friend invited him to come and learn to "read the little book," he was more intrigued with Dembeli than with the book. He joined his friends but he held back a little as the children once again listened to the story of salvation. Without thinking, Dembeli casually took off his hat and laid it on the step beside him, exposing his rather bald head. The little boy could no longer contain his curiosity and exclaimed, "Oh my, what happened to his hair?" Before Dembeli or anyone else could answer, the little five-year-old neighbor girl explained. "It is okay. His hair is in his room in the house."

Once that was taken care of, the kids could go back to the learning process. Some of them told Dembeli that they thought they could now read the book. So Dembeli took the little cloth book and asked them to read it to him. All who could correctly tell the story of salvation were permitted to keep a Wordless Book for themselves. They went away jubilant!

Soon however, they returned and asked Dembeli if they could have another book to give to their friends. He assured them that if they taught their friends to "read the book," they could bring them and he would give each of them a copy also. The next day some of the children came to Dembeli with their friends and clamored for the opportunity to show him that they had taught their friends to "read" too.

Dembeli wondered if they really understood the concept that the little book taught. After the story had been shared a couple of times he went through it with them again. This time he asked if any of the children would like to accept Jesus as their Supreme Sacrifice and put their faith in Him. Six little voices responded that they would like to do that, and together they prayed and asked Jesus to come into their hearts. Dembeli wondered if they really understood, because some of them were so young. Then the Holy Spirit pointed to the little neighbor girl and reminded Dembeli that he was about her age when he had accepted Jesus as his personal Savior and Lord and that Jesus is just as real today as He was back them. It was a gentle reminder that Jesus loves the children and they can believe in Him.

That evening at the Bible study with the adults, Dembeli asked the children to show the adults that they could read too. They proudly displayed their wordless books and "read" the story of salvation to the "big people." As Dembeli watched, it suddenly dawned on him that all six of the children were from Folk Muslim, or animistic homes, and that there would be no one to teach, encourage and disciple them. He challenged the Church to care for and take responsibility for these precious little ones who now love the Lord.

Eight years later, following the war, Dembeli was able to track down all but one of the children that accepted Christ that day. What joy he experienced when he discovered that all of them are still walking with the Lord. God is faithful!!!

Tensions continued to mount. Sunday morning some of the men came to visit Dembeli and the pastor. After a cup of coffee and lively conversation, they decided they should worship inside the house instead of out under the trees where they usually meet. They meandered over to the house and stood around talking on the veranda while they waited for the women and children to join them. Suddenly, a police officer showed up with one of the Christian young men in custody. He asked if anyone there knew the man and of course the Christians responded that they all knew him. He was from their hometown back across the border, and some of them had grown up with him. Apparently that was what the officer had in mind in the first place. Once his suspicions had been confirmed, he proceeded to arrest all the men in the congregation on the simple charge that they were Kurankos from across the border.

He demanded that each of the men produce their identification cards. Interestingly enough, these were the very cards that the former chief of police had helped the men acquire following Dembeli's arrest the previous year. Once he had all the cards in hand, the officer ordered the men to follow him to prison. They tried to reason with him, but he would not listen to them and so they turned to Dembeli for help. The pastor had not been arrested since he is known in town as a tailor, and the officer apparently figured that he was a local resident. Dembeli was the only other one of the men who was not under arrest, and that was probably because he was known due to the his previous arrests, and the officer figured that Dembeli would just be released anyway. Dembeli suggested that since the men all had official ID cards that had been acquired through the police headquarters it would probably be wise to go see the district officers in charge of the area before carting the men off to jail. The discussion continued for a couple of hours. Finally the officer said that he would return that evening to finish the business and he left, taking all the ID cards with him, but leaving the men free to move around town.

Sunday evening the officer did not show up as he had promised he would. Monday morning Dembeli and the Christians took things into their own hands and began a tour of the leaders in the town to explain the situation and to see if they could get the ID cards back since the men could not travel anywhere in the area without proper identification. The highest political leader was rather upset that someone had arrested the Christians in his area without his knowledge. He said that he would need more information so that he would be able to find the officer who had arrested the Christians. The police chief let the believers know in no uncertain terms that he had not ordered their arrest and that it was not one of his officers who had arrested them. It was his office that had been instrumental in helping the men obtain the ID cards in the first place.

Then the men went to see the commander of the all the military troops and border patrol in the area. They discovered that a new commander had just been stationed in town and they did not know him. Proper protocol required that they first congratulate him on his transfer into the area and then welcome him as the top military man in the region. Following that courtesy the men began to explain their situation. The commander listened carefully, asked a few questions, and then responded by stating that he had not ordered the arrest of the Christians. He then asked them to provide him a list of all the believers who were active in the church in town and assured them that they would not be bothered again as long as they "behaved themselves." The request for the names of all the Christians in town threw up red flags in Dembeli's mind.

The men expected professionalism, and they saw that in the commander immediately. The believers certainly were not asking to be given any special privileges. On the other hand, they did not want to go to jail again either. After a brief discussion, they decided to comply with his request and assured him that they would identify all the active Christians in town.

When the conversation ended, the commander looked at the Christian men seated in his office and assured them that he would investigate the case on their behalf and recover their ID cards and return them to the men. Thinking that the session was over, the men prepared to leave. Then the commander told the men that indeed he was new in the area, but that he was a Christian from the Forest region farther east. He asked how the Church in the district was doing and invited the men to go with him to his home church so they could visit a large group of thriving believers there and be encouraged in their walk with Jesus. To their total surprise, the commander asked if he could pray with them before they left his office. The commander led them in prayer and asked God's richest blessing and protection on the believers and on the Church in the area. It was a precious time, and the men left with a new awareness that we serve a great and awesome God. Who else could have engineered the transfer of a Christian into the highest military position in the area at exactly the right time? Dembeli and the men left with hearts full of praise for such an incredible God.

True to their word, the three leaders that the believers had approached, did investigate the case. They found the officer who had arrested the men that Sunday morning. They discovered that he had come from another area and that he had decided to arrest various individuals without contacting the local authorities in the area. The believers were given back their ID cards, and heard that plans were being made to send the officer back to the capital minus his uniform since he had acted on his own without giving proper respect to the local authorities. The uniform was to be delivered to his commanding officers in the capital later.

—

Each morning and evening, the believers continued to gather for a time of worship, Bible study, and prayer. One Saturday a great number of Christians walked in to the market from the surrounding villages for the market on the coming day. The Sunday market draws people from miles around to buy, sell, trade, or just to enjoy the holiday spirit that is felt in the town on market days. On Saturday evening the believers join the regular evening Bible study and prayer time. Right at the beginning one of the young church planters suggested that the group spend the time together in worship and then have a praise and prayer service. He reasoned that it would be good to hear what God was doing for the believers from other towns, especially from across the border. His idea was readily accepted and the meeting proceeded without a designated leader as various ones gave their testimonies or led in a song of worship and praise.

After some time it was suggested that a row of rough stick benches be cleared. Anyone who wanted to could ask the Church to pray for them and then move over and sit on the stick benches. When all had made their requests, the Church would then pray for them. Dembeli noted that the requests were not for material possessions or for comfort. The believers were asking for courage and strength to face their trials. They asked for prayer that they might have courage to stand firm in Christ and that they might be good testimonies for Him. They sought wisdom so that they could speak His Word clearly and boldly to others. All agreed that they needed to pray that peace would come to their home country and that the terrible rebel activities would cease.

Soon the benches were full and the Church began to pray for those who had expressed needs. Dembeli was asked to close in prayer. Sensing that the Lord wanted him to place his hands on each of the individuals, Dembeli stood behind each person in turn. As he led the Church in prayer for each individual, he placed his hands on their shoulders. He moved slowly down the line as the prayers were offered. Somewhere in the process it seemed that heaven opened and the Holy Spirit moved upon His people. They began to weep as they interceded for each other. It was not just one or two people weeping, but the body of Christ. It seemed that the Church caught a vision for the needs of their people. In the midst of all the trials and oppression, they began to pray for those who had still never heard the Gospel of Christ. In his mind Dembeli pictured some of the towns where the Gospel had never been taught and the people have never heard of God's plan of salvation. As much as the Church longs for Christ to return quickly and take them home, the prayer that night seemed to be that Jesus would wait just a little longer until the they could win their loved ones to Christ.

Dembeli finished walking down the line and returned to his seat on a stone. The Church continued to weep and pray. Since it is an outdoor church, there are no walls. The only ceiling is the leafy branches of the avocado pear tree which shades the stones and crude stick benches. A path about ten yards away runs from the town to the farms out in the bush. Normally people walking by on the path will greet their friends in the church, and the believers will respond in a culturally appropriate manner. On that particular night, nobody passing by greeted as they quietly continued on their way home from the farms. The awesome presence of God moved among His people as they sat weeping and praying.

Nobody checked the time. Nobody cared. People prayed and wept before God as they worshiped and interceded together on holy ground. Then one of the young men stood and with tears streaming down his cheeks he began to sing a little chorus that Dembeli had heard so often in the past. Actually, Dembeli never appreciated or enjoyed, that particular chorus because it seemed that whenever they started singing it they would sing it into the ground. Dembeli remembers the evening when they repeated it thirty seven times in a row. But this time, the song made sense!

The young man stood and with his hands raised toward heaven he began to sing, "Father in heaven, we glorify your name. We bow down before you. Oh, Father in heaven we glorify your name, we bow down before you." Half way through the first verse, the whole Church rose to their feet and joined in worship. Tears glistened in the light of the little kerosene lamp as the beautiful song of worship ascended toward heaven. There was no worship leader nor was there a song leader, but after a few repetitions the group sat down and continued interceding.

Some time later another young man stood and began to sing, "You are a miracle working God; You are a miracle working God; You are the Alpha and Omega; You are a miracle working God; You made the blind to see ..." Once again the people rose to their feet and joined in a song of worship and adoration. As they sat back down their hearts seemed to cry out a new last line to the song, "And we worship you, Oh, Lord." They continued to intercede.

Then it seemed that in a divine moment Jesus stepped in and walked through His Church. He started where young men were sitting on the rocks under the shade tree and moved among His people drying their tears. He tenderly moved among the rocks and through the structure of the crude stick benches where worshipers were sitting, and dried the eyes of all His children. As their tears were dried the worshipers fell silent. Then something happened that Dembeli had never experienced before. When all the tears were dried, there was total, absolute, silence in the Church. It seemed that each person sat silently basking in the presence of the Master. The Church was worshiping on holy ground.

The challenge of reaching the rest of the Kuranko people stills remained. The tensions of war continued. The hurt and the heartache were still real. A nation still has to be rebuilt. But God is still in control and each believer left the service that evening with a new sense of His presence and power and an awareness of the fact that He will keep His promises and that He will never leave or forsake His children.

Part 4: Current Affairs

Chapter 33: The Transition

The year 2000 closed with bitter conflict. An African proverb states: "When two elephants fight the grass gets hurt." This was certainly true as the governments battled the rebel forces, and innocent men, women and children suffered. Yet the Church remained strong. Some of the Upper Kuranko people moved back to their home area in the Heredugu area to try and rebuild their homes and their lives on the ashes of destruction. Many believers returned with the first groups of those headed home, and two churches were reopened. Within a few months one of those churches reached out to another town, and a daughter church was started with believers being discipled to reach others.

Within a couple years a peace agreement was reached (2002) with the rebel forces and peace was slowly restored ending a bitter conflict which had lasted ten years. The people were free to return home and start over. As stability came the Church continued to grow. As they returned home, the Believers reopened the former churches. New believers who had just accepted Christ during the war started churches in their home towns. Gospel Team members found each other, and rejoicing in the fact that they had survived the war, they began to move out together to share the gospel in the towns in their area. Together, with the pastors who returned, they were soon reaching over fifty towns with a consistent Christian witness.

It has been extremely hard to keep statistics on Church growth at this point in time. One is not counted until baptism because it is easy to profess being a Christian, but when it costs something to identify publicly with the Church it can be difficult to get the professing Christian to really take a stand. Baptism declares to the community that the individual is identifying with Christ and the Church, and it is then that they are recognized as believers. Knowing that Christ is their only hope causes the believers to share with anyone who will listen to the simple yet powerful message of salvation. It is the story of having their heads pulled, of having their feet planted on a road to an eternal refuge, and knowing that they are on their way Home. It is the knowledge that only as "new creatures in Christ" will they be able to meet the deep needs of a hurting people and offer hope to rebuild a nation. It soon became apparent that during the war years the Church in the area had doubled, that opposition had purified the hearts of believers, and others had seen Christ in them. New believers had been discipled and the Churches were keenly aware of the fact that their spiritual leaders lacked Biblical training.

—

The Church continued to grow and it soon became apparent to leaders in other organizations that God is moving among the Upper Kuranko people. Several other organizations offered to help fan the flames of the movement to Christ by sending a team to show the *Jesus* film. Another organization offered a vehicle to carry the team. They sent word to Dembeli in the States, and he was able to raise the funds for the fuel that would be necessary for this tremendous endeavor.

About two months later reports came back to America that the *Jesus* film project had been a great success. Over one hundred sixty people had accepted Christ in the various villages where the team had gone. Among them were prominent community leaders. However, the rains had started and many villages could not be reached. One of the Paramount Chiefs asked that the team come back in the dry season and show the film throughout his chiefdom. Because it had such a tremendous impact on him and his people, he wanted all to have the opportunity to see it.

Chapter: 34 A Vision For The Future

As the churches multiplied the leaders continued to ask Dembeli to help them train spiritual leadership which would give direction for each of the local Churches. In an effort to meet this need Dembeli stepped up his endeavors to enroll as many of the new pastors and Gospel Team members in TEE courses as possible. The courses were effective and as the pastors studied they passed on to their people what they were learning. However, even with the increased efforts the leaders expressed their feeling that more training was needed for their pastors.

When peace came the Heredugu District was able to reestablish contact with the other Churches in the Northeastern State of Sierra Leone and they discussed the problem of leadership training with leaders from the other areas. They felt that a Bible School was definitely needed, but the one in Kurela had been dismantled as a result of the war. As their leaders met with pastors from other evangelical groups they discovered that they all shared two things in common : they wanted to reach the rest of the northeastern part of the country with the Gospel, and they needed a Bible School where they could train their own men.

After times spent in prayer and fasting God gave them a vision to rebuild the Bible School. Later Dembeli learned that during this time two separate individuals had had dreams that the Bible School campus had been restored and was operating to the glory of God. They felt that this was such an impossibility that they were afraid to share the dreams they had had in the night with anyone, so they kept them to themselves. When Dembeli returned Church leaders contacted him and shared the vision for the Bible School that they had with him. They were persistent enough that when he was back in America they contacted him again and asked him to consider helping them reach their goal.

Finaba knew that Dembeli would take on the challenge of building roads and constructing bridges, but he was not sure that Dembeli felt comfortable building buildings. Therefore he was not surprised when Dembeli called one of his mentors, Jake Schierling, who had built the Bible School buildings back in the seventies and asked him to accompany him on a survey trip back to Kurela to check out the site. Pa Schierling, now in his eighties accepted the challenged and joined Dembeli in the venture.

In 2006, the two men returned to Kurela to find the Bible School campus in ruins. During the twelve years that the school had been shut down due to the war, the trees and undergrowth had taken over to such an extent that trees were growing up inside some of the building. The beautiful campus which had once been such a vital part of the ministry was now but a ghost town. What was left of the walls were crumbling, the wells were polluted, and the orchard had been swallowed up by the heavy fast growing African bush.

Dembeli and Pa Schierling spent days meeting with leaders from various evangelical groups. They talked to government and tribal leaders, as well as the local people. They soon discovered that it was not only the pastors and Church leaders who wanted the Bible School rebuilt, but the state leadership and people on the grassroots level as well.

The Church leadership had a vision that God had given them. Pa Schierling and Dembeli walked the campus with some of the believers and listened to their ideas and heard them share their dreams for the future. They measured buildings, priced materials in the capital, and put together a list of what they felt was needed to reconstruct each building. They spent time in prayer with pastors and various church leaders as they sought the mind of Christ in this new aspect of Kingdom building ministry. The national church leaders invited government and tribal leaders to a meeting with Pa Schierling and Dembeli and together they made a formal request for help in rebuilding the Bible School. They felt that if the buildings could be rebuilt that the National Church, could handle the administration and teaching aspect of the Institution. They shared their vision and asked the two missionaries to join them in reaching the goal that they felt God had set before them. Dembeli asked many questions as the two missionaries tried to discern what needs the Church felt they had and how those needs could be met.

The two missionaries returned to the States and Dembeli completed their cost analysis. After much prayer and discussion they began to present the project to various individuals and churches. One day Dembeli called Pa Schierling and told him that the first donation had come in to help reconstruct the Bible School in Kurela. Jake wisely encouraged him to contact a National Church leader in Sierra Leone and let him know that God was moving. When the leaders shared that information with the people the two individuals who had had the dreams were now longer silent as they began to praise the Lord for what He was going to do. They shared their dreams and challenged the people to trust God to rebuild the campus.

Dembeli asked his intercessors to pray with him because he knew that God was asking him as a "bush missionary" to step out of his comfort zone and take on a new challenge. Realizing that this is God's Project, Dembeli and Jake prepared to begin the reconstruction of the Bible School. In 2007 Dembeli returned to Sierra Leone as the front runner for the project and began making the necessary arrangements to begin the work and to prepare for a Work Team that Jake would be leading in just a few short weeks although he was already eighty five years old. The Work Team helped "jump start" the program and then they returned to America to encourage individuals and Churches to get involved. Dembeli stayed continue supervising the reconstruction of the campus.

In 2008 an Evangelical Church in Nigeria began partnering with the Bible School by sending two missionaries to help. They designed the curriculum and set up an administrative structure. When classes began one was asked to serve as the Principle and both of them began teaching advanced classes. Several Sierra Leone teachers also teach classes so that classes can be taught in the local language and students can be taught English so that they are qualified to take the advanced classes if they choose to pursue their education.

After being closed for fourteen years the Bible School reopened in a "Grand Celebration" in the newly re-constructed chapel. Then in 2010 the first post war graduating class achieved their goal, completed their studies, and received their certificates for a job well done. What a time of rejoicing that was!!!

Realizing that the Church needs to help rebuild a war torn country, the National Church leaders proposed that a Technical Vocation Training Center be added to the Bible School. This is so that pastors and their wives can be trained in a vocation which they can use not only to support themselves when they graduate, but it will enable them to become valuable assets to their communities in the rebuilding process. Plans to develop this program are in progress as Dembeli and the National Church leadership look to the future needs of the school as it pertains to buildings, programs, and instructors. Orchards and a plantation are being planted so that when the harvest is sold it can be added to the income from the school fees paid by the students and the Institution will become self supporting.

The vision is to build a top level Institution which will meet the needs of the Church in Northeastern Sierra Leone. Dembeli spends most of each year in Sierra Leone working with church leaders and local people to take another step in achieving the vision that God has given them in ministry. Once the old campus, which was destroyed during the war is rebuilt, new buildings to accommodate the increase in students will need to be added. For this reason the project is not seen as a "sudden fix" but as a development program under the capable leadership of the Church.

The National Church in Sierra Leone has a vision that God has given them and their desire is to train young men and women to reach the rest of their nation with the Gospel of Jesus Christ. (See Appendix C on page 331.)

In 2010 Dembeli and Clare were married. Clare shares her husbands vision for the Bible School and for village evangelism and walks beside him as they answer God's call on their lives and serve together. Later that same year, in response to God's call on their lives, Roy and Faith Hill joined the Reifels at the Bible School. They come with the technical skills to help the Institution achieve the goals in the area of technical training. With her skills as a nurse Faith is able to build bridges to reach the hearts of the people. Roys training as a pastor, and his skills in computers and printing equipment will enable him to train men who can publish the material needed to spread the Gospel beyond the present borders.

Chapter 35: A Sense of Urgency

Dembeli had often expressed a sense of urgency when asking people to pray with him about the Church among the Kuranko people. Many of us in America do not understand the urgency that national believers feel when they share the Gospel with their loved ones who are unreached or who have never heard the Gospel.

Some years ago, buffalo were destroying farms in the foothills of the mountains. Forest buffalo are cousins to the cape buffalo of the plains which is considered by many hunters to be the most dangerous animal in the world to hunt, simply because he would just as soon kill you as look at you. The forest buffalo, although somewhat smaller, shares the same sentiments. Finaba mused that many hunters down through the generations of African hunters discovered that when you set out to kill an African buffalo, one of you is going to die, either the animal or the hunter.

On this occasion the Paramount Chief asked various hunters to gather and drive the buffalo out of the swamps so the farmers in the area could have a harvest. Dembeli and Barnabasi joined others who were willing to respond to the call. They drove to the town where the Paramount Chief lived and then walked back in to the area where the buffalo were most active. As evening approached, other hunters arrived and the two friends found themselves part of a group of seventeen hunters who were participating in the hunt.

The first day was spent tracking and locating the buffalo to find their favorite resting and feeding grounds. The buffalo were finally located, and the second day the man who was leading the hunt had the hunters stationed around a swampy forest. He then sent men down into the forest to make as much noise as possible to drive the buffalo out into the open. Dembeli had climbed a tree and was patiently waiting with his little hunting dog, Chippewa, tied at the bottom of the tree when the men began to holler and make a terrible racket down in the forest. They scared the herd of buffalo and it split up. Three of the buffalo came charging up out of the swamp and forest into Dembeli's view. Dembeli sighted his rifle and squeezed the trigger, hoping that a buffalo would fall. Nothing happened except that the buffalo changed the course of their travels and came charging right under the tree where Dembeli was perched. Dembeli managed to get off a second shot, but due to a tree branch that jumped in the way he was not able to get a good sight on the buffalo and knew he had missed. Upset with himself for having missed a fantastic opportunity and knowing that the buffalo were on their way to the next county, Dembeli climbed down out of his tree to where Chippewa was having fits. As he was looking around, Dembeli found a drop of blood about the size of the head of a hat pin and realized that he had not missed completely. He turned his dog Chippewa loose.

Chippewa had been given to Dembeli by a Fullah friend who was a nomadic cow herder, and had most likely never been touched by human hands until he was caught and handed to Dembeli. Dembeli found him to be one of the hardest dogs to train that he had ever worked with, and although he was an excellent watchdog and loved to hunt, he basically did what he did on his own terms. Past experience had taught Dembeli that his little dog that weighed in at about forty pounds was solid muscle and speed, and was totally fearless regardless of the odds.

When Chippewa started barking down in the middle of the forest, Dembeli knew that he was communicating with a buffalo. Dembeli hurried to the spot where he figured his dog was and found Chippewa snout to snout, trading meaning words with the wounded buffalo. Finaba laughed when Dembeli voiced his longing for a camcorder, because words could not capture the scene that Dembeli found there in the forest as his little hunting dog took on the fearful buffalo. Small saplings were knocked down as the buffalo tried to get one of his fearsome horns hooked into the little snarling, barking machine that was tormenting him. Finaba chuckled as he recalled that hunters will tell you that a buffalo is not afraid of a dog, but he certainly dislikes the man that is following the dog. After watching the battle for a few brief moments, Dembeli decided it was time to pronounce the winner and put another bullet into the buffalo. The buffalo hit the dirt with the little dog snapping and snarling at its hindquarters. Dembeli then gave a hunter's call and waited for some of the other hunters to show up. Meanwhile, Chippewa was trying to get a meal of steaks off the immobile beast.

Barnabasi was the first to respond to Dembeli's call. When he stepped into view he asked Dembeli if he should shoot the buffalo again because he knew that Dembeli "always" put the finishing shot into a dangerous animal, which then guaranteed that it was actually dead. Dembeli pointed out that he had put the buffalo down, Chippewa was chewing on it, and there was no evidence of life, so he did not feel that Barnabasi needed to waste another shell on the buffalo. Leaning his gun against a tree, Dembeli took a small hatchet that they carried to help break up bones when they were butchering large animals. Dembeli walked up to the buffalo and hit it as hard as he could between the base of the horns and the ears. When it did not move Barnabasi relaxed a little bit and then commented, "Hit him again."

Again Dembeli swung the hatchet and hit the buffalo. But this time was different. Something had motivated the buffalo and that huge chunk of "mean" started to get up. Dembeli jumped back and called out to Barnabasi, "Shoot him Barnabasi! Shoot him! Shoot him! Shoot him!" Finaba chuckled. No, he rolled hysterically on the ground wrapped in gales of laughter as Dembeli scurried out of the way so Barnabasi could guarantee that the "dead" buffalo did not claim a victory. Suddenly things had changed. Now there was a sense of urgency!

Do you ever sense urgency about reaching the lost? Is there a lingering thought in the back of your mind that time is running out—that the summer is over and the harvest is past, and our loved ones and friends are not saved (Jeremiah 8:20)? It is a deeper sense of urgency than the feeling that you might get caught on the horns of a buffalo and end up dead. It is the sense of knowing that eternal lives hang in the balance. Christ's return is close at hand, and every day thousands are going into eternity never having heard that they can have their heads pulled, the fire of the Holy Spirit in their lives, and their feet planted on the road to an "eternal refuge." It is that sense of urgency that we know when we consider that time is running out and realize that how we invest our lives, our incomes, and our energies will have eternal implications. It is almost like we can hear the drum still beating as another person for whom Jesus died goes on into eternity never having heard that He died for them.

In the book of Revelation God showed the Apostle John a scene in heaven. He speaks of the "four living creatures and the elders" who fell down and worshiped the Lamb. They were "holding golden bowls full of incense, which are the prayers of the saints" (Revelation 5:8). It seems from this verse that as the prayers of the saints ascend to heaven, God gathers them and puts them in the golden bowls. Could it be that somewhere up in heaven, perhaps on a great golden altar, there is a little golden bowl for each tribe, nation, or people group all around the world? As the prayers for a particular people group reach the throne, does God take them and put them in the little golden bowl ascribed to that particular ethnic group?

Dembeli has often challenged people to consider what happens when the little bowl for a particular people group is filled up with the prayers of the saints. He suggests that revival breaks out in the church. Renewal takes place. Believers fall in love with Jesus all over again. A spiritual awakening takes place among the people, and hearts are turned toward God as sinners believe, repent, and are recreated by His awesome love.

This leaves us with the challenge to do our part. Will you intercede for the Kuranko people until the little golden bowl labeled "Kuranko" is full of the prayers of the saints and in one divine moment God walks among men once again? Will you help reach them through your prayers so that the empty, echoing agony of the drum will be replaced with a song of the glorious hope that only Christ can give?

The voice of Amos could not be silenced by the religious leaders of his day, nor could his words be snuffed out by the power of a disagreeable king. They could not be negated by an uncaring nation. They were the words of Creator God, given by His Spirit through the voice of His prophet. The words of Amos echoed through the nation as each man passed them on in hushed and whispered tones.

Yet in the midst of the judgments pronounced against her, Israel found the promise of restoration that brought peace and comfort in spite of her heartache and defeat. The Lord God Almighty declared that He would not forsake His people, that they would someday be restored, never to be uprooted again.

Through the voice of His chosen prophet the Lord declared, "The days are coming when the reaper will be overtaken by the plowman and the planter by the one treading grapes." (Amos 9:13) What greater description do we have of a coming harvest? Is that also a promise for a spiritual harvest among the Kuranko people? Will there come a day when the drum no longer cries out the agony of a departed loved one, but the Church triumphant stands around the grave and sings songs of victory and triumph—songs of heaven?

Appendix A

Appendix B

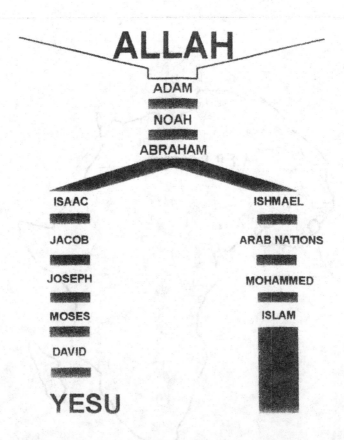

Appendix C

DIAGRAM DEPICTING SIERRA LEONE CHURCH STRUCTURE
FOR EVANGELISM / DISCIPLESHIP / PASTORAL TRAINING

Advanced Training

Bible Schools

T.E.E.

Literacy Programs

GOSPEL TEAMS
(Trained in Evangelism)

Discipleship / Mentoring

Evangelism = New Converts

NOTE : This diagram is not intended to convey statistics, percentages, or numbers. It is designed to express the pattern of training being used to reach, and to teach others to reach, people for Christ. The shape of a triangle has been chosen due to the authors lack of artistic ability. It is not intended to place a greater value on any type of training, or to degrade any individual who has not achieved a given level of education. All are equal, but the role of the individual may vary depending on the training received.

EVANGELIZED : Ideally all who accept Christ will be discipled, but unfortunately this does not actually happen in real life. Hopefully a large portion of those who do accept Christ will be assimilated into the Church and will be discipled to disciple and mentor others creating a growing, reproducing Church. NOTE : The bottom of the structure has no lower boundary. This is an endeavor to depict the unfinished task that continues to welcome individuals from all walks of life into the Church family.

DISCIPLED / MENTORED : Ideally all of those who accept Christ as Savior and Lord will be discipled and mentored to the point where they will "pass it on". It is not necessary that these individuals know how to read or write, but many of the students in the literacy classes begin their learning at this point. The picture association to Scripture continues to be a valuable part of this aspect of the training program.

GOSPEL TEAMS : In addition to the discipleship program these men are trained in an active "hands on" outreach program that is more advanced then basic sharing of the faith which comes in the Discipleship level.

LITERACY PROGRAM : Some trained in outreach (Gospel Teams) will join a literacy class. However, not all who join a literacy program have been trained like the Gospel Team members. Hopefully, they have all been discipled and are being mentored.

THEOLOGICAL EDUCATION by EXTENSION (TEE) : Some who study TEE have received formal training in public schools. Others will be those who have learned to read by being tutored by a pastor or literacy teacher in a very simple setting. Either way, the ideal is that they will continue to be part of the discipleship/mentoring program that brought them to this point. It is to be noted that TEE is also structured to add continuing education for pastors who have completed their Bible School training.

BIBLE SCHOOLS : Some individuals will go from the literacy classes right to Bible School. As the center for TEE in the north, the Bible School is prepared to offer TEE to all prospective students so that they will be able to handle the level of training which they will receive at the Bible School. Bible School training is built on the other aspects depicted in the broader levels of the triangle and offers in-depth training for the spiritual leadership of the Church. Just as there comes a time when a building gives identity to a local church in a small village, so there has come a time when the Bible School, as an institution, gives identity to the evangelical Church in the country.

ADVANCED TRAINING :
This educational level could take one or more of many forms, but there will be those that God leads on to higher education who will become the leadership, and the voice, of the Church in the nation. They will also encourage and enable those in the broader sections of the "triangle" to keep pressing on so that the Church moves on triumphantly together, evangelizing, discipling, mentoring, and training the next generation of believers. NOTE : There is no "lid" on this because one can never be sure how far the Lord will lead some of our African brothers in their pursuit of education and into a field of influence that we may not even imagine at this point in time.

Each segment pictured in this "Triangle of Training" is important. It can readily be seen that the broader levels are the base for the smaller segments of the triangle and therefore even the most educated is dependent on the training they received while involved at those levels. What is not readily seen in the diagram is that the upper levels are often the ones who lead, encourage, and train those in the other segments of the triangle. All are dependent on each other and thus they need each other. A much better diagram would be that of a vine and branches. One would then be compelled to observe that it is the same Spirit running through ALL the branches that gives the plant, in this case the Church, life. What an analogy!!!!

The Sierra Leone Church has experienced growth in the most adverse circumstances (war) because they were trained and were obedient to the command of our Lord to make disciples. The goal is to continue the same pattern of evangelism and discipleship that brought growth in the toughest of times and now to add to it the next level of training. They have no intention of forsaking the broader segments of the "triangle". They are just adding the smaller segments in order to expand the ministry knowing that there is less chance of false doctrine and heresy creeping into the Church if the spiritual leadership is adequately trained to reach, to teach, and to train others.

God has given the National Evangelical Church in Koinadugu a vision to rebuild and expand the Bible School. It is their dream and they have taken ownership of it. They are asking that we join them to help make their vision become a reality, because their ultimate goal is to reach the rest of their people and nation with the Gospel.

Appendix D

For more information on the redevelopment of the Institution and the status of the Technical Vocational Training Center please visit

Ripe For Harvest World Outreach,
1375 E. Grand Ave. #103-333
Arroyo Grande, CA 93420

Ripe for Harvest is an evangelical interdenominational mission organization with the purpose of enabling missionaries to minister effectively where God has called them to serve. Ripe For Harvest World Outreach is a member of the Evangelical Council for Financial Accountability (ECFA). You may find out more about them by looking up their website at **www. ripeforharvest.org.**

If you would like current information of the development of the Bible School check the web site : WestAfricaBibleSchool.com

Respectfully Submitted, Earl L. Reifel